"Peter Leithart is one of our best and most c
book Leithart shows that doctrine is not some abstract entity disconnected from
contemporary life but is in fact deeply relevant and pregnant with social and political insights. Leithart is biblically, theologically and culturally literate—a rare
combination—and thus able to produce the sort of work we so badly need today.
Attending to the doctrines of the atonement and justification, he writes in the best
tradition of apologetics, namely that of creative, orthodox, contextual theology."

Craig Bartholomew, professor of philosophy and religion and theology, Redeemer
University College

"Among contemporary theologians, only Leithart has the biblical erudition, theological breadth and rhetorical power necessary for writing a book like this one. His
Christian creativity and love for Jesus Christ jump off the page. As an account of
atonement, this book is also an account of the entirety of Christian reality, and
indeed of the reality of Israel as well, in light of pagan and secular cultures and in
light of the church's own failures to live what Christ has given. At its heart is an
urgent call for all Christians, living in the Spirit, to share the Eucharist together
against every fleshly barrier and Spirit-less form of exclusion. Leithart's dazzling
biblical and ecumenical manifesto merits the closest attention and engagement."

Matthew Levering, Perry Family Foundation Professor of Theology, Mundelein Seminary

"When you read Peter Leithart, you suddenly realize how timid most Christian theologians are, tepidly offering us a few 'insights' to edify our comfort with the status
quo. Leithart is like a lightning strike from a more ancient, more courageous
Christian past, his flaming pen fueled by biblical acuity and scholarly rigor. In this
book, he does it again—here is the *City of God* written afresh for our age, asking a
question you didn't know to ask but now can't avoid: Why is the cross the center of
human history? Couldn't God have found another way? Leithart's answer—this
book—is a monumental achievement."

James K. A. Smith, professor of philosophy, Calvin College, editor, *Comment* magazine

DELIVERED FROM THE ELEMENTS OF THE WORLD

ATONEMENT, JUSTIFICATION, MISSION

✝

PETER J. LEITHART

IVP Academic

An imprint of InterVarsity Press
Downers Grove, Illinois

InterVarsity Press
P.O. Box 1400, Downers Grove, IL 60515-1426
ivpress.com
email@ivpress.com

©2016 by Peter J. Leithart

All rights reserved. No part of this book may be reproduced in any form without written permission from InterVarsity Press.

InterVarsity Press® is the book-publishing division of InterVarsity Christian Fellowship/USA®, a movement of students and faculty active on campus at hundreds of universities, colleges and schools of nursing in the United States of America, and a member movement of the International Fellowship of Evangelical Students. For information about local and regional activities, visit intervarsity.org.

All Scripture quotations, unless otherwise indicated, are the author's own translation.

Cover design: David Fassett
Interior design: Beth McGill
Images: Ascension, Laila Shawa. Private Collection / Bridgeman Images

ISBN 978-0-8308-5126-3 (print)
ISBN 978-0-8308-9971-5 (digital)

Printed in the United States of America ♾

 As a member of the Green Press Initiative, InterVarsity Press is committed to protecting the environment and to the responsible use of natural resources. To learn more, visit greenpressinitiative.org.

Library of Congress Cataloging-in-Publication Data
Names: Leithart, Peter J., author.
Title: Delivered from the elements of the world : atonement, justification,
mission / Peter J. Leithart.
Description: Downers Grove : InterVarsity Press, 2016. | Includes index.
Identifiers: LCCN 2015050901 (print) | LCCN 2016002356 (ebook) | ISBN
9780830851263 (pbk. : alk. paper) | ISBN 9780830899715 (eBook)
Subjects: LCSH: Atonement. | Jesus Christ--Crucifixion. | Justification
(Christian theology) | Mission of the church.
Classification: LCC BT265.3 .L45 2016 (print) | LCC BT265.3 (ebook) | DDC
234/.5--dc23
LC record available at http://lccn.loc.gov/2015050901

P	23	22	21	20	19	18	17	16	15	14	13	12	11	10	9	8	7	6	5	4	3	2	1
Y	36	35	34	33	32	31	30	29	28	27	26	25	24	23	22	21	20	19	18	17	16		

To Peter Miles Taylor Tollefson

May the Lord who welcomed you at the font

keep you at his table forever.

CONTENTS

ACKNOWLEDGMENTS

✝

Delivered from the Elements of the World follows up on themes I started to explore twenty years ago in my doctoral dissertation, *The Priesthood of the Plebs*. It began to take its current form several years ago, when I realized in a flash of folly that three books I wished to write—on sacrifice, on justification, on religions—might be squoozed between two covers.

I have many people to thank for their encouragement and help. During the last few years of full-time teaching at New St. Andrews College in Moscow, Idaho, I restructured my theology course around the themes of this book. I am grateful both to the college and to the many students who went through my theology course during those years, and for their often enthusiastic reception of my somewhat eccentric treatment of these questions.

I received direct assistance from Donny Linnemeyer, who served as a research assistant during the 2012–2013 academic year. Donny and I read through a number of classic treatises on the atonement together, and his insights and notes were a great help as I developed the themes of this book. I am, as usual, indebted to James Jordan, both for a few brief exchanges about this book and more generally for his inspiration over the last couple of decades. Pastor Rich Lusk's preaching on Mark helped me think through a number of issues, as did follow-up conversations with Rich. Michael Gorman responded to my review of one of his books and clarified several points for me, and Matthew Levering gave me some pointers about literature on Thomas. Dan Reid and his team at IVP were again a delight to work with.

This book is dedicated to my latest grandchild, and my namesake, Peter Miles Taylor Tollefson. So far, my main contribution to his life has been to allow him to nap in my arms. I look forward to watching him grow over the years with his two big sisters, and trust that in the future I will be more to him than an animate bed. I witnessed Miles's baptism, so I know that the Lord has welcomed him as a member of his new Israel, and I trust that the Lord will keep Miles forever, eating, drinking and rejoicing unveiled before the face of God.

one

ATONEMENT AS SOCIAL THEORY

✝

No purely secular society exists or has ever existed. Define religion how you will: As a matter of ultimate concern, as belief in something transcendent, as the organizing master narrative for history and human lives, as a set of practices. However religion is defined, all institutions, structures and patterns of behavior have religious features. All cultures are infused with values and actions that have religious dimensions and overtones. Whether they name the name of a known God or not, societies and cultures are always patterned by some ultimate inspiration and aspiration.

By the same token, all religions have social aspects; they all are embedded in and rely on patterns of interaction among persons. Even the retreat of a solitary ascetic into the desert is a social act, since it is a retreat from social relation. And all religions deal with artifacts, symbols and rituals that might as well be called "cultural."

Religion is not the "soul" of culture, nor culture the "body" of religion. Religions have bodies, and cultures have souls. It is rather the case that in dealing with any group of human beings, we are always dealing with socio-religious or religio-cultural entities. The common contemporary rhetoric of conflicts between religion and politics obscures the reality. Conflicts are never between politics and religion. Conflicts are always between rivals that are both religious and both political.

Islamic terrorists kill themselves and innocent bystanders for overtly religious reasons. In response, the United States sends troops to the Middle East to make the world safe from terrorism, but also to sacrifice themselves to preserve and advance America's values, freedom and democracy. To say that the terrorist and the Marine are both motivated by religious values is not to make a moral equivalence. But we misread the times unless we recognize that the war on terror is a religious war on *both* sides.

We think ourselves all secular, all grown-up, but we have our taboos, our pollution avoidances, our instincts of recoil and disgust. Not so long ago, many found homosexual sodomy disgusting. In a matter of decades, the disgust has turned inside out, and now those who consider homosexual conduct sinful and unnatural are outcasts, treated with contempt. The freedom to engage in any form of consensual sex is now considered a right, and a *sacred* one, as inviolable as the sacred precincts of an ancient temple.

When the religious character of society is stressed, the emphasis is often placed more or less exclusively on beliefs. It is thought that societies and cultures are religious because they express religious ideas. Contemporary American culture is religious because it is founded on a belief system that Christian Smith has labeled "Moralistic Therapeutic Deism." That emphasis on ideas is misplaced, not because beliefs are insignificant, but because beliefs and practices are inseparable. Exclusive focus on beliefs misses the habitual, often instinctive actions that form the stuff of social relationships. Rules of etiquette are, deep down, based on a set of beliefs, but few mothers teach their children those beliefs. What they teach is, "Say thank you" and "Shake hands with the nice man" and "Don't pick your nose!"

My references to purity and holiness are not accidental. I will argue in this book that the fundamental physics of every socioreligious, cultural-religious formation consists of practices concerning holiness, purity and sacrifice. Locate the sacred center of a group; its boundaries of tolerable and intolerable persons, objects and behavior; its rituals of sacrifice—discover all this and you have got down to the elementary particles that determine the group's chemical composition. Relocate the sacred, rearrange the boundaries of purity and pollution, revise its sacrificial procedures, and you have changed the fundamental physics of the society. A revolution *here* is the most profound of social revolutions, and it is the revolution achieved by Jesus in his cross and resurrection.

Cur Deus Homo

Delivered from the Elements of the World addresses questions internal to Christian theology. That is not a limitation. Christians believe the gospel encompasses everything, and so all Christian theology that is worthy of the name strains beyond the confines of "theology" to the ends of the earth.

The main questions I attempt to answer can be posed in several complementary ways.

They can be posed as a variation on the interrogative form of Anselm's classic treatise on the atonement, *Cur Deus Homo*? At one level, my aim is the same as Anselm's. It is an attempt to unravel the rationality of the central claims of the Christian gospel: Jesus died and rose again to save us from our sins. Like Anselm, I assume *that* the gospel is true and probe to discover *how* it happened. How can the death and resurrection of a Jewish rabbi of the first century, an event in the putative backwaters of the Roman Empire, be *the* decisive event in the history of humanity, the hinge and crux and crossroads for *everything*? Even here we can assume a partial *that*: because of the history of the church founded by Jesus, it is clear *that* his death and resurrection changed a great deal, perhaps everything. Again, my question is about the mechanics: *How* did that happen?

Unlike Anselm, however, I have self-consciously asked *Cur Deus Homo* as a question of social and political theology, as an exploration of the cultural and public settings and consequences of the event of the cross and resurrection. We are social and political creatures. If humanity is going to achieve a state of health (what Christians call salvation), we are going to have to be saved *in* our social and political situations; our social structures and political institutions are going to have to become conducive to harmony and justice, peace and human flourishing. For Christians, the health of the human race turns on the work done by Jesus, and that means that the good of social life must somehow have its source there, on Calvary and at the empty tomb. Ultimately Jesus died and rose again to bring the human race to its final end in glory, to gather a people who will one day be a spotless bride, without blemish or wrinkle or any such thing, a perfected humanity to be presented to the Father. While I keep that eschatological qualification in mind throughout, my focus is on the already of the eschatological dualism. *Cur Deus Homo* for the salvation of human society *in history*? What need do we have of a God-man, or of the death and resurrection of a God-man, to restore human culture and society? Why can we not simply establish institutions that promote peace and justice? Why can we not found our common life on our common humanity?[1]

---

[1]For much Christian theology, the answer is, in part, that we *can*. Human flourishing in society is *here*, and the salvation of humanity in relation to God is over *there* someplace else, in heaven,

That is one way to ask the question. Another is in terms of sacramental theology: the church cannot exist without rites, any more than any society. For there is no religious society, Augustine insists, whether true or false, whose separate members are not "coagulated" into common life by sacraments and signs. According to Augustine, old figural and prophetic sacraments are fulfilled in new sacraments, more powerful, easier and fewer than the sacraments of old (*virtute maiora, utilitate meliora, actu faciliora, numero pauciora; Contra Faustum* 19.13). Fine. I agree. But again my question is, Why do we need a dead and risen Christ to accomplish this? When Moses instituted the sacraments of the old law, there was opposition, occasional threats on his life, but in the end he survived to see Torah established. Why could Jesus not be another Moses? Why could he not be a teacher and founder of a new cultus and a new sect? Why does he need to die in order to institute new signs and sacraments for the new society he forms? Why the cross if the task is simply to relocate the sacred and change the rules of purity and sacrifice?

The question can be posed in another way. Old Testament acts of judgment and redemption were inescapably acts of social and political salvation, and if Christian faith takes the Old Testament as canon, and if Jesus and his body fulfill Israel's history, then judgment and redemption in Christian theology *must* take social and political form. It must at least coagulate that new society around those new sacraments, but, beyond that, if the gospel is about the salvation of humanity it must carry a message of hope for the salvation of human society.

The problem is this: Old Testament acts of judgment and redemption were comprehensibly acts of judgment and redemption. Many today will think the story of Adam's sin in Eden's garden to be a bit of implausible mythology. But it is *comprehensible* mythology: Adam is put in a garden and told not to eat the fruit of the tree on pain of death. Yahweh forms Eve to be a helper suited to him. We know what will happen: Satan tempts Eve, she and Adam eat, and they are expelled from the garden, exiled from the tree of life. Many regard it as a children's story; even the skeptic can agree that it has at least one virtue: it possesses the bright clarity of a fairy tale.

---

in the eschaton, in the church. This entire book is an implicit polemic against that dichotomy, and I address its soteriological manifestations directly in appendix 1.

So too do the other stories of judgment and deliverance throughout the Old Testament. Seeing his world ruined by violent heroism, Yahweh regrets having created in the first place, so he wipes out the world in the flood. Yet he rescues Noah by disclosing the threat ahead of time and giving him instructions for an ark. Again, many sniff out mythology here, but it is not a difficult myth to understand. Catastrophe falls on wrongdoers (yay!), and the one righteous man is delivered (yay! again). It happens in the exodus (oppressive Egypt and Pharaoh decimated, Israel delivered); it happens again and again in the time of the judges; it happens in David's battles with Goliath and with Philistines; it happens on a national scale when Israel is handed over to exile and then brought back to the land. The Old Testament records a long and complex history, but throughout judgment and salvation are perfectly clear: Judgment means that bad things happen to bad people; salvation means that God rescues the righteous, those who trust and walk with him.

Not only are these judgments and rescues comprehensible, but they are comprehensible as *historical* events, events in the political history of nations, even if one does not believe they happened. Yahweh devastates Egypt and brings Israel to Sinai to give them a tabernacle and a constitution for their national life: a clearly *political* rescue. So too for the battles of judges, the deliverance of Jerusalem from Assyrians, the return from exile.

It is not at all clear that the death and resurrection of Jesus is an act of judgment and salvation on anything like the same scale. If God wanted to save the whole world, why not another global flood—or, failing that, since he promised not to flood the world again, a Stoic conflagration that surgically targets bad guys? Why not, at least, a David with a sword (or five stones), a Gideon, a Jehu? Why not a freedom fighter to liberate Israel from Rome? That would be *comprehensible*, and comprehensibly political.

Yet Christians say that *this* event of Jesus' crucifixion and resurrection— *not* the flood, exodus or return from exile—is *the* decisive moment for the salvation of the world. If it is comprehensible at all, the death of a supposed Messiah is not immediately comprehensible as a saving act, though resurrection is certainly good news for the dead Messiah himself. The problem is intensified when we add that this event is supposed to be the source of social, economic and political justice and peace. The problem becomes nearly impossible when Christians say, as we often have over the years (starting with Jesus, Lk 24), that *these* events form the fitting, even the *inevitable* climax, to that comprehensible history of political judgment and deliverance we read about in the Old Testament. *This* is what Israel's history was all aiming at?

So: God destroys the world with water and rescues Noah; he demolishes Egypt and leads Israel through the sea to Sinai and to the land; he raises David and Solomon to glorify Israel among the nations; in his wrath, he casts Israel into exile, but then draws them back in love—he does all this, and the key to what this means is the life of a Galilean teacher crucified on a Roman cross, raised from the dead on the third day. *This* is the concluding chapter that ties up all the loose ends of the Bible's story?

Something *very* odd is going on here. Christianity's claim has become domesticated by its success, but to grasp the logic we need to *un*domesticate it and recover a sense of the word made strange. Either Christianity's good news is incomprehensible delusion, or it operates by a logic that violates much of the logic we believe explains the world. It is either irrational, or it reveals that the world itself has a rationality quite different, more subtle and certainly odder, than we believe.

This is not a book of apologetics, nor a history of theologies of the atonement. But in writing it I have been conscious that skepticism about the atonement found in Kant and, behind him, Faustus Socinius, has been central to modern assaults on the rationality of Christian faith. The attack on the rationality of the cross was an attack on the rationality of Christianity and the Bible. For Kant and many moderns, atonement theology was an invention of priests. *Real* atonement is self-help, repentant turning from evil and doing right. *That*, like the story of the fall, is perfectly comprehensible. It has all the clarity of, though less plausibility than, a fairy tale.

This has direct bearing on the social and political questions that animate this book, for if we can correct ourselves by our own natural powers, surely we are also capable of establishing social and political structures that embody the kingdom of God. Kant's Pelagian atonement is intimately linked to Kant's advocacy of liberal political order. If, by contrast, Christians say that individuals can be put back on the track of justice only by the death and resurrection of Jesus, then we also raise fundamental questions about the adequacy of liberalism to achieve our political ends.

Satisfaction theories came under special criticism from Socinians and others, and penal substitution makes an appearance in what follows. I affirm it, with appropriate cautions and qualifications. More than cautions, I offer *context*, because we cannot make sense of Jesus' suffering the penalty for others' wrongs unless we see it as a summary of the plot of the gospel story. Jesus' substitutionary death is one moment in a *sequence* of redemptive acts, in a complex sacrificial movement, and without the other moments before and after, it is no redemption at all. Isolating the moment of substitutionary death does havoc to our theology of atonement and our soteriology generally, not to mention our ecclesiology and sacramental theology and practice.

Thus, though I focus on the sociopolitical dimensions of the atonement, I hope that this focus illuminates traditional questions about the atonement. Indeed, I hope to show that atonement theology *must* be social theory if it is going to have any coherence, relevance or comprehensibility at all.

How This Book Proceeds

Methodological excursions are boring, and I do not want to bore the reader. But I do want to sketch out the framework in which this book operates and the criteria that I have used to test the success of the venture.

I have described *Delivered from the Elements of the World* as my Big Red Book About Everything, and its scope is evident in the variety of "discourses" that make appearance in the following pages: anthropological studies, especially of sacrifice and ritual; postmodern "cultural studies," especially the theories of René Girard; research on ancient Near Eastern religion (chapter three); classics, especially studies of Greek religion and sacrifice (chapter three); Old Testament studies, particularly on Leviticus and the Levitical system of temple, purity and sacrifice (chapter four); historical Jesus studies, studies of the Gospels as narrative and political studies of the gospel (chapters five and six); Pauline studies, including the new perspective on Paul, apocalyptic readings of Paul, political treatments of Pauline theology and recent work by Continental philosophers and political thinkers on Paul (chapters one and seven; appendix three); dogmatic studies of soteriology and the doctrine of justification like those of Karl Barth and Eberhard Jüngel (appendixes one and two); historical-theology studies of atonement theology, justification and soteriology (appendixes one and two) and comparative world religions (chapter ten); Reformation studies, especially those focusing on the ritual dimensions of the Reformation battles (chapter eleven); secularization theories and critiques of secularization (chapter eleven); and counter-Enlightenment Continental philosophy (chapter eleven). The reader who is looking for extended discussions of the scholarship in any of these areas will be disappointed. I interact with these various fields along the way, but this is not a treatise on the scholarship concerning the atonement. I *use* the scholarship of various disciplines, responsibly I hope, to construct an argument that does not fit neatly into any of them. My treatment is not comprehensive at any point, neither is my research. I am sure there are dozens of highly relevant works in each of these fields of which I am utterly ignorant. For reasons that may be clear by the end of the book, I have tried to learn to be cheerful, even giddy, in my limitations.

There *is* a master discourse, and it is the discourse of biblical theology or a typological reading of Scripture. Atonement theology has sometimes been dislodged from Scripture, working out the "mechanics" of atonement using categories other than biblical ones.[2] Jesus himself explained the "must" of his death and resurrection by starting with Moses and working through the Psalms and Prophets to show that the whole of Scripture was about the suffering and glory of the Christ (Lk 24, again). Moving from typology to another discourse is not moving from the poetic to the rational; it is simply to change rationalities. Typology is a way of reading history, so any atonement theology that abandons typology is in danger not only of leaving Scripture behind but also of constructing a timeless account of the atonement.[3] Timelessness here is disastrous because it belies the subject matter: Atonement theology offers an interpretation of *historical* events that happened precisely to have a decisive effect *on history*, as well as eternity. It must matter for atonement theory that sin entered the world, that God called Abraham and

---

[2]This is far *less* true than some critics of the tradition allege. In the early centuries, typological accounts of the atonement predominated (see Frances Young, *The Use of Sacrificial Ideas in Greek Christian Writers from the New Testament to John Chrysostom* [Philadelphia: Philadelphia Patristic Foundation, 1979]). Even Anselm's more rational treatise on the atonement, which does use the categories of the penitential system and (perhaps) a feudal concept of honor, still makes use of biblical categories. Origen, Athanasius, Aquinas, Luther, Calvin and many others return constantly to the biblical text to answer questions about the mechanics of atonement. This is not to say they do everything as well as they might have done. I fully agree with Robert Jenson's complaint that atonement theology has tended to ignore Jesus' connection with Israel's history, and has focused too much on the death of Jesus without reference to the atoning effect of the resurrection (Jenson, *Theology as Revisionary Metaphysics: Essays on God and Creation* [Eugene, OR: Cascade, 2014], 127-35). For an account of the reasons for this oversight, see appendix 2.

[3]Readers may not recognize what happens in this book as "typology." But it fits what I describe as typological reading in *Deep Exegesis: The Mystery of Reading Scripture* (Waco, TX: Baylor University Press, 2009).

gave Torah, and that Jesus lived, died and was exalted to send the Spirit. If an atonement theory "works" without reference to those historical events, it is not a Christian atonement theory. An ahistorical account of atonement is an absurdity.

Specifically, the book is organized by Pauline themes, drawn especially from Galatians and, to a lesser degree, Romans.[4] The organizing theme is a rather marginal one in Paul's letters—Paul's brief treatment of *ta stoicheia tou kosmou*, the "elements of the world," in Galatians 4:1-7. Yet this book deals with central Pauline themes—Torah, the Abrahamic promise, God's justice, the faith of Jesus Christ, his death and resurrection, justification. My (postmodern, Derridean, deconstructionist) assumption is that staring hard at the marginalia of Paul's discussion of "elements" will do much to illumine the center. My treatment is confessedly, deliberately idiosyncratic as a treatment of Paul. At times I offer close exegesis of Pauline texts; in other chapters I fill in a Pauline argument or concept, page after page, by surveying passages of the Old Testament. I do not claim that I necessarily explain *Paul's* thinking on these points, but I do aim to offer something of a midrash on Paul that coheres with Paul's (typological) reading of the Hebrew Scriptures. To offer a full reading of Paul, I gleefully violate the boundaries of Pauline scholarship, taking as my defense that Paul himself did not confine himself to Pauline letters but ranged over the whole canon of Scripture. The result may read more like a treatise in systematic theology than an excursion in biblical theology. So be it: systematic theology is nothing but tidily presented typology.[5]

During the course of my research and writing, I have formulated several criteria of a successful, comprehensible theory of the atonement.

- Historically plausibile: Atonement theology is an *interpretation* of events, not a recital of "bare facts," which is impossible in any case. But that interpretation must make sense of the historical events, not by transcending phenomena into a noumenal realm of meaning, but by tracing and

---

[4]I might have constructed a similar argument using Hebrews, and I have made glancing references to that letter. Since this was already a big book, I did not deal with Hebrews in detail.

[5]Systematics of course deals with questions raised in the history of theology, but its basic categories arise from typology. "Christology," for instance, is nothing but an explanation of how Jesus fulfills all the messianic hopes, titles, saving actions of Israel—how he is last Adam, greater Abel, Abraham's seed, new Moses, greater Aaron, David's son, a prophet like Jeremiah.

perhaps extrapolating the logic of the events.[6] Successful atonement theology must, for instance, make sense of Jesus as a figure in a first-century Judaism dominated by Rome. A successful atonement theory has to show how the death and resurrection of Jesus is the key to human history, which means that atonement theory has to provide an account of all human history. It has to be a theory of everything.

- Levitical: A successful atonement theology treats Jesus' death (at least) as a sacrifice, and it must be able to show that Jesus' sacrifice fulfills Levitical ritual in historical events.

- Evangelical: Successful atonement theology must arise from *within* the Gospel narratives rather than be an imposition from outside (even a *Pauline* outside).

- Pauline: Atonement theology must make sense of the actual words and sentences and arguments in Paul's letters.

- Inevitable: A successful atonement theology should leave an impression of inevitability: "Was it not necessary for the Christ to suffer these things and to enter into His glory?" (Lk 24:26 NASB). Jesus should appear to be the *obvious* divine response to the human condition. Like the denouement of a well-constructed drama, the cross and resurrection should emerge as the most fitting climax to the history of Israel among the nations, as the climax of a history of sacrifice.[7]

- Fruitful: A successful atonement theology must offer a framework for making sense not only of the history of Jesus but also of the subsequent history of the church and of the world. It must, for instance, not shrink from addressing the apparent *failure* of the atonement, the palpable fact that the world Jesus is said to have saved is self-evidently *not* saved.

---

[6]This is perhaps the key apologetic issue in atonement theology, at least against modern critics of atonement: How can this odd sequence of events so long ago have any bearing on me now?

[7]The best exemplar of "inevitable" atonement theory in contemporary theology is the work of René Girard. As will be clear in my discussions of Girard below, I believe Girard makes some fundamental errors in his theory of sacrifice, scapegoating and religious violence. Yet Girard's theory explains in precise terms how the specific events of the gospel story answer to the disorder of human life and human societies. Given the fact that human beings are gripped by mimetic desires that produce sacrificial crises that are relieved by scapegoating, God *must* achieve salvation through the cross. Though my treatment of Girard is relatively brief, his work is always lurking in the shadows and peeking through the empty spaces. In a sense what I have to offer is a biblical and Pauline revision of Girardian theory.

I will indicate throughout the book where I think I meet these criteria, but the final determination is for others.

A CHANCE TO JUMP SHIP

Methodological excursions are boring. Introductory summaries are for the lazy. I would not insult the reader by assuming you are lazy. I do you the compliment of assuming the best: that you fully intend to read every page of my Big Red Book.[8] You will discover that I occasionally pause, like Virgil on a terrace of Mount Purgatory, to summarize along the way. But if you want to know what this book is about, turn the page, and then another and another until you see the back cover over the horizon. If you do *not* care to find out, feel free to leave it behind for a different reader, and go find a more pleasant way to spend the day.

---

[8]Alas, the designers decided not to use a red cover. Yet one can dream, can one not?

PART ONE

UNDER THE ELEMENTS OF THE WORLD

two

THE PHYSICS OF THE OLD CREATION

†

The apostle Paul shows little interest in the natural world or its hidden parts and processes. He does not catalog plants and animals or attempt to penetrate to the basic particles that compose the physical world. He rarely uses the terminology of Greek physics or metaphysics, and when he does he no longer uses them as Aristotle or Greek scientists had. Paul is more sociologist than scientist, more priest than philosopher, and this is nowhere more obvious than in his knack for "humanizing" and "socializing" terms borrowed from Greek philosophy and science.

This chapter begins our excursion into atonement theology by examining two related Pauline terms, "nature" and especially "elements," *physis* and *ta stoicheia*. Paul transforms both terms by relocating them in the history of Israel, the law, the arrival of faith and the gospel. Instead of being permanent features of the physical world, as they are in Greek philosophy and science, the elements are redescribed as features of an old creation that Christ has in some way brought to an end. This chapter works at a fairly high level of abstraction. Only later will we examine in detail what the elements are or how they work. It will be some time before we venture a theory about how Jesus disassembled and reassembled the world. All that will have to wait. But if the particular pieces of the puzzle come later, this chapter gets the shape of the final picture in front of us.

That picture looks, in general, like this: Prior to the coming of Jesus, the social worlds of Jews and Gentiles were both organized by practices, structures and symbols to which Paul assigns the label "elements of the world." Minimally, these involved distinctions between purity and impurity, between sacred and profane, and practices that both enforced those distinctions and, to some degree, provided sacrificial pathways of transfer from one to the other. My principal aim will be to show that Paul gives a socioreligious meaning to the phrase "elements of the world," so that, having made that case, we can assemble a Periodic Table of Old Creation Elements in the following chapters. Over the course of the book, we will find that, according to the apostle, Jesus delivered Jews and Gentiles from the elemental world into a new social world that operates by different sociophysical laws.

To make this sketch plausible, though, we need some evidence.

Paul's Social Physics

In contrast to the church fathers, the New Testament's vocabulary rarely overlaps with the standard vocabulary of Greek philosophy or science, and the scattered biblical uses do not bear the philosophical or scientific weight they had in classical thought. Nature (*physis*) is a crucial concept in Aristotle. Physics studies those things that exist by nature (*physei*), things, as Heidegger put it, that "arise on their own"[1] and that are moved and develop by an inner principle. Physics thus studies animals and their components, plants and the elements, their motions and changes. Each of these "has within itself a principle [*en heautō archēn echei*] of motion and stationariness in respect of place, or of growth and decrease, or by way of alteration" (Aristotle, *Physics* 2.1, 192b). Artificial things possess an inner principle insofar as they are made from natural things that naturally possess it, so Aristotle's more precise formulation is that nature is the "source or cause of being moved and of being at rest in that to which it belongs primarily, in virtue of itself and not in virtue of a concomitant attribute" (*Physics* 2.1, 192b22-23).[2] Nature is the answer to the questions, why does this thing remain the thing that it is? and, why does *this* thing mature along *these* particular lines? The inner principle of *physis* is the ground for saying that the seed and tree are "the same" in some way, and *physis* also determines the trajectory of the seed as it moves toward fulfillment as a tree. Physics is not first philosophy, for

---

[1]Martin Heidegger, *The Principle of Reason*, trans. Reginald Lilly (Bloomington: Indiana University Press, 1991), 62.

[2]Helen S. Lang, *The Order of Nature in Aristotle's Physics: Place and the Elements* (Cambridge: Cambridge University Press, 1998), 40. The Greek is *hōs ousēs tēs physeōs archēs tinos kai aitias tou kineisthai kai ēremein en hō hyparchei prōtōs kath' auto kai mē kata symbebēkos.* Unless otherwise indicated, I draw my translations of Greek texts, and the Greek originals, from the Perseus Digital Library, www.perseus.tufts.edu/hopper.

first philosophy has to do with more essential questions about substance (*ousia*). Physics is, however, second philosophy (*deutera philosophia*; Aristotle, *Metaphysics* 7, 1037a14-15).

In the New Testament, *physis* is rare and its meaning variable. Same-sex desires (*pathē*) are, Paul says, *para physin* (Rom 1:26), since people overcome by such passions abandon the natural function (*aphentes tēn physikēn chrēsin*). "Nature" does not describe an inner principle of movement and rest but rather a moral order rooted or at least reflected in the physical differences between the sexes. Paul's usage is closer to the Stoics Zeno and Chrysippus than to Aristotle, but in Paul there are no hints of the metaphysical supports for Stoic ethical appeals to nature. Given the Jewish and theistic context of the passage, *para physin* is best understood as "against God's intended order for sexuality."[3] In this passage, *physis* names a *permanent* structure of creation. From the beginning, God made them male and female, and the gospel does not dissolve the created structures of human sexuality. Human desires should be conformed to the Creator's design, which Paul calls "nature."

Paul's other uses of the word are neither Aristotelian nor Stoic. Those Gentiles who do not have Torah "by nature" (*physei*) may still do what Torah requires, and thus they become a law to themselves, showing the law written on the heart (Rom 2:14-15),[4] and Paul writes of Gentiles who are "uncircumcised by nature" (*ek physeōs akrobystia*, Rom 2:27). In Galatians 2:15 he identifies himself and Peter as Jews *physei*, and the tree of Israel has both natural Jewish and grafted Gentile branches, branches *kata physin* and branches

---

[3]See Richard B. Hays, "Relations Natural and Unnatural: A Response to John Boswell's Exegesis of Romans 1," *Journal of Religious Ethics* 14:1 (1986): 184-215, esp. 192-95. Hays writes, "Though he offers no explicit reflection on the concept of 'nature,' it is clear that in this passage Paul identifies 'nature' with the created order. The understanding of 'nature' in this conventional language does not rest on empirical observation of what actually exists; instead, it appeals to an intuitive conception of what ought to be, of the world as designed by God. Those who indulge in sexual practices *para physin* are defying the creator and demonstrating their own alienation from him" (p. 194). This is a first hint that whatever Paul says about the transformation of social physics, he does *not* teach that it dissolves the created difference of male and female, nor does he undermine the Old Testament's sexual ethics that is grounded on that difference.

[4]Against most translations, I follow Simon Gathercole, N. T. Wright and others in seeing *physei* as a modifier not of the doing but of the Gentiles themselves. They have the law written on their hearts because they are Gentile believers, participating in the New Covenant. See Simon J. Gathercole, "A Law Unto Themselves: The Gentiles in Romans 2:14-15 Revisited," *Journal for the Study of the New Testament* 85 (2002): 27-49; N. T. Wright, "The Law in Romans 2," in J. D. G. Dunn, ed., *Paul and the Mosaic Law* (Grand Rapids: Eerdmans, 2000), 131-50.

para physin (Rom 11:24). Paul draws ethical conclusions from an appeal to *physis*, but in an anti-Sophistic way. He argues that *physis* teaches that men should have short hair (1 Cor 11:14), apparently an appeal to social custom.[5]

Paul's few and scattered uses do not raise physics anywhere close to the level of *deutera philosophia*. If Romans 1 condemns same-sex desire because it violates God's created order of sexuality, the other uses have to do with God's covenantal ordering of humanity through the division of Jew and Gentile. Possession of Torah, which is a contingent historical and cultural fact, can be "by nature"; circumcision, a deliberate modification of the male penis, can also be "by nature." Cultural and religious distinctions that would in Sophist classification fall under the heading of *nomos* Paul categorizes as differences of *physis*.[6] There *is* a "natural" order, but for Paul constructed orders also have the force of "nature." Some human beings are "naturally" Jews, others "naturally" Gentiles. One of the burdens of Paul's teaching is that these different human "natures" are being joined into one in a new humanity, of which Jesus is the head.

Two explanations for this usage suggest themselves. It may be that Paul sees possession of Torah, circumcision and Jewishness as "natural" because they are part of an ancestral inheritance. They are "natural" because they are genetic, tied to descent from Abraham. That which is born of flesh is by nature flesh; that born of Abraham is by nature Jewish; that not born of Abraham is by nature Gentile. Paul's idea of "nature" might be closer to modern biological concepts of nature than it first appears. While this may well have been part of what Paul had in mind, Jewishness and circumcision were not *necessarily* linked to descent. Any Gentile might be circumcised and become Jewish. Circumcision would transform him from one who is Gentile "by nature" to a natural possessor of Torah, a natural Jew. Alternatively, we

---

[5]Troy Martin has recently argued that Paul is influenced by Greek medical thought in which *peribolaion*, usually translated as "covering," can refer to testicles. Men store semen in hair, and so long hair is a shame to men who should eject rather than store semen; women are glands that draw in semen to form into fetuses, and female hair provides storage for male seed, and is considered part of the woman's genitalia. Thus long hair enhances a woman's *physis* but is contrary to a male's natural purpose ("Paul's Argument from Nature for the Veil in 1 Corinthians 11:13-15: A Testicle Instead of a Head Covering," *Journal of Biblical Literature* 123 [2004]: 75-84). Intriguing though this is, I find it more plausible, given Paul's usage elsewhere, to see this as another example of Paul using *physis* to designate what we would describe as *cultural* differences. Paul is not making a "scientific" argument in 1 Corinthians 11 any more than he does in Romans 2 when he speaks of "natural" circumcision.

[6]See W. K. C. Guthrie, *The Sophists* (Cambridge: Cambridge University Press, 1971), 55-134.

might try to unify Paul's uses of *physis* by noting that Torah, circumcision and Jewishness were all divine institutions. Human beings performed circumcisions, taught and applied Torah, but the fact that Israel was marked by circumcision and possessed Torah was as determined by Yahweh as the order of created sexuality. Jewishness was not a cultural construction; or, if it was, the constructor was God himself. Thus Paul might use *physis* in a fairly consistent manner to describe "an order created by God"—whether created or covenantal. That works, but the point noted above remains: Paul has "socialized" and "historicized" the language of "nature." Even if it describes a divine institution, it is one revealed in history.

For Paul, *physis* and *nomos*, physics and law, nature and culture, are not finally separable. Human beings can be "naturally" Jews, not simply by birth but by conformity to the nomic regulations and patterns of life of Torah. One can be "naturally" circumcised. What we would separate into "ritual" and "natural" Paul joins together. And this expresses an anthropology: Human beings are defined by the social and cultural setting in which they live, move and have their being. Jews are not simply generic human beings who happen to practice and live Jewishly. Conformity to Jewish norms, performance of Jewish rites and adherence to Jewish institutions give them Jewish *nature*.

Against this background, we can make better sense of Paul's use of the scientific phrase "the elements of the world." If human *physis* is intertwined with human and divine *nomos*, then the elementary particles of physics are also linked to law, custom and practice. And if *physis* is so closely linked to *nomos*, then a change of law might also involve a change of nature and its elements.

THE ELEMENTS OF THE COSMOS

Stoicheion ("element") had a range of meanings in pre-Christian Greek.[7] The

---

[7] For surveys, see Gerhard Delling, "Στοιχειον," in *Theological Dictionary of the New Testament*, ed. Gerhard Kittel and Gerhard Friedrich, trans. Geoffrey Bromiley (Grand Rapids: Eerdmans, 1971), 7:670-68; J. Louis Martyn, *Galatians*, Anchor Bible (New York: Doubleday, 1997), 394-95; Eduard Schweizer, "Slaves of the Elements and Worshipers of Angels: Gal 4:3, 9 and Col 2:8, 18, 20," *Journal of Biblical Literature* 107 (1988): 455-68; David Bundrick, "Ta Stoicheia tou Kosmou (Gal 4:3)," *Journal of the Evangelical Theological Society* 34 (1991): 353-64; Dietrich Rusam, "Neue Belege zu den στοιχεια του κοσμου (Gal 4, 3.9; Kol 2,8.20)," *Zeitschrift für die neutestamentliche Wissenscahaft und die Kunde der alteren Kirche* 83 (1992): 119-25; Bo Reicke, "The Law and This World According to Paul: Some Thoughts Concerning Gal 4:1-11," *Journal of Biblical Literature* 70 (1951): 259-276; Martinus de Boer, "The Meaning of the Phrase τα Στοιχεια του Κοσμου in Galatians," *New Testament Studies* 53 (2007): 204-24; de Boer, *Galatians: A Commentary*, New Testament Library (Louisville, KY: Westminster John Knox, 2011), 252-61; Linda L. Belleville,

noun is etymologically related to the verb *systoicheō*, which means "to arrange in contrasting columns" or "to arrange in ranks," and the term was applied to ranks of soldiers, bricks and blocks in building, and organized packs of hunters.[8] By a natural progression, the noun came to refer to one of the particular items ranked in the series.[9] This can be misleading, because a single *stoicheion* is what it is only in rank with others. A *stoicheion* is not precisely an individual, but forms part of a system, and the interrelated, systematic aspect often has more emphasis than the notion of "elementary" or "simple." The *stoicheia* of a building form a ranked ordering, and the related term *stoichos* describes an "order" of interlocking items.[10]

"Elementary principles" is often taken to refer to "simple" teaching, and there is some basis for this conclusion in Paul. In Greek texts generally, the term does not connote simplicity but the foundational character of what is being described, with a further hint that the particulars form an interlocking system. Euclid's *Stoicheia* and the *Harmonika Stoicheia* of Aristoxenos are not books of "elementary school" mathematics or harmony, but lay out the main topics of their chosen subjects in a systematic, orderly fashion.[11] Similarly, in Aristotle the term refers to fundamental axioms or premises from which ethical and political conclusions may be drawn.[12] Menaechmus distinguished two meanings of the term in mathematics: Common postulates

---

"'Under Law': Structural Analysis and the Pauline Concept of Law in Galatians 3:21–4:11," *Journal for the Study of the New Testament* 26 (1986): 53-78; Clinton E. Arnold, "Returning to the Domain of the Powers: 'Stoicheia' as Evil Spirits in Galatians 4:3, 9," *Novum Testamentum* 38 (1996): 55-76; Ernest De Witt Burton, *The Epistle to the Galatians*, International Critical Commentary (Edinburgh: T&T Clark, 1920): 510-18. For Aristotle, see Lang, *Order of Nature*. D. R. Lloyd examines some aspects of Plato's theory of elements in "Symmetry and Asymmetry in the Construction of 'Elements' in the *Timaeus*," *Classical Quarterly* 56 (2006): 459-74. For Epicurean theory, see Michael Wigodsky, "Homoiotetes, Stoicheia and Homoiomereiai in Epicurus," *Classical Quarterly* 57 (2007): 512-42.

[8]Walter Burkert, "Στοιχειον. Eine semasiologische Studie," *Philologus* 103 (1959): 182.

[9]Wigodsky, "Homoiotetes," 524. Wigodsky is summarizing the analysis of Burkert, "Στοιχειον," a crucial essay on the subject in classical studies. J. Louis Martyn, *Theological Issues in the Letters of Paul* (Nashville: Abingdon, 1997), 113-18. For the prominence of binary oppositions in Greek thought, see G. E. R. Lloyd, *Polarity and Analogy* (Bristol: Bristol Classical Press, 1992).

[10]Burkert, "Στοιχειον," 181: "Die gewohnliche Paraphrase von στοιχος und seinen Ableitungen ist ταξις."

[11]As Burkert, ibid., 192 says: "Kein mathematischer Satz steht allein, er gehört in einem System."

[12]Aristotle argues that it is a major political principle (*stoicheia prōta*) that the supporters of the state must outnumber the critics (*Politics* 1309b 16, quoted in ibid., 169), and finds the ethical notion of the mean offers a valuable principle (*stoicheion*) for forming political judgments (*Politics* 1295a 35, quoted in Burkert, "Στοιχειον," 169-70). Burkert argues that in these contexts, the term does not mean "rudimentary" but fundamental, foundational and axiomatic.

and "any theorem used to prove another," adding that "in this sense many theorems are also *stoicheia* of each other." Drawing on the work of Walter Burkert, Michael Wigodsky glosses this comment by observing that "*stoicheion* must originally have referred to a presupposition as something paired with its consequence like an object with its shadow, and was then generalized to presuppositions common to many proofs."[13] The implied binary structure of the *stoicheia* will be relevant below.[14]

Most commonly, "elements" referred to the basic constituents of physical reality, and this is especially true when modified by "of the world." *Stoicheion* was not synonymous with *atomos*. Atomism was a particular theory about the basic constituents of material reality; using the term *stoicheia* did not commit the user to any particular theory: "Stoicheia . . . means 'the basic constituents of matter, whatever they may be.'"[15] Empedocles first isolated four "roots" of physical reality (water, air, fire, earth), though without using the *stoicheion* as a general category. Plato identified "the four" as *stoicheia*, tentatively suggesting that "we call [the four] *archai* and presume that they are *stoicheia* of the universe [*tou pantos*], although in truth they do not so much as deserve to be likened with any likelihood [*hōs en syllabēs*]" (*Timaeus* 48B). In Plato, *stoicheion* sometimes refers to the geometric shape that in his theory gives each element its particular properties: "that solid which has taken the form of a pyramid [is] the *stoicheion* and seed [*sperma*]

---

[13]Wigodsky, "*Homoiotetes*," 524. He notes that "one of the earliest-attested meanings of the word is 'shadow' . . . presumably because an object and its shadow form . . . a set" (524).

[14]As a linguistic term, *stoicheion* was a letter of the alphabet or an "elementary sound," and was used in a similar fashion in music theory, close to the English "tone" (Hermann Koller, "Stoicheion," *Glotta* 34 [1955]: 161-74; Burkert, "Στοιχεῖον," 177). Plato and others distinguish *stoicheion* from *gramma* as referring to a basic sound of spoken language that is "in rank" with other sounds. It is not a letter but a syllable or basic word (*Cratylus* 393d, 424b-d, 433a, 434a-b). The elementary things are sometimes elementary sounds set over against the spaces of silence that make up a large part of any spoken language. In some ancient linguistics, letters have particular power, and *logos* has to mediate between them so that they cannot destroy one another. *Logos* keeps the powerful letters in their ranks. *Logos* ensures that particular *stoicheia* stay in their *stoichos*—they stay in their ranked place. By the same token, keeping elements in their proper place is a way of ensuring the viability of *logos*. Vowels are seen as especially powerful, and this accords with the fascination with the mystical name YHWH, rendered in Greek as ΙΑΩ, the middle, first and last vowels of the Greek alphabet. Thus alphabetic uses of the word expand into cosmological uses. Letters are the fundaments of creation in some forms of linguistic mysticism: "The 7 heavens constantly sound forth the 7 vowels; their echo becomes the creator of earthly existence. . . . The elements from which this world is made are generated from the sound of a letter which rings forth in the upper world" (Delling, "Στοιχεῖον," 7:671; quoting the Valentinian gnostic Marcus).

[15]Wigodsky, "*Homoiotetes*," 525.

of fire" (*Timaeus* 56B).[16] According to a widespread theory, the elements exhibited different combinations of wetness and temperature. Earth is cold and dry, water cold and wet, air hot and wet, and fire hot and dry. *Stoicheia* was capable of combining with other genitive phrases ("of language" or "of music," for instance), but a number of scholars have concluded that when it is used in the specific phrase *ta stoicheia tou kosmou* it invariably refers to the four (or five) elements of physical reality.[17] For some, physics shades over into politics, and the fact that men share the same elements becomes a democratic principle; others press the point to formulate evolutionary theories of brotherhood between men and animals.

Aristotle theorized extensively on elements as constituent parts of the physical universe. An element is a "body into which other bodies may be analyzed, present in them potentially or actually . . . and not itself divisible into bodies different in form" (*On the Heavens* 3.3, 302a15). *Stoicheia* regularly appears alongside plants and animals as "things that are by nature" (*Physics* 2.1, 192b1011, where they are described as *ta hapla tōn sōmatōn*). Elements are key to Aristotle's understanding of motion, and hence crucial to his theory about the order of reality. Things are ordered according to place, by their inclination up or down. Because they exist *physei*, each element has an inner principle of motion and rest, unique to itself. Each element has its own lightness or heaviness—not weight, but a natural inclination to move toward a particular place of rest. Being light, fire inclines upward; being heavy, earth inclines downward.[18] By moving naturally, the element actualizes itself and comes to rest in its intended, telic place. Aristotle acknowledges that the motion of things sometimes goes contrary to nature. Fire may move downward or be arrested in its upward motion, and heavy earth may be moved upward. Unnatural motion is a result of violence, and the cause behind the interruption of natural motion is usually obvious

---

[16]Wigodsky describes this as a "tentative" statement, an indication that Plato's terminology is innovative (ibid., 525).

[17]E.g., Rusam, "Neue Belege," 124: "Die Wortverbindung στοιχεια του κοσμου dagegen schliesst aus, dass es sich hier um andere Elemente als um die vier bzw. Funf physicalischen handeln könnte. Der lexikalische Befund lässt keinen anderen Schluss zu."

[18]Lang, *Order of Nature*, 167. Lang describes the tensions in Aristotle's physics as follows: Elements do not share a common nature and thus "although they are included among the things that are by nature and all things within nature are composed of them, there is no one universal element, nor is there a universal nature that is shared by the elements." As a result, they are not included as a separate topic in the *Physics*, which attends only to nature, motion and common and universal things (167). My summary of Aristotle's theory relies on Lang's account (part 2).

(e.g., a boy threw an earthy rock). Natural motion of elements, however, comes from a hidden source, and it is because of this natural motion that the cosmos has an orderly configuration.[19]

Aristotle's cosmos is a stately dancehall, each element and substance smoothly growing toward its telos. That is an altogether too harmonious world-picture for those ancient thinkers who claim that elements do not remain what they are but resolve into one another. Burning turns something earthy into something fiery; evaporation is heavy water translated into light air. Following Heraclitus, who spoke of the "mighty strife among the members" that make up the universe, Empedocles theorized that the world is characterized by a "continual exchange which never ceases." The four "unite in love" or are separated "by the hate of the strife."[20] Ovid mentions the Stoic-inspired fear that earth, water and sky will someday be reduced to one element, fire. In the following lines, he worries about inundation with water, a flood that would end the world as we know it. Philo believed the elements to be immortal, but claimed that they exist in a constant circular exchange and round of apparent death and rebirth. And human beings get caught in the machinery.[21] While the elements once were in harmony, they are now in a state of constant strife due in part to their never-ending shape-shifting. Death brings relief, as the elements making up the physical body disperse and return to their origins, but even death does not bring peace to everyone. Drawing on this thread of theorizing, Plutarch lays out a remarkable theory of theosis: "In the same manner in which water is seen to be generated from earth, air from water, and fire from air, as their substance is borne upward, even so from men into heroes and from heroes into demons the better souls obtain their transmutation. But from the demons a

---

[19]Aristotle also argued from an analysis of the motion of the four elements that a fifth *stoicheion* must exist. Motion, he presumes, is either linear or circular. Both are simple and natural motions. Depending on their heaviness or lightness, the four elements move either toward or away from the center, so the four elements move only linearly. If circular motion is a simple, natural motion, there must be some element whose nature it is to move circularly. This fifth element Aristotle calls *aithera*. See *On the Heavens* 1.2. Lang provides a lucid analysis of the argument (*Order of Nature*, 173-80).

[20]Empedocles is from *Fragment* 30, quoted in Schweizer, "Slaves," 456. See Rusam, "Neue Belege," 124, who cites a passage in which Empedocles indicates "dass die Liebe die verbindende Macht unter den Elementen ist."

[21]All the references in this paragraph are from Schweizer, "Slaves." Ovid is from the *Metamorphoses* 256-28 (quoted p. 459); and Philo from *De aeternitate mundi* 109-11 (quoted p. 459), though the Philonic source of the quotation is disputed. See Schweizer's summary statement on p. 464.

few souls still, in the long reach of time, because of supreme excellence, after being purified, come to share completely in divine qualities."[22]

Even when defined as physical elements, *stoicheia* are often intimately linked with religious beliefs and practices. This is the case partly because "elements" can refer to spiritual entities. In the Greek Magical Papyri, the term refers to stars, spirits or gods, and sometimes to the astral decans that rule over ten-degree sections of the celestial sphere.[23] Biblical scholars have noted that some Jewish texts use *stoicheion* to describe elemental spirits (perhaps Wis 7:17; 19:18; 4 Macc 12:13, though the last seems to use the word in its more common scientific sense).[24] Rites of purification and sacrifice, as well as ascetic renunciations, become a means for overcoming the deleterious effects of the strife of the elements.[25] Human salvation depends on

---

[22]Plutarch, *De defectu oraculorum* 10, quoted in Schweizer, "Slaves," 462.

[23]Arnold ("Returning," 57-58) notes that "in the Greek Magical Papyri, the term *stoicheia* is used most commonly in connection with the stars and/or the spirit entities, or gods, they represent. In a related sense, *stoicheia* was also used to refer to the 36 astral decans that rule over every 10 degrees of the heavens. . . . Each of these astral decans could also be represented by a magical letter. Given one of the common usages of *stoicheia* as letters of the alphabet, it is easy to see how this usage could have arisen." He argues that "it is quite probable that the term *stoicheia* was used of astral decans in the first century A.D. or prior." See also Clinton E. Arnold, *The Colossian Syncretism: The Interface Between Christianity and Folk Belief at Colossae* (Tübingen: Mohr Siebeck, 1995), 158-94; and N. T. Wright, *Colossians and Philemon*, Tyndale New Testament Commentary (Downers Grove, IL: InterVarsity Press, 1988), 101-2, who links *stoicheia* to the tribal tutelary deities that are hinted at in various places in the Old Testament (Deut 32; Dan 11).

[24]Many have questioned whether there is any evidence that this "personalized-cosmological" (Bundrick's term, "*Ta Stoicheia*," 357) was current prior to the third century AD. Walter Wink exclaims over the "utter lack of a single scrap of evidence that anyone prior to the third century C.E. had regarded the stoicheia as personal beings, fallen angels, or demons in any form" ("The 'Elements of the Universe' in Biblical and Scientific Perspective," *Zygon* 13 [1978]: 244). Clinton Arnold's evidence from the Greek Magical Papyri is strong, but he can offer no more than a "quite probable" on the question of whether the term was used for astral decans in the first century AD.

[25]The Pythagorean Alexander Polyhistor explained the process in a rich passage: "the four *elements*, fire, water, earth, air . . . wholly undergo changes and are altered. And from them the animate, intellectual world came into being, globular encompassing in its middle the earth, also globular and inhabited all around. . . . In the world light and darkness, warm and cold, dry and wet are equivalent. By a predominance of warm summer comes, of cold winter. . . . The best (parts) of the year are when there is an equal share. . . . The growing Spring is healthy, the waning Fall unhealthy. Also the dawn of the day is growing, the evening waning and therefore unhealthy. The ether around the earth is unshakeable and unhealthy, and everything in it mortal; the highest ether, however, is always moving and pure and healthy, and everything in it immortal and therefore divine. . . . Hermes . . . escorts the souls away from the bodies, out of earth and sea, and the pure ones are brought to the highest (place or circle or element), the impure . . . are bound by untearable chains. The whole air is filled by souls, and these are considered to be the demons and heroes. . . . To them go purifications, averting sacrifices, all oracular practice, prayers and similar (rites). . . . Not the same honors are, as they think, due to the gods and to

observing rites and disciplines of purity, which include purging baths, sacrifices, prayers and avoidance of sexual defilement. Participation in these rites of purification enabled the performer to ascend eventually beyond the four elements into the fifth element, which was "always moving and pure and healthy." The rites, in fact, ensure the continuing stability of the cosmos. The structures and interactions of the elements form a complex and shifting *taxis*, and that order is saved from chaos only by rites of worship. The blocks of the universe stay in their ranks only as the boundaries of pure and impure, holy and profane, are drawn and protected from transgression. Ritual and liturgical performance regain and retain some semblance of primordial harmony.

In a Jewish context, Philo linked this Pythagorean complex of ideas to the rites of Torah. In *On the Special Laws* (2), he explains that the Jews used trumpets at the beginning of the climactic seventh month because the "trumpet is an instrument used in war." The war involved in the feast included the strife of nature with nature. God keeps the world in a state of peace, and the feast of trumpet-war expresses Israel's thanks for his constant peacemaking.

> The forces of nature use drought, rainstorms, violent moisture-laden winds, scorching sun-rays, intense cold accompanied by snow, with the regular harmonious alternations of the yearly seasons turned into disharmony. . . . The law instituted this feast . . . to be as a thank-offering to God the peace-maker and peace-keeper who destroys factions both in cities and in the various parts of the universe.

In other places (*Life of Moses* 2), Philo indicates that Israel's temple liturgy itself had a cosmic effect and that the ministry of the high priest in particular maintains the order of creation: "We have in (his vesture) . . . a typical representation of the world and its particular parts. . . . The three *elements*, earth, water and air, from which come and in which live all mortal and perishable forms of life, are symbolized by the long robe. . . . The three said *elements* are of a single kind, since all below the moon is alike in its liability to change

---

heroes, but for the gods they always clothe themselves in white and purify themselves with prayer and praise, for the heroes only in the afternoon. Purity is (reached) by purifications and baths and besprinklings and by being clean from sexual connexion and marriage bed and all defilement, and by abstaining from eatable animal-corpses, meat, mullets, blacktails, eggs and egg-laying animals, beans and other things about which orders are given to those who accomplish the initiations in the temples" (Quoted in Schweizer, "Slaves," 458).

and alteration."[26] Thus what we call "physics"—the study of the basic constituents and forces of the natural world—coheres in Greco-Roman and Hellenistic Jewish thought with religious activities. For Philo the institutions of Torah provide the physics of the religious universe, but we should add that Jews observe Torah in order to pacify the physical elements.

ELEMENTARY PAUL

What *Paul* does with the phrase remains to be seen, but the starting point is to see that he is doing something with a phrase that possesses a prior, recognized public meaning. *Ta stoicheia tou kosmou* means primarily the organized parts that constitute the system and order of the physical universe. Even in the strictest scientific sense, *ta stoicheia* are features of a religious and political outlook that included purificatory rites, sacrifices and intense spiritual disciplines. It is particularly against this latter background that we can understand the Pauline variations on this Hellenic theme.

We will examine Paul at length later, when we finally return, along a long and forked path, to Galatians. For now I make a few preliminary points, just as much as is necessary to get this aircraft of a book off the ground.

Paul[27] uses the phrase *ta stoicheia tou kosmou* in three passages (Gal 4:3; Col 2:8, 20), and once uses *ta stoicheia* by itself in the same sense (Gal 4:9). My focus will be on Galatians.[28] Galatians 3–4 is the theological core of the letter.[29] Paul responds to the Judaizing crisis by recalling the promise to Abraham (3:1-14), explaining how Torah fits into God's program for international blessing promised to Abraham (3:15-22), and then turning to an explanation of the role of Torah in the preparation of the world for the coming of the Christ (3:23–4:11). The two references to *stoicheia* occur in the third section of his argument, and come on the heels of several other images

---

[26]Both passages from Philo are quoted in Schweizer, "Slaves," 460. Schweizer summarizes Philo's position: "If the Jewish high priest did not bring God's Logos and the whole universe into the temple of God, so that in the war of the elements peace is restored and God established as guardian of peace every year, the world would break down" (464).

[27]I call the author of Colossians Paul because I believe it is Paul, but my argument does not depend on this attribution of authorship. Hebrews uses the term once in the arresting phrase *ta stoicheia tēs archēs* (Heb 5:12) and Peter writes of a conflagration of the "elements" (2 Pet 3:10, 12).

[28]My exegesis of the passage closely follows the clear, careful treatment in de Boer, "Meaning," though I arrived at most of my conclusions independently of his excellent article. On the question of the meaning of the phrase, however, my conclusions diverge significantly.

[29]For a structural outline of the center of this section, see Belleville, "Under Law," 54-55, and below, chap. 9.

and claims. Before *pistis* arrived, that is, before the advent of the faithful Jesus Christ,[30] "we" were in custody under Torah (*hypo nomon ephrourou-metha*), as if guarded by sentries (Gal 3:23). During that time, Torah functioned as a *paidagōgos* guiding those under its oversight toward Christ, so that justification could come by faith (Gal 3:24). After swiftly summarizing the new situation that has come into being since Christ, Paul returns to his characterization of the world prior to Christ, extending the image of humanity as a minor child kept under guardians who act *in loco patris*. While the heir is a child, he is no better than a slave to the *epitropoi* and *oikonomoi* that the father assigns to oversee him (Gal 4:1-2). Like a minor child under such guardians, "we" were children enslaved (*dedoulōmenoi*) under *ta stoicheia tou kosmou* (Gal 4:3). Paul's charge is that by reverting to Torah, the Galatians have turned *back* to those same elementary things rather than accepting the inheritance that has now come to them.

Who is the "we"? That it is not generically inclusive is evident from the fact that Paul switches to second person at the end of Galatians 3 (Gal 3:26-29) before returning to the first person at the beginning of Galatians 4. Since Paul is writing about the role of Torah in the history of Israel (Gal 3:23-24; 4:4-5), "we" must mean "we Jews."[31] "Under Torah," "under guardians and managers" and "under *ta stoicheia tou kosmou*" are parallel descriptions of Israel's childhood. They all refer to the life of Israel prior to Christ, but bring out different aspects of that pattern of life.[32] This supposition is confirmed by the fact that Paul thinks that the Galatians revert to *ta stoicheia* when they submit to Jewish demands that they be circumcised and maintain purity and food laws prescribed by Torah (Gal 4:9; see Gal 1-2). In a reenactment of the exodus, God sends the Son and Spirit like Moses and the pillar of cloud to bring Israel, his slave-sons, to maturity, to deliver them out from their immature bondage to the elements and to bring them to full sonship. Turning back to the elements is like returning to Egypt.

Redemption of *Israel* from the elements is only the beginning. In Galatians 4:8-9 Paul addresses "you," the Gentile Galatians, who once "did not

---

[30]See below, chap. 6.

[31]De Boer, "Meaning," 209-10. See the similar alternation of first and second persons in Eph 1-2.

[32]This is a truism of exegesis on the passage. De Boer, however, argues that Paul does not equate the law with the elements but rather the *doing* of the law with *veneration* of the elements ("Meaning," 215n50). The string of *hypo* phrases suggests otherwise: Custody *hypo nomon* and *hypo paidagōgon* is explained by reference to *hypo epitropous . . . kai oikonomous*, which leads to the conclusion that "we also" were *hypo ta stoicheia tou kosmou*.

know God" and were "slaves to that which by nature are no gods." This cannot refer to Israel, yet Paul charges that they are in danger of reverting (*epistrephete palin*) to *ta stoicheia*. If they are turning *again* to the elements, they must have been under the elements at some time in the past. Jews under Torah are under the elements, but Gentiles who had no Torah were *also* under some form of *ta stoicheia*. Paul dramatically, radically flattens the difference between Jew and Gentile.[33] The topography of Jewish life for millennia had been organized by the binary opposition of Jew and Gentile, circumcision and uncircumcision. As J. Louis Martyn says, Paul announces a world beyond old polarities, a world in which "there is neither circumcision nor uncircumcision" but only the reality of new creation (Gal 6:15: *oute gar peritomē ti estin oute akrobystia alla kainē ktisis*).[34] Paul describes this change as a transformation of the elements that constitute the world of Jew and Gentile. A new social physics comes to Jew first, then Greek: In the Son and Spirit, Jews are first rescued from Torah, but their rescue is the down payment on the rescue of the nations. In Christ, Gentiles too have come into their majority, and they ought not revert to Torah nor to any Gentile form of stoicheic life.[35]

What *are* the elements? Clearly Paul does not mean what Aristotle or Greek scientists meant. He does not claim that the gospel announces a change in the constitution of the physical world. As with *physis*, he uses *stoicheia* to describe a change in the basic constituents of the social and cultural cosmos. We can be more specific. While *stoicheia tou kosmou* is sometimes linked with attachment to gods or other spiritual beings, it is more often linked to religious practices.[36] The controversy in Galatia is about

---

[33] De Boer, "Meaning," 209-10, also helpfully highlights the "blurring" of the Jew/Gentile distinction, though he argues that it occurs from the beginning of the passage. I believe that Paul distinguishes Israel from Gentiles until Gal 4:6.

[34] Martyn, *Galatians*, 570-77, and passim.

[35] As Mark Heim says, Paul puts Jesus "in an unavoidably comparative context" (Heim, *Saved from Sacrifice: A Theology of the Cross* [Grand Rapids: Eerdmans, 2006], 24).

[36] De Boer concludes that "the phrase *ta stoicheia tou kosmou* in 4:3, a technical expression referring specifically to the four constituent elements of the physical universe, is being used by Paul as a summary designation for a complex of Galatian religious beliefs and practices at the center of which were the four elements of the physical cosmos to which the phrase concretely refers. In Paul's usage, then, the phrase is an instance of *metonymy* whereby a trait or characteristic stands for a larger whole of which it is a part. In this case τα στοιχεια του κοσμου—the four elements of physical reality—stand for the religion of the Galatians prior to them becoming believers in Christ. Calendrical observances and the physical phenomena associated with such observances—the movements of the sun, moon, planets, and stars—were an integral part of these

whether Gentile disciples of Jesus must accept circumcision, observe Jewish purity regulations and renounce table fellowship with the impure. Do Gentiles have to become Jews to be followers of Christ, members of the new Israelite community? Must they subject themselves to Torah? In Galatians 4:10, Paul expresses his exasperation that once they have come to be known of God, they would subject themselves to enslaving stoicheic regulations, which he goes on to specify: "You observe days and months and seasons and years." Observance (*paratēreisthe*) of a festival calendar is a reversion to stoicheic life in more than one sense: It involves subjection to the heavenly bodies (sometimes called *stoicheia*) that kept time for all ancient people; but even if the Galatians revert to the *Jewish* festival calendar, that still constitutes a fall back into stoicheic life, a return to "Egypt."

This point is confirmed by Paul's use of the phrase in Colossians.[37] He has warned about seduction by philosophy and human tradition, which are according to (*kata*) the stoicheic patterns of life (Col 2:8). He is more specific in Colossians 2:20. The Colossians who died with Christ came out from under (*apo*) the elements, but they act as if they are still living in the world constituted by the elements (*ti hōs zōntes en kosmō*). Their actions betray their convictions, for they act as if Christ has never come. The world they died to is a world of purity prohibitions: "Do not handle, do not taste, do not touch." A purity system is relevant in a world mapped by the distinction of holy and profane space: Only the pure can draw near to God; only the holy can approach what is holy, for holy things are for holy people. In most civilizations of the ancient world, sacrifice, performed by priests, was the primary ritual for traversing the boundaries of sacred and profane in order

---

religious beliefs and practices. The gods the Galatians worshiped were closely linked to the four στοιχεια so that worship of these gods could be regarded as tantamount to the worship of τα στοιχεια themselves" ("Meaning," 220-21). He adds that the use of this phrase plays a strong rhetorical role in Paul's argument, associating embrace of Torah with a reversion to the paganism from which the Galatians had so recently converted. Conversely, liberation from *ta stoicheia*, Paul argues, includes liberation from Torah. He connects his conclusion to that of J. Louis Martyn, who argues that the central question in Galatians is, what time is it? Paul's answer is that "God's own (apocalyptic) 'time-keeping scheme' as revealed in Christ . . . has brought an end to the 'time-keeping schemes' associated with τα στοιχεια του κοσμου, whether by Jews or by Gentiles" (24).

[37]De Boer is correct that in Galatians calendrical observances are "the *only* relevant point of contact . . . between the observance of the Law and the veneration of τα στοιχεια του κοσμου" ("Meaning," 222), but that narrow conclusion, true enough regarding Galatians, obscures the fact that the same phrase appears in Colossians, where slavery under the elements manifests itself in adherence to rules of purity and avoidance.

to approach the gods, and these approaches were often made according to a schedule determined by observation of the sun, moon and stars. "Do not handle, do not taste, do not touch" thus implies an entire system built from the binary oppositions of holy and profane, clean and unclean.

Practices of purity imply a cosmos, a way of organizing and construing reality. Distinctions between clean and unclean map the social world into distinct regions. Purity regulations form an economy of signs, a symbolic universe, but the symbolic universe is not self-enclosed. A symbolic map works with the world divvied up in specific ways. Purity regulations trace out a world that comes to seem natural to those who inhabit it.[38]

Rites of purity are not only *signs* of a cosmology that exists apart from the rites and practices. They are *efficacious* signs that ensure the coherence, the stability of the social world. Indeed, these practices *alone* ensure the continuance of the social world they signify. The order of the social cosmos *depends* on purity practices. Symbolic boundaries exist only if they are maintained in the minds and habits of a people. Israel's temple is a divine shelter because Yahweh comes to dwell there. Priestly guardians and worshipers treat it as inviolable holy space because of the divine presence. Without the presence of Yahweh and the sacred activity of priests, it is just a building. Bodily functions are impure only insofar as they are *considered* impure. Whether or not the Galatians and Colossians were worshiping the elements or considered them divine, they might well have considered them unruly powers that needed to be managed by regular sacrifice, careful observance of calendars, avoidance of defilement, prayer. Ancient thinkers are not primitive when they believe order depends on maintaining their stoicheic boundaries and rituals. It does indeed, because the order is a construct. They are not being primitive; they are being sociological. Paul is, of course, a theological sociologist, who believes that the stoicheic boundaries and rituals were instituted by God. Yahweh gave Moses instructions for building his holy tent, but Israel had to build it. He told them the rules for maintaining his holy space, but they had to do the maintaining. Stoicheic order is a divine-human construct. It is instituted by God but kept intact (or not) by human action.

Sacred space, purity rules, sacrifice and priesthood thus constitute the foundational reality of religious and social life in the ancient world, both

---

[38]Mary Douglas, *Purity and Danger: An Analysis of Concepts of Pollution and Taboo* (New York: Praeger, 1966).

Jewish and Gentile. These practices and boundaries are *stoicheia* because they are arranged in ranks; they are *stoicheia* because they constitute the basics of religious and social life. They are very appropriately called "elements of the world," and it is these that Paul says have now lost their force.

CONCLUSION

Paul, I said, is a sociologist, transposing terms from Greek thought into a social, covenantal key. He does so with *physis* and with our key phrase, *ta stoicheia tou kosmou*, which he translates from its normal home in Greek physics into the realm of biblical sociology. He recognizes that the social *kosmoi* of Jews and Gentiles stay together only because both maintain their great Nos: do not handle that, do not step there, do not touch that, do not eat this. Focusing on stoicheic order and its transformation by the gospel will enable us to meet our criteria of success: It will enable us to develop a successful atonement theology that is historically plausible, evangelical, inevitable, Levitical, fruitful and, of course, Pauline. It will enable us to develop an atonement theology that is simultaneously an atonement sociology.

Paul tries to convince everyone to *stop*: everything is pure; no more circumcision/uncircumcision; no holy space other than the human being and human community indwelt by the Spirit of Jesus. Paul told everyone that the physics of religion and society had been transformed, and that the end of the old elemental system was the great moment of maturation, when the human race grew up from slaves to sons. A world beyond stoicheic order— that is a *saved* world, a world fulfilled as new creation.

All this seems anticlimactic to us who live on the far, far side of this transformation. We look at the fewer, simpler, easier rituals of the Christian church and wonder, Is that *it*? How can *this* be salvation? Jesus died for *this*? Here we need to catch the full force of Paul's rhetoric. To say that Paul announces a transformation of "order" is not to say that he advocates a change in the "external" institutions and practices of Jews and Gentiles that leaves the persons themselves unchanged. The humanity of Jews and Gentiles is determined by different *nomoi*, and because of that they have different "natures." A change in the cultural, ritual and institutional patterns that define those natures is a change of human nature, a transformation of a dual *physis*, divided between Jew and Gentile, into one new, universal human *physis*. God divided the human race, and now the same Creator God has reunited it. Nothing could express the root character of the change brought by the gospel more stunningly than the language of physics. Jesus did not merely rearrange the surface. The world *works* differently now, because it is no longer made up of the same stuff. It is as if Paul announced that Jesus transformed the world right down to the quarks.

For many Jews and for pagan Gentiles, giving up rules about tasting, touching, handling meant giving up hope for salvation. For Jews like Philo, for Egyptians, Babylonians, Greeks and Romans too, the end of *ta stoicheia* could only mean the end of the cosmos—for some, *literally* the end. It was *unthinkable* that human beings could outgrow subjection to *ta stoicheia* or the practices that express that subjection. Liberation from *stoicheia* simply means liberation from order itself, for there appears to be no conceivable order besides stoicheic order. For many, the gospel Paul announces is no good news, it seems, but a threatening wave of chaos.[39]

---

[39]It is not entirely clear whether Paul believes that the world *once* operated as Philo thought it did. His focus in Galatians is not on the cosmology but on the practices of stoicheic religion that imply a continuing attachment to a world that has passed. Colossians makes the cosmological issue more central. Jewish observances of festivals, new moons and Sabbaths are no more than shadows, but the substantial something that casts a shadow is Christ (Col 2:16-17). Believers die to the world of *ta stoicheia* by dying with Christ (Col 2:20), and rise again with Christ as their life (Col 3:3-4). Christ is himself the new cosmos of the believer, as he is the principle of coherence and unity in the cosmos as a whole, for in Christ the Creator all things cohere (Col 1:17). What ensures the persistence and harmony of creation and of the church is not the continuation of sacrifice, purity regulations, festivals and other stoicheic observances. Now at least, if not before, what accounts for the harmony of the world is rather a fifth element, Christ the Quintessence. Laying aside the sacrificial knife and eating a bit of pork required an act of radical faith in Christ, which was also a radical shift of cosmology.

three

AMONG GENTILES

AN ANCIENT JEWISH TRAVELOGUE

✝

You are a Jew." He regarded me with the haughty disdain that is second nature to noble Egyptians. He was utterly clean shaven—not only beardless but also hairless and eyebrowless. His white robe hid his chest, but I was certain that every hair had been plucked from his breast too.

He was right. I am a Jew. Circumcised on the eighth day, of the tribe of Benjamin, a Hebrew of Hebrews. I was in Thebes on my way to visit the Jews of Elephantine. I had business in Elephantine, business that I hoped would eventually take me to the East, to Greece, finally home to Jerusalem by Pentecost.

I was sitting under a shade tree outside the temple of Horus, cooling and drinking. I had had a long journey.

"You were once our slaves." His handsome mouth twisted into a smirk.

I nodded. I did not want to talk to him.

"I know the whole story," he continued. "You Jews are the most execrable people. You would perform abominations in our land, offering our sacred animals in sacrifice. You caused a great plague to break out among us. You were lepers among us, and we expelled you for our own safety. We had to expel you to maintain our order of *ma'at*, the purity of Egypt."

He spoke falsely, but I did not want to argue.

"You would have infected us if we had not driven you out. We had to purge our sacred land of your impurities. Purity is the main element of our worship. We gathered many thousands of you lepers and drove you out of the land. It saved Egypt."

"It saved the Jews," I responded, and immediately regretted it.

He smiled condescendingly. "Is that what you tell? I have heard otherwise. I have also heard of your religion. It is horrible. You regard as profane everything we hold sacred, and permit all the gods we abhor. You have a statue of a donkey, and you offer to it sacred bulls because we worship Apis. We Egyptians had to get rid of you because we are the most religious of all the nations of men, excessively religious. We honor all the gods, with great ceremony."

It occurred to me to answer that he was nothing but an idolater who did not know the true God, but I held back. I wished I had some appointment that offered escape, but there was none. It would be rude to leave him, rude to argue with a man in his own country. I resigned myself to the barrage. Perhaps I could learn something.

"We are most scrupulous for cleanliness," he was saying. "We believe that purity is necessary if we are to please the gods. We drink from cups of bronze and rinse them out every day. We wear garments of linen that are always newly washed." He gestured elegantly at his robe, which was indeed dazzling white. "We priests—we are called *wab* because we are purified—we shave ourselves all over our bodies every other day, so that no lice or any foul thing comes on us. We wear only linen, and sandals of papyrus. We wear no wool in the presence of the gods. We wash ourselves in cold water twice a day and twice in a night, in the sacred lake near the temple. Before we enter the temple, we have to chew natron to cleanse our breath and we have to fumigate ourselves with incense. We must keep ourselves from women during the days before we are to serve the god. We have countless services to perform for our gods, so they will be favorable to us."

"We have similar statutes," I ventured. "We too must be clean before entering the presence of our God, who is the God of heaven and earth," I added. "Our women cannot enter the presence of God during the time of their flow, nor after childbirth. Men and women who lie with one another must wash before entering."

"We believe that we must obey our God if we want to please him," I said. "We can wash ourselves clean but have unclean hearts. We can be circumcised in flesh, but Yahweh also wants us to have hearts that are circumcised."

"That is not entirely unfamiliar. 'I am pure, pure, pure, pure!'" he suddenly cried. "'I am pure from evil.' That is from our *Book of the Dead*. We must be pure from evil to please the gods. We all will stand to have our deeds judged, weighed in the scales of Anubis, measured by the standard of *ma'at*, to see if we are righteous. We are weighed against the feather of *ma'at* in the scales."

"And we must be purified from death," I added. "Death above all."

He looked astonished. "You believe that death pollutes?"

"It is the worst of pollutions. We cannot be in a room with a dead body without being defiled by it. Every form of impurity is a form of death. Flesh is mortal and spreads impurity. When flesh dies it spreads death."

"We Egyptians do not believe that. The realm of death is not a realm of evil. It is paradise. Our dead have great powers that can help us who remain alive. We do not avoid them because they can help us. When we die, we go closer to the gods. We go into the realm of Osiris. It is darkness, a realm of terrors. The West is a land of sleep. Darkness weighs on the dwelling place. Those who are there sleep in their mummy forms. They don't awake to see brothers. They don't see fathers, or mothers. Their hearts forget their wives, their children. But it is not a place of impurity. No one who has eaten abominable food can enter a tomb. If I enjoy my wife, I cannot go into a tomb until I have been purified. We must be pure to enter into the realm of the dead."

He paused for a moment considering, glancing at me from his browless eyes.

"My father was a priest before me," he explained, "and the king gave him a tomb among the priests. It is a great privilege to receive a tomb from the king. On my father's tomb we have inscribed this dedication: 'The king gave me this location, for I always did what the king favors.' It is true. He was a very loyal priest, and deserved the privilege. We have to keep the tomb supplied with all necessary provisions, where we leave the things that our dead need to enter and live in the west country. They need food and drink, cakes, meats, beer, wine, fruits, vegetables. They need to have those things that adorn them, oils and paints to make them beautiful in the West." He scoffed silently. "I have heard of some who do not bring food to their dead, but only statues of food or baking or cooking. A woman kneading bread in one statue, a man offering a bird in another. They leave these in the tomb and think that this will suffice. I do not agree. The dead live differently, but they live, and they need all that we need to live. We need to supply the dead for the same reason we serve the gods—to keep the world orderly."

He stopped and looked at me as if I were a peasant. "We believe that we all have a body, a *ka* and a *ba*. When we die, we make mummies of our bodies and put them in tombs. But the *ba* and *ka* remain. But they need to be united if we are to live in the west country. They need to be united in an *akh*. Our rituals are *akh*-makers, akhifiers. When we do the rites, our *akh*s become united with the life-giving Sun and with Horus. You see, each night the Sun dies and goes into the place of the dead, into Duat and Akhet, the two zones of the world of the dead. Re's journey each day is from birth in the morning to death at night. But the Sun can only come to life if it receives power from Osiris. Every night the Sun merges with Osiris in his tomb, and by uniting with Osiris the Sun takes new life. Every morning he is reborn on Nut's thighs, and sails along the Winding Canal across the body of Nut that stretches over us, over Geb, the earth, her husband. The dead die and are reborn each day with Re, with the power of Osiris. We offer our prayers and spells to protect our dead from the dangers of the underworld—snakes and scorpions and crocodiles. Our kings ascend from the world of the dead to become stars, to join the great Giant in the night sky, to sit on a pure throne of heaven. Do you understand?"

I understood nothing. But he ignored me.

"I can remember the day of my father's embalming. My mother and sisters and all the women of our house covered their heads and faces with mud. They went around the city beating their breasts, their robes drawn up and their breasts exposed. We men beat ourselves too, lamenting and mourning the great father we had lost. Embalming is a great art. Some of our people are employed regularly for this."

His eyes swept toward the hillside behind us, where the necropolis stood. Momentarily he looked wistful. "My father's funeral," he said. "My father's funeral was the most impressive thing I have ever witnessed in my life. We processed up to the necropolis—bier, family, mourners, porters with his canopic jars. He was taken into the burial chamber, and his face turned to the south to be bathed in light. 'May your mummy be set up in the sight of Re in the court of the tomb,' we prayed. The priest chanted a prayer:

Hail great god, lord of the place of the Two Goddesses of What is Right.
I have come before you so that you may bring me to see your perfection.
I know you, I know your name,
I know the name of these forty-two gods who are with you in this broad
    court of the Two Goddesses of What is Right.

I have not orphaned the orphan of his goods;

I have not done the abomination of the gods;

I have not slighted a servant to his master;

I have not caused affliction; I have not caused hunger; I have not caused
    grief; I have not killed;

I have not harmed the offering-cattle; I have not caused pain for anyone;

I have not reduced the offerings in the temples;

I have not harmed the offering-loaves of the gods;

I have not taken the festival-loaves of the blessed dead;

I have not penetrated the penetrater of a penetrater; I have not masturbated;

I have not reduced the measuring-vessel, I have not reduced the measuring
    cord;

I have not encroached on the fields; I have not added to the pan of the
    scales;

Nothing evil can befall me in this land, in this broad hall of the Two
    Goddesses of What is Right,

because I know the names of the gods who dwell in it."

It was an impressive prayer, and I said so.

"But the most important moment was the one to come. It was the Opening of the Mouth. If my father was to live in the West, he had to have the use of his eyes, his ears, his tongue. A *sem* and two lectors circled the mummy chanting 'Be pure! Be pure! Be pure! Be pure!' Four times. Then the *sem* went into a trance and became the son of the dead. The other priests woke him, and the *sem* said that he had seen his father—my father—in all the forms that he has. The other priests called on the *sem* to protect his father. The *sem* becomes Horus, and the dead is Osiris. Then they brought a young calf with its mother, and while the mother cow looked on, they slaughtered the calf before her. She bellowed and cried, because she too was lamenting the death of my father, and the priest took the foreleg of the calf and ran to the mummy. The foreleg makes the *ba* go above and the corpse go below. Then the *sem* touched the face of the statue and the mummy with his finger, as if he were cleaning the mouth of a newborn baby. He poured out water and grain. Then it was done. He said, 'I have given breath to those who are in hiding. The breath of life, it comes and creates his image, his mouth is opened. His name endures forever, because he is an excellent *akh* in the netherworld.'"

He took a breath, then continued. "We have many priests, but not everyone is a priest. A priest is pure, has to be pure more than anyone else. The priests take three offerings that are brought to the god every day. They are his meals. Before he can serve the king, the priest has to wash his body with water, purify him with incense, cleanse his mouth with natron. He recites some chants as they enter. He carries in a candle and first has to wake the god: 'Awake in peace! May your awakening be peaceful!' He has to break the seals of the door bolts and draw back the bolts."

"Your god is difficult to wake," I said, mischievously. Then I remembered the psalm, and knew that Yahweh too sometimes seems to sleep.

He ignored me and continued, "The priests set the table with flowers, food, drink. We offer grain, vegetables, wine, meat, fowl. After the god is finished, we take the food away and purify him for sleep. He is returned to the shrine until the next time when the priests will serve him a meal. It is all necessary if Egypt is to survive and flourish. What we do in the temple for the god, the god does for us in the land."

He paused. "Of course, those of us who are without the temple also can communicate with the gods. There are listening holes at some temples where we can speak. I saw a stela once that was covered with carvings of ears, the ears of Ptah, who would listen when we prayed toward his rock. And we can leave surrogates to serve in the temple."

My look must have been skeptical, because he continued somewhat defensively. "We cannot go into the presence of the god, but we can place an image there. My family has left many offerings at the temple of Hathor— figures of women, one nursing a child, plaques with cows, ears, eyes, male members."

I did not even attempt to hide my horror.

"Yes, male members. The gods are gods of life. Some of their figures are in the shape of a male member, and we offer them an image of a male member so they will make us fertile, vibrant, alive. Male and female members."

"And these are placed in your temples?"

"Of course." He was getting agitated. "Every time your priest goes into the temple, there is a male member in the temple, is there not?"

"Yes, but our priests take care to hide their nakedness when they are in the presence of God."

He looked genuinely puzzled. I changed the subject.

"Do you not offer sacrifice?" He did not seem to understand, so I added, "Do you kill and burn animals in your worship?"

"Yes. Or perhaps I should say that we have something that is somewhat like that. We offer animals to the gods, and then butcher them for a feast. These are usually pigs."

"We cannot eat pigs or sacrifice them," I said, interrupting him. "We can eat sheep, goats, oxen, deer. But we cannot eat pigs or bears or any fish that does not have scales."

"Yes, we too have to be careful of what we eat. We cannot look at beans. Different gods have different rules for us. Re abhors fish, so the priests of Re do not eat fish. Some of our spells should not be recited after eating pork. In some temples, cows, pigs, ewes, pigeons, fish are not eaten. We are not allowed to eat some parts of a slaughtered animal. All the gods are different."

"We serve only one God, so we always know what we are to do."

With that, our conversation ended.

◆ ◆ ◆

"My fathers were here," I mused as I wandered the dusty streets of Babylon. They had been captured and transported to this very place. Perhaps the palace where Daniel had served Nebuchadnezzar was still standing, or the place where the king had set up his great image and commanded all in Babylon to bow to it. Perhaps this square was the place of the great furnace where the three children sang as they stood in the fire with the son of God.

The temples of the land between the rivers are very impressive. As I have traveled along the Euphrates, I have seen great houses of the gods, some standing strong like fortresses, some in ruins. Some structures rise up above the landscape like mountains made by human hands, with a temple at the top that seemed to scrape the edge of heaven. They must have been one hundred cubits tall.

I spoke to an old man who sat by the gate of the city. Temples, he said, were the main elements of worship in Babylon. They are divided into three main areas, a *babu*, a gate, and then the *bitu*, the house of the god itself, and the inner sanctuary is the *kissumu*, the dark room, the place that knows not daylight. He told me that the man-made mountains were called *ziqquratu*, which meant a place highly built. The temples were called the "bonds of heaven and earth," or the "highly built house." I could almost hear Sennacherib's great boast at the walls of Jerusalem, and the boast of the king of

Babylon of which Isaiah told. The temples of Babylon and Assyria are there to puff up the pride of kings.

And he told me of the great temple to the goddess Ishtar that once stood at that place. Its entrance was guarded by two pillars rising thirty or forty cubits. The walls were uneven, with buttresses pushing out alternating with recesses. Some of the recesses contained statues of goddesses with hands folded in intercession for the worshipers. On either side were images of fierce lions, or winged bulls with the heads of great kings—the old man could not remember, or had heard different stories. He told me that temples were always guarded by fierce beasts, bison, fish-men, goat-fish, dogs, bulls, scorpions, lions, heroes, eagles. I could not help but think of the great cherubim on the ark of the covenant, and the oil-wood cherubim that guarded the throne of Yahweh in Solomon's temple.

Once you had passed between the great pillars, he said, you came into a huge court surrounded by high, thick walls. To one side were steps leading to a higher area, another entrance that passed between two more great pillars into a smaller interior court. Still you were not at the heart of the house of this god, for there was yet another entrance to one side that led into an enclosed inner chamber. Even here, to enter the presence of the god, one had to turn once again. Even if all the gates were wide open, you could not see into the heart of the sanctuary, the dark inner room, the room that no light enters. A worshiper had to take a forked path, moving to the left, then the right, then the left again before entering the presence of Ishtar.

Around the courts and sanctuaries were hallways and corridors with high walls and forbidding passages. All around there were storage rooms for clothing, furniture and utensils. The house had a bakery and a kitchen and a brewery. Everything was designed to make it difficult to get into the presence of the goddess. The temple was the house of Ishtar, but like Yahweh our God, Ishtar did not open up her house to everyone.

Like our temple in Jerusalem too, these temples looked plain on the outside, and became richer and richer as you entered. The outside was brick, but within everything was covered with gold and lapis lazuli. At the very center, on an elevated platform or in a recess of the wall, was the image of the goddess, and this was the richest of all. The old man quoted a great king boasting of the rich adornments that he gave to the image of the goddess: "With the wisdom and understanding of, and according to the desire of, the great gods who love me, I created an icon of the goddess Ishtar, my mistress, which had never before existed. (I created it) from the finest stones, fine gold, making her great divinity resplendent. I set up her dais for eternity. I made this temple suitably resplendent." Another boasted that his temple had brought heaven to earth: "I decorated the house like the interior of heaven. I decorated its walls as splendidly as the brilliance of rising stars." He told me of a sacred barge for one of the gods, "adorned with silver wrought with gold throughout, the great shrine is of electrum so that it fills the land with its brightness, its bows made Nun [water] to shine as when the sun rises in heaven, to make his beautiful voyage of a million millions of years."

Like a human homeowner, he said, the god took the house as his own. To call the temple a "house" for the god meant that the god at rest in the temple was like a man at rest in his home. At times the house became almost identical to the god. The god's glory and light and sacredness was so strong in the house that the house itself became divine. He mentioned the temple of the god Ningirsu in Girsu, which was known as E-ninnu, the flashing thunderbird, which was another name for the god himself. Another was called "House rising sun" because it was the house of the sun god Utu. Another was "House causing light" because it was the home of the moon goddess.

"It is a great risk, then, for a man to build a house for a god, if the house is the god himself," I commented.

He looked at me carefully before he answered. "Men do not build the houses. The houses of the gods have been built by the gods, from the very beginning of all things. When Marduk had overcome Tiamat and established order in the world, he raised the summit of Esagila against the Apsu, then built the temple tower, a house with foundations of heaven and earth. That is why the temple has a *du-ku*, a pure hill, in the forecourt. It is a brick pedestal, and that is the sacred mound that came from the waters of chaos. The temple is the center of the world, with the chaos surrounding it. That is why the walls of our temples are so thick and the gates so strong. We must keep the house of the god safe. He must keep us safe, within the great fortress of the world."

I recalled an old myth of the detestable idol Baal, who also won a victory over the sea, over Yam, and then built his house on the mountain of Zaphon in the sacred city of Ugarit. And I thought again of my fathers, rescued from the sea by our God Yahweh, and then taken to a high mountain to build

Yahweh's house. And I thought of Noah in his great ship, filled with all the creatures of the earth, saved from the raging waters. And I thought of the creation of the world when Yahweh made the land come from the sea and called on plants to grow in it.

I thought again of Babylon and of my fathers carried into exile. I recalled the great visions of the prophet-priest Ezekiel, who saw the glory of Yahweh departing from his house because of our abominations, leaving his own house to desolation.

I spoke carefully, not wishing to offend. "If the god and his house are one," I said, "then the god will be there as long as the house is there. No matter what happens, the god remains."

He gestured to the ruins around him and shook his head sadly. "Does it look as if our gods have remained, and the houses of the gods have stood firm?"

I had to agree with him.

"No," he said sadly. "The gods do get angry, and when they get angry they leave their house and leave it in ruins. Marduk once abandoned his lofty shrine because he and the gods of heaven were angry with the shepherd of the people. Our priests are reminded of this danger every day."

I was curious. "What do you mean?"

"Every day, the priests of our temples awaken the temple and do the *pit babi*, the opening of the gate. Everyone who is within the temple is called to awaken—the gods and the priests. But we know that the gods do not always stay, and we worry that during the night, while the priests slept, the god has slipped away. We worry that perhaps we have done something to offend him, and that we do not know what we have done. So our priests begin the day with the *taqribtu* and the *ershemakku*, hymns of lamentations and pleas for our god to remain in his place and not to leave us. The sun goes dark every night, dying, and the god might too. So we call on the god like the sun, 'Appear like the Sun! Appear like the Sun! Watch your city!' Sometimes our priests even sing the great songs that lament the destruction of a city or temple. If we lament as if the temple is destroyed, perhaps the gods will have pity and not leave our city to destruction. When we lament, the lost powers that we can never recover come again."

He began to chant, quietly, mournfully, a solemn prayer of one abandoned by the god and goddess. I was much moved, and said so.

"This is why we must serve the gods. The gods created us to serve them, made us to be priests. The lower gods were unhappy serving the higher gods, and so the higher gods made us to take their place, to serve in their stead. If we do what we are required to do, the god will be satisfied and he will remain in his house and we shall be safe. There are butchers and cooks for the meat, bakers for the bread and brewers of beer. The temple is supplied by farmers and milkmen, fishermen, oxherds, orchard keepers. Some are specialists in setting the table of the god, and others are artisans who work with reeds, clay, gold, jewels or wood. There are weavers and there are washers. To entertain the god during his daily meals, we have singers, singers who specialized in lamentations, acrobats. Gatekeepers guard the gates of the temple and keep out the unwanted people. Barbers are there to ensure that all of the priests are pure."

"We too have our priests who serve our God in his house," I said.

He nodded. "Then your priests must have learned what it is like to serve the god his daily meals. Once the house is awakened, the priests must go to the god and prepare him for his morning meal. They wash and purify him, crown him with a tiara and put on his robes. They offer incense to cleanse the air around him, to make sure that he smells nothing that is evil in his nostrils. He is a king and he is treated as a king. Our priests set the glowing golden *passuru* table before him, lay out the dishes and bowls and plates to serve his meal. Drink and bread and fruit and meat. Beer and wine and milk, loaves of bread and sweet cakes, meats of oxen and fat of sheep, chicken, duck, pigeons, fruit of raisins, dates, grapes, and figs and dried figs, abundant vegetables. He is served honey and butter. Nothing cheap or common is brought to his table, no pork or mutton. He is a king and he eats like a king. He receives only the best of our food. While he eats, he is entertained with music, which our priests have learned to play. After he is done, his fingers are greasy and we bring a bowl of water for him to wash in. We do the same every evening as the day ends, when the temple goes back to sleep and the doors are closed. If we do not serve the gods, they will leave us, and all good will go with them. If we do not keep the gods happy, the world will fall back into the waters of death from which we all came."

"And so the priests eat with him."

He looked startled. "Eat with the god? Our priests eat with the god?"

I shrugged. "You do not eat with the god?"

"No. Our gods are too great to eat with us. The priests do not even see him eat. The priests receive food that comes into the temple, but they never eat with the god. That would be disgusting, if a human being ate before a god. Even the *king* does not eat with the god. When they have set the table before him, they pull the *siddu* around him, curtains that hide him from the priests during his meal. Each god and goddess eats alone, behind tent curtains."

I was feeling mischievous. "And when they draw back the curtains, the food is now gone?"

He looked at me with dismay, and some anger. "No, no. The gods are not men. The gods do not eat like men. They do not chew. Food does not go into their stomach. They are gods, and they eat like gods, and when they are done eating, when they have taken their fill and drunk as much as they wish, they still leave as much food as they began with, which belongs to the king to eat."

He paused, thinking. "Do your people share a meal with your god?"

"Yes. Sometimes an entire animal is burned on the *mizbeach*, but often it is only some of the best pieces, and the rest is given to the priests or the people."

"Your god is a god of fire."

I agreed. "He is a consuming fire."

I was feeling mischievous again. "You do all this before your god, you say. But your god is a statue. He is made from wood, and covered with gold plating, with jewels for eyes. He has eyes and a mouth, ears and a nose, hands and feet, but he cannot see or speak, hear or smell. He cannot taste the food you give him because his mouth cannot open. His fingers do not get greasy because his hands do not move, and he cannot leave the temple because he has no feet. How then can you say that your god eats your food and drinks the drink you place before him?"

The old man was aghast, and for a moment I thought our conversation had come to an abrupt end. "Do you not believe in the gods? Do you not worship any god?"

"I worship one God, the God of my fathers."

"But your god comes to you. He is near to you." His voice trailed off in confusion.

"Yes, he is near to us at all times. He is our Maker and our Lord."

"Then he is there in your temple. Your priests, at least, see him there?" He seemed to become more relieved.

"No. We have no images in our temple. We do not worship wood or gold. We believe that such images are dead, and we worship the living god."

He took a deep breath. "No, you misunderstand. You misunderstand us completely. The wood that our workmen use to make the images of our gods is not dead. It is alive. It is alive from the beginning. It already is filled with the power of god as soon as the craftsmen begin to make it."

I was ready to speak back, but I held my tongue.

"And the image does not remain as it was. It is true what you say. Until its mouth is opened, the god cannot smell incense, cannot eat food, cannot drink water. But it does not remain with the artisans and craftsmen. It must pass through the *mis pi*, the ceremony of the mouth-washing, and the ceremony of the mouth-opening. The image is taken from the workshop to the river bank, to the orchard and finally to the temple. At each place, its mouth is washed and its mouth is opened. As it goes from one place to another, it grows up. It is like a newborn at the beginning, but it is still a god. When the priests say their prayers over it, its mouth and nose are opened so it can smell incense and eat food and drink water. The craftsmen do not make the image, and the priests do not make the image. The priests sing a hymn, 'Born in heaven by your own power, born in earth by your own power.' The god makes the image, and when the mouth-washing is finished the statue is the god. He can receive our bread and our drink. He can dine in his place. He can pick up the food with his fingers, and he can walk away from his house with his feet. Ea, Shamash, Ashalluhi grant that his mouth eats and his ears hear. He becomes pure as the heavens as it goes through the ceremony. He is being filled with the fullness of the god. It comes into the fellowship of the gods, as he is fumigated and cleansed and his mouth is opened. He is dressed in his royal regalia and makes his first public appearance."

I had heard similar things in Egypt, and I wanted to change the topic. But he talked on and on about the rites of purity, the shavings and clippings and washings, the fumigations of breath and body. He mentioned the danger of impurity, and told me a story of a man who was not saved from death even though he called to his personal goddess for help.

I saw an opportunity and seized it. "Our god is more powerful than impurity. He has given us his word to tell us how we may be delivered from impurity."

He paused. "Sometimes our gods are powerless before the demons of impurity," he mused. "You shall see. I did not finish my story. The man was suffering from the torments of a *gallu*-demon, which had been placed on him. Silence and an evil malediction had been placed on him, had cut his throat like a slaughtered sheep. But Marduk saw and helped. Marduk went to his father Ea and cried out about the man afflicted by the *gallu*-demon. But what did Ea say? Ea said, 'What is it that you do not know, my son? What more can I give you? Marduk, what do I know that you do not know?' Do you see? Our gods are far, far above us. We cannot understand or fathom them. They do not mingle among us. Their ways are beyond our grasp. Even if we try to comprehend what they want and what they do, we cannot understand them."

A shadow passed across his wrinkled face. "The world is full of evil forces," he said quietly, as if trying not to be heard. His speech turned rhythmical, as if he were reciting a memorized song: "They are gloomy, their shadow dark, no light is in their bodies, ever they slink along covertly, walk not upright, from their claws drips bitter gall, their footprints are full of evil venom. Over high roofs, over broad roofs like a floodwave they surge, from house to house they climb over, doors do not hold them, locks cannot restrain them, through doors they glide like snakes, through the hinges they blow like wind." He stopped and took a deep breath. "The world has many powers. Some are evil, and seek to harm. Some are good. We try to cling to those that are good. We try to keep them in our temples. And we do all we can to ward off the evil."

"Our God too is great and high. He is also beyond our thoughts," I said. "And yet." I struggled to say what I meant. "And yet, our God has shown himself. We know him. He has spoken to us, and we have his word with us. We know what is good, what he delights in. He is mysterious, but he has shown us what he wants and he is good and a God of truth."

"Our gods also act to deliver us from impurity," he continued. "It is not true that the *sagga* makes one pure. The gods are the ones who give birth to their image, and the gods are the ones who purify the priests and others who approach them." He began to chant again, a hymn to Enki who consecrates the sky. "Kusu, the goddess of purity, cleanses us, and all the gods. We do not and cannot make ourselves pure without the gods. Here is what we think. We can protect ourselves if we placate the anger of the gods, if we plead with the gods to change their decision to give us an evil fate, if the impurity is removed, along with the impurity of the house and the surroundings, if we are able to return to an intact life and if we can find permanent protection against omens that come later. If we do all these things, we are safe. Then we are free."

Then you are never free, I thought. *You will always be slaves to your mighty gods and your proud kings who boast in their own flesh.*

But I did not speak it.

◆ ◆ ◆

Before I saw the parade, I heard the pipers wailing and the *choros* singing, mingled with the bellowing of a frantic bull. "We sing of Pallas Athene, the glorious goddess, bright-eyed, inventive, unbending of heart, pure virgin!"

My day in Athens had already convinced me that they are a deeply religious people, their city so full of altars and shrines, a god on every hill and under every tree. My soul churned to see such riches and so much passion devoted to vanities.

I turned a corner and the parade was before me, a surging, dancing line of people, all dressed in brilliant white robes, making their way toward the altar of Athena at the acropolis. At the head of the parade was a young man crowned with laurel. He wore a flowing cloak that covered only his shoulders, his nakedness showing beneath. He held an image of the goddess, who stood upright bearing shield and spear. Behind him came a man carrying a basket on his head that held the fillet and the knife. Then the bull, a huge thing, bellowing and rearing so that the man who led him could barely keep him in check, his horns glistening with the foil wrapped around them. Colorful fillets tied to sticks and to the heads of the worshipers streamed in the breeze. Fortunately, the animal's back legs were tied, the ropes held by a man who followed it in the procession. Behind him was a piper, then a line of men, some carrying wreaths and another with a small vessel of purificatory water. In the midst of the procession was an important-looking man who must have been a priest. He wore an elaborate *himation*, while all the rest of the men were naked or wearing short loincloths, *chitōnes*. A cart pulled by a donkey carried worshipers with wreaths and more instruments. The sweet aroma of incense trailed behind them as smoke streamed from a censer that sat on top of the head of the figure of a woman that formed the pillar of the censer. The air was bright with their joy.

I turned white when I saw what followed. An almost naked man brought up the rear of the procession carrying a large uncircumcised male member made of bronze. Others were bearing portraits of one whose flesh extended before him like the flesh of a donkey. It was disgusting, a sacrilege.

The procession wound up the hill along the narrow street toward an ornate altar. I have seen many altars on my travels, but this was the most magnificent. At the base was a stone pedestal, from which rose a column of stone. The altar was terra cotta, the sides decorated with carvings of strange creatures—a winged horse on each side with a neck like a serpent and a tail curling in an *s*. They were attacking a doe beneath.

Beyond the altar rose the temple of Athena itself. Four large steps went up to the floor of the temple. The entrance was guarded by four huge pillars whose capitals were like scrolls. The pillars held up a frieze that depicted the swirl and turmoil of a great battle. Some of the figures were dressed like Greeks, the others like Persians, and I learned later that the scene was from the great battle of Marathon. Strong Greek men swung heavy swords against crouching, desperate Persians. One Greek, his robe flying like a wing behind him, stood over a dead body as he attacked a Persian rider on horseback. I had heard of this temple, celebrating the victory of the goddess Athena, Athena Nike. It is a simple temple, for behind the pillars is only a single large cella, but it stands impressively at the side of a steep cliff above the city.

The great statue of Athena showed a sexless warrior. She was covered with long robes, her breast covered with an aegis and a corset full of snakes. On the aegis she wore the head of a Medusa, snakes curling out of her open mouth. On top of her helmet was a sphinx. In one hand she held a spear and in the other a shield depicting the Athenian slaughter of the Amazons. Another battle, between gods and giants, was depicted on the inside of her shield, and her sandals were decorated with scenes of the war between the Lapiths and the centaurs. The rest of the building was decorated with other scenes of the tale of Athena—her birth from the head of her father Zeus on the east pediment. Their temples are temples to gods of battle, but I wonder if the Athenians are not more worshipers of their own strength than the strength of the gods. I wonder if they do not boast more in their own flesh than in their gods.

To the east I could see the top of the Parthenon, which I had heard is one of the great wonders of the world. There, a large graven image of Athena sat enthroned, holding a spear, receiving her worshipers and keeping them in great fear.

As I watched, I saw a young man standing to the side of the procession. I bowed slightly. He seemed ready to talk.

"*Kalē*, isn't it?" he said. "Nothing is too good for the gods. We want to please them. All this music, this singing, it is all for them. We bring the best we have, and carry it from our homes, from our common world, into the sacred place where the goddess lives. The gods are dangerous. We cannot walk up to their altar without winning their approval. We want to call them down to us from Olympus, from the sky, wherever they may be, so that we can be with them. We dance now on the way to the high place so that the goddess will be there when we get to the top, and we can dance in her presence."

I restrained myself from replying. The youth had so much right, but so much was wrong too. I was sickened.

I gestured toward another phallic statue borne aloft by another nearly naked worshiper.

The youth smiled. "Priapus," he said. "He is one of our gods, a son of Aphrodite and Dionysus."

"You offer worship to this thing?"

"Yes, he is divine. He ensures our fertility, that our grapes and grain grow and that fathers have sons and daughters."

I had heard of such deities, but seeing one was different.

He looked at the procession for a few moments and then kept the conversation going on his own. "They say it began many ages ago, when the earth was very young. Prometheus tricked Zeus into accepting the bones of the sacrifice as his portion, bones turned to smoke. When we see smoke, we know there is a fire, and that the fire is probably from a man. When we send our smoke signals to the gods, we hope that they will come to meet us because they enjoy the smell of smoke. We need the gods. Without the gods, the world is nothing. We make them happy to keep them near us."

He paused. "My teacher tells me that sacrifice is our link with the gods above. It is the elementary thing of our friendship with gods. But at the same time every time we sacrifice we know that the gods are above and we are below. We eat the flesh, and are flesh. We are meat sacks, while the gods feast on ambrosia and smoke." He started chanting quietly:

often there comes
from Naxos for the sacrifice

of richly-fed sheep, together with the Graces,
to the slope of Kynthos, where
they say dark-clouded, thunder-flashing
Zeus.

He pointed at the altar and the procession. "We live on meat and on other dying things because we are dying things. And the gods are deathless. We send our *knisē* up to them, and we feast on flesh below. They are gods, we are rotting flesh. And yet, each time we kill an animal, we are also showing that we are not beasts."

I frowned. "Beasts kill beasts."

"Yes, but not as we do. We use knives. We make clean cuts. You will not see anyone tear into the raw flesh of that bull with their teeth. We roast and boil the flesh. We are those who cook, not those who eat raw meat. So every time we offer a *thysia* we are reminded of our place, our place between the gods and the beasts."

"Lower than the *Elohim*," I muttered. He did not hear me, and we both fell silent.

"You are a very religious people," I said.

The youth nodded. "Everything we do is done through sacrifice. All of our groups are formed by sacrifice. I am not a member of my *oikos* by birth but because a sacrifice was given to purify me from my birth. The mother is just a nurse for the man's seed, but our fathers are our real parents. But we are defiled by our mothers, and need to be brought into the house. My father recognizes me as his son because I have been brought into the family cult by sacrifice. Our *polis* is what it is by sacrifice."

It seems that the male member rules in Athens, I thought but did not say. What I said was, "Why aren't you in the parade? You seem eager to offer your prayers and worship."

He pointed to a line of stoups that encircled the altar. "The altar is in a sacred area. That is the place of the gods, and only the pure can draw near." He looked at the ground. "I am *akatharos*."

The word was unfamiliar, yet I knew exactly what he meant. "How?"

"My grandfather died."

"I'm sorry. You have been to the funeral?"

"No. I haven't seen him in many years. He doesn't live in Athens."

"Yet you are impure because of his death?"

"It is the way in Athens. When a close relative dies, the entire family is polluted."

"Not those who are in the house with the body?"

"Oh, those too, as much as any. But the pollution of death is powerful. It works at a distance and runs along the lines of blood."

"My people believe that death defiles, but that it is not so powerful. It defiles those who touch the body and those who enter the death house. No others."

"I don't agree. Death is out of our control. It can't stay inside a house. All the other things that are outside our control pollute us too." He pointed to some women on the other side of the road, watching the procession. "They are probably polluted too."

"They are in their blood?"

He looked puzzled. "No, why?"

"Among my people, when women are in their blood, they are unclean and cannot come to the place of our God."

"We have no such custom," he answered. "No, they are unclean because they are pregnant."

Now it was my turn to be puzzled. "Being pregnant pollutes a woman?"

He nodded. "But not through the whole pregnancy. They are polluted for the first forty days, but after that they are clean. Priests encourage them to come into the temples in the later stages of their pregnancies. Once they give birth, though, they are unclean again, though only for a few days."

"Our God has given us similar ordinances."

"Purification is the science of division," he said, somewhat pompously. It sounded like something he had learned in school, and he admitted it. "I heard a great philosopher say that once. It seems to be true. The gods are not like us. They are immortal, and they don't need food and drink to live. The priests teach us rules to remind us that the gods are not like us. Their homes are sacred. They keep death from their presence. They keep intercourse from their presence, and anything connected with intercourse. That is why pregnant women and women with newborns are not allowed into the temple."

"Blood, the blood of the innocent, that defiles," I said.

The youth knew what I meant about blood. "Yes, we have a famous story about blood. One of the great heroes of the war with Troy came home to his wife, who slaughtered him like an ox for sacrifice, slaughtered him in his own bath. She set a trap for him and treated him like an animal. Her son—his name was Orestes—needed to avenge his father, but to do so he had to kill his mother. It was a horror, but he did so. But then he had to flee because he was polluted by bloodshed. The Erinyes pursued him here to Athens, where he sought protection from our goddess. It was the beginning of our Athenian way, because our goddess, wise and just, gathered citizens of our city to judge Orestes. Ever since, blood is no longer avenged by blood. We have courts and judges who decide, who bring an end to the bloodshed. Still," he paused and reflected, "we believe that blood pollutes the murderer and the city where he lives. A murderer has to be tried by the court, but if he is guilty, he has to be driven from the city. If he stays, he pollutes us all."

The parade was at the altar now, circling the altar, entering or forming that sacred space where the god's image would be placed and served. One of them must have been carrying a coal in a censer and some wood, because the fire blazed up on the altar. A man with a brush swept the area, followed by the *hydrophoros*, wearing a purple *chitōn* and an olive garland, who sprinkled water on the altar, on the still-bellowing bull, on the worshipers dancing around the altar. Another man called for silence as he drew handfuls of barley from a basket and strewed them around on the altar and the ground. He took the sacrificial knife and cut off a few hairs of the bull, which he scattered into the altar fire.

The young man seemed eager to tell me more. "Pollution is an important thing for us Athenians. We believe that a man must be clean if he wishes to be in the presence of a god. But that is not all. The gods show favor to *good* men. We cannot cover up an evil life with sweet smoke or the thighs of bulls. The gods delight in thighs, to be sure. We read of it in Homer—that the gods enjoy the feasts they receive. These are the words of Chryses to Apollo when Agamemnon refuses to return his daughter."

He recited it, intoning ancient words with the solemnity of youth. I had never heard the words before, and they stirred me.

"Chryses can pray to Apollo because he has been a faithful servant of Apollo. The gods remember and honor those who honor them. But that was not my point. I was saying that the gods love good men, not just those who burn thigh bones and fat. I got distracted. Homer does that to me. But one of our great philosophers has said that men who pile up injustice without limit bring down divine accusations on themselves. They think they can bribe the gods by sacrifices and prayers. But the gods know better, and the whole people is rewarded harshly for the impiety of one of its members."

"I know of that," I answered. "We believe the same. Our God looks for pious sacrifices. He doesn't need the blood or flesh of bulls and goats."

We were interrupted by the bull's intensified bellowing. Seven or eight strong young men, bearded and nearly naked, were pulling the bull toward the altar fire. One held a heavy axe. When the bull got close enough to the altar, he swung the axe with all his might, striking the front of the bull's forehead with a dull thud. The bull's front legs buckled under him, so that he appeared to kneel in piety before the god. The bull went limp, and the men who had been dragging him forward stepped closer, bent over the bull and began to lift the bull on their shoulders. Two others steadied the animal, one with a rope that looped around its limp neck and the other with a strong rope tied to the bull's tail. The bull's head was pointed to the altar, and as they lifted, the head slumped down, stretching its neck above the shoulders of two of the men. Another young man crouched nearby with a *sphageion*.

A *mageiros* drew near with a large knife and slid it across the soft neck of the bull. It twisted and gurgled, but the men holding the animal held steady. Blood poured down into the *sphageion* below. The leading *hiereus* dipped a leafy branch into the pool and flicked the blood at the altar, bloodying the altar with small specks that trickled for a moment and then dried. The bull twitched and twisted and noises of suppressed bellowing came from its mouth and the deep bloody cut in its throat. Soon it went quiet, twitching now and then, even after the assistants began to butcher the meat.

The man with the *sphageion* hurried over to a large stone *trapeza* nearby, while the men bearing the bull carried it over and laid it on the table. Three of them took out carving knives and began to cut the bull into pieces. Larger pieces they hung on hooks that were dangling over smaller tables from the arm of a frame nearby. Blood dripped down the flesh into *sphageia* below.

"What are they doing there?" I pointed to the basins filling with dripping blood.

"They need the blood to make black pudding."

"And you eat that?"

"You do not? Is blood also *akatharon*?"

"No. Many animals have flesh that is unclean to us—pigs, horses, donkeys. But that is not why we refuse to drink blood. The life of the flesh is in the blood, and the blood is given on the altar for atonement. Blood belongs to God. That is what our God teaches us."

"You eat neither pigs nor dogs nor donkeys nor blood? *Can you eat anything at all?*"

I ignored him and attended to the butchering. One of the sacrificers had made a long cut down the middle of the bull's underside and began pulling out the internal organs. They were carefully separated from the rest of the bull, and the upper organs were further separated from the lower organs, the slick shiny intestines. Every now and then the flesh of the bull still twitched. Another butcher was cutting off the hind legs. After he had cut through the joint, he stripped off some of the meat, exposing the white bones here and there. When he was finished, the bones still had meat on them. He took some of the fat from the abdomen and wrapped the bones in the fat. Along with the tail and the attached portion of the sacrum, he carried the fat-wrapped bones to the officiant, who placed them on the altar, where they sizzled in the leaping flames. The pipers played and the *choros* sang as the fire licked around the fat and turned it into thick, greasy, black *knisē* that floated up and was taken away by the breeze. The bones of the sacrum stuck up on the altar, pointing like a finger to heaven.

The young man was excited. "It is a good sign," he almost shouted, gesticulating at the bone. "It is a sign that the sacrifice has been accepted."

While the portion of the gods burned on the altar, one of the sacrificers pulled out and cleaned some of the inner organs—heart, lungs, liver, spleen, kidneys. Another man, the *mantis*, bent low over the entrails to perform the *hieroskopia*. He stared intently for some moments, pushing the entrails with his finger now and then. Finally, he stood upright, face relaxed, and announced, "*Hiera kala*. It is good." A young boy was commissioned to run down from the Acropolis to spread the news. The gods had accepted the sacrifice.

One of the other assistants sliced the *splanchna*, thrust sticks through the slices and put them into the fire. They busied themselves slicing the rest of the bull's flesh for cooking and eating. After a few minutes, one of the *parasites* took a spit of *splanchna* from the altar and carried it to the image of the god. Bowing with great ceremony, he placed the food into its hands.

Steam billowed up around the god's head and greasy fat dripped off its hands to the ground.

"Do you always have a meal during a sacrifice?"

"This is a *thysia*, and yes, every *thysia* ends with a feast. The god receives his portion, and we receive some for ourselves. All sacrifices and the whole province of divination—these are the arts of communion between gods and men."

"In many of our sacrifices, our God is the only one who receives meat from the sacrifice."

"Yes, we do have such *holokausta*. I have never attended a sacrifice to the *hērōs* Herakles, but I have heard that they offer him *holokausta*."

As we spoke, some of the worshipers filed up toward the altar to receive a small portion of the roasted meat, along with a cake from the *kanoun*. One splendidly dressed man received a large strip of meat from the back of the bull, the most delicious meat on the animal. The youth nudged me.

"He is one of the leading magistrates of the city, so he gets his *gēras*. At city feasts like this one, the important men always get more food than the rest of us."

The sacrificers cut the rest of the meat into chunks and placed them on flesh hooks hanging from the tree. Nearby they had built fires and placed pots full of water into the flames. Some of the worshipers came forward with bowls and dropped pieces of meat into the boiling pot.

"The boiling pot!" said my Athenian friend. "It is the great equalizer."

I looked at him questioningly.

"Whatever they put into the pot, however good or bad, gets boiled together. It all comes out the same—all tender, all sharing the same taste. And all *hagios*. They killed it at home or on the hunt, but they bring it here and put it into the pot, and it is all sacred food."

Through the entrance of the temple, I noticed a neat arrangement of figures—a broadly smiling man who carried a small calf on his shoulders, small statues of cows and pigs and sheep, a tableau scene of a sacrifice.

I nodded in the direction of the display with a questioning look.

"Votive offerings," he explained. "The sacrifice is so brief. The animal is slaughtered, blood is spilled, we eat the food and that is all. The gods may be with us for a moment, but then the feast is over, and our sacrifice has simply gone up into the smoke. The votive makes the offering everlasting. It reminds the gods that we have sacrificed. It is a permanent smoke signal to the gods."

As the people found places to sit or recline to enjoy the meal, the dancers and musicians began playing. What had begun as a procession of joy ended with joy, with the worshipers filling themselves, their "meat sacks" with the meat of the sacrifice, enjoying the good things that lie to hand in the presence of the gods.

◆ ◆ ◆

I have just got my first glimpse of the Holy City, gleaming high above in the evening sun. I still have a day to travel, but I can see where I am going now. I am nearly home, and I will be glad to be there.

Everywhere the world is ruled by things that are not gods, ruled by death and sin and weak flesh. Egypt is half in love with death, half in utter terror. Babylon's temples are nothing but imposing glory, but when I look I can only hear Sennacherib's foolish taunt. The Babylonians forget they are men when they make temples that say they are all but gods. I cannot erase the vision of that Athenian image from my mind. I wish I could but I cannot. Of all the gods of Greece, the one they call Priapus may be the most important. They all seem to be cowering under the reign of the phallus. Everywhere I go, flesh reigns.

In Jerusalem I will be home. Pentecost is at hand, and I have longed to celebrate with my brothers and hope for the redemption of my people. All is not well with us Jews. But at least we know what God to worship, the Creator of heaven and earth, the God of our fathers. At least there, in Jerusalem, is one place where sin and death do not reign.

Bibliographical Note

Though fictionalized in this chapter, the information is based on current scholarship on Egypt, Babylon and Greece. For the purposes of this sketch, I have ignored diachronic issues. It may be that some of the rites described by the Theban priest were no longer performed in the time of our Jewish explorer. Yet the general sketch makes the point: Gentiles had their own systems of sacred space, priesthood, purity and sacrifice, just as Israel did. Part of the aim is to begin to fulfill the Girardian aims of this book by showing how the cross fits into the religious history of humanity.

Sources for Egypt. The Egyptian's account of the exodus and his under-standing of Jewish religion is a mishmash of Manetho, Apion, Pompeius Trogus and Tacitus. For a summary see Jan Assmann, *The Mind of Egypt: History and Meaning in the Time of the Pharaohs* (New York: Metropolitan, 2002), 398-403. "You regard as profane . . ." is a virtual quotation from Tacitus, *Histories* 5.3-5. The claim that Egyptians are religious beyond all peoples is from Herodotus, *Histories* 2.36-37, and the description of purity practices is taken from Herodotus, *Histories* 2.37, with some additional details provided by Yohan Yoo, "A Theory of Purity from the Perspective of Comparative Religion" (PhD diss., Syracuse University, 2005), 79-80. See also Alan B. Lloyd, ed., *Gods, Priests and Men: Studies in the Religion of Pharaonic Egypt by Aylward M. Blackman* (London: Kegan Paul, 1998), 3-22.

The discussion of moral purity is indebted to Yoo, "Theory of Purity," 90. Emily Teeter, *Religion and Ritual in Ancient Egypt* (Cambridge: Cambridge University Press, 2011), 125-26, emphasizes the need for purity to approach tombs. The quotation is spell 125 of the *Book of the Dead*. See Yoo, "Theory of Purity," 118-20, for discussion of Egyptian dietary regulations, and the distinction between Egyptian and Israelite (and Greek) notions of death pollution is emphasized by Yoo, "Theory of Purity," 108-11.

For Egyptian beliefs about death and salvation, see especially Jan Assmann, *Death and Salvation in Ancient Egypt* (Ithaca, NY: Cornell University Press, 2014); also the brief summary in James P. Allen, ed., *The Ancient Egyptian Pyramid Texts* (Atlanta: Society of Biblical Literature, 2005), 7-12. The various descriptions of the ascension of the king are taken from Pyramid texts, compiled in R. O. Faulker, ed. and trans., *The Ancient Egyptian Pyramid Texts: Translated into English* (Oxford: Clarendon, 1969). From "the west is a land of sleep," the Egyptian is quoting the au-tobiography of Taimhotep of the first century BC, quoted in Teeter, *Religion and Ritual*, 120. The description of tomb-building, and the quotation from the Egyptian priest's father's tomb, are from Teeter, *Religion and Ritual*, 121-28. For a description of mummification, see Herodotus, *Histories* 2.85-90, the most complete ancient record of Egyptian em-balming techniques. See also Lloyd, *Gods, Priests and Men*, 73-114. The priest's funeral prayer is from a text in the tomb of Dheuty at Thebes, quoted in Teeter, *Religion and Ritual*, 137. The full text is in the *Book of the Dead*, chapter 25, placed in the ritual at the moment that Assmann suggests. The description of the rite for Opening the Mouth comes from Teeter, *Religion and Ritual*, 139-43.

For further details on the rankings of Egyptian priests, see Teeter, *Religion and Ritual*, 19-26; Lloyd, *Gods, Priests and Men*, 117-44. See also the description of the order of priests in a procession in Clement of Alexandria, *Stromata* 6.4. The myth of Seth and Osiris is told in many versions. See Assmann, *Mind of Egypt*.

The description of the temple at Karnak is taken from Teeter, *Religion and Ritual*, 39. Richard Wilkinson's *The Complete Temples of Ancient Egypt* (London: Thames & Hudson, 2000) provides lavish illustrations, floor plans for temples, alongside concise descriptions of the temples and the rituals of Egyptian worship.

The description of the temple rites is from Teeter, *Religion and Ritual*, chap. 3; see also Lloyd, *Gods, Priests and Men*, 168-82, 215-37. See the prayer "When few offering breads" from the Papyrus Jumilhac from the Thirteenth Dynasty in Assmann, *Mind of Egypt*, 404. See the description of the Feast of the Valley in Teeter, *Religion and Ritual*, 66-73.

The Egyptian's confusion about the notion of sacrifice is described in David Frankfurter, "Egyptian Religion and the Problem of the Category 'Sacrifice,'" in *Ancient Mediterranean Sacrifice*, ed. Jennifer Wright Knust and Zsuzsanna Varhelyi (Oxford: Oxford University Press, 2011), 75-93. Frankfurter problematizes the notion that sacrifice can function as a catch-all term for very different rites.

Sources for Babylon. For my purposes the differences between Assyrian and Babylonian, and between earlier and later, have been blurred. Several scholars, however, emphasize the continuity and stability of Babylonian religion. I could have extended the comparative section by including ancient West Semitic worship, closer in some ways to that of Israel. For Ugarit, see Dennis Partee, *Ritual and Cult at Ugarit* (Atlanta: Society of Biblical Literature, 2002).

The discussion of the relationship between cities, gods, temples and images is based on Jeffrey Niehaus, *Ancient Near Eastern Themes in Biblical Theology* (Grand Rapids: Kregel, 2008), 86-89, 94-99, 108-15. The old man's description is of the temple of Ishtar-Kititum in today's Ischali; for a possible reconstruction and floor plan, see Michael Hundley, *Gods in Dwellings: Temples and Divine Presence in the Ancient Near East* (Atlanta: Society of

Biblical Literature, 2013), 55. I have relied on Hundley, *Gods in Dwellings*, chapter three, for much of the information about the physical structure of Mesopotamian temples. The names for the dark inner room are from Hundley, *Gods in Dwellings*, 53n11; the distinction of *babu* and *bitu* is from Hundley, *Gods in Dwellings*, 70. See also the hymn comparing the house to a mountain in M. J. Geller, "Deep-Rooted Skyscrapers and Bricks," in *Figurative Language in the Ancient Near East*, ed. M. Mindlin, M. J. Geller and J. E. Wansbrough (London: School of Oriental and African Studies, 1987), 13. See also Anne Lohnert, "Das Bild des Tempels in der sumerischen Literatur" in *Tempel im Alten Orient*, ed. K. Kaniuth et al. (Wiesbaden: Harrassowitz, 2009), 263-82. For the various forms of guardian figures, see Hundley, *Gods in Dwellings*, 66. The etymology of "ziggurat" is also from Hundley, *Gods in Dwellings*, 70. Not all Mesopotamian temples were bent-axis temples. See Othmar Keel, *Symbolism of the Biblical World: Ancient Near Eastern Iconography and the Book of Psalms* (New York: Seabury, 1978), 153.

The quotation regarding the image of Ishtar comes from Ashurnasirpal II in the ninth century BC, quoted in Niehaus, *Ancient Near Eastern Themes*, 109. The boast about the heavenly splendor of the temple is from Tiglath-pileser, quoted in Niehaus, *Ancient Near Eastern Themes*, 98. The barge was for the god Amon, and the description is quoted in Niehaus, *Ancient Near Eastern Themes*, 92.

For the identification of the god with his house, see Thorkild Jacobsen, *Treasures of Darkness: A History of Mesopotamian Religion* (New Haven, CT: Yale University Press, 1978), 16-17. On the connection of temple-building and creation, and the connection with the "pure hill," see Keel, *Symbolism of the Biblical World*, 113; also Hundley, *Gods in Dwellings*, 79-80.

The description of the daily service of the Mesopotamian temples is taken from Hundley, *Gods in Dwellings*, 270-81, and A. Leo Oppenheim, *Ancient Mesopotamia: Portrait of a Dead Civilization* (Chicago: University of Chicago Press, 1977), 183-98. The main feasts are summarized briefly in Jacobsen, *Treasures of Darkness*, 14. Marc Linssen's *Cults of Uruk and Babylon: The Temple Ritual Texts as Evidence for Hellenistic Cult Practice* (Leiden: Brill, 2004) covers the feasts and daily rituals of a later period in great detail but also includes information about earlier Mesopotamian festive calendars. Linssen is the source for the detailed description of the procession of Anu at Uruk (p. 73). For the list of foods, see also Caroline Waerzeggers, "The Babylonian Priesthood in the Long Sixth Century," *BICS* 54, no. 2 (2011): 62. Hundley emphasizes the lamentations that begin the day (*Gods in Dwellings*, 272). See the chant of lamentation titled "Prayer to Every God" in James B. Pritchard, *Ancient Near Eastern Texts: An Anthology of Texts and Pictures* (Princeton, NJ: Princeton University Press, 1958), 391-92, which Pritchard dates to around the time of Ashurbanipal (seventh century BC). The "magical" quality of the lamentation is emphasized by Jacobsen, *Treasures of Darkness*, 15. See also Anne Lohnert, "Manipulating the Gods: Lamenting in Context," in *The Oxford Handbook of Cuneiform Culture*, ed. Karen Radner and Eleanor Robson (Oxford: Oxford University Press, 2011), 402-17; Lohnert, "Scribes and Singers of Emesal Lamentations in Ancient Mesopotamia in the Second Millennium B.C.," in *Papers on Ancient Literature: Greece, Rome and the Near East*, ed. Ettore Cingano and Lucio Milano (Padova: Sargon, 2008), 421-45. Oppenheim stresses the absence of *communio* and commensality in Mesopotamian sacred meals (*Ancient Mesopotamia*, 191). For the details of the "mouth washing" ceremony and its meaning, I have relied on Hundley, *Gods in Dwellings*, 239-70.

The list of priestly specialties comes from Waerzeggers, "Babylonian Priesthood," 63. The discussion of prebends and the qualifications and ceremonies for the installation of priests is from Waerzeggers, "Babylonian Priesthood," 62-68; Waerzeggers and Michal Jursa, "On the Initiation of Babylonian Priests," *Zeitschrift für Altorientalische und Biblische Rechtsgeschichte* 14 (2008): 1-35; Lohnert, "Reconsidering the Consecration of Priests in Ancient Mesopotamia," in *Your Praise Is Sweet*, ed. Heather D. Baker, Eleanor Robson and Gabor Zolomi (London: British Institute for the Study of Iraq, 2010), 183-91; Anne Lohnert, "The Installation of Priests according to Neo-Assyrian Documents," *State Archives of Assyria Bulletin* 16 (2007): 273-86. For the Hellenistic period, see Linssen, *Cults*.

My summary of Mesopotamian standards of nonpriestly purity is drawn from Michael Guichard and Lionel Marti, "Purity in Ancient Mesopotamia," in *Purity and the Forming of Religious Traditions in the Ancient Mediterranean World and Ancient Judaism*, ed. Christian Frevel and Christophe Nihan (Leiden: Brill, 2013), 47-113. A very useful overview of purity concerns in the ancient Near East is found in Karel van der Toorn, "La pureté rituelle au Proche-Orient Ancien" *Revue de l'Histoire des Religions* 206 (1989):

339-56. The list of physical disqualifications, which overlaps with Leviticus 21–22, is from Waerzeggers, "Initiation," 4. The similarities between the mouth-opening rite for the god's image and the purification of priests is pointed out in Waerzeggers, "Babylonian Priesthood," 67. The connection between purity and brightness is made in Guichard and Marti, "Purity," 50-51. See the story of rotten dates and pomegranates presented to the Lady-of-Uruk, told briefly in Waerzeggers, "Babylonian Priesthood," 64. For the purification of a diviner, see Guichard and Marti, "Purity," 81. The lists of forbidden foods and daily taboos are found in Guichard and Marti, "Purity," 75, 83. The transmission of impurity is described in Guichard and Marti, "Purity," 88-90. See the ancient chant about evil powers in Jacobsen, *Treasures of Darkness*, 12-13. The story of the man who was unable to escape his misfortune is from the *Ludlul bel nemeqi* ("I want to praise the lord of wisdom"), and is recounted in Guichard and Marti, "Purity," 91-92. The summary of what Babylonians did to deliver themselves from omens is from Stefan M. Maul, "How the Babylonians Protected Themselves Against Calamities Announced by Omens," in *Mesopotamian Magic: Textual, Historical, and Interpretative Perspectives*, ed. Tzvi Abusch and Karel van der Toorn (Groningen: Styx, 1999), 123-29. Maul describes in detail the ritual for release from an ill fate pronounced by the gods; see also the ritual for escape from the growling cat omen described in Guichard and Marti, "Purity," 96-97.

Sources for Greece. The young Athenian is well-informed, probably a future priest who has taken some time to study at the Academy in Athens. More surprisingly, he anticipates debates among contemporary classicists.

The description of music and the Orphic sacrificial songs are from F. S. Naiden, *Smoke Signals for the Gods: Ancient Greek Sacrifice from the Archaic through the Roman Periods* (Oxford: Oxford University Press, 2012), 53-54. The order of the parade is from Naiden, *Smoke Signals*, 24-25, which describes the depiction of a sacrificial parade from a Boeotian *lekanis* of the sixth century BC. The censer is pictured in Naiden, *Smoke Signals*, 73. For a portrait of the image of a god being carried to a sacrificial site, see Naiden, *Smoke Signals*, 46. See also the song to Athena in the Homeric Hymn to Athena.

For the phallus as part of the procession, see Eva Keuls, *The Reign of the Phallus: Sexual Politics in Ancient Athens* (Berkeley: University of California Press, 1993). The description of the Acropolis and the color of the temples is taken from William Stearns Davis, *A Day in Old Athens: A Picture of*

Athenian Life (1910; repr., New York: Biblo & Tannen, 1960), 191-92. The description of the statue of Athena in the Parthenon is taken from Keuls, *The Reign of the Phallus*, 38-39. The altar described is a real Greek altar, but it was not in front of the temple of Athena Nike. The Athenian youth has been reading some feminist literature regarding the connection between sacrifice and patrilineal descent, especially Nancy Jay, *Throughout Your Generations Forever: Sacrifice, Religion, and Paternity* (Chicago: University of Chicago Press, 1992), 43-45, 98.

Without knowing it, the young Athenian makes an intervention in current debates about Greek sacrifice. Walter Burkert (*Homo Necans: The Anthropology of Ancient Greek Sacrificial Ritual and Myth* [Berkeley: University of California Press, 1986]) has emphasized the violence of Greek sacrifice, lending some support to the broader theory of sacrifice from René Girard. French classicists Marcel Detienne and Jean-Pierre Vernant, by contrast, argue that sacrifice is primarily an event of commensality (*The Cuisine of Sacrifice Among the Greeks* [Chicago: University of Chicago Press, 1998]). Naiden has charged that both ignore the role of the gods in Greek sacrifice, and argues that sacrificial procedures were intended to call the gods to meet with the worshipers and to grant petitions. Apparently the young Athenian's teacher was Hesiod, as interpreted by Marcel Detienne. The young Athenian knows his Lévi-Strauss (*The Raw and the Cooked: Mythologiques*, vol. 1 [Chicago: University of Chicago Press, 1983]). The Athenian's list of animals is taken from Gunnel Ekroth, "Meat in Ancient Greece: Sacrificial, Sacred or Secular?," *Food & History* 5, no. 1 (2007): 256-57.

The discussion of purity rules in Athens is taken from Robert Parker, *Miasma: Pollution and Purification in Early Greek Religion* (Oxford: Clarendon, 1996). I have ignored differences of time and place to give a composite portrait of Greek notions of impurity. The Athenian youth's explanations anticipate the theories of Mary Douglas, as well as Parker. "Purification is the science of division" comes from Plato, *Sophist*. The notion that the Greeks had laws governing religion is controversial, but see Robert Parker, "Law and Religion," in *The Cambridge Companion to Ancient Greek Law*, ed. Michael Gagarin and David Cohen (Cambridge: Cambridge University Press, 2005), 61-81. Naiden, *Smoke Signals*, also argues that the Greeks had regulations of purity and sacrifice. The youth's comment about the absence of sex in Greek and Egyptian religion is from Herodotus. For an extensive survey of the evidence that concludes that Herodotus was wrong, see Rebecca Anne Strong, "The Most Shameful Practice: Temple Prostitution in the Ancient Greek World" (PhD diss., University of California at Los Angeles, 1997). The story of bloodshed the youth tells is obviously from Aeschylus's *Oresteia*. The discussion about the impurity of various forms of intercourse is based on Parker, *Miasma*, 96-99. On intercourse and education, see Jan Bremmer, "Greek Pederasty and Modern Homosexuality" and "An Enigmatic Indo-European Rite: Pederasty," *Arethusa* 13 (1980): 279-98.

By emphasizing the moral prerequisites for sacrifice, the Athenian youth shows his agreement with Naiden, *Smoke Signals*, over against the common contemporary claim that ancient sacrifice worked more or less "automatically." See the prayer to Apollo in book one of the *Iliad*. The philosopher who warns that sacrifices cannot cover an unjust life is Plato in *Laws*. The prayer that accompanies the sacrifice is the Orphic Hymn to Athena.

Many scholars doubt the evidence of vase paintings that show men lifting sacrificial victims on their shoulders. F. T. van Straten (*Hierá Kalà: Images of Animal Sacrifice in Archaic and Classical Greece* [Leiden: Brill, 1995], 109-13) persuasively argues that the vase depictions are accurate. For the description of the use of blood on the altar and in the sacrificial feast, see Gunnel Ekroth, "Blood on the Altars? On the Treatment of Blood at Greek Sacrifices and the Iconographical Evidence," *Antike Kunst* 48 (2005): 9-29. The description of the butchering of the animal is taken from van Straten, *Hierá Kalà*, 117-31. On the distribution of sacrificial meat, see van Straten, *Hierá Kalà*, as well as Detienne and Vernant, *Cuisine of Sacrifice*, 3-13. Naiden estimates the number of participants and the amount of food they received in "Blessed Are the Parasites," his contribution to *Greek and Roman Animal Sacrifice: Animal Victims, Modern Observers*, ed. Christopher A. Faraone and F. S. Naiden (Cambridge: Cambridge University Press, 2012), 55-83. "All sacrifices and the whole province of divination"—the young man is quoting Plato, *Symposium* 188b-c. "Communion" translates *koinōnia*.

The practical importance and symbolism of the boiling pot is brought out by Ekroth, "Meat in Ancient Greece," 266-68. See also Ekroth, "Meat, Man and God: On the Division of the Animal Victim at Greek Sacrifices," in *MIKROS IERPOMEMON: Meletes eis Mnemen Michael H. Jameson*, ed. A. Matthaiou and I. Polinskaya (Athens: Hellēnikē Epigraphikē Hetaireia, 2008), 259-90. On votive offerings, see Naiden, *Smoke Signals*, 122; Richard

Neer, "Sacrificing Stones: on Some Sculpture, Mostly Athenian," in Faraone and Naiden, *Greek and Roman Animal Sacrifice*, 99-119; and W. H. D. Rouse, *Greek Votive Offerings: An Essay in the History of Greek Religion* (Cambridge: Cambridge University Press, 1902). The young Athenian skirts Jane Harrison's claim that *holokausta* were reserved for chthonic deities.

four

FLESH

†

Our Jewish traveler found that he had much in common with the Egyptians, Babylonians and Greeks he met. Like Jews, Egyptians were obsessed with purity. Like Jews, the Babylonians constructed monumental houses for their gods and served the gods who resided in them. Like Greeks, Jews slaughtered animals and burned them on altars, feasting on the flesh. What Paul implies in Galatians 3–4 is borne out by the evidence we have from the ancient world: the same elements constructed the worlds of Jews and Gentiles—purity, temple, sacrifice.

And yet: the *stoicheia* of religious life combine differently among Jews and Gentiles. Jews observe purity, build temples, offer sacrifice, just like Gentiles. The building blocks are similar, if not the same, but the way they fit together into an overall socioreligious pattern is not the same. Paul implies that Jews and Gentiles are both *hypo ta stoicheia*, but he also writes that there are "Jews *physei*," Jews who are Jews *by nature*, which implies that there are also Gentiles who are Gentiles *physei*. The way the elements combine differs so much that it produces humans who have divergent natures.

Israel's form of stoicheic life is described in detail in Exodus–Deuteronomy. But to understand the structures of Torah and its purpose, we need to go back to the beginning, to Adam and Eve, the first human society and first liturgical assembly, who were placed under stoicheic regulations as soon as they were created.

ADAM UNDER ELEMENTS

Adam in the garden was a child, naked as a newborn, formed of flesh. As a child, he was under "guardians and managers" until the time set by his

Father, Yahweh. Created to be lord of all, to share in the Creator's creative rule over creation, Adam would one day be elevated to kingship. At the moment of his birth from earth and breath, he was a trainee, a servant in the Lord's garden, his earthly dwelling place, the original sanctuary. It was a place of festivity: Adam could eat from the tree of life, communing in life with his Father. He could not, however, eat from the tree of the knowledge of good and evil, the tree of judgment that signified his eventual entrance into mature kingly wisdom. At the beginning, Adam was placed under the elements, *hypo ta stoicheia tou kosmou*, and "Taste not, touch not" was the first lesson of his pedagogy.[1]

"Taste not, touch not" was the first human ethics, the first human religious practice. It was a fundamental element in the socioreligious physics of the original creation.

Adam and Eve were created as flesh—limited, weak, vulnerable, touchable, woundable. That was good, *very* good. They might have accepted their vulnerability and the precariousness of their fleshly life, trusting the Father to care for them. Adam might have been content to wait for the Lord to open his hand to satisfy his desires, might have trusted his Father to give him his full inheritance when the Father saw that he was ready. Eve might have rejoiced in fleshly weakness and trusted her Father to supply whatever strength she needed.

Instead, they were discontented and impatient. Created good, *very* good flesh, they wanted to be more, and they wanted to be something more *now*. They ate the fruit on the promise that it would enable them to transcend fleshly weakness and limitations so they could be as God. It worked in some fashion or other. Their eyes were opened, they saw they were naked, and even Yahweh acknowledged that "the man is become as one of us" (Gen 3:22 KJV). But it did not enable him to escape the vulnerability of flesh. After eating, Adam was still weak, vulnerable, dependent, woundable. Only now in his flesh he was cut off from the gift of life, which Yahweh had offered him through the fruit of the tree of life.

Outside Eden, Adam and Eve were still flesh, but something had changed. Adam and his children were not only weak and dependent but also now

---

[1]My treatment of the original situation of Adam is indebted to the work of James Jordan. See Jordan, "Merit Versus Maturity: What Did Jesus Do For Us?," in *The Federal Vision*, ed. Steve Wilkins and Duane Garners (2004; repr., Monroe, LA: Athanasius Press, 2014).

delivered over to the reign of Death and Sin, in corruptible, shameful and now *mortal* flesh. By Adam's sin, the whole human race came under wrath, God's punishment expressed in his expulsion of Adam and Eve, his handing-over of humanity to the power of the death and sin that they chose. Adam's sin affected everyone after. Cain did not eat the forbidden fruit, but he too was exiled from the tree of life. Because of Adam's sin, death came to *all*. According to Paul, death came into the world on the heels of sin, so that after Adam death spread to all people (Rom 5). And when death spreads, sin spreads.[2]

From the beginning, the garden was a unique location. It was Yahweh's earthly home, where Adam and Eve could commune with him through the fruit of the tree of life. It was "holy space" because the holy God was present.[3] After Adam's expulsion from the garden, holy space became taboo, inaccessible space. Yahweh stationed cherubim at the gate of the garden to guard against every attempt at reentry. From Adam on, if anyone wanted to enter the presence of God, he would have to pass through the sword and fire of the cherubim. No man could return to feast in the presence of God unless he first died. Yahweh performed the first sacrifice by providing animal skins for Adam and Eve, and from that point on no one could approach God's presence unless he were clothed in an animal. He could return to life, feasting and the presence of God only by passing through death.

Salvation would mean the reversal of this fallen condition. Salvation would bring readmission to eat and drink in God's presence. Salvation would involve deliverance from mortal flesh, and from the taboos and exclusions that resulted from it. Anyone who could achieve *that* would be the Savior of Adam's race.

WHAT FLESH DOES

Adam's condition after the fall is what Paul describes as life in the "flesh" (*sarx*), "sarkic" life. For Paul, "flesh" is not merely a term for the bone and

---

[2]See my "Adam, Moses, Jesus: A Reading of Romans 5:12-14," *Calvin Theological Journal* 43, no. 2 (2008): 257-72, for a defense of this reading of Rom 5.

[3]That the garden was a sanctuary has become "common knowledge" among Old Testament scholars. See Meredith Kline, *Images of the Spirit* (Eugene, OR: Wipf & Stock, 1999); Gregory Beale, *The Temple and the Church's Mission: A Biblical Theology of the Dwelling Place of God* (Downers Grove, IL: InterVarsity Press, 2004); James Jordan, *Through New Eyes: Developing a Biblical View of the World* (Eugene, OR: Wipf & Stock, 1999); L. M. Morales, *The Tabernacle Pre-Figured: Cosmic Mountain Ideology in Genesis and Exodus* (Leuven: Peeters, 2012), 51-119, 248-52.

muscle and gristle of human bodies. Drawing on the Old Testament, Paul uses "flesh" as a "master metaphor" to describe the condition of humanity following the fall.[4] Humanity's fleshly condition is the presumption behind Paul's talk about the "elements of the world."[5]

As a master metaphor, "flesh" is multidimensional. It is *not* incoherent. The concept ranges from a description of physical vulnerability to genetic ancestry and descent, and often takes on moral connotations, but these various meanings are interconnected.

We may start with the obvious. Physically, "flesh" (Heb. *bāśār*; Gr. *sarx*) is musculature, the layer between the outer skin and the bones and internal organs, the "meat" of human and animal bodies. In some contexts, "flesh" has a more specific focus on the genitals (Lev 15).[6] Male "flesh" is where Yahweh commands Abraham to place the covenant sign (Gen 17:11, where the mark in the *bāśār* is an *ʾôt bərît*). Circumcision is a sign in the *flesh* not

---

[4]J. Louis Martyn has rightly emphasized the "cosmic" scope of flesh. Much of what he says is suggestive, but I have attempted to offer a more concrete explanation of flesh, and one that sticks more rigorously with the text of Scripture. In particular, I have tried to fill out Paul's understanding of flesh by bringing Levitical notions of flesh into play. For a summary of Martyn's argument, see Joshua Davis, introduction to *Apocalyptic and the Future of Theology: With and Beyond J. Louis Martyn*, ed. Joshua B. Davis and Douglas Harink (Eugene, OR: Wipf & Stock, 2012), 39. Drawing on Hebrews, John Dunnill gives a concise summary of the range of meanings of *sarx* in *Sacrifice and the Body: Biblical Anthropology and Christian Self-Understanding*, new ed. (Farnham, UK: Ashgate, 2013), 95-96. For other discussions of Paul's use of *sarx*, see James D. G. Dunn, *The Theology of the Apostle Paul* (Grand Rapids: Eerdmans, 1998), 62-73 (who examines the overlap and difference between *sarx* and *sōma*, "body"); Rudolf Bultmann, *Theology of the New Testament*, trans. Kendrick Grobel (1951–1955; repr., Waco, TX: Baylor University Press, 2007), 1:232-46.

[5]The connection between the *stoicheia* and *sarx* is clearest in Col 2:8-23. Paul reminds the Colossians that they have been circumcised with a divine circumcision, the circumcision of Christ. In the death of Jesus, the "body of the flesh" was stripped away, and by baptismal participation in the death of Jesus the flesh of the Colossians is removed. They have died to the flesh, buried with Jesus in baptism (Col 2:11-12). Later Paul states explicitly that they have died to the *stoicheia*, specifically to purity prohibitions. They therefore ought not to follow purity rules, since they no longer live in the world determined by those elements, by stoicheic physics (Col 2:20-21). Death with Christ thus is both a stripping of flesh and a death to *ta stoicheia tou kosmou*. Though the connection is not as explicit in Galatians, the flow of Paul's argument seems to assume it. The Son and Spirit are sent to deliver Jews and Gentiles from *stoicheia* (Gal 4:1-11) and to bring them to the life of the Spirit. When Paul speaks of the old way of life in Gal 5, he describes it in terms of adherence to the mind and desire of the flesh (Gal 5:16-17).

[6]The discharges enumerated in Lev 15 are not bodily discharges in general, but genital discharges—menstruation, seminal emissions, gonorrhea. For argument, see Gordon Wenham, *The Book of Leviticus*, New International Commentary on the Old Testament (Grand Rapids: Eerdmans, 1979), 217-18. Not all discharges from the genitals produce impurity; urination does not. Flows of body fluids from other parts of the body (a bloody or runny nose, for instance) do not defile at all.

only in the generic sense that it is a cut in the body, but also in the more specific sense that the organ that is cut off is the organ designated as "flesh." In Romans 2:28, Paul speaks of the open, apparent circumcision that is in flesh (*en tō phanerō en sarki peritomē*), and virtually every use of *sarx* in Galatians is haunted by the fact that circumcision is the subject in debate. *Flesh* is the target of the cut of the covenant.

As a symbol of procreation, *sarx* is used in an extended sense to describe genealogy, ancestry or descent. Jesus is the Son of David *kata sarka* (Rom 1:3), Abraham is a forefather *kata sarka* (Rom 4:1), Paul mourns for the fate of Israelites, who are his kinsman *kata sarka* (Rom 9:3), from whom Jesus received his fleshly descent (Rom 9:5). According to Hebrews 7:16, Israel's priests were qualified by "flesh" (*kata nomon entolēs sarkinēs*), that is, by descent from Aaron. Descendants are according to flesh because they are conceived by the sperm that comes through the "flesh" of their ancestor. Because they share a common original flesh, they share a common "flesh." "Flesh of my flesh, bone of my bones" is kin language in the Old Testament (see Gen 29:15; Judg 9:2; 2 Sam 5:1).

As the physical organ of procreation, "flesh" signifies human potency and power. Flesh, we might say, *is* a potency, especially *male* potency.[7] Life under the flesh is thus life under the "reign of the phallus,"[8] domination by the virile and the strong and the fecund. By producing children as the fruit of flesh, flesh extends itself in time, attempting to transcend its limitations and achieve immortality. Achievements in war, art, politics, piety are "fleshly" achievements, expressions of flesh's potency. In Philippians 3, Paul declares that he has no confidence in flesh, and then enumerates the reasons why he might have put confidence in flesh: "Circumcised the eighth day, of the nation of Israel, of the tribe of Benjamin, a Hebrew of Hebrews; as to the Law, a Pharisee; as to zeal, a persecutor of the church; as to the righteousness which is in the Law, found blameless" (Phil 3:5-6 NASB). Paul is privileged, and has grounds for boasting in flesh, in part because of physical descent: he is a flesh descendant of Abraham and Jacob through Jacob's son Benjamin. His attainments as a Pharisee and zealot for the law, however, are not

[*handwritten marginal note:* is this why the promise of the woman's seed?]

---

[7]I take the term from Stanislas Breton, *A Radical Philosophy of Saint Paul*, trans. Joseph N. Ballan (New York: Columbia University Press, 2011), 112.

[8]Eva Keuls, *The Reign of the Phallus: Sexual Politics in Ancient Athens* (Berkeley: University of California Press, 1993).

products of descent. "Flesh" here is stretched out to include not only privileges that arise from being a "blood descendant" of Abraham and Jacob but also status that arises from his pedagogy in the Torah. "Flesh" covers everything from birth to training and education to heritage to achievements as a member of a particular race. Everything that makes Paul a "natural" Jew is "flesh," even if it is cultural rather than biological.[9]

At the same time, *sarx* calls attention to the finitude of human beings as creatures. "Flesh" or "flesh and blood" is a biblical metonymy for human existence under postfall conditions of mortality, weakness, shame (1 Cor 15:39-49). Flesh denotes the vulnerability and weakness of human beings, and especially our vulnerability to death and the small forms of death that afflict us during life. To say that someone is "under flesh" in this sense is only to say he is a postlapsarian human, a human who exists after death entered the world with the first man's one act of disobedience (Rom 5). This is the irony of fleshly boasting: the flesh that seems so potent in battle and sex, in production and reproduction, is *mortal* flesh. Achilles may be dipped in the river, but his skin is not armor and his heel can be pricked by Paris's arrow.[10]

The dialectic of fleshly weakness and fleshly prowess is not as paradoxical as it might appear. Vulnerability to loss, lack, death and damage leads to fear, and fear produces protectiveness, protectiveness produces violence and aggression. Weakness is the source of boastful displays of strength and virility. Those who live in the fear of death—in fleshly weakness—are thus prone not

---

[9]Jews who are Jews by nature are those who have descended from Abraham. As argued above, *physei* cannot simply describe physical descent, because what makes Paul a Jew is not merely ancestry but circumcision. To repeat: in Paul's usage, "flesh" and "nature" both extend beyond what we normally think of as "nature" to include what we could classify as "culture."

[10]Entire philosophies are built on the foundation of supposed honest confrontation with mortality, not only existentialism but also the philosophy of Bertrand Russell, who wrote in his 1903 "A Free Man's Worship": "That man is the product of causes which had no prevision of the end they were achieving; that his origin, his growth, his hopes and fears, his loves and his beliefs, are but the outcome of accidental collocations of atoms; that no fire, no heroism, no intensity of thought and feeling, can preserve an individual life beyond the grave; that all the labors of the ages, all the devotion, all the inspiration, all the noonday brightness of human genius, are destined to extinction in the vast death of the solar system, and that the whole temple of man's achievement must inevitably be buried beneath the debris of a universe in ruins—all these things, if not quite beyond dispute, are yet so nearly certain, that no philosophy which rejects them can hope to stand. Only within the scaffolding of these truths, only on the firm foundation of unyielding despair, can the soul's habitation henceforth be safely built" (available at www3 .nd.edu/~afreddos/courses/264/fmw.htm). Absent faith in resurrection, death is the ruling power in human life, always pronouncing the last word. If it is a noble ethic, it is a tragic nobility.

only to "feelings of insecurity, low self-esteem, obsessions, perfectionism" but also to "ambitiousness, envy, narcissism, jealousy, rivalry, competitiveness, self-consciousness, guilt, and shame."[11] Insofar as it is mortal and vulnerable, flesh desires pleasure and avoids pain. It can express itself in desire for luxuries and wealth, in greed and all the cruelty that greed produces. It can express itself in a desire for power and dominance; it is the source of *libido dominandi*. Life according to flesh can take the form of confidence in one's achievements. Jews boast in their zeal for the law. Greeks boast in their potency in battle, in public debate, in sexual conquest.[12] Achilles boasts in the strength of his flesh, his sheer battle prowess and *biē*, and the exploits of Greek heroes are depicted along with the exploits of the gods on Greek temples. Insofar as public debate is a form of battle, riposte and quick wits are displays of flesh. In a more specific Levitical sense, sexual prowess is a display of the power of flesh, a compensation for mortality. All these are phallic displays, phallic competitions, fleshly rivalries.

Life in the flesh is life under postfall conditions. Life *kata sarka* is life conformed to what flesh dictates, both in its potency and its weakness. Adam could have lived in flesh without sin. But when human beings live according to flesh, flesh is no longer flesh, but *sinful* flesh (see Rom 8:1-4). Flesh is good. Even *mortal* flesh is not evil in itself. Flesh becomes a motivator of sin and evil when human beings seek to compensate for finitude, mortality, weakness, when they refuse to accept their vulnerability and trust

---

[11]Richard Beck, *The Slavery of Death* (Eugene, OR: Wipf & Stock, 2014), 28-29. Elsewhere in his book, Beck observes, "As vulnerable, biodegradable creatures in a world of real or potential scarcity, we are prone to act defensively and aggressively toward others who might place our survival at risk" (11). Weakness, once again, inverts into aggressiveness. For my review of Beck's stimulating book, see "Slavery of Death," Theopolis Institute website, January 20, 2014, theopolisinstitute.com/slavery-of-death. See the similar observations of Theodore Jennings Jr., *Outlaw Justice: The Messianic Politics of Paul* (Stanford: Stanford University Press, 2013), 118-19, who traces the phenomenology of flesh back to the fact of our vulnerability to touch. "Flesh is the weakness of the human. . . . It is the way we are vulnerable, exposed. Our life is subject to touch, that is, to what gives pleasure and pain, gives joy, and makes wounding possible." This very vulnerability explains "how sin is able to overcome Adamic humanity, especially that Adamic humanity that is under law." Fear of our weakness, anxiety at our vulnerability, overtakes us, and we use the instruments of law, power, justice, and violence as protection. The "sense of weakness or vulnerability [seizes] control of that which intends life . . . to accelerate injustice, to hyperbolize violence and violation." Thus "flesh comes also to name hostility to justice or to God, the very hostility that crucified the messiah as son of David."

[12]Jerome Neyrey has explored the honor-shame systems of the ancient world in many works. See, for instance, *Honor and Shame in the Gospel of Matthew* (Louisville, KY: Westminster John Knox, 1998).

their Creator for all good gifts. Sin and evil are human attempts to *compensate* for having, for *being*, mortal flesh.

Flesh is not only a motivating power for individuals but also a principle of religious life and social organization. It is a "power" in the Pauline sense, a transpersonal reality that dominates and may enslave human beings. Fearing death, fleshly humans create machines for immortality, what Ernest Becker called "hero systems" that offer recipes for immortality, prelaid paths toward everlasting fame.[13] Greed is not only a personal vice, one of the traditional seven deadly sins, but also can become the organizing principle of economic life. As such, it expresses fleshliness in both a direct and an inverted way. Economies motivated by fleshly avarice make material wealth the highest value and congeal into structures that promote that value. The wealthy find ways to protect and enhance their wealth, often at the expense of the poor, and because they embody the social ideal there are few restraints on their pursuits. But greed can also express the weakness of flesh. Faced with the precariousness of fleshly existence, a person might put his trust in the fortress that wealth provides. An entire society can put its trust in its GNP and its stock market averages: so long as wealth is growing, all is well.

Flesh has direct and indirect *political* effects too. Tyrants from Babylon to modern totalitarian systems, and not a few democratic demagogues, act out phallic political scripts, pursuing power for its own sake, to make a name, to establish a legacy, to bid for immortality. Political systems can be structured in a way that promotes these direct fleshly ambitions: only the most ruthless and violent were able to ascend the Soviet bureaucracy, often the most ambitious and narcissistic end up holding power in democratic regimes. But political power, diplomacy, military programs can also be covers for the weakness of flesh. It is a dangerous world, and we need protection, and so we trust in horses and chariots, in drones and missiles and brute force. If you want to see a concrete, structural expression of flesh, take a look at the budget for the US Department of Defense or the protective system of Homeland Security.

The old Hobbesian charge is true: religion may well be a response of fear, the fear of loss, vulnerability and death.[14] Religious orders are fleshly also

---

[13]Ernest Becker, *The Denial of Death* (New York: Free Press, 1997).
[14]Bertrand Russell's *Why I Am Not A Christian* (1927, available at www.users.drew.edu/~jlenz/

when their structures of priestly service are determined by descent from a priestly ancestor (as in ancient Israel), when religious life largely revolves around the care of the dead (as in ancient Egypt) or when religious institutions are set up to stave off threats from the gods (as in the tendency of religions to turn into protection rackets). A stoicheic order of sacred space, purity, sacrifice and priesthood can become a screen to hide the worshiper from an irascible god.

Human life organized by flesh produces a community organized by common ancestry, "genetic" or what we consider "blood" bonds.[15] Internally, a fleshly society may be divided among families (like the Italian cities of the Renaissance) or between the well-born patricians and the lowborn commoners and slaves. Externally it stands in tension with other communities. Greek flesh is *superior* to barbarian flesh, and that is an accurate way to speak even if the Greek boast is a boast in Greek culture, for culture is an achievement of the flesh and an occasion for boasting in the power of flesh. Only those of the right flesh can be trusted, only they are worthy of honor, and anyone with slave's flesh or female flesh is of lesser worth. Only those born from the right line of descent can be full members of the political community. Ancient communities organized by flesh created fictive kin relations. Someone born with lesser flesh can be elevated by adoption or a grant of citizenship. Slaves can be manumitted. "Flesh" is not always literally flesh. But the fundamental organizing principle remains the same.[16]

---

whynot.html) made the claim that "religion is based primarily upon fear" of the unknown, as well as "fear of the mysterious, fear of defeat, fear of death." This fear, he went on, is the "parent of cruelty, and therefore it is no wonder if cruelty and religion have gone hand in hand." In place of religion, Russell proposes that Science can deliver us from "craven fear."

[15]Gil Anidjar, *Blood: A Critique of Christianity* (New York: Columbia University Press, 2014) highlights the difference between Old Testament and modern European terminology.

[16]Leviticus also recognized fictive flesh relations. In the incest laws of Lev 18, Israelite men are prohibited from uncovering the nakedness of those who are "flesh of flesh." In the first instance, a flesh relation is a strictly biological/genetic relation. The first prohibition is against uncovering the nakedness of a mother; because the mother is "flesh," a direct biological ancestor, it is illicit to uncover nakedness (also the sister, Lev 15:9). "Flesh of flesh" relations exist in cases of immediate relatives of one's immediate ancestors. Your aunt is not a direct ancestor, but she shares flesh with your father, and so she is off limits, flesh of flesh (Lev 15:12-13). More interestingly, "flesh of flesh" relations exist where there is no biological connection at all. Lev 15:8 prohibits uncovering the nakedness of your father's wife, who is presumably not a mother. You have a direct biological flesh relation with your father, and while you have no biological flesh relationship with a stepmother, she's still off limits. Lev 15:14 prohibits uncovering the nakedness of your father's brother's wife. That is, your father has no direct blood relation with this woman—she is his sister-in-law. And she certainly has no blood relation with you. Yet she is prohibited, and

Fleshly society is exclusivist, divided and competitive. Flesh produces "enmities, strife, jealousy, outbursts of anger, disputes, dissentions, factions, envying" (Gal 5:20-21 NASB). It produces sexual immorality, not only because flesh is a drive toward pleasure,[17] but also because flesh is a drive to mastery: sexual conquests are honor displays. The works of the flesh express the aggressive self-protectiveness of the weak. On the basis of early humanity's propensity to violence, Yahweh judges that man "is also flesh" (Gen 6:3).

Disgust polices the boundaries between one form of human flesh and another.[18] Disgust is a boundary psychology. We are not disgusted by blood flowing peacefully in our or another's veins; when the blood flows out, though, breaching the boundary of the skin, the gorge rises. In some cultures, certain persons or behaviors are disgusting in a similar way: beggars, slaves, untouchables are the pus oozing from the wounds of the social body. Purity rules regulate the boundaries of disgust and maintain distinctions between races, classes and other groupings. As our Jewish traveler found, these fleshly exclusions are institutionalized, architecturalized, in temples and holy spaces, in purity rules and observances, in rituals of purification, expulsion and scapegoating. These practices constitute the basic elements of the social world of flesh.

In both its prowess and its weakness, flesh militates against the flourishing of human life, against the fair ordering of society. Human society cannot be just or harmonious if each is at war with each and all, if everyone tries to compensate for his or her mortality by striving for heroic immortality, if society forms structures, myths, habits, pedagogies that encourage

---

presumably because she is "flesh of flesh" with you. In addition to the direct biological flesh relations, the prohibitions of "flesh of flesh" relations also count what we can call "covenant flesh" relations as flesh, as kin. The logic of prohibiting uncovering the nakedness of a stepmother is this: You have a *biological* flesh relation with your father; he has a *covenant*-flesh relation with his wife, since by virtue of his marriage he is one flesh with her. Through your biological connection with your father, you also have a secondary covenant-flesh relation with his wife.

[17]The Bible links flesh and desire only rarely (see Ps 63:1). Typically, the *soul* is the seat of desire, need, longing (see Ps 84:2). Paul speaks of the "desire" (*epithymia*) and "passion" (*pathēma*) of the flesh more frequently than any other biblical writer, especially in Galatians (Gal 5:16-17; 24; see Gal 6:12-13; cf. Eph 2:3). The desire of the flesh may refer to the desires that the flesh produces in individual humans (e.g., the desire to overcome vulnerability and death) or the desire of the abstract, personified culture of flesh. In Paul's usage, "flesh" and "soulish" (*psychikos*, 1 Cor 15) are closely related, both depicting human being as perishable, mortal, weak and shameful.

[18]See the brilliant analysis in Richard Beck, *Unclean: Meditations on Purity, Hospitality, and Mortality* (Eugene, OR: Wipf & Stock, 2011).

flesh, and if it inculcates the values of flesh. Flesh is suicidal, since in militating against the flourishing of human life it militates against itself. Fleeing death, flesh finds death—literally in violence, metaphorically in the exclusions that dismember social bodies.

If the Creator is going to fulfill his purposes for his creation, he will have to destroy flesh. Just so: Genesis records the beginning of Yahweh's centuries-long war against flesh, institutionalized in the stoicheic system that imposes an antisarkic pedagogy on his people.[19]

A Cut in Flesh

The mind set on flesh is at war with the Spirit and the Spirit against the flesh.

Human beings can live as God intended only if flesh is put to death. In opposing flesh, Yahweh is not opposing humanity. He is acting to deliver humanity from everything that makes it bestial, every attempt to become more than human that makes humanity inhuman. In his war against flesh, Yahweh is at war with pride, heroic bravado, violence, the cascade of reciprocal vengeance, against Adam's impatience and Cain's envy and Lamech's brutality and the lusts of the sons of God for the daughters of men. In seeking to kill flesh to save the human race, Yahweh ultimately aims to prosecute, condemn and execute *mortality*, to put death to death.

The flood is the first great exemplification of this theme, as Yahweh's Spirit wearies of the struggle with flesh (Gen 6:3) and grieves over the damage to creation (Gen 6:6-7), the violence that flesh invariably produces (Gen 6:13). In the flood, Yahweh wipes the world clean of all flesh (Gen 6:13, 17; 7:21).

Even after the flood, though, Yahweh sees that humankind is flesh and that the imagination of the heart is only evil from youth (Gen 8:21). Yahweh's evaluation of postdiluvian humanity is quickly confirmed in the fall of the postdiluvian nations at Babel (Gen 11:1-9). The peoples who refused to

---

[19]As explained in chap. 2, the word *institutionalize* is somewhat misleading. The Bible does not share our materialist or atomized anthropology, according to which human beings remain what they are no matter what shape their social setting takes or what direction their cultural values impel them. "Institutional" patterns determine nature, so that a person who lives under Torah is "naturally" a Jew, naturally one *hypo nomou*. Paul even uses the language of birth to describe this, speaking of Jews not only as the "seed of Abraham" but also as those who have their source from the works of the law (*ex ergōn nomou*, Gal 3:10). I will continue to use terms like *institutional* and *order* throughout the book, but they refer, and rather clumsily, to *one* dimension of the complex reality of human nature and human society, without implying that this dimension is separable from human beings themselves or their nature.

scatter end up scattered and the men who sought to make an immortal name for themselves are left with the insulting name "Confusion." Humanity, descended from one man and woman, and reborn after the flood in the sons of Noah, becomes fragmented and divided. Outside Eden, human flesh is distant from God. Long before Babel, this distance from God manifested itself in interpersonal division—Adam accused Eve, Cain murdered Abel and the prediluvian world was filled with violence. Under Babelic conditions, division becomes institutionalized and permanent. After Babel, flesh separates from flesh.

This is the context for the call of Abram. Tenth in descent from Noah as Noah was tenth from Adam, Abram is a new Noah, through whom Yahweh continues his war against flesh. Yahweh's call to Abram does not *create* the exclusion from Eden but presupposes that exclusion. It does not *create* the division of the nations but assumes it. Through Abram, the nations divided at Babel will be reunited as they are reconciled to the Creator to receive his blessing through Abram's seed. Through Abram, humanity will somehow be forgiven of the sin of Adam and pass by the cherubim to reenter Eden. Fleshly divisions and rivalries will be overcome as Abram becomes Yahweh's agent to insert a fresh principle of social cohesion and order into human society. Through Abram, God's Spirit will overcome the sinful flesh of fleshly sons of Adam and Eve.

Beginning with circumcision, Israel's stoicheic regulations signified this vocation. Israel's rites were parodies of those in other ancient cultures, many of whom already had stoicheic systems prior to the exodus.[20] Gentiles had temples and priesthoods long before Israel, where they performed rites of sacrifice, observed purity regulations and holiness taboos, enjoyed a rich festival life. At every point, these similarities serve to highlight differences.[21] Israel was told to employ the same elements as Gentiles, but to assemble them so as to form a different human *physis*.

The covenant of circumcision came in the context of a promise of an abundant seed (Gen 17:17) that would inherit and inhabit and therefore

---

[20]The term *parody* is taken from Douglas Knight, *The Eschatological Economy: Time and the Hospitality of God* (Grand Rapids: Eerdmans, 2006), though I do not use the term in exactly the same sense as Knight.

[21]I am in part following the discussion of Howard Eilberg-Schwartz, *The Savage in Judaism: An Anthropology of Israelite Religion and Ancient Judaism* (Indianapolis: Indiana University Press, 1990).

be fertile on the land that Yahweh promises.[22] Circumcision removed an obstacle to fertility even as it marked an Israelite child as a fulfillment of the Abrahamic promise. Yahweh promised a land to Abram (Gen 15:12-21) and also the seed to make the land fruitful (Gen 17). Circumcision sealed the deed of inheritance for the land, but demonstrated that Abraham's children were not going to inherit the land by the power of their arm of flesh, their battle prowess or heroism. Yahweh promised fertility, but indicated that Abraham would father the seed only when he gave up fleshly hope.[23] Circumcision was the "fruitful cut" in Abram's flesh. It is no accident that Abram could father the child of the promise, Isaac, only *after* he was circumcised.[24]

Circumcision has been widely practiced in many cultures, but outside Israel *infant* circumcision is unknown. In the ancient world, and in tribal cultures studied by anthropologists, circumcision is typically a puberty rite.[25] That makes sense if it is a sign of fertility, a pruning to make the boy's penis a fruitful tree. If it is a sign of fertility, why inflict it on infants?[26]

---

[22]Ibid., 147-48. He points out that fertility comes up seven (!) times in Genesis.

[23]The notion that Israel is a circumcised people transplanted to be fertile in the land is strengthened by the language of Lev 19, which forbids Israel from taking the produce of "uncircumcised" trees. For three years, fruit would be considered "uncircumcised." Its fruit during that period is classified as "foreskin," and therefore taboo to Israel (Lev 19:23-25). The analogy works because trees must be pruned to bear fruit. Circumcision is pruning of Israelite males so that they may bear fruit, the seed of Abraham (ibid., 149-54).

[24]Though Paul does not mention circumcision in his allegory of Abraham's wives and sons (Gal 4:22-33), it is glaring by omission, and essential to the argument. Abraham becomes fruitful only by removing flesh, not by boasting in it—his flesh had been impotent in any case. See my essay, "Mother Paul and the Children of Promise (Galatians 4:19-31)" in *Obedient Faith: A Festschrift for Norman Shepherd*, ed. P. Andrew Sandlin and John Barach (Mount Hermon, CA: Kerygma, 2012). For discussions of the covenant of circumcision, see David Bernat, *Sign of the Covenant: Circumcision in the Priestly Tradition* (Atlanta: Society of Biblical Literature, 2009); Gordon H. Wenham, *Genesis 16–50*, Word Biblical Commentary 2 (Waco, TX: Word, 1994), 13-32; Elizabeth Wyner Mark, *The Covenant of Circumcision: New Perspectives on an Ancient Jewish Rite* (Lebanon, NH: Brandeis University Press, 2003).

[25]For crosscultural evidence, see Bruno Bettelheim, *Symbolic Wounds: Puberty Rites and the Envious Male* (Glencoe, IL: Free Press, 1954); Leonard Glick, *Marked in Your Flesh: Circumcision from Ancient Judea to Modern America* (Oxford: Oxford University Press, 2005).

[26]Eilberg-Schwartz explains it in the context of patrilineal descent, especially for priesthood. Circumcision of infants showed that "a boy's procreative powers were granted by God as a privilege for having been born into Abraham's line. They were granted in fulfillment of the divine promise that Abraham and his descendants would be fruitful, multiply, and inherit the land. A male's ability to reproduce was not simply the outcome of his maturation but also a privilege of having a certain genealogy. Circumcision was thus a rite which simultaneously conferred and confirmed one's pedigree" (Eilberg-Schwartz, *Savage*, 175-76). That is insightful. What I offer here is a "Pauline" corrective.

From the beginning, circumcision ritualized the impotence and infertility of flesh. Flesh is not the solution to the human dilemma, to death. Flesh is the problem. The obstacle that needs to be removed is flesh itself, and given the connotations of "flesh" in Scripture, circumcision hints that fertility comes only when the phallus itself is cut off. Circumcision is a sign of "descent" only when we think of descent in a paradoxical way: the children of Abraham were marked by a sign of *distrust* in flesh, a signifier of flesh's impotence. At the same time the circumcised renounce flesh, they are entrusted to the life-giving God. The mark in the flesh is an *absence*—an absence of the normal power of procreation. From Abraham on, the most productive, the most fertile, are those *without* powers of flesh, those who *cut off* whatever powers of flesh they might possess, and are fruitful by the power of the Spirit, who gives fruit. To drive home the point, this mark of flesh's impotence was imposed on the already-impotent, on eight-day-old boys. Jesus was repeating something his Father taught him when he pointed to little children as model disciples.

As noted above, "flesh" denotes genetic relation, and a social order grounded on flesh is a social order organized around such flesh relationships. In a fleshly social order, ancestry, heritage and birth are determinative. To be well-born is to be well-set, for life. Flesh societies are therefore exclusive. The in-group is defined by sharing the potent flesh of a founder, out-groups by having flesh of a different, lesser patriarch. After Babel, the nations each represented a separate line of descent, a trail of flesh through time.

If circumcision is a renunciation of *flesh*, it is also a renunciation of ethnic separation and division.[27] Circumcision separated Israel, but the character of that division needs to be carefully specified. God's judgment against Babel, not God's command of circumcision, created the divided world. Circumcision was given in the context of Babel, but it was not a Babelic, that is, a *fleshly* marker. On the contrary, it was a renunciation of the fleshly patterns of division, rivalry, competition, strife that characterized the world after Babel. Circumcision was *anti*-Babel, signifying the promise that Yahweh would bless all nations through Abraham.[28] Circumcision is a division, but

---

[27] I have argued elsewhere that it was a "deeper cut" within divided humanity, an act of separation from the Gentiles, but did not recognize that it was cutting Israel off from a fleshly principle of *division*.

[28] That circumcision is not a sign of a fleshly covenant is evident in the fact that Abraham had only one son, Ishmael, when he circumcised his household (Gen 17). The "males in your household"

it marked a division *from* division, a separation from the rivalrous project of scattering and domination that characterizes the nations, a negation of the negation and a death to the death that is fleshly existence. This is why circumcision itself can be seen as a type of Jesus' cross, what Paul calls "the circumcision of Christ": in his death, Jesus decisively cut off flesh (Col 2:11).[29] Thus we further pursue the effort to provide a historically plausible account of the atonement, an account that shows how the specific history and institutions of Israel answer to the condition of humanity as a whole.

Circumcised Israel was not another tribe. It was a *parody*-tribe. Its tribal emblem did not mark the triumph of fleshly virility or manly endurance, as would be the case if circumcision were a puberty rite that involved pain. Circumcision was a casting-away of flesh that began in infancy. Sexual potency and procreation are paths to immortality, two of flesh's main strategies for overcoming the fear of death. A cut in the flesh of the foreskin, a cut in the *male* organ of generation, is a counterattack on the flesh's strategies of flesh-avoidance, its tactics of death-denial. Circumcision brought an end to the reign of the phallus by symbolically cutting off the phallus: there is not much room left for phallic display when there is no phallus to display.[30] With a stroke of the knife, an Israelite child was cut off from the necrophobia that inspired the necrophilia of Egypt, from the pompous displays of Babylonian warrior kings, from the honor system of Greek heroes. Circumcised in the flesh, he was called to renounce flesh with all its pomp.

---

were not sons but servants and soldiers (Gen 12–13). From the beginning the household of Abraham was a *fictive* or symbolic kin group, not a fleshly one, a covenant people, not a race.

[29]See J. A. T. Robinson, *The Body* (London: SCM, 1952), 41, who writes of Col 2:15: "The dying Jesus, like a king, divests himself of that flesh, the tool and medium of their power, and thereby exposes them [powers] to ridicule for their Pyrrhic victory." Thanks to Dan Reid for this reference.

[30]As some Jews discovered during the Hellenistic period, when their circumcised penis was a source of shame when they participated in Greek games. In Abram's story, the renunciation of natural procreative power is fulfilled in the Aqedah, when Abraham willingly gives his son, his hope for the future and immortality, into Yahweh's hands. Insofar as the *Aqedah* is the foundation of Israelite sacrifice, we can see that Israelite sacrifice fulfills the flesh-renunciation of circumcision. This point will be expanded in somewhat different terms below. Because she is fixated on finding patrilineal biases in "P," Nancy Jay botches the *Aqedah* (*Throughout Your Generations Forever: Sacrifice, Religion, and Paternity* [Chicago: University of Chicago Press, 1992], 102). She argues that Isaac's sacrifice "restores him to patriliny," but it is rather Abraham's ultimate renunciation of fleshly patriliny, his relinquishment of his fatherly rights to Yahweh, and an affirmation of divine Fatherhood. By offering Isaac, Abraham confesses his flesh has no future; because Isaac is "raised," that future comes as gift, as Isaac is confirmed as the child of the Spirit.

Conclusion

Circumcision initiated a pedagogy in weakness.[31] Paradoxically, this anti-sarkic pedagogy is both more fertile and more fleshly than the fleshly *stoicheia* of the Gentiles. It is more fertile because in renouncing his own potency, Abram's flesh became a conduit for infinite divine power. His seed was conceived not by natural means but by a miracle; Isaac was a resurrected child in his birth, not only in his death-and-resurrection at Moriah (cf. Rom 4). By renouncing flesh, Abram was able to overcome the limitations of flesh.[32] Yet, deprived of flesh, Abraham's children were *more* fleshly because circumcision encouraged an honest admission and even embrace of the limitations, weakness and vulnerability of flesh. Circumcision was the beginning of the overthrow of the fear of death because it imposed a fleshly death at the *beginning* of life. For Abram too it might be said that "he died and his life was hid in God." Because the circumcised man trusted God's power rather than his own, his own powerlessness was no longer shameful. He was not anxious about his weakness. *Weakness* became a point of boasting. Abram could have boasted, like Paul, in his weakness, because in his weakness God's power was made known.

Circumcision enlisted the circumcised in Yahweh's opposition to flesh. By cutting away the flesh of the foreskin, Israel was incorporated into Yahweh's war against flesh. Yahweh's aim was not only to wipe out flesh in order to establish his kingdom of justice. He intended to do that by gathering an army of fleshly humans who in the very midst of the flesh make war on flesh, using something other than weapons of flesh.

Circumcision was the first *stoicheion* of Israelite social life, and it set the trajectory for the Torah that was later added to the promise. When the full stoicheic system was established at Sinai, it institutionalized Yahweh's anti-sarkic program for his people and advanced the cause of his saving war against enslaving flesh.

---

[31] In calling the stoicheic regulations of the law a "pedagogy," I am of course drawing on Paul's analogy in Gal 3.

[32] Though Paul does not mention circumcision in his allegorization of the Abraham narrative (Gal 4), circumcision is crucial to his argument. Both Isaac and Ishmael were circumcised, but the crucial circumcision was Abraham's. Only *after* he had cut off flesh was he prepared to be father of Isaac, and hence father of us all.

five

WHAT TORAH DOES

†

Adam was created flesh, vulnerable, finite and weak. Because of his sin, his flesh became *mortal* flesh, subject to the ultimate vulnerability of death. In the fallen world, flesh is both human potency and human weakness; it is the arm of the flesh and the power of procreation, but it is also the woundable body. To compensate for our vulnerability, we carry out fleshly displays of military, athletic, sexual, intellectual or economic prowess. We try to cheat death with hero games, like the game of writing big books, and fleshly cultures cooperate by creating hero-creating systems that lay out well-worn pathways to immortal glory. Fleshliness gets embodied in habits and practices of pollution, restrictions on access to holy space, in socioreligious boundaries that separate one form of human flesh from another. Flesh is the background condition that gives rise to the *stoicheia* that constitute the *physis* of the Gentile universe. In all these senses, flesh is inimical to human life. If human beings and human society are to be saved, someone will have to strip us of our flesh.

As we saw in the last chapter, circumcision signified precisely this—Yahweh's intention to destroy flesh so as to save the human race. As the first *stoicheion* that constitutes the world of Israel, the first ingredient in the forming of an alternative human *physis*, circumcision was a confession of the impotence of the flesh and the beginning of a pedagogy of weakness and dependence, a pedagogy of faith. It was the beginning of the removal of flesh that would allow Israel to return to Eden; it was a separation from the Babel world of fleshly division and the beginning of a pedagogy that would end with the reunion of the human race in Abraham's seed.

Israel's later stoicheic regulations extended this parodic, antifleshly pedagogy, extending Yahweh's war against flesh, and further called Israel to share in that war. Torah was given to Israel outside Eden, after Babel, and it accepted the conditions of Edenic and Babelic curse. Torah did not restore open access to the garden. Torah did not get the cherubim to lay down their fiery swords. Torah did not reunite the nations in one flesh or make them all one flesh with God. Simply by the fact of its being given to Israel and *not* to everyone, Torah established a hierarchy of access and responsibility to God and his oracles. Torah was accommodated to the fleshly condition of the human race. It was a new, divine version of *ta stoicheia tou kosmou*, adding elements to the world that circumcision began to form. By revealing Torah, Yahweh continued the process of creating a new type of human being, modifying human nature Jewishly, Torahly. What is born of flesh is flesh, and sons of Abraham continued to be born of flesh. Eight days later, their flesh was cut away and they were reborn as Jews *physei*. Israel was not a child of the Spirit, but it was no longer precisely *ek tēs sarkos* either. Israelites and Israelite society became naturally Jewish by taking their origin from Torah: their world was the social formation that emerged *ek nomou* (see Rom 4:16) or *ek tōn ergōn nomou*. It was a cultural and religious world constituted by Jewish elements. This formation of a Jewish *physis* was the first stage in the Creator's renewal of human *physis*.

Rooted in the fruitful cut of circumcision, Torah instituted a "civilization" of weakness, a culture patterned on renunciation of flesh. In one of his studies of Sophocles,[1] Charles Segal points to several Greek terms that might be translated as "civilization" and that capture various aspects of civilized life.

nomos = the established institutions, customs and norms of a people

politeia = the form of government, especially the constitutional forms

paideia = culture as manifested and transmitted in poetry and art[2]

---

[1] Charles Segal, *Tragedy and Civilization: An Interpretation of Sophocles* (Norman: University of Oklahoma Press, 1999). See also Segal, *Sophocles' Tragic World: Divinity, Nature, Society* (Cambridge, MA: Harvard University Press, 1998).

[2] All of these, Segal suggests, are to be contrasted with *physis*, "nature," which when applied to humankind describes humans in a semibestial or savage state. Segal, following the lead of structuralist criticism, examines Sophocles in terms of the conflict of *physis* and *nomos*. Segal points out the optimism that gripped Athens in the Periclean period, an optimism about the ability of human *logos* and *nomos* to stave off the savage potential of humanity's *physis*. But that was short-lived: The Peloponnesian Wars broke out, marked by several horrific acts of savagery (detailed by Thucydides), which had an affect on Athenian consciousness not unlike the effect of World War I on the confidence of European civilization. Intriguingly, Segal points to a shift in the meanings of *nomos* and *physis* during the course of the fifth century BC: At the beginning of the

For Paul, Torah is all three, especially *nomos* and *paideia,* a set of established institutions and customs, an idealization of social life that is used as a standard not only for moral decisions but also for the patterns and habits and values of social life.[3] These norms are understood within the poetry and narrative of creation, Adam, flood, Babel, the call of Abraham and the lives of the patriarchs. For Paul, Torah—broadly conceived as including narrative, rules of behavior and sanctuary regulations—foreshadows the Messiah, and so prepares Israel for the arrival of a messianic order. By speaking of the pedagogy of Torah that leads to Christ, Paul also hints that doing the law—performing sacrifices, keeping purity laws, attending feasts at the temple, approaching God through the priest—inculcates habits of weakness, which means a habitus of faith and a vocation to assail

---

century, *nomos* was seen as liberating, a structure that suppressed the savage nature of humans and enabled them to live in political community. By the end of the century, in an almost Freudian move, *nomos* is "seen as repressive and destructive" while *physis* is liberating. This is the ground on which the Sophists operated, bringing a "natural" critique against the injustices of the "legal" order. Part of the Sophist innovation was to argue that Athenian *nomoi* were products of human action rather than gifts of the gods, and therefore as susceptible to change and deterioration as any human institutions or creations. This is also the ground on which tragedy staked its claim: "The triumph over the beastlike life of savagery, so proudly celebrated by Sophocles in the *Antigone,* by Euripides in the *Suppliants,* by Critias in the *Perithous,* rings hollow when set against the recrudescence of bestiality and savagery in man's own nature. To this paradox the tragic poets return again and again." Euripides, writing in the midst of the shocking events of the war, clearly depicts this dissolution of civilized order into bestiality; Sophocles, at some chronological remove, deals with the issues more subtly but still explores the power of humans to civilize themselves. The Parthenon was completed in the year just before the outbreak of the Peloponnesian Wars and the production of Euripides's *Medea.* Segal points out that the hero's relationship to place (and hence his moral "standing") is ambiguous. Places that should be safe havens become threatening (e.g., Agamemnon's bath). In part, this is because of the ambiguity of the hero's relationship to the polis. On the one hand, the hero's energy and physical strength is necessary for the survival of the polis; on the other hand, the hero's energy is so boundless that he threatens to break the order (*nomos*) of the polis. There is a conflict, in Reinhold Niebuhr's terms, between the hero's vitality and the law. The hero has no safe and fixed place, either socially or geographically or politically, and has to make his own character, has to invent himself (Segal, *Tragedy and Civilization,* 5). As I observed in chap. 2, Paul's use of *nomos* and *physis* appears to cut across these distinctions. Instead of polarizing the two in either direction, he sees that the variety of *nomoi* established a different set of elementary social physics, thus establishing a variety of different *physeis.* For a careful review of the various meanings of *nomos* in Paul, see Michael Winger, *By What Law? The meaning of Νομος in the Letters of Paul* (Atlanta: Society of Biblical Literature, 1992). Winger, though, does not consider the expansive definition offered here.

[3]Paul, of course, uses the Greek *nomos* everywhere to refer to written Torah (e.g., Rom 2:12-13), which includes commandments to individuals but also forms the constitution for Israel's social and political life. That Paul calls the law a *paidagōgos* (Gal 3:24) hints at the notion that the law functions as *paideia* in something like Segal's sense. For Paul, it is not only the imperatives that comprise Torah but the narratives of Abraham and his wives and sons (see Rom 4:21). Since Paul can speak of Christian training as *paideia* (Eph 6:4), it seems likely that he could say the same of Torah.

fleshliness.[4] Insofar as Torah opposes mortal, sinful flesh, flesh that kills and dies, it is what Paul says it is: a law intended to give life.

SANCTUARY

Similar as biblical sanctuaries were to the temples of the ancient world, there are notable divergences. Solomon's temple was grand, but it did not depict the military glories of Israel the way Babylon and Greek temples displayed the exploits of their respective armies. The dead had no place in Yahweh's house as they did in Egyptian temples, nor did the worship of heroes. Yahweh was the sole occupant of his house: there was no divine council, no consort, no defeated foes.[5] Of course there was not even an image of Yahweh himself. That alone made it a parody sanctuary: for what is the purpose of building a house for the god if the god does not plan to reside there visibly?

The accent of Israel's sanctuaries is not on fleshly display. The accent lies elsewhere. Eden is the Bible's first form of temple.[6] Creation itself is Yahweh's three-story house, and Eden is his earthly sanctuary: Yahweh walks there; there is food and abundant water; Adam is given a priestly role to guard and to tend, to serve and guard.[7] The garden is the original holy space, and after the fall becomes the original form of restricted space.

Torah instituted a partial recovery of Eden—a *real* recovery, though partial. The construction of the *miqdāš* and Yahweh's habitation of the house created a distinction between holy and common space, and thereby between holy and common people and things. The tabernacle was the center of an ordered map of the entire world that revolved around the binary oppositions of holy and profane, clean and unclean.[8] These were the elemental regulations

---

[4]Fernando Belo, *A Materialist Reading of the Gospel of Mark* (Maryknoll, NY: Orbis, 1981), 51, interprets Israel's refusal of images as a signifier of the renunciation of human strength.

[5]What I am describing is the normative ideal of the sanctuary as described in Ex 25–40, 1 Kings 5–7 and in the related passages of 1–2 Chronicles. Scripture itself indicates that Israel added all of these things, and archeological evidence confirms that some in Israel believed Yahweh had a wife and that he was head of a pantheon. Those beliefs and practices, though, represent a drift from Israel's calling, and conformity to the norms of ancient Gentile religion.

[6]See Meredith Kline, *Images of the Spirit* (Eugene, OR: Wipf & Stock, 1999); Gregory Beale, *The Temple and the Church's Mission: A Biblical Theology of the Dwelling Place of God* (Downers Grove, IL: InterVarsity Press, 2004); James Jordan, *Through New Eyes: Developing a Biblical View of the World* (Eugene, OR: Wipf & Stock, 1999); L. M. Morales, *The Tabernacle Pre-Figured: Cosmic Mountain Ideology in Genesis and Exodus* (Leuven: Peeters, 2012), 51-119, 248-52.

[7]On the priests as new Adams, see Morales, *Tabernacle Pre-Figured*, 97-100, 258-61.

[8]The term is taken from Philip Peter Jenson, *Graded Holiness: A Key to the Priestly Conception of the World* (London: T&T Clark, 1992). Though organized around binaries of holy/common and

of the world under which Israel lived. The holiness system set up a symbolic universe in Israel, a "world" organized around the sanctuary. This system constituted the physics of Israelite social and religious life. It was part of the pedagogy of Torah, since it demonstrated that while in the flesh Israel cannot live in Yahweh's house.

The intention behind the sanctuary is, however, frequently misunderstood. Israel's holy places were restricted spaces, off-limits to all but authorized personnel, priests who had "filled the hand," been consecrated and wore their robes of glory and beauty that made them at home in Yahweh's glory house (Ex 28–29; Lev 8–9). But the building of the tabernacle and later the temple did not *create* the conditions of exclusion and distance. In fact, the sanctuary was a *counter*movement to the curse of Eden. Yahweh drove Adam and Eve *out* of the garden; he invited Aaron and his sons *in*. For the first time since Eden, a human being stood before the Creator to serve. Not Noah, not Abraham, not Jacob or Joseph: none of them passed by the cherubim to take up the Adamic task to stand and serve within Yahweh's garden. For the first time since Yahweh stationed cherubim at the gate of the garden, Torah allowed *human beings* to take over the Adamic task to "guard" the garden (*šāmar*, Gen 2:15).[9] For the first time since Adam, holy men walked on holy ground, with only a veil embroidered with cherubim between them and Yahweh. The tabernacle was still holy space, but the boundaries of holy space had become porous. Yahweh expelled Adam from the garden in wrath, and put Adam under wrath. In the tabernacle system, Yahweh went out into the howling waste to find his unfaithful bride and bring her back home. He went outside Eden to give a taste of Eden to Adam's children who lived east of Eden.

---

clean/unclean, the system of Torah is more complicated; it can be summarized as seen in table 1, following Jenson.

Table 1. System of Torah

Spatial	Social	Animal	Material	Cosmic	Food
Most Holy	high priest	goat	pure gold	highest heavens	Most Holy
Holy	priests	bull	gold/silver	firmament	Holy
court	laity	lamb	bronze	earth	peace offering
land	sojourners	clean animals	earth	clean	
world	Gentiles	unclean animals	sea	unclean	

[9] See the seminal work on guard duty at the tabernacle by Jacob Milgrom, *Studies in Levitical Terminology*, vol. 1, *The Encroacher and the Levite: The Term 'Aboda* (Berkeley: University of California Press, 1970).

Having taken up residence among the Israelites, Yahweh invited them to his house to share his goods. Why would Yahweh set up his house in Israel and then refuse to let Israel draw near? Why would Yahweh live among his people but show no hospitality?[10] Under the circumstances, Yahweh's hospitality must be restricted, the welcome must be a *controlled* welcome, *stoicheic* access. But Yahweh set up his house so fleshly people, who were marked by the renunciation of flesh, could draw as near as possible. Torah was a form of *ta stoicheia tou kosmou*, but it was a form that permitted limited access. It introduced a new world of worship and held out the possibility of even freer, more open access in the future. By rearranging the elements, Yahweh began to form a new creation, and a new nature, in the midst of flesh.

One allegorical portrait of the tabernacle reinforces this point. According to Ezekiel 16, the sanctuary was a gift of bridal clothing (Ezek 16:8-14).[11] Though this is not explicit in Exodus, it is implicit. Yahweh entered into covenant with Israel in a kind of wedding feast. Then he built a house where he could dwell within his court in the midst of Israel. The tabernacle was the Lord's glory wing stretched out over Israel his bride. The tabernacle curtains and adornments were bridal adornments, and the tabernacle was the bridal tent where Yahweh and Israel had their appointed meetings.[12] It was a tent

---

[10]Daniel Block has emphasized that the sanctuary is a place of hospitality. See Block, *How I Love Your Torah, O Lord! Studies in the Book of Deuteronomy* (Eugene, OR: Cascade, 2011), 98-117. I do not see tension between Leviticus and Deuteronomy at this point, contra John Dunnill, *Sacrifice and the Body: Biblical Anthropology and Christian Self-Understanding*, new ed. (Farnham, UK: Ashgate, 2013), 96-97, who claims that the Levitical notion of sacrifice is purely expiatory and not holistic. Such a conclusion is plausible only if Leviticus is isolated from the rest of the Torah.

[11]Ezekiel 16 is an allegory of Judah's promiscuity and harlotry, but begins with Yahweh discovering Israel as a discarded child, writhing in birth blood. He cares for her, and as she grows to maturity he adorns her with cloth, porpoise skin sandals, bracelets, gold, silver and linen, and feeds her with the goods of the land—flour, honey and oil. Yahweh's initial care follows an ordination sequence: washing, anointing, clothing (see Ex 28; Lev 8). And the materials with which he adorns his daughter-bride are tabernacle materials: porpoise sandals (see Ex 25:5; 26:14; 35:7, 23; Num 4:6); fine linen (see, e.g., Ex 25:4; 26:1, 31, 36); earrings and nose rings (see Ex 35:22). In the allegory, in short, Yahweh clothes his bride like a tabernacle, for she is the image of his glory.

[12]The tabernacle is described as a "tent of meeting" ('ōhel mô'ēd, first in Ex 27:21), though this phrase might more specifically refer to the holy place, the portion of the tabernacle complex that is "outside the veil which is before the testimony" (Ex 27:21 NASB). After Ex 27, the phrase is used thirty-four times in Exodus—a total of thirty-five (7 × 5). Significantly, Ex 27:21 is also the first time that the tabernacle texts refer to Aaron and his sons as ministers in the tent, and the text moves on to describe the priestly garments and to lay out the rite of priestly ordination. The tent is described as a tent of appointment at the very moment when the text introduces those who are qualified to keep the appointments. *Mô'ēd* has a specific connotation in the Hebrew Bible.

of meetings, a tent for trysts, a place for communion of Yahweh and Israel, not for the self-isolation of Yahweh. For Yahweh is not flesh but Spirit.

WASHED TO DRAW NEAR

The sanctuary established a double-sided pedagogy, both a reminder of Israel's distance from Yahweh and a partial overcoming of that distance. The sanctuary was both an invitation to flesh and a constant reminder of the inadequacy of flesh. Purity regulations capture that double-sidedness even more clearly.

Purity regulations have everything to do with access to the sanctuary.[13]

The word is first used to describe one of the functions of the sun, moon and stars, to "be for signs and for appointed times" (Gen 1:14), and the other uses in Genesis describe a specific designated time set aside for an event. In the rest of the Pentateuch, a *mô'ēd* refers more specifically to the appointed times for Israel's assemblies. Israel is to observe the Feast of Unleavened Bread at the "appointed time" (Ex 23:15), and Lev 23 lays out the schedule of Yahweh's appointed times during which Israel will proclaim holy convocations, gatherings for festivity and worship (Lev 23:2 [2×]; cf. Lev 23:4 [2×]; Lev 23:37, 44). Yahweh comes near to establish times of communion with his people, to set up a calendar of trysts with his bride.

[13]Despite popular confusion, and a surprising amount of confusion among scholars, purity and holiness are not identical. There are two spectra in the Levitical system: a spectrum from profane or common on the one side and holiness or sanctity on the other, and a spectrum with unclean or impure on one side and clean or pure on the other. Though the spectra overlap, the Hebrew terminology is different. The root *ṭm'* refers to impurity; it is both a verb ("become unclean") and an adjective (the status of "unclean"). Impurity can be contracted from touching a carcass of an animal (Lev 5:2), eating unclean food (Lev 11:8), having skin disease (e.g., Lev 13:11, 15), various forms of discharge from the genitals (Lev 15:2, 25-26) or being in the presence of a human corpse (Num 19:13). The opposite of *ṭāmē'* is *ṭāhēr* (verb, "become clean" or "pronounce clean") or *ṭāhŏrâ/ṭāhôr* (noun, "purity" or "purification"). Many impurities are removed by a simple washing. Other things are purified when put into water until evening (Lev 11:32), or through a waiting period and an offering (women after childbirth, Lev 12:7-8), by washing body and clothes and receiving the declaration of cleanness from a priest (Lev 13:6; 15:13, 28) or being sprinkled with special water of purification (Lev 19:12, 19). Through the ritual of purification, the person takes a state of cleanness. It is the priest's job to distinguish between the *ṭāmē'* and the *ṭāhēr* (Lev 10:10). The root word for holiness or sanctity or sanctification is *qdš*. This too functions both as a noun or adjective, describing persons, places, objects, and as a verb meaning "consecrate" or "sanctify." Things are consecrated by being set apart as Yahweh's own (the firstborn, Ex 13:2), by rituals of consecration that include washing (Ex 19:10, 14), by rituals of ordination (Ex 28:3, 38, 41; 29:1; Lev 8:10-12, 15) or by rituals of consecration (Ex 29:36-37). Yahweh himself consecrates his house and his priests (Ex 29:44) and consecrates the holy place by coming near in his glory (Ex 29:43). Israel is to be consecrated to Yahweh (Lev 11:44; 20:7), partly by avoiding ritual defilements (Lev 11:44). The opposite of *qādaš* is *ḥōl* (Lev 10:10). Idolatry causes "profanation" (Lev 18:21; 19:12) and so does sexual sin (Lev 19:29). The form *ḥālal* is used of offenses against holy things (Lev 19:8) or persons (Lev 21:4, 6, 9, 12, 15).

Though distinct, the two spectra are interrelated. There is only defilement only where there is holiness. Before Israel came to Sinai, they didn't have Yahweh living in their midst, no tabernacle, no singular altar or holy place. Once that tabernacle is set up and Yahweh moves in, the place becomes holy, and access to that holy place, even the outer court, requires ritual purity. The first

Clean persons were permitted to enter the court of the sanctuary; unclean persons were not allowed, or at least they might not do so in safety. Purity regulations also had to do with sacrifice, since Israelite worshipers and priests were to be in a clean state to offer acceptable sacrifices.

Purity regulations are frequently explained as expressions of disgust—distance-making boundaries.[14] In Leviticus, they are the opposite. Yahweh is a consuming fire, and he has cherubic guardians around his throne. He specifies the conditions that make Israel unacceptable in his house, but then invites Israel in by publicizing how Israel can approach in safety. The purity regulations of Torah *are* prohibitions: taste *not*, touch *not*.[15] But the prohibitions are imposed for the sake of access. The No to impurity is ordered to the Yes of welcome. Yahweh did not descend from Sinai to the ark asking, "What fences can I set up that will keep my neighbors from disturbing my peace?" He came saying, "You can draw near, but only under certain conditions, only in a state that makes it safe for you to approach." The accent in the rules of impurity is not on the exclusion, which is presupposed. The texts focus on the details of purity, but the telos of these regulations is to describe mechanisms for *removal* of impurity, which means the closure of distance. Usually that closure of distance involves a simple washing. Sometimes it includes more elaborate rites of purification that include sacrifice. In either case, the purity rules do not exclude Israel permanently but allow Israel to draw near.

---

hint, for instance, that God's presence requires sexual abstinence occurs at Sinai (Ex 19). They are similar also in the fact that both are "graded" systems. On purity in Torah, see Walter Houston, *Purity and Monotheism: Clean and Unclean Animals in Biblical Law*, Journal for the Study of the Old Testament Supplement 140 (Sheffield: JSOT Press, 1993); Baruch J. Schwartz et al., eds., *Perspectives on Purity and Purification in the Bible* (New York: T&T Clark, 2008); Jacob Neusner, *The Idea of Purity in Ancient Judaism* (Leiden: Brill, 1973), esp. 7–31. Neusner extends the analysis to rabbinic notions of purity in *Purity in Rabbinic Judaism: A Systematic Account* (Atlanta: Scholars Press, 1994).

[14]This is the mistake in Richard Beck's superb analysis of uncleanness, *Unclean: Meditations on Purity, Hospitality, and Mortality* (Eugene, OR: Wipf & Stock, 2011).

[15]Jonathan Klawans offers this useful summary of what he calls "ritual impurity": "Birth, death, sex, disease, and discharge are part of normal life. Ritual impurity is also generally unavoidable. While certain defiling substances are relatively avoidable (e.g., touching carcasses), discharge, disease, and death are inescapable. Some ritual impurities are not just inevitable but obligatory. All Israelites (priests included) are obligated to reproduce (Gen. 1:28, 9:7). All Israelites (except the high priest) are required to bury their deceased relatives (Lev. 21:10–15; cf. 21:1–4). Priests are also obligated to perform cultic procedures that leave them defiled as a result (Lev. 16:28; Num. 19:8)" (Klawans, *Purity, Sacrifice, and the Temple: Symbolism and Supersessionism in the Study of Ancient Judaism* [Oxford: Oxford University Press, 2009], 54). There is no sin involved in ritual impurities, though it is a sin to refuse to perform the rites of purification or to enter the sanctuary of Yahweh in an impure state. Ritual purity is often contagious, and it lasts for varying lengths of time, but is never permanent (ibid., 54).

Purity regulations perpetuate and extend the antisarkic pedagogy estab-lished by circumcision.[16] Priests are distanced from flesh in unique ways, though it is important to specify how this is the case. On the one hand, they are under tighter regulations than other Israelites. They may not engage in mourning rituals or have contact with the dead except for close relatives, and the high priest may not defile himself even for family members. They have to be perfect physically, and no descendant of Aaron who is deformed can approach Yahweh's altar (Lev 21–22). This might seem to be an affir-mation of flesh, since it celebrates fleshly perfections, but the rite of ordi-nation belies that conclusion. During the rite of "filling" (Lev 8–9), blood is smeared on the ordinand's right ear lobe, right thumb and right big toe, extending circumcision to three other "corners" of his body. By this rite, the priest is symbolically maimed—made deaf to anyone's voice but Yahweh's, symbolically deprived of the use of his weapon hand, symbolically lamed. It is only as a living sacrifice, circumcised in four dimensions, that the priest may enter into the sanctuary. It is not enough for a priest to be cut in the flesh of the foreskin, renouncing sexual prowess. He must be cut off from *all* fleshly power if he is going to stand and serve before Yahweh.

For ordinary Israelites too, access to Yahweh only happened if they washed away the stains of flesh. "Flesh" (*bāśār*) recurs over twenty times in the purity texts of Leviticus 12–15, and the condition of flesh is central to

---

[16]The logic of the purity rules is an ongoing point of debate. Many commentators on Leviticus have linked the purity laws with death. See Jacob Milgrom, *Leviticus 1–16*, Anchor Bible 3 (New Haven, CT: Yale University Press, 1998), 766-68, 1000-1004. Loss of blood is a loss of life, but not all loss of blood pollutes. Only certain kinds of animal flesh are impure, and they are not in any noticeable way connected with death. Klawans, *Purity, Sacrifice, and the Temple*, 28-29, 57-58, disputes Milgrom's claim, arguing that not all the forms of impurity are obviously connected with death. Following Tikva Frymer-Kensky and David Wright, Klawans suggests that there is a double source for impurity, sex and death. The curse of Eden is the curse of death, but that curse takes specific forms. Adam is cursed in his work, Eve in her childbearing, the serpent by being forced to go on the ground. Purity rules are specifications of the curse of Eden, as James B. Jordan has argued in many places. David Biale (*Blood and Belief: The Circulation of a Symbol Between Jews and Christians* [Berkeley: University of California Press, 2008], 34) goes to the opposite side of the spectrum, arguing that menstrual blood defiles not because it is deadly or represents death but because it represents the potency of fertility. Mary Douglas's claim that a pure animal embodies an ideal form of a species needs to be more specific to be successful, though her claim that purity rules represent regulations of the social body is, in my judgment, exactly right (*Purity and Danger: An Analysis of Concepts of Pollution and Taboo* [London: Routledge, 2002]). I suggest here that the broad, flexible category of "flesh" is inclusive enough to cover most if not all of the data. Many of the purity rules explicitly specify that *bāśār* is the source of uncleanness; flesh is linked with both death and with sex, and an explanation of uncleanness in terms of flesh links the purity laws to the removal of flesh in circumcision.

determinations of purity and impurity. Israelites are forbidden to eat the flesh of certain animals (Lev 11)[17] and are prohibited from eating the life of the *bāśār*, which is in the blood (Lev 17:11). To eat blood is to seek life from flesh, and Yahweh is training Israel to seek life in him alone. Childbearing, that great expression of flesh's triumph over death, *defiles* (Lev 12). Israelites cannot make themselves pure by being fruitful and multiplying in the flesh. Skin disease pollutes when flesh shows through the outer covering of skin (Lev 13–14). Emissions from the genitals pollute, and Leviticus uses *bāśār* (flesh) to describe genitals (Lev 15:2, 3, 7, 13, 16, 19). Emissions may flow from various orifices of the body, but they do not make anyone unclean. Only flows from the "flesh" defile. Sex itself, a display of fleshly prowess, makes both the man and woman unfit for entry into Yahweh's presence (Lev 15:18).[18] Dead flesh defiles (Num 19).

Flesh is not only a static source of defilement. Flesh *spreads* pollution (see Rom 5 on the spread of death), so that the woman with a flow of blood defiles any who touch her, and dead flesh spreads death to the entire space where it lies. Flesh is a potency whose power must be controlled and arrested if Israel is to be near Yahweh's house. And every time an Israelite

---

[17]That the purity laws have ethical weight is the argument of Leigh M. Trevaskis, *Holiness, Ethics and Ritual in Leviticus* (Sheffield: Sheffield Phoenix, 2011). It is part of a pedagogy that is not simply liturgical but for life among the covenant people in general. Forbidden foods are not arbitrary but teach Israel what kinds of things they are to avoid taking in. The word "belly" in Lev 11:42 is used only in Gen 3:14: these are serpent-like creatures, and Israel, the new Adamic people, is to refuse to eat those animals that represent the serpent. Leviticus 13:2 makes an unusual reference to an *'ādām* who contracts skin disease—a reference, Trevaskis argues, to the original *'ādām* in the garden. In the laws of skin disease, the focal point of uncleanness is the exposure of flesh. "Live flesh" is "explicitly identified as unclean" in Lev 13:14-15, and when the underlying flesh is completely covered with skin disease, the person is clean. He notes that skin disease is often described with the word "stroke," suggesting that Yahweh has smitten the person. Overall, the laws symbolically depict "human rebellion under divine judgment," an exposure of flesh that God "strikes" with fire or wound. Skin disease incarnates God's judgment on "flesh." In Lev 15, exposure of flesh is like exposure of nakedness in God's presence: As Trevaskis says, "While 'one flesh' lives happily in God's presence within the Garden of Eden, it is the object of divine punishment in Genesis 6–9. . . . We may speculate that God's immediate presence is no longer accessible to 'naked flesh' in the way it was in the Garden" (142). For a more complete exposition of the relationship of impurity and death, see James B. Jordan, *The Meaning of Clean and Unclean*, Studies in Food and Faith 10 (Niceville, FL: Biblical Horizons, 1990).

[18]Mira Balberg goes so far as to say that semen is the only substance that is "impure in and of itself" (*Purity, Body, and Self in Early Rabbinic Literature* [Berkeley: University of California Press, 2014], 20). This evaluation of semen stands in stark contrast to the elevation of semen as the essential life force and life fluid in other religious traditions. See Natalie Gummer, "Sacrificial Sutras: Mahayana Literature and the South Asian Ritual Cosmos," *Journal of the American Academy of Religion* 82, no. 4 (2014): 1091-1126.

washed away the stains of flesh when he drew near, he was carrying on, in a small way, Yahweh's war with flesh.

As Jonathan Klawans observes, certain *sins* also pollute, and the land is the "victim" of the pollution:

> Moral impurity results from committing certain acts so heinous that they are considered defiling. Such behaviors include sexual sins (e.g., Lev. 18:24-30), idolatry (e.g., Lev. 19:31; 20:1-3), and bloodshed (e.g., Num. 35:33-34). These 'abominations' bring about an impurity that morally—but not ritually—defiles the sinner (Lev. 18:24), the land of Israel (Lev. 18:25, Ezek. 36:17), and the sanctuary of God (Lev. 20:3; Ezek. 5:11). This defilement, in turn, leads to the expulsion of the people from the land of Israel (Lev. 18:28; Ezek. 36:19).[19]

Unlike some forms of sanctuary defilement, land defilement is not contagious, but its consequences are long-lasting and may be permanent. Land pollution is all but impossible to rinse away. It does not go away at sundown after washing one's clothes.[20] It is removed only when Israel is expelled from the land into the grave of exile, and rises again to her inheritance.[21]

Land defilements, like sanctuary defilements, arise from flesh, flesh now understood in the extended sense in which Paul uses the term. Idolatry, *porneia* and angry strife are among the works that the flesh does (Gal 5:19-20). Violence is an expression of the power of flesh, a straightforward claim to dominance, one of the main pathways in the hero systems of the ancient and modern worlds. Nation conquers nation to enrich itself, to display its power over others, to have something to boast in. Violence is compensation

---

[19] Klawans, *Purity, Sacrifice, and the Temple*, 55. For an earlier treatment of the polluting effect of sin, see A. Büchler, *Studies in Sin and Atonement in the Rabbinic Literature of the First Century* (New York: Ktav, 1967), 212-374. Klawans's terminology can be misleading, since it suggests that the rituals themselves have no moral weight. It is preferable to speak of the distinction spatially: What Klawans calls "ritual" defilement pertains to the sanctuary, while "moral" defilement involves pollution of the land. That, it needs to be added, is not an absolute distinction.

[20] In contrast to ritual defilement, moral defilement doesn't exclude a person from the sanctuary, though it does defile the sanctuary: "Since moral impurity does not produce ritual defilement, sinners—in contrast to those who are ritually impure—are not excluded from the sanctuary. In the case of the suspected adulteress (Num. 5:11–31), the woman is brought into the sanctuary itself in order to determine her moral status. It also appears that Israelite murderers sought sanctuary in the sanctuary (Exod. 21:14; cf. 1 Kgs. 1:50-53 and 2:28-30). Moral impurity does indeed defile the sacred precincts (e.g., Lev. 20:3). But the effect of moral impurity does not penetrate the holy realm by the entrance of sinners into it. Moral impurity is a potent force unleashed by sinful behavior that affects the sanctuary even from afar, in its own way" (Klawans, *Purity, Sacrifice, and the Temple*, 55).

[21] On the differences between "unclean" and "abomination," see James B. Jordan, *The Meaning of the Mosaic Dietary Laws*, Studies in Food and Faith 1 (Niceville, FL: Biblical Horizons, 1989).

for the vulnerability of the flesh and the fear of death. Perverse sexuality, especially incest that forms "flesh of flesh" relations (Lev 18:6), defiles the land. Sexual immorality arises not only from sheer desire for pleasure but also from the desire for glory, the enhancement of reputation. Incest is an extreme of endogamy that creates an enclosed society of flesh. Israel was to avoid these fleshly indulgences so as to keep the holy land holy.

The civil regulations of Torah have the same aim: to preserve Israel's inheritance of the land and to provide for Israel's flourishing in the land. Even the "harshest" regulations of Torah aim at restorative justice. Idolaters, sexual sinners and the violent defile the land and endanger the whole community. If Israel wants to remain in the land and enjoy Yahweh's blessing, idolaters, sexual criminals and murderers have to be purged. When a murder is executed, the blood of the murderer pays for the innocent blood of the murdered, and the land rests. This is an altogether imperfect justice. A perfect justice would execute the flesh of the sexual pervert, of the murderer, of the idolater without executing the pervert, the murder or the idolater. Torah cannot target flesh in that fashion. It cannot kill the flesh without killing the man or woman who bears flesh. And so Torah cannot bring the restorative justice of God but only a proximate form of justice, which restrains violence by counterforce. If a law could have been given that could impart life to Israel, a law that both killed and made alive, such a law would have been given.[22]

Nothing in the Torah's purity regulations prohibits interaction between Israelites and Gentiles. _Nothing_ suggests that Israelites become impure simply by contact with Gentiles. A Gentile who dies in a room with an Israelite defiles the Israelite, but he defiles because he is dead and not because he is a dead Gentile. A Jew might be defiled by inadvertently touching a menstruating Gentile woman in the marketplace, but a Jewish woman would have caused defilement just as readily.[23] Perhaps a Jewish woman would have kept herself at a greater distance than a Gentile woman in order to prevent defilement. A scrupulous Israelite who has visited the market during the day and taken the precaution of bathing in the evening will be

---

[22] Alternatively, it may be that those guilty of capital crimes, like the human race before the flood, are flesh through and through, flesh all the way down. Killing them is simply killing flesh. Thanks to James Jordan for this suggestion.

[23] On the other hand, it is possible that Gentile menstruants would not defile at all since they were not under Torah. If true, this would strongly reinforce my point: though a Jew might avoid a Jewish woman with a flow of blood, he would not have to avoid a Gentile. Gentile contact would be less defiling than contact with a Jew. Thanks to James Jordan for raising this question.

cleansed in any case (Lev 15:19-24). In Torah, a Gentile is no more defiling than an Israelite. Nor do Israel's purity regulations trace out "class" or caste differences within Israel. Priests are qualified by descent from Aaron and by ordination, and so are under stricter purity regulations than the rest of Israel. Otherwise, every Israelite is equally susceptible to impurity, equally capable of achieving purity. There are no Brahmins, no untouchables.

The Torah that came four centuries after Abraham did not nullify the promise to Abraham that he would be the father of many nations and bring blessing to the Gentiles. Torah did not reverse the significance of circumcision; it was not a reaffirmation of flesh after four centuries of renunciation. Torah was an instrument in the realization of the promise and a further stage in the deliverance of humanity from flesh. Torah did not turn the Abrahamic promise to bless all nations into an exclusive possession of Israel. Like circumcision, Torah expressed Israel's separation from the Babelic world of fleshly divisions.

How did Torah express Israel's separation from separation, her negation of the politics of flesh? In part it achieved that by giving Israel access to Yahweh, the Creator of Israel and the nations. Yahweh's life, blessing and gifts were available in the sanctuary, and he drew near to Israel to distribute those gifts, not only to Israel but also through them to the world. He gave his oracles to Israel so that Israel may become a light to the nations and a teacher of the wise. While Israel alone was the priestly people, the caretaker of Yahweh's house, Israel cared for the house on behalf of the nations.[24] At the Feast of Booths, she offered seventy bulls for the seventy nations, and so offered up the world to the Creator. When Solomon dedicated the temple, he asked Yahweh to hear the prayers of strangers as well as of Israelites, making the temple a house of prayer for the nations (1 Kings 8). Based on Numbers 15, it seems likely that Gentiles could offer sacrifice at the Lord's house.[25] It is arguable that Israel bore the sins of the nations for the nations. As we will see below, the sanctuary and priest bore Israel's sins, and it seems fitting that Israel, as priestly nation, also bore the sins of the nations.[26] Later Gentiles

---

[24]Mark George, *Israel's Tabernacle as Social Space* (Atlanta: Society of Biblical Literature, 2009), 193, emphasizes that the tabernacle elevates Israel's status among nations in a way similar to the elevation of the high priest in Israel.

[25]The argument is made in Jacob Milgrom, *Numbers*, JPS Torah Commentary 4 (Philadelphia: Jewish Publication Society, 1989).

[26]See Jacob Milgrom, "Israel's Sanctuary: The Priestly Picture of Dorian Gray," in *Studies in the Cultic Theology and Terminology* (Leiden: Brill, 1983), 75-84. N. T. Wright argues that Israel's sanctuary is a "magnet" for sin and uncleanness, and that the system is set up to make Israel a sin-bearing people and the high priest the sin-bearer among sin-bearers.

recognized Israel's importance as a nation of intercessors on behalf of the nations (Ezra 6:6-12). Apart from the specific roles Israel played, their orientation to serve Gentiles was implicit in the promise to Abraham that stood behind the stoicheic system of Torah.

Torah assumed the conditions of separation among nations, and it gave form to Israel's consecration to bring blessing to the nations. Torah did not overcome Babel. Babel is a system of flesh, and the elementary things of Torah could not overcome flesh. Because Torah could not overcome flesh, it could not dismantle the elementary things of the world either. So long as Israel remains in the flesh, she is under Torah, under managers, under elements, and if Israel is then so is the rest of the world. As Paul says, Torah is holy, righteous and good, but its purpose and achievements are limited: it enables communion with Yahweh and promotes peace among nations *under the conditions of flesh*.

SACRIFICE

Many Christian thinkers have recently argued that salvation has to come in a fundamentally *anti*-sacrificial fashion because sacrifice is violence.[27] We

---

[27]The literature on sacrifice is of course vast and stretches over several millennia. For a clear survey of recent theories, see Maria-Zoe Petropoulou, *Animal Sacrifice in Ancient Greek Religion, Judaism, and Christianity, 100 BC to AD 200* (Oxford: Oxford University Press, 2012), 1-31. Petropoulou's book also surveys ancient theories, as does Daniel Ullucci, *The Christian Rejection of Animal Sacrifice* (Oxford: Oxford University Press, 2011). See also Bruce Lincoln, "From Bergaigne to Meuli: How Animal Sacrifice Became a Hot Topic," in *Greek and Roman Animal Sacrifice*, ed. Christopher Faraone and F. S. Naiden (Cambridge: Cambridge University Press, 2012), 13-31. In the same volume, Fritz Graf, "One Generation After Burkert and Girard: Where Are the Great Theories?," 32-51. Recent studies of the subject have been dominated by the work of the prolific René Girard. See, to begin, *Violence and the Sacred* (Baltimore: Johns Hopkins University Press, 1979) and *The Scapegoat* (Baltimore: Johns Hopkins University Press, 1989). Mark Heim's *Saved from Sacrifice: A Theology of the Cross* (Grand Rapids: Eerdmans, 2006) is a balanced Girardian study of atonement. Moshe Halbertal, *On Sacrifice* (Princeton, NJ: Princeton University Press, 2012) mounts an exegetical critique of Girard. Less popular but influential is the work of Walter Burkert, *Homo Necans: The Anthropology of Ancient Greek Sacrificial Ritual and Myth* (Berkeley: University of California Press, 1986), who claims that sacrifice is a sublimation of the aggression of hunting communities. Girard and Burkert engage in direct conversation, triangulated by Jonathan Z. Smith, in *Violent Origins: Ritual Killing and Cultural Formation*, ed. Robert Hamerton-Kelly (Stanford: Stanford University Press, 1987). In *Defending Constantine: The Twilight of an Empire and the Dawn of Christendom* (Downers Grove, IL: IVP Academic, 2010), I was too much influenced by this perspective. In chap. 9 below, I attempt to make a similar case about "sacrificial modernity" on a sounder basis.

Several writers have challenged Girard's and Burkert's claims that violence is the central meaning of sacrifice. F. S. Naiden complains that these "atheistic" theories do not fit the Greek evidence; see *Smoke Signals for the Gods: Ancient Greek Sacrifice from the Archaic Through the Roman Periods* (Oxford: Oxford University Press, 2012), and my review at *First Things* (blog),

are not saved *by* sacrifice but *from* it.[28] Here we have a rare convergence of tradition and contemporary innovation because historic theologies of atonement sometimes assume a view of sacrifice quite similar to Walter Burkert and René Girard.[29] On all sides, it is assumed that substitutionary killing is *the* sacrificial act.[30]

February 2, 2014, firstthings.com/blogs/leithart/2014/02/smoke-signals-for-the-gods. Also see Dunnill, *Sacrifice and the Body*, 13-16, 143-62. Dunnill points out that, contrary to Burkert's theory, sacrifice does not arise among hunters but in pastoral communities, and that sacrifice requires a certain level of technical sophistication and social organization (ibid., 34-49). One of the key problems with Girard is his equation of sacrifice and scapegoating. Heim assumes throughout that sacrifice is virtually equivalent to scapegoating, both acts of religious violence (*Saved from Sacrifice*, 10, 16, 48). The key truth about sacrifice is that it is violent (ibid., 40), though the Bible is unique in its honesty about the violence (ibid., 66) and unmasking the scapegoat mechanism (ibid., 98-99, on Is 53). B. Hudson McLean rightly distinguishes between sacrifice and scapegoating but eventually conflates the two, arguing that by the first century the scapegoat of Yom Kippur was killed (McLean, *Cursed Christ*, Journal for the Study of the New Testament Supplement 126 [Sheffield: JSOT Press, 1996], 75, 82). While Girard's claims may be extreme, *pharmakoi* rituals of removal were common in antiquity (Martin Hengel, *The Atonement: The Origins of the Doctrine in the New Testament* [Eugene, OR: Wipf & Stock, 2007], 23-25).

Various alternative accounts of sacrifice are currently on offer. Marcel Detienne and Jean-Pierre Vernant, *The Cuisine of Sacrifice Among the Greeks* (Chicago: University of Chicago Press, 1998) propose that sacrifice is fundamentally about commensality. Kathryn McClymond, *Beyond Sacred Violence: A Comparative Study of Sacrifice* (Baltimore: Johns Hopkins University Press, 2008) observes that "sacrifice" sometimes does not involve killing at all, stresses the sequence of sacrificial actions, and argues for a "polythetic" understanding. See ibid., 3-17, for a review of theories of sacrifice. Klawans also distances himself from Girardian and Burkertian theory, arguing that sacrifice is an *imitatio Dei* that involves a separation from the least Godlike aspects of human life (sex and death) to perform Godlike acts (summarized at *Purity, Sacrifice, and the Temple*, 72). Daniel Ullucci contests the notion that there is a discernible crosscultural "essence" to sacrifice (*Christian Rejection of Animal Sacrifice*) and stresses that in the ancient world sacrifice was a site of "competition" among "culture producers" who wanted their particular views of sacrifice to prevail.

Unsurprisingly, there are "splitters" among theorists of sacrifice, those who shy away from grand theory and stress local and regional differences. See Anne Porter and Glenn Schwartz, eds., *Sacred Killing: The Archaeology of Sacrifice in the Ancient Near East* (Winona Lake, IN: Eisenbrauns, 2012), which focuses on the material remains of sacrifice—bones, pottery, burnt wood, etc. Gunnel Ekroth has done something similar with Greek sacrifice. See, for instance, Ekroth, "Bare Bones: Osteology and Greek Sacrificial Ritual" in *Animal Sacrifice in the Ancient World*, ed. I. S. Hitch and I. Rutherford (Cambridge: Cambridge University Press, 2013). For detailed studies of ancient Hebrew sacrifice in comparison with Mesopotamian, see the two-part essay by JoAnn Scurlock, "The Techniques of the Sacrifice of Animals in Ancient Israel and Ancient Mesopotamia: New Insights Through Comparison," *Andrews University Seminary Studies* 44, no. 1 (2006): 13-49; 44, no. 2 (2006): 241-64.

[28]This is an allusion to Mark Heim's book *Saved from Sacrifice*.

[29]This is even *more* evident in recent efforts to formulate "nonviolent" theories of atonement. Nonviolence is often equated with "nonsacrificial." What Klawans says about Girard applies also to his theological disciples: sacrifice is injustice (*Purity, Sacrifice, and the Temple*, 25). On that basis, it is very difficult to avoid Marcionism.

[30]Admittedly, there might seem to be some New Testament warrant for this emphasis. Hebrews

Whether these theories are crossculturally useful, whether we can even begin to isolate the "essence" of sacrifice, these theories do not fit the specifics of the Levitical system.[31] Sacrifice is a "gate liturgy,"[32] a liturgy of return and access, designed for worshipers who are in the flesh, excluded from full enjoyment of the presence of God. Yahweh himself performed the first sacrifice, taking skins from animals to cover Adam and Eve. Sacrifice does not transform Adam or restore him to Eden. But under fleshly conditions it does what *can* be done: Yahweh's original sacrifice *covers* Adam's flesh. To *kāpar* is to cover, and by covering to put out of sight and to wipe away.[33]

Sacrifice enacts distance as well as proximity.[34] Worshipers themselves do not draw near to Yahweh's table to offer themselves as "bread" for God (see *leḥem ʾĕlōhîm*, Lev 21:21-22). They send animals to act as priest on their behalf. Worshipers do not pass by the cherubim in their own persons, but send substitutionary animals to represent them in Yahweh's presence, to submit to the sword and to be translated to divine smoke and fire on their behalf.[35] The animal is killed in the course of its approach to Yahweh's fire;

---

highlights the crucial significance of blood in covenant-making and in forgiveness: "Without the shedding of blood, there is no forgiveness" (Heb 9:22). But the writer to the Hebrews is sufficiently schooled in the Levitical system to know that death is only one moment in the sacrificial rituals of the tabernacle and temple.

[31] Throughout this section, I am indebted to decades-long conversation and note-comparing with James B. Jordan.

[32] Morales, *Tabernacle Pre-Figured*.

[33] Jay Sklar's argument that *kāpar* connotes both ransom and purgation has merit, but the argument is too narrowly focused on linguistic, semantic issues. Even if Sklar's conclusions are entirely correct, one is still left with the large task of determining how *these* particular ritual actions in *this* sequence perform a ransom and purgation. Sklar too quickly dismisses the view that *kāpar* has the meaning of "cover" when used in the sacrificial system. See Sklar, *Sin, Impurity, Sacrifice, Atonement: The Priestly Conceptions* (Sheffield: Sheffield Phoenix, 2005).

[34] This point is developed brilliantly in Detienne and Vernant, *Cuisine of Sacrifice*.

[35] The claim that the sacrificial animal is a "substitute" is hotly controversial, but incontrovertible when the Levitical system is placed within its narrative context. The sacrificial system assumes exile from Eden; the worshiper approaches a God who is enthroned behind a screen of cherubic guardians with swords of fire. The worshiper cannot draw near without dying; so he sends an animal ahead on his behalf. The animal is sent to bring the worshiper into God's presence; the animal dies and is turned to smoke, and the worshiper remains quite alive and nonsmoky. The only word that fits what happens is "substitute." It is important to recognize the "inclusive" character of the substitution: the animal does what the worshiper cannot do, but he does it so that, represented by the animal, the worshiper himself can have his sins covered and can draw near. Further, the Aqedah and Passover stand behind the sacrificial system: every worshiper is Abraham offering Isaac, and every sacrifice reenacts the deliverance of Passover. In both cases, an animal took the place of a human, a son, who was in danger, and the animal died in place of the son. Levitical offering can be called "inclusive place-taking" insofar as the animal goes ahead of the worshiper as a means of bringing the worshiper near. But that has to be balanced with the

it cannot be otherwise, since worshipers approach Yahweh from a condition of "flesh," under wrath, exiled from Yahweh's cherub-guarded house. The animal cannot get into God's presence without suffering death at the hands of the cherubic priests with their swords and fire.

Sacrificial smoke arises to heaven while the worshiper remains on earth. While worshipers draw near through the animal and the ritual, the rite itself reinforces their distance from God. As it depicts the boundary between the holy God who is a consuming fire and the fleshly worshiper, it also reinforces and maintains the boundaries of holy and common. Sacrifice is one of the elements that keeps the world in working order.[36] The world of Israel is ordered by the separation of Israel from Yahweh, and every sacrifice reinforces that separation. The world of Israel is ordered by proximity to Yahweh, and every sacrifice gives limited access, while instilling hope that Yahweh might someday fully open up his house, or that there may someday be a sacrifice that can carry the worshipers *themselves* into Yahweh's house.[37] Sacrifice is part of Yahweh's antiflesh pedagogy: if worshipers are going to ascend to God, they have to shed their skin and be translated into something other than flesh. Every Israelite who sacrifices does what Yahweh did in the flood—destroys flesh in order to make room for a new creation. So long as they are flesh, they will have to be content to let the animal pass into Eden for them.

Augustine's definition of sacrifice (*City of God* 10.6) as any act by which the actors seek to be united to God in holy society captures the sense of Levitical sacrifice. Augustine's definition is teleological, and thus includes

---

recognition that the animal's ministry takes place *outside* the worshiper. On the varieties of "place-taking," see Bernd Janowski, "He Bore Our Sins: Isaiah 53 and the Drama of Taking Another's Place," in *The Suffering Servant: Isaiah 53 in Jewish and Christian Sources*, ed. Bernd Janowski and Peter Stuhlmacher (Grand Rapids: Eerdmans, 2004), 48-74.

[36]Speaking of Aaron's use of incense as a screen to protect Israel from Yahweh's wrath, David Janzen puts the point nicely: the high priest "must bring in incense to separate himself from the presence of YHWH, and so spare his life (Lev 16:13). Aaron now uses incense to do the same for Israel, separating the nation from the holy to keep it alive. In other words, he erects the cultic wall between the Israelites and the sacred that the people had removed through their moral disposition" (Janzen, *The Social Meanings of Sacrifice in the Hebrew Bible: A Study of Four Writings* [Berlin: de Gruyter, 2004], 102). Janzen makes it clear elsewhere that the tabernacle is a new creation structure (ibid., 98), so maintaining the boundaries of holy space *is* a matter of maintaining the order of creation.

[37]This is the significance of the generic term *qorbān*, used for the offerings in Lev 1. Taken from the verb *qārab*, "to draw near," the *qorbān* is a "near-bringing," a gift brought to Yahweh through which the worshiper himself "draws near" to Yahweh.

not only the moment of death but also the ascent and incorporation that follows. Sacrifice traverses the boundary between sacred and profane space, as the animal serves in a priestly capacity to enter the sanctuary on the worshiper's behalf.[38] It includes a moment of substitutionary death, but the point is that the animal dies in the process of drawing near to God.

Sacrifice is ministry to Yahweh in his house. It is the "bread of God" (Lev 21), his meat, grain and wine. Every sacrifice is a meal, offered on Yahweh's altar-table and often involving human beings in table fellowship with Yahweh. In some offerings (the ʿôlâ or "ascension" offering), Yahweh is the only one who "consumes" (ʾākal, meaning "eat," see Lev 6:10; 9:24) the meal. The ʿôlâ is a meal prepared for the great King by servants. But the central innovation of the Sinai covenant is not that Israel performs table service. Abel, Noah and Abram all offered "offerings of ascension." Like Noah, Israel offers ascensions, "sons of the herd," recapitulating the exodus of Israel as a son prepared to take a throne beside Yahweh his father (Ex 4:23).[39]

---

[38]See Hartmut Gese, "The Atonement," in *Essays on Biblical Theology*, trans. Keith Crim (Minneapolis: Augsburg, 1981), 93-116. Matthias Grebe summarizes Gese's understanding of sacrifice as a "symbolic offering up (*zeichenhaft*) of the person's life through the shedding of the animal's blood. The animal's death becomes the sinner's own death [*real*], taken over by the sacrificial animal in substitution. Finally, through the blood-rite the *nepes* is dedicated and incorporated into the holy. Thus, the cultic atonement is a surrender, a 'total substitutionary commitment of a life' in which the sacrifice of the animal's life *includes* the one bringing the sacrifice. The sacrifice of the animal and the blood ritual should be seen as a holy rite in which the animal is not punished for the guilty, but brought into the sanctuary 'where it comes into contact with what is holy.' It is not merely a death and removal of sin that accomplishes the atonement but an inclusive *Stellvertretung* and the commitment of life to what is holy—this 'ritual brings Israel into contact with God'" (Grebe, *Election, Atonement, and the Holy Spirit: Through and Beyond Barth's Theological Interpretation of Scripture* [Eugene, OR: Pickwick, 2014], 76). This is a fine statement, though I disagree with Gese's and Grebe's claim that the "animal is not punished for the guilty."

[39]The bull of the ascension offering (whole burnt) are described as "sons of the herd" (Lev 1:5). This is often translated as "young bull," but it is a different phrase from the one we find in Lev 4:3 ("bull of the herd"). Only the ascension bull is explicitly described as a son. Only in the ascension offering is the "head" of the animal placed first on the altar (Lev 1:8, 12; cf. Lev 1:15). The head of a purification offering for priests is mentioned (Lev 4:11), but it is not placed on the altar; it is burned outside the camp. Though the head is not mentioned specifically, the head of a purification offering for the whole congregation is disposed of in the same way (Lev 4:20). Worshipers laid their hand on the head of the animal, but apart from the ascension offering there is no indication that the head played a significant role in the arrangement of pieces on the altar. Since only the internal organs and fat were burned in the peace and some purification (and trespass) offerings, it seems that the head was retained, perhaps as part of a meal (cheeks especially, mentioned as a delicacy in sacrificial accounts from outside the Bible). The import of this is that the ascension offering has a unique filial, capital role in the sacrificial system. It is the offering made morning and evening; it is the "head" offering, and the head of this head offering, the first thing put into the altar each day, was the head of an ascension. If we link this

The novelty at Sinai is that once Yahweh has received his bread, he shares his food and his table with Israel. Prior to the exodus, no one eats a sacrificial meal, a "peace offering," in the presence of God. The first use of *šəlāmîm* is in Exodus 20:24, at the beginning of Israel's covenant-cutting wedding ceremony. The patriarchs may have enjoyed sacrificial feasts in the presence of God, but we are never (or rarely) told so. After Sinai the tabernacle becomes a place of continuous feasting. The word for peace offering is used sixty times (12 × 5) in Leviticus. The new thing at Sinai is Israel's privilege of sharing a meal with Yahweh. Yahweh has moved into his house in the midst of Israel, and he makes it a house of hospitality (see Deut 12).

The marital/covenantal dimension of this innovation is underscored by the introduction of another novel term into the sacrificial vocabulary of the Old Testament: *'iššeh*. This term is used for the first time in the instructions for the priestly ordination rite (Ex 29:18, 25, 41), but after that it is used of every one of the five major offerings (Lev 1:9; 2:2-3; 3:3; 4:35; 7:5). There is no consensus about the translation of the term, which is often rendered as "fire offering," sometimes as "food offering." James Jordan has made the suggestive observation that *'iššeh* is closely linked to *'îš* (man) and *'iššâ* (woman) and that both are aurally and conceptually, if not etymologically, linked with fire, *'ēš*. The gendered words are first used in Genesis 2, after the creation of Eve. Given this background, Jordan has suggested that the sacrificial term *'iššeh* carries the connotation of "bridal food."[40] When Israel has entered into marriage covenant with Yahweh, she offers herself continuously as bridal food for his delight (see Song 5:1) in a continuous marriage feast. This new term fits the new-creation pattern in the exodus: Yahweh tears a "rib" from Egypt, brings it to the wilderness where he builds a Bride (people and bridal tent), where they bring near *'iššâ* to Yahweh's table.[41] "Let us go that we may

---

with the uniquely filial dimension of the ascension offering, we may say: Each morning, Israel's worship started with the head of a son on the altar. The son took the head position in the sacrificial system, and the bride follows.

[40]James B. Jordan, *Leviticus 1: Translation and Commentary* (Niceville, FL: Biblical Horizons, 2003).

[41]If the tabernacle is a bridal chamber, we can also speculate on the marital dimensions of sacrifice. Hos 2:14-20 allegorizes the exodus as a love story. Yahweh lures Israel from Egypt to the wilderness, speaks to her heart, becomes her *'îš* (man) and no longer her Baal (lord). Yahweh promises to take Israel out to the wilderness for a second honeymoon, but that implies that the *first* wilderness excursion was a honeymoon too. Israel starts out its Egyptian sojourn in Goshen, a fertile garden-land suitable for shepherds where Israel is fruitful and multiplies. Eventually Israel becomes mingled with the Egyptians, and Yahweh performs the radical surgery of plague and

sacrifice to Yahweh" can be glossed as "Get me to the church on time." Israel is ripped from Egypt, like a rib from Adam, so that she can be built (see Gen 2:22) into a bride for Yahweh. Israel goes from Egypt as a bride built for her husband,[42] to build a bridal chamber where the priestly "friends of the bridegroom" prepare the bride for her Husband. The sacrificial system is an ongoing wedding feast, presided over by the bridegroom priest (see Is 61:10-11).

Yahweh's advent among his people is an occasion for joy, the beginning of continuous divine hospitality and festivity, as Israel eats, drinks and rejoices before and with her Lord. Yet Yahweh's arrival poses a danger to flesh.

Passover to extract Israel from Egypt and bring her to his mountain of marriage to initiate the marriage supper.

Prior to the appearance of the woman, the man is *'ādām*, from the *'ādāmâ*, the ground; with the presentation of the woman, he becomes *'îš*. He is an earthen, unlit altar; when the woman comes, he catches fire. And *speaks*. Similarly, the arrival of the bride "transforms" Yahweh. He has not been silent in Genesis, but nowhere do we hear anything like the discourses of Ex 25–40, and then nearly the whole of Leviticus. He is the divine *'ādām*, whose tongue is loosed when he sees the Bride he has made for himself (see Zeph 3:17). Yahweh himself becomes associated with *'îš* only as the exodus approaches (Ex 3:2), as he leads Israel from Egypt (Ex 13:21-22; 14:24), at Sinai (Ex 19:18), in the finished bridal tent (Ex 40:38) and at the inauguration of the sacrificial system, when he breaks out in fire for the first time in the Bible to eat an *'iššeh*, bridal food (Lev 9:24). Not surprisingly, the first use of "jealousy" in connection with God is in Exodus (Ex 20:5; 34:14). Both of these are in connection with idolatry. In Ex 20:5, Yahweh the Lover demands that his Bride devote themselves to *him*, not to an image; Ex 34:14 prohibits spiritual adultery or, as Yahweh calls it, "harlotry" (v. 15). When *'iššâ* arrives, Yahweh reveals himself the divine archetype of the *'îš*. For the first time, he is shown to be the consuming *'îš* fired with jealous passion for his beloved. Sacrifice provided a way for bride Israel to approach Yahweh while remaining at a distance. It provided a way for the ravished divine Husband to "consume" his Bride.

[42]The biblical history of sacrifice depicts this story line. After the flood, Noah builds an altar (*mizbēaḥ*) and offers ascension offerings (*yaʿal ʿōlōt*). It is the first altar and the first ascension offering in biblical history (Gen 8:20). After the flood, Noah is the first king. Every clean animal and bird is included. There is not yet a distinction between sacrificial and nonsacrificial beasts, only between pure and impure. That further distinction is introduced only after Israel is separated as Yahweh's flock from the nations. And it's also the first time the Lord breathes in the smoke and enjoys the soothing aroma. The Hebrew has *wayyāraḥ yəhwâ 'et-rêaḥ hannîḥōaḥ*, which includes multiple puns. *Rāwah* and *rêaḥ* (verb and noun for "smell") recall the *rûaḥ*-Spirit of the original creation. The word for soothing or pacifying (*nîḥōaḥ*) is a pun on the name of Noah (*nōaḥ*), whose name means "rest" (Gen 5:29). Noah is the Sabbath bringer (appropriately also a vinedresser), and he brings rest by offering an ascension that delights Yahweh for its Noahroma. What Yahweh smells when sacrifices ascend is Noah, the "righteous man, blameless in his generation," who "walks with God" (Gen 6:9), the Noah who finds favor before Yahweh (Gen 6:8). Yahweh sniffed out the righteous Noah before he ever offered a sacrifice. The ritual of sacrifice does not have to be "allegorized" morally. It is an enacted allegory from the beginning, always already a symbol of self-offering and Yahweh's gracious acceptance of the offerer. Torah makes it clear that the offering of faithful obedience pleases Yahweh, just as the prophets had said. Torah already ties right worship with the requirement of a just life. For a detailed analysis of the extensive wordplay in the flood narrative, see Carol M. Kaminski, *Was Noah Good? Finding Favour in the Flood Narrative* (New York: T&T Clark, 2014).

did he?

In commanding that Israel build him a tent and then a house, Yahweh inserts a new factor into Israel and the nations, a holy space that is highly sensitive to the pollutions of flesh and the defilement of sin.[43] A land with Yahweh's temple is a holy land, so Israel's land too needs to be kept clean. Israel's festivity would continue only as long as Yahweh's residence, people and land remained pure. To maintain the continuous offering of ascension and peace offerings, Israel needs a mechanism for keeping the house clean to ensure Yahweh's presence.[44]

So in addition to the "peace offering," Torah gives Israel instructions about the *ḥaṭṭā't* and *'āšām* offerings that enable Yahweh to remain near in a world of flesh.[45] "Purification" offerings cleanse the sanctuary from the effect of inadvertent sins and various forms of "ritual" impurity, ensuring that the worshiper, the priest, or the community can retain access to the house of God. When a worshiper offers a purification offering, the priest eats the flesh of the animal, thereby bearing the *'āwōn*, the worshiper's guilt, his liability to punishment.[46] The priest becomes a guilt-bearer on behalf of the worshiper; the worshiper's sin or impurity, which puts him in danger of punishment, is absorbed by the priest. Further, by eating the flesh of the animal that has become a representation of the worshiper's flesh, the priest transforms that flesh into himself, into flesh that is ordained to enter into the presence of Yahweh. The priest is a living altar, a cooker of Yahweh's bread who eats and digests flesh, transforming it into the holy person.

Not only the priest but the sanctuary itself becomes a bearer of sin, specifically of the impurities (*ṭām'āh*), rebellions (*pešaʿ*) and sins (*ḥaṭṭā't*) of Israel.[47] Each is in its own way a manifestation of flesh. Impurity infects

---

[43]The classic statement of this is Milgrom, "Israel's Sanctuary," 75-84.

[44]James Jordan puts it nicely: Referring to Ex 35:21-22, he points out that Israel gave as their hearts moved them. The tabernacle is constructed from what comes from the hearts of Israel, and so the defilements of the tabernacle represent the defilements of their hearts. The people are cleansed by the cleansing of the sanctuary at the heart of Israel.

[45]The focus in the text is on purification offerings. The "trespass" offering has the same aim, but works from the opposite direction. Instead of purifying defilements, it makes compensation for sacrilege or trespasses and ensures the continuing presence of the God who has come near.

[46]This is a controversial point. I am convinced by the arguments of Roy Gane, *Cult and Character: Purification Offerings, Day of Atonement, and Theodicy* (Winona Lake, IN: Eisenbrauns, 2005), 91-105. On this issue, see also the idiosyncratic but stimulating work of N. Kiuchi, *The Purification Offering in the Priestly Literature: Its Meaning and Function*, Journal for the Study of the Old Testament Supplement (Sheffield: Sheffield Academic, 1987); and Kiuchi, *A Study of Ḥaṭa' and Ḥaṭṭā't in Leviticus 4-5* (Tübingen: Mohr Siebeck, 2003).

[47]See the summary chart in Gane, *Cult and Character*, 299. Gane's book is largely an argument

because it is the spread of flesh—menstruation, seminal emission, flesh showing through the skin. High-handed, defiant rebellion expresses the pride of flesh, its refusal to accept creaturely limits and its desire to be as God. Inadvertent sin is a product of the weakness of flesh, which violates God's commandments without willing to do so, often when willing to do the opposite. Together with his priest, Yahweh offers his sanctuary as a place for the temporary disposal of Israel's sin.

The agent for the purging of the impure, the removal of liability and the transfer of guilt to the house of Yahweh was the blood of the sacrificial animal.[48] The key text, Leviticus 17:11, emphasizes the life (*nepeš*) in the blood, but that does not resolve the question, since the blood that performs *kāpar* is no longer inside a living animal. The animal must yield its fleshly *nepeš* in order to cover the worshiper.

The problems surrounding this text can be somewhat ameliorated by recognizing that the efficacy of blood is not treated here as natural but as attributed or "given."[49] What lends it atoning power is that Yahweh has "given it to you on the altar" (*ʾănî nətattîw lākem ʿal-hammizbēaḥ*). Manipulating blood atones for the same reason that anointing consecrates and the rite of filling makes a priest and, for Christians, baptism unites one to Christ: it is because Yahweh has "given" that *this* physical material used in *these* ways achieves *this* effect. There is no magic. All is the gift of Yahweh. The

---

with Milgrom concerning the object of the *ḥaṭṭaʾt* offering: Does the offering purge the sanctuary, or the person who offers it? Though I suspect that this is a both-and, I find Gane's argument for a two-stage purgation convincing. Each purification offering cleanses the worshiper of sin or uncleanness by removing it and transferring it to the priest and sanctuary. Then, on the Day of Atonement, these are removed from the priest and sanctuary by offerings and by the removal rite with the scapegoat.

[48]Commentators are divided between those who see blood primarily as a source of life and those who argue that *shed* blood is proof of death. For the former viewpoint, see the concise discussion of Royden Keith Yerkes, *Sacrifice in Greek and Roman Religions and Early Judaism* (London: Black, 1953), 42-50. Leon Morris argued that blood signified death ("The Biblical Use of the Term Blood," *Journal of Theological Studies* 3, no. 2 [1952]: 216-26). Frances Young offers a critique of Morris, pointing to the mythologies in which blood as a principle of life is released in order to fertilize more teeming life (*The Use of Sacrificial Ideas in Greek Christian Writers from the New Testament to John Chrysostom* [Philadelphia: Philadelphia Patristic Foundation, 1979], 53-57). Milgrom argues that blood functions as a detergent to clean up the sanctuary and so preserve Yahweh's presence among his people. On the blood ritual in the "peace offering" specifically, see Martin Modeus, *Sacrifice and Symbol: Biblical Selamim in a Ritual Perspective* (Stockholm: Almqvist & Wiksell, 2005), 135-47. See also Dennis J. McCarthy, "The Symbolism of Blood and Sacrifice," *Journal of Biblical Literature* 88, no. 2 (1969): 166-76; McCarthy, "Further Notes on the Symbolism of Blood and Sacrifice," *Journal of Biblical Literature* 92, no. 2 (1973): 205-10.

[49]In Augustinian terms, it is a *signa data* rather than a *signa naturalia*.

machine works because One with authority to delegate responsibility has authorized *x* to do *y*.

Yet the symbol is not arbitrary, and blood has natural properties that make it a suitable agent for atonement. What is most decisive, at least for my purposes, is the qualifying phrase attached to *nepeš*: What is in the blood is not life per se, but the life *of the flesh* (*nepeš habāśār*).[50] What is poured out in sacrifice is *fleshly* life. Against the background of the Torah's narrative, the blood rites of the offering system are shown to be part of Yahweh's antisarkic pedagogy. As a "son of the herd" (Lev 1:3), an ascension offering recapitulated the sacrifice of Isaac, the fruit of Abraham and Sarah's flesh. By offering up the life of the animal to God, the worshiper expresses both the renunciation of flesh and the faith of Abraham, who abandoned his *fleshly* future to God to do with what he would—and received a "new son" back in return. In their blood rites especially, every sacrifice recapitulated Passover, the night on which a lamb or goat was slain in place of a firstborn son. The blood of the Passover animal had to be displayed to ward off the angel of death, who went through Egypt destroying the last remnants of "flesh" in a way analogous to the destruction of flesh in the flood. Under the stoicheic system, worshipers did not experience this in their own person, but through the vicarious ministry of an animal. But every sacrifice was a renewal of circumcision, a confession of the impotence of the *nepeš* that is in flesh, an offering of fleshly life to God, as a way of moving toward the transfiguration of flesh into Spirit and smoke. Once the animal's fleshly life is drained, the animal is ready to ascend into Yahweh's presence. Every sacrifice was another moment in Yahweh's pedagogy of weakness until Faith should come.[51] The blood of the animal, emblematic of the fleshly life of the worshiper, is spread on the furniture of the sanctuary so that the sanctuary bears the guilt and impurity of the worshiper. Torah's sacrifices enact a ministry of condemnation—a condemnation of *flesh* for the purpose of transforming it to Spirit.

---

[50]This intimate link between flesh and soul may provide background for Paul's use of *psychikos* to describe what sounds like "fleshly" existence—weak, perishable, shameful (1 Cor 15).

[51]Blood is also "blood of the covenant," the blood of covenant renewal (see Ex 24). That too coheres with the theme of flesh: Israelites could not become "one blood" with Yahweh on their own, but only by the blood of an animal substitute. Yet as the animal yielded up its fleshly life to God, it renewed a covenant bond between Yahweh and the worshiper.

Purification offerings pressurized Israel's situation: Yahweh's very presence in Israel was a danger, and as the sins, rebellions and impurities mounted on the priest and in Yahweh's house, the danger intensified. Without a mechanism for decompression, it would rapidly become intolerable. Yahweh graciously provided a pressure valve in the complex ritual of *yôm hakkippurîm*, the Day of Coverings (Lev 16). These rites provided an annual reboot for the sanctuary and an annual removal of impurity and reinvestiture of the high priest. Atonement explicitly removed from Yahweh's house the impurity, rebellion and sin of the people (Lev 16:16), while the scapegoat bore the liability that the priest had taken on himself by eating the sin offerings of Israel (Lev 16:21).[52] The priest put off his garments of glory to minister before Yahweh and then put them back on at the end of the rite. That renewal of the priesthood and sanctuary was possible because of the unique offering of a double purification, a bull and a goat offered as purification offerings whose blood is sprinkled before the ark cover, and a "scapegoat" expelled from the community bearing the sins and uncleanness of Israel. Atonement is Israel's judgment day, Yahweh's annual condemnation of sin in the flesh, and his annual raising up of priest and people to share his life in his presence.

On the Day of Atonement, Yahweh himself takes responsibility for Israel's impurity, rebellion, sin and liability to punishment. Throughout each year, the sins and rebellions of Israel were "covered" (*kāpar*) because they were taken up under cover of Yahweh's house. Finally, on the Day of Atonement, the fleshly life of the offerings was pushed all the way into Yahweh's throne room, the Most Holy Place. He did not impute sin and rebellion to his bride, but bore the burden of her sin.[53] As he revealed to Moses on Sinai, he "keeps *hesed* for thousands, who bears [*nāśā'*] iniquity [*'āwōn*], rebellion [*peša'*], and sin [*ḥaṭṭā'*]; yet he will not leave unpunished" (Ex 34:7).[54]

---

[52] See again Gane's chart for a summary (*Cult and Character*, 299).

[53] As Paul says in Rom 5:13, "sin is not imputed where there is no law" (*hamartia de ouk ellogeitai mē ontos nomou*). That is not a generic principle of legal theory, but a specific statement about Torah, the obvious referent of *nomos* earlier in the same verse (*achri nomou*). Before Torah, sin was spread out in the world, but before Torah entered there existed no mechanisms of imputation that could deter the spread of sin. Torah does have the effect of specifying guilt because it specifies infractions and sentences for infractions. It "imputes" in that sense. But it also introduces a system by which Yahweh himself can become the bearer of Israel's sin.

[54] Note: The text does not say Yahweh "forgives" sin. That is true (Lev 4:20, 26, 31; the verb is *slḥ*). But in Ex 34, Yahweh informs Moses that he carries sin, no doubt to remove it.

To say that these sacrifices are types of Jesus' work is not to say merely that he dies on behalf of his people, that he plays the role of the sin-bearing priest, that he bears the curse for his people and becomes sin who knew no sin. That is all true, but it is inadequate to express the shape of Levitical sacrifice. The whole movement of Jesus' life, death, resurrection and ascension is a single sacrificial sequence, and *that* is the sacrifice necessary to save. The history of humanity can, indeed, be seen as a sacrificial history: Torn in pieces at Babel, Israel cut off from flesh by the Abrahamic covenant of circumcision. Humanity remains a corpse until a new Adam comes to recapitulate this history of sacrifice and to reunite the nations with God and one another in the smoke of the Spirit, living by a lifeblood that is *not* life of the flesh, at Pentecost. When we apply the whole sequence of sacrifice to Jesus' work, we can formulate a fully Levitical account of the atonement, fulfilling one of our criteria of success.

Attending to sanctuary, purity and sacrifice, we begin to discern the shape of the life Yahweh envisions for his people. Life means Yahweh living among his people; Yahweh opening his home to welcome humanity to commune with him and providing pathways of purification; Yahweh giving blood on the altar to cover sin and give Israel a fresh start; Yahweh consuming animals to transform them into his fiery Spirit. Torah establishes a realm of life in a world under the dominion of death. Yahweh does not withdraw his Edenic or Babelic curse. The cherubim are still there, and circumcision is a mark of difference. Yet having cursed, Yahweh loves humankind too much to leave them excluded and divided, and in Torah he begins to overcome the curse and form a new Adamic race that can draw near, commune with the Creator and be translated from flesh to Spirit. Torah begins to bring the nations back into one. In Torah, in short, Yahweh makes use of fleshly elements to begin to construct one new man.

WHAT TORAH DOES AND DOES NOT DO

No flesh (*sarx*) will be justified by the works of the law (*ex ergōn nomou*) because the law only brings knowledge of sin. Whatever "justify" means here, it is something Torah cannot accomplish, nor presumably any other form of human law or *paideia* of culture. Paul makes this point explicitly in his axiom about the impotence of law in Galatians 3:21: "If a law had been given which was able to impart life, then righteousness would indeed have been based on law" (NASB). Torah is capable of killing flesh, or at least *some* flesh. It cannot target flesh without killing the human being. No law—neither Torah nor Roman law nor any hypothetical law—is capable of giving life and bringing in righteousness (or justice, *dikaiosynē*). No law can overcome flesh; therefore, no law is capable of bringing in the justice of God.

Here we can see, with elegant simplicity, why Torah cannot justify: Torah was accommodated to a *fleshly* people, to an Israel marked in the flesh of the foreskin, to a people whose priesthood was qualified by genealogy, to a nation partly defined by descent from the patriarchs and, most especially, to a people that still lived on the outside of Eden. Like Gentile *stoicheia*, the law institutionalizes fleshly institutions of priesthood, purity, temple and sacrifice, even as (unlike Gentile *stoicheia*) it imposes an anti-sarkic pedagogy on Israel, even as it enlists Israel in Yahweh's own battle against flesh. Yahweh lets Israel come as near as they can in flesh, but they can only get so close without being consumed. If they are going to enter into the presence of the glory, they have to be glorified themselves. If they are going to commune in Spirit, they have to become Spirit. That, Torah *cannot* do. *No* law can do that, Paul insists (Gal 3:21), and thus there can be no justice by law (Gal 3:21 again). Justice depends on human beings overcoming their mortality, their vulnerability, their fear of death and their reactiveness to harm. Conquering death is beyond the power of all law, not least a law designed for human beings in flesh. Torah is a form of *ta stoicheia tou kosmou*, and so it clearly cannot release anyone from fleshly subjection to *stoicheia*.

It is more difficult to grasp what Paul says about what Torah actually does. Far and away Paul's most extensive analysis of the problem of Torah is in Romans 7:7-25. Within the letter, Romans 7 demonstrates the law's inability to achieve the righteousness of God. Whoever the "I" is, he is one who receives the law. The law itself is holy, righteous and good (Rom 7:12), but it is turned into an instrument of death because the one who receives it is under the dominion of sin (Rom 7:13). The contrast in Romans 7:14 is stark: the spiritual law comes to one who is "of flesh, sold into bondage to sin," and it cuts the fleshly person in two. In their heart, they desire to do what the law requires, but their flesh resists and so they cannot accomplish what they wish to do. Torah creates schizophrenics, and precisely because it divides the "I" in two, it kills. The law that causes this division cannot be the healer of the division. Paul describes a sacrificial movement here: the law is the sword that divides, and nothing but the Spirit can join together what the law has torn asunder. The law is spiritual, and only the spiritual can fulfill its righteous requirements. As long as Torah comes to those who are in the flesh, it can only kill. What is needed is something that can kill the flesh and raise up in the Spirit. What is needed is a form of sacrifice that does not rely on an animal substitute.

Torah cannot bring the life of justice, but it *can* invigorate latent sin.[55] Paul's example is about moral consciousness: he would not have known sin without the commandment (Rom 7:7).[56] Torah identifies and names sins, raising them from mere sins to the level of "transgression," a violation of an explicit command (cf. the distinction in Rom 5). Spiritual Torah exposes Paul's fleshliness, his bondage to sin (Rom 7:14). Nothing good dwells in his flesh, but instead his flesh has become a lodging place for sin. Torah is commandeered by the flesh so that Torah itself becomes a killing weapon, an instrument of injustice. Paul hears a prohibition against coveting; that is a reminder that his neighbor has what he does not, and sets him at odds with his neighbor; his flesh rears up in envy, makes him a rival to his neighbor for his neighbor's goods. This is not simply desire misdirected. It is flesh—its vulnerabilities and fears, its weakness and reactiveness—being aroused and lashing out in covetousness and envy. The command "Do not covet" arouses the self-protective instincts of the flesh. Thus commands intended to curb the destructiveness of flesh end up only increasing the damage.

Paul is not merely concerned about individual struggles with besetting sin.[57] Israel was chosen to bring blessing to the nations, but Israel turned the law into a symbol of national privilege and boasting in flesh. Levitical purity offered rules of controlled *access*, and were rules of exclusion only because all flesh was *already* excluded. As we have seen, Torah's purity rules were rules of access and welcome. Over time, Israel turned the good laws of purity

---

[55] As Theodore Jennings Jr. nicely puts it, the law "supercharges" sin (*Outlaw Justice: The Messianic Politics of Paul* [Stanford: Stanford University Press, 2013], 118).

[56] I am not taking a position here on the disputed question of the identity of the "I," except to say that it is clearly a recipient of Torah, and so either an individual Jew, perhaps even Paul himself, or a representation of Israel. The crucial part of the argument, for Paul and for me, is that Paul is explaining the effect that Torah actually has in practice.

[57] Theodore Jennings Jr. rightly insists that Rom 7 has to do with our engagement with the world, not with personal internal struggles (*Reading Derrida/Thinking Paul: On Justice* [Stanford: Stanford University Press, 2005], 151).

into instruments to bar the way not only to Gentiles but also to other Jews. Jews come to regard impurity as even more virulently contagious than Torah says it is, and those who fail to follow the extended purity system of clean Jews are treated as outcasts. Purity laws, designed to provide access to God for people in the flesh, designed to regulate social connections within Israel, designed to prepare Israel for her mission to the nations, become instruments of exclusion and brute marginalization. At its worst, Pharisaical oral tradition is the law turned to flesh—turned into a means for reinforcing fleshly distinctions, restrictions and enhancing fleshly boasting—which is why Jesus so ferociously attacks the Pharisees.[58]

Flesh turns Torah, given to offer life by making war on sinful flesh, into an instrument of death.[59] Because Torah cannot overcome death, it cannot overcome the fleshly instincts inspired by the fear of death. Flesh turns Torah into its opposite, accomplishing not the life and justice that Torah intends but the injustice and desolation Torah was intended to inhibit.[60] Instead of bringing blessing, either to Israel or the nations, Torah leaves Israel under a curse. It is a just curse; it is the curse Torah itself warned about (most centrally in Lev 26; Deut 28–31). By Paul's day the curse might be characterized as the curse of continuing exile,[61] but the curse is more fundamental than Israel's contingent failure to keep Torah and the judgment that came on her as a result. The curse is the inevitable result of the work that God's good Torah does among a fleshly people. In the end, it is nearly as relentless as another flood, sweeping Israel away. Israel has no claim, but if the pattern holds, Israel can hope that the God who left Eden to search out humans, the God who came down from Sinai to live among Israel, will also enter *this* wrath to rescue his beloved.

Only a handful of scholars have raised the possibility that this is what Paul is talking about when he uses the phrase *ta erga nomou*, "the works of the law."[62] It is grammatically possible that the phrase is a subjective genitive;

---

[58]See below, chap. 6, for further discussion of this point.

[59]Flesh's sense of vulnerability is aroused by the law's punishments, so that in the face of law flesh is not complacent but suspicious and wary, and if wary then often violent (Jennings, *Outlaw Justice*, 49).

[60]Contrary to Stanislas Breton (*A Radical Philosophy of Saint Paul*, trans. Joseph N. Ballan [New York: Columbia University Press, 2011], 87), *this*, not the mere "proliferation" of the law, is Paul's concern. He is not worried about the number of rules but about the way the rules get deployed to impose rather than relieve burdens.

[61]As N. T. Wright has long argued.

[62]The most extensive discussion of this option is that of Lloyd Gaston in his *Paul and the Torah*

the law is the "subject" or "actor" in the implied sentence. Hence we could translate, "what Torah accomplishes," "what Torah does." If "righteousness of God" means the righteousness that is done by God, and "faith of Christ" means the fidelity of Jesus in his life and death, then "works of the law" may refer to the works that the law performs, the effects that Torah effects. No one is justified by the "works worked by the law" because the Torah brings wrath (Rom 4:15); it kills and condemns. That is the work it does.[63]

All this directly raises questions about the rationale for the giving of the law in the first place. If God intended to bring blessing to the nations through Abraham, and the law inhibits the fulfillment of that promise, why give the law at all? If the law is going to become an instrument of injustice and death, if it is going to be commandeered by sin, why Torah? Paul answers that Torah was added "for the sake of transgressions" (Gal 3:19: *tōn parabaseōn charin prosetethē*). That has often been taken as a reference to the public uses of the law as a restraint on evil and sin, but such an interpretation is hard to square with Paul's pessimistic analysis of the "works of the law." Inevitably, it seems, the actual operation of Torah was to bring

---

(Eugene, OR: Wipf & Stock, 2006). He cites Ernst Lohmeyer's opinion that "the only natural grammatical possibility" of the phrase is a "*genetivus auctoris*," meaning "the works worked by the law" (101). Lohmeyer cannot believe that this is what the phrase means, but after a long article still cannot give a plausible grammatical alternative. The phrase *ta erga nomou* has been central to the debates over the "new perspective on Paul" over the past three decades. The notion that the phrase refers to ceremonies of the Torah in distinction from moral requirements has its origins in the Middle Ages and was held by some Protestant interpreters, and that view has been given fresh impetus by James Dunn's claim that the phrase refers to the role of Torah as a "boundary marker" between Jews and Gentiles. See, for instance, Dunn, *The Theology of Paul the Apostle* (Grand Rapids: Eerdmans, 1998), 354-66; Dunn, "Works of the Law and the Curse of the Law (Galatians 3:10-14)," *New Testament Studies* 31 (1985): 523-42. The majority of Protestants have taken the phrase to refer either to the moral deeds demanded by Torah, which cannot justify because no one can keep the law perfectly, or to the intention of the doers of law to merit justification by obedience. For a review and assessment of the debate, see Robert Rapa, *The Meaning of "Works of the Law" in Galatians and Romans* (New York: Peter Lang, 2001).

[63]It would be a mistake to conclude that *ta erga nomou* excludes human action, especially the human effort to obey the Torah. Torah does what it does not merely by being present to Israel, available to Israel as the oracles of God, but by establishing a pattern of national life. The law comes to Israel, they might delight in the law in the inner man. They strive to obey it, but in their very striving to obey it they discover that the law kills. So while the phrase means "what the law works" or "the works that the law accomplishes," the phrase evokes a larger reality that includes human action. Thus the traditional Protestant interpretation of the phrase is not lost, but it is not foregrounded as the key to the phrase. Paul's point in denying that justification comes by the works of the law is to highlight the impotence of Torah itself, *not* the failure of human efforts to keep the law. In fact, the impotence of Torah to bring life is revealed in the failed efforts of human beings to keep it.

Israel under a curse. Paul has insisted that the law brought a curse instead of blessing to Israel because Israel did not obey the law and could not do so. If the law was added to inhibit transgressions, it failed miserably in its stated purpose.

Paul's claim could, however, be taken to mean that the law was added to provoke transgressions or to "define" transgressions. That is the argument of Romans 5, where Paul claims that there is no transgression where there is no law. There is moral wrong, and certainly sin, without law, but those sins do not rise to the level of transgressions in the absence of law. Law raises the profile of generic sin, and so exposes sin for what it is. Paul makes a related point in Romans 7, as we have seen, where the evil of sin is evident in the fact that it can even turn the law—holy, righteous and good—into an instrument of death.

This "negative" effect of Torah is not the end of the story, because Yahweh uses flesh's perversion of Torah as another piece of evidence in his lawsuit against flesh. He turns the fleshly twisting of his law into an instrument for the redemption of Israel and of humanity. The perversion of Torah by sin, death and flesh is, in the end, a cunning tactic in Yahweh's continuing prosecution of flesh. It is another stratagem in his war against flesh. It is not the final piece of evidence, but it is a crucial piece in the trial that will condemn flesh and justify humanity. He uses the fleshly manipulation of the elements of Jewish *physis* to bring an end to those elements and constitute a new humanity.

CONCLUSION

We know what the law cannot do: it cannot justify. We do not yet know what that means, but we might surmise that "justify" is an antidote to the mayhem that sin and flesh and death do, and the mayhem that these forces make the law do. Whatever *justify* means, however it is accomplished, it must involve the overcoming of sin, death and flesh, and consequently must involve release from bondage to the elemental practices that assume the existence of sin, death and flesh. Justification must involve a full and final overcoming of the curses of Eden and Babel, a full and final restoration of humanity to God and of the nations to each other. It must involve a transfiguration of the elements and a reconstitution of the socioreligious physics of humanity.

Only this can overcome the curse of Eden and the curse of Babel. Only justification, whatever it is, however it is accomplished, can ensure the erection of a just society. The failure of Torah to create just society is one dimension of the answer to our question, *Cur Deus Homo*? Who can save from slavery to our own flesh? No law can do it. Only a God can save.

PART TWO

GOOD NEWS OF GOD'S JUSTICE

six

THE JUSTICE OF GOD

✝

Jesus came preaching the kingdom.[1] For a kingdom to come, one needs a king. One also needs something for that king to do—a mission to right wrongs, deliver the beleaguered, shine down like sunlight on mown grass after rain. One needs people for the king to save and rule, and a realm for that people to live in. If this kingdom is coming to Israel, the king needs to be a descendant of David, a king who embodies and represents the whole people, and the mission needs to have something to do with the restoration of Yahweh's people.[2]

Paul does refer to the kingdom of God (see Rom 14:17; 1 Cor 4:20; 6:9-10; 15:50; Gal 5:21; Eph 5:5; Col 4:11; 1 Thess 2:12), but it is not one of his major themes. Yet Paul speaks of precisely the same thing that Jesus announced—the arrival of a king who sets things in order for his people—and makes it the theme of what is regarded as his most important letter. Where Jesus calls it the coming of the kingdom, Paul calls it the apocalypse of the justice of God.

As we shall see, for Paul the arrival of justice has everything to do with the themes we have examined in the previous chapters—with Torah and flesh and the elements of the socioreligious cosmos and the nations. Though part of God's campaign to deliver humanity from sin, death and flesh, Torah

---

[1]While I make some use of "historical Jesus" studies and research on the Gospels in this chapter and the next, this is neither an exercise in historical Jesus studies nor a contribution to the study of the Gospels. As the chapter title indicates, I offer instead a *Pauline* reading of the gospel story.
[2]Ben F. Meyer, *The Aims of Jesus* (1979; repr., Eugene, OR: Wipf & Stock, 2002), 133-34, points out that the kingdom, salvation and the restoration of Israel are inseparably connected ideas in the first century. On the Davidic king as the embodiment and representative of "son" Israel, see 2 Sam 7 in the light of Ex 4:23. This is a constant theme in my *A Son To Me: An Exposition of 1 and 2 Samuel* (Moscow, ID: Canon, 2003), esp. 208.

is accommodated *to* flesh, arranging the elements of religious life in a way appropriate to a fleshly people. For that reason, if for no other, Torah cannot deliver from flesh: even as it partially overcomes the effects of flesh, Torah and every other form of *ta stoicheia tou kosmou* institutionalizes a world of flesh. And so long as human beings are in flesh, the justice of God will not reign among the nations; as long as they remain under the elements, flesh will feel right at home. Fleshly human beings will remain at a distance from the God of justice, and will be estranged from one another. Torah cannot bring the justice of God. Torah cannot justify. Only God can.

At the heart of Paul's gospel, and at the heart of the Gospels, is the announcement that he has done just that.

THE JUSTICE OF GOD

Paul introduces the theme of the letter to the Romans in the declaration of Romans 1:16-17, where he summarizes the good news that is the power of God to salvation as the "revelation of the righteousness of God," revealed "from faith to faith." Paul bolsters the summary with a quotation from Habakkuk 2:3, typically rendered as "the righteous [one] shall live by faith." The Greek *dikaiosynē* is innocent of the English distinction between "righteousness" and "justice," so we can translate the phrase as either the "justice of God" or the "righteousness of God." And of course those terms are not free of ambiguity: What *sort* of justice?[3] The genitive too is ambiguous, possibly expressing all sorts of relationships between "God" and his "righteousness." "Righteousness of God" could name an eternal divine character quality; it could name a righteousness that has its *source* in God; it could refer to some *activity* of God—an act of punishment, or an act of deliverance, or a gracious donation of righteousness—that is a righteous act or results in righteousness. Whatever it means, it has something to do with salvation, because the good news that is the power of God to *sōtēria* is the gospel that unveils the righteousness of God. In fact, it appears to be the power of God to salvation *because* it reveals God's righteousness.

Dikaiosynē tou theou is Paul's theme, but what *is* this theme?[4]

---

[3]Historians make clear that there is no single concept. For a deft recent overview, see David Johnston, *A Brief History of Justice* (Oxford: Wiley-Blackwell, 2011). On pre-Hellenistic ancient ideas of justice in Egypt and Mesopotamia, see Enrique Nardoni, *Rise Up, O Judge: A Study of Justice in the Biblical World*, trans. Sean Charles Martin (Peabody, MA: Hendrickson, 2004), 1-41.
[4]Since Luther, Protestants have understood the "righteousness of God" as the gift of righteousness

Two considerations are decisive, one general and one specific. Generally, Paul claims at the outset of Romans that the gospel to which he is set apart as an apostle is "promised beforehand through His prophets in the holy Scriptures" (Rom 1:2 NASB), and later states that the righteousness of God is revealed in that gospel (Rom 1:17). Whatever the righteousness of God is, then, it must be something that was promised earlier through the prophets of Israel. Paul refers later in Romans to Genesis 15:6, which informs us that Yahweh regarded Abraham as righteous, but one looks in vain for a prophetic text that promises imputed righteousness.

---

from God to sinners, often specified, borrowing the language of Rom 4, as the "imputed" righteousness of God. Many have been convinced by Luther's argument that the medieval understanding of *dikaiosynē theou* as the *iustitia Dei*, and particularly as God's retributive justice, cannot constitute good news. What kind of relief is there in knowing that God deals out punishments to the wicked when we know *we* are among the wicked? Luther's claim that Paul is talking about the unmerited gift of righteousness is widely understood as *the* Reformation breakthrough.

In recent years, this standard Protestant reading has been widely questioned, even among Protestant interpreters. While not necessarily disputing Luther's theological conclusions, they have disputed his exegesis of the passage. Commentators who read Paul as a political theologian have taken *dikaiosynē* as God's "justice," understood dynamically as a justice that is known only in action. God's justice is revealed in his acts of doing justice, however those acts might be defined. Liberation theologians were among the first to press for a more political understanding of *dikaiosynē*. See, for example, Jose Miranda, *Marx and the Bible: A Critique of the Philosophy of Oppression*, trans. John Eagleson (Maryknoll, NY: Orbis, 1974), 160-92. For N. T. Wright the righteousness of God is God's own righteousness, interpreted as his faithfulness to his covenant promise, enacted in the work of Jesus; most recently, *Paul and the Faithfulness of God* (Minneapolis: Fortress, 2013), 795-804. Given the nature of God's promises and his commitment to keeping them, "righteousness" includes his determination to set things right, to enact restorative justice; on this see Wright, "Paul's Gospel and Caesar's Empire," in *Paul and Politics: Ekklesia, Israel, Imperium, Interpretation*, ed. Richard A. Horsley (Harrisburg, PA: Trinity Press International, 2000), 170-73. James Dunn similarly defines God's righteousness as "God's fulfillment of the obligations he took upon himself in creating humankind and particularly in the calling of Abraham and the choosing of Israel to be his people" (*The Theology of Paul the Apostle* [Grand Rapids: Eerdmans, 1998], 342). Theodore Jennings Jr. points out that Paul's terminology in his letter to the church at Rome (!) is the terminology of ancient political theory, particularly his use of *nomos* and variations of the *dik-* root (Jennings, *Outlaw Justice: The Messianic Politics of Paul* [Stanford: Stanford University Press, 2013], 1-2; Jennings, *Reading Derrida/ Thinking Paul: On Justice* [Stanford: Stanford University Press, 2005], 5-9). Ernst Käsemann is often cited as the source of the dynamic, apocalyptic understanding of the righteousness of God; see Douglas Campbell's discussion in *Deliverance of God: An Apocalyptic Rereading of Justification in Paul* (Grand Rapids: Eerdmans, 2009), 677-711. Though this "political" view of the righteousness of God has the appearance of being cutting edge, it is in some respects a throwback to a late patristic understanding of justification. Augustine was well aware of the links between justice and justification in Paul, and aware too of what this implied about the "political" concerns of the New Testament. See, from different angles, Alister McGrath, *Iustitia Dei: A History of the Doctrine of Justification*, 2nd ed. (Cambridge: Cambridge University Press, 1998), and Robert Dodaro, *Christ and the Just Society in the Thought of Augustine* (Cambridge: Cambridge University Press, 2008). For a brief discussion of how the New Testament got "de-justicized," see Nicholas Wolterstorff, *Justice: Rights and Wrongs* (Princeton: Princeton University Press, 2008), 96-108.

Many prophetic passages promise that Yahweh will one day establish justice, among his people and among the nations. The prophets hold out the promise that Babel's curse will be overcome as the promise to Abraham is fulfilled. We can draw an impressive, albeit still partial, list from Isaiah alone:

- Zion the harlot city, once full of justice, is now full of murderers (Is 1:21), but Yahweh promises to "restore your judges as at the first. . . . After that you will be called the city of righteousness [Heb. ṣedeq; LXX, polis dikaiosynēs], a faithful city. Zion will be redeemed with justice and her repentant ones with righteousness" (Is 1:26-27 NASB).

- A child will be born to the throne of David who will uphold his kingdom "with justice [Heb. mišpāt] and righteousness [Heb. ṣədāqâ; LXX en dikaiosynē] from then on and forevermore" (Is 9:7 NASB [9:6 LXX]).[5]

- A Spirit-anointed "Branch" will appear who will judge the poor "with righteousness" (Heb. ṣedeq) since he wears "righteousness" (LXX dikaiosynē) as the belt around his waist (Is 11:4-5).

- When the Spirit comes, "justice will dwell in the wilderness, and righteousness [Heb. ṣədāqâ; LXX dikaiosynē] will abide in the fertile field. And the work of righteousness [Heb. maʿăśēh haṣṣədāqâ; LXX ta erga tēs dikaiosynēs] will be peace, and the service of righteousness, quietness and confidence forever" (Is 32:16-17 NASB).

- "I will bring near My righteousness [Heb. ṣidəqātî; LXX dikaiosynē mou], it is not far off; and My salvation will not delay" (Is 46:13 NASB).

- "Preserve justice and do righteousness [Heb. ṣədāqâ; LXX dikaiosynē], for My salvation is about to come and My righteousness to be revealed [LXX to eleos mou apokalyphthēnai]" (Is 56:1 NASB).

- "For Zion's sake I will not keep silent, and for Jerusalem's sake I will not keep quiet, until her righteousness [Heb. ṣədāqâ; LXX (differently) dikaiosynē mou] goes forth like brightness, and her salvation like a torch that is burning" (Is 62:1 NASB).[6]

---

[5]This is all the more impressive as a background to Rom 1, where we note that Paul's gospel centers on the announcement of a Davidic king (Rom 1:3). Paul's sketch of the gospel in Rom 1 can be summarized as follows: the good news of a Davidic king, promised by the prophets, by whom the righteousness of God is revealed. That almost seems a gloss of Is 9!

[6]The point could be belabored, once again drawing only on Isaiah, by a glance at Is 45:8; 51:5-6, 8; 58:2, 8; 61:1-11; 62:1-2.

Anyone coming from Isaiah to Romans would conclude that Paul's good news was (1) the good news of God acting justly (2) through a Davidic king and (3) to save humans or some humans from their own disorder and from their enemies in a way that (4) enables humans or some humans to gleam with Yahweh's own radiant righteousness. In Isaiah, God's justice is clearly a *saving* justice, bringing rescue and restoration in a sociopolitical context. Yahweh will come in his charitable righteousness to bring justice to the poor, beleaguered and oppressed.[7] No one coming to Romans from Isaiah would think Paul is answering Luther's putative question. Paul answers Zion's question, Jerusalem's yearning that her sin be covered and her warfare ended.

More specifically, Paul supports his summary of the gospel by citing one of the prophetic texts that promised the righteousness of God, Habakkuk 2:4. That passage is the source of several of the characteristic themes and phrases of the letter to Rome. Not only does it mention a "righteous one" (*dikaios*), but it also uses the phrase "out of faith" (*ek pisteōs*) and promises life (*zēsetai*) to the one who is righteous by faith. Like Isaiah, Habakkuk is a prophet of the justice of God. Israel is full of violence and wickedness (Hab 1:2-3), and Torah is impotent to restore order (Hab 1:4). Yahweh has done nothing to deliver Israel from this desperate condition (Hab 1:2), and when Yahweh *does* respond to Habakkuk's anguished pleas, Yahweh threatens to send the Chaldeans to punish them (Hab 1:5-11), a medicine worse than the disease. The opening section of Habakkuk, in short, sets up the prophecy to propose a double theodicy: What is Yahweh going to do to repair a broken Israel? And how is Yahweh *himself* just if he uses the violent and vicious Chaldeans to accomplish his purposes?[8] Habakkuk looks to Yahweh to justify his people and himself publicly, in history, among the nations.

In the New Testament as a whole, we know that this justice will not be utterly realized until death is overcome in the final resurrection of the dead (1 Cor 15). Whatever justice is achieved before the final judgment will be an

---

[7]See Rivka and Moshe Ulmer, *Righteous Giving to the Poor: Tzedakah ("Charity") in Classic Rabbinic Judaism* (Piscataway, NJ: Gorgias, 2014), for a discussion of the "charity" of righteousness in Jewish thought.

[8]This summarizes the brilliant article of Rikki Watts, "'For I Am Not Ashamed of the Gospel': Romans 1:16-17 and Habakkuk 2:4," in *Romans and the People of God: Essays in Honor of Gordon D. Fee on the Occasion of His Sixty-Fifth Birthday*, ed. Sven Soderlund and N. T. Wright (Grand Rapids: Eerdmans, 1999), 3-25.

imperfect justice. But that necessary qualification should not cancel out the central thrust of the gospel, which is that God's justice has been revealed here and now, in Jesus and in the proclamation of the gospel of Jesus. Whatever Paul says in the letter about God's righteousness, justification, the law, faith, Christ and his death and resurrection, it must be an answer to the sociopolitical questions that the prophets pose, which are simultaneously cosmic and metaphysical/theological questions. Paul's answer is that God has revealed his justice in Jesus Christ, the seed of David and the Son of God (Rom 1:3-4). God reveals his justice in the justification that is effected by that Davidic king.

WRATH FROM HEAVEN

John the Baptist warned the winnowing fork was in the hand of the farmer, who was ready to clear the threshing floor, the temple (Mt 3:12; Luke 3:17).[9] Jesus' message was also a warning: "Repent! The kingdom is coming." The good news of the kingdom includes, and seems to be first and foremost, the *bad* news of judgment.

Does Paul believe in *iustitia distributiva*, a justice that discriminates between right and wrong and punishes and rewards, a justice that renders to everyone according to their deeds?[10] It is difficult to fathom how this could become a serious question, either for Scripture as a whole or for Paul.

---

[9]On the temple as the threshing floor, the place for separation of wheat and chaff, see 2 Sam 24; 2 Chron 3.

[10]It has become de rigueur to claim that justice in the Bible is restorative *rather than* punitive (see, e.g., Sharon Baker, *Executing God: Rethinking Everything You've Been Taught About Salvation and the Cross* [Louisville, KY: Westminster John Knox, 2013], 91-99). The opposition can be maintained only by being selective about biblical texts, about which Baker is at least refreshingly honest, offering an "everybody does it" defense. Nicholas Wolterstorff argues that Jesus rejects retribution in the sense of "redressing the harm done to some victim by the imposition of an equivalent harm on the victimizer." For the New Testament, he argues, punishment expresses wrath and terrorizes evil, but "nothing is said about retribution, about getting even, about reciprocating evil with evil, about redress, about vengeance. Punishment as a condemnation of the wrongdoer is a good in his life and serves the social good of deterring such wrongdoing" (Wolterstorff, *Justice in Love* [Grand Rapids: Eerdmans, 2011], 128-29). Wolterstorff develops a "reprobative" view of punishment (ibid., 183-99). Wolterstorff is right to stress that God never does evil, and never acts in peevish spite. But he is mistaken to claim that civil authorities have nothing to do with vengeance. Rom 13:4 says that the ruler is "an avenger who brings wrath upon the one who practices evil," and the term *avenger* (*ekdikos*) echoes the description of God's vengeance (*ekdikēsis*) in Rom 12:19. God never returns *evil* for evil, but it seems clear throughout Scripture that Yahweh "turns the wickedness of the wicked on his own head." See Garry Williams, "Penal Substitution: A Response to Recent Criticisms," *Journal of the Evangelical Theological Society* 50, no. 1 (2007): 71-86.

Immediately after Paul writes of the good news of the righteousness of God, he announces that the wrath of God is revealed from heaven against injustice and those who unjustly suppress truth (Rom 1:18). He warns that those who pass judgment but do the evils they condemn face "wrath . . . in the day of wrath and revelation of the righteous judgment of God, who will render to each person according to his deeds" (Rom 2:5-6 NASB). God distinguishes between those who persevere in doing good, who will be rewarded with eternal life, and those who obey injustice rather than truth, who will be condemned to destruction (Rom 2:7-8). God cannot be unjust, for if he were he could not judge the world (Rom 3:6). That God *does* judge the world by punishing evildoers and rewarding the righteous is for Paul so axiomatic that any argument that leads to its denial *must* be wrong (Rom 3:5-6). One has to ignore large stretches of Paul's letters to conclude that he denies that God punishes and rewards according to works, that Paul denies that he is just in that straightforward, classical sense.[11] That God's justice is *more than* punitive is evident from Isaiah. That it includes punitive justice is unquestionable. Clearing out the wicked is, after all, one of the main things a king is expected to do (Ps 72).[12]

Again, a brief catalog of passages from Isaiah will indicate that Yahweh's justice includes his discipline and punishment of the wicked.

- Promising that a remnant will return from exile, Yahweh declares that "a destruction is determined, overflowing with righteousness [Heb. *ṣədāqâ*; LXX *dikaiosynē*]" since Yahweh has decreed to execute a "complete destruction" in the whole land (Is 10:22-23).

- Yahweh promises to uphold Israel with his "righteous right hand" (Heb.

---

[11]Ignoring vast stretches of Paul is what Douglas Campbell ends up doing, treating the early chapters of Romans not as Pauline theology but as "speech in character" representing the views of Paul's opponents.

[12]As Mark Seifrid says, "Administration of justice in the biblical contexts, as in the ancient world generally, is simultaneously judicial, legislative and executive." Seifrid, "Righteousness Language in the Hebrew Scriptures and Early Judaism," in *Justification and Variegated Nomism*, vol. 1, *The Complexities of Second Temple Judaism*, ed. D. A. Carson, Peter T. O'Brien and Mark Seifrid (Grand Rapids: Baker, 2001), 422, 426-27. Seifrid cites scholars who define "forensic" uses of the *ṣdq* word group as those that have to do with "'status' and not activity or behavior." As Seifrid points out, this does not match the biblical categories: "Especially from the start of the monarchical period, legislative and executive decisions appear to have been effected primarily in the judicial setting. In such instances one cannot legitimately separate 'status' from the vindicating act of the king, nor should one . . . treat 'legal activity' and 'governing, ruling activity' as separate categories." This is also one of the key emphases of Campbell, *Deliverance of God*.

bîmîn ṣidqî; LXX *te dexia te dikaia mou*), one of the results of which is that "those who are angered at you will be shamed and dishonored" and Israel's enemies "will be as nothing and will perish" (Is 41:10-11).

- Yahweh promises to establish his people in righteousness, which includes an assurance that the destroyer will be ruined and weapons raised against Israel will not prosper (Is 54:14-17). In short, Yahweh displays righteousness by protecting his people from their enemies, destroying their enemies if need be.

- Yahweh puts on a breastplate of righteousness (Heb. *ṣədāqâ*; LXX *dikaiosynē*) to repay everyone according to their deeds, "wrath to His adversaries, recompense to His enemies, making recompense to the coastlands" (Is 59:17-18). This is part of the righteousness that brings salvation (Is 59:16).

- "Yahweh comes from Edom in righteousness [Heb. *biṣdāqâ*; LXX *dikaiosynē*], mighty to save, His garments red from trampling the wine press of Edom" (Is 63:1-2).

Paul raises the conundrum that, according to popular history, stymied the young Luther: How can God's punitive justice, his distributive or retributive justice, be *good* news? How can *sinners* take heart from the fact that God reveals his justice by punishing sinners? The conundrum is partly removed when we see that Paul's argument is about public justice, rather than in the first instance about the sinner of anguished conscience. In the setting of public justice, enacting restorative justice must involve removal, correction or even destruction of whatever inhibits justice. A city cannot be in harmony if looters roam the streets, looting with impunity. Forcibly removing the looters from the streets is an act of restorative justice precisely because it is an act of retributive justice. In Isaiah, the two dimensions work in tandem, and the final end is always restoration. God punishes Israel's enemies *in order to* deliver Israel, to preserve her, to provide the conditions for her flourishing. Yahweh punishes the wicked in Israel to save Israel from them. Yahweh even punishes *Israel* to save Israel, to arrest her flight to Sheol and to turn her back to himself. The justice Paul talks about is punitive, distributive justice, but that distributive justice, promised by the prophets and revealed in the gospel, aims at the ultimate restoration of Zion. Yahweh aims to rescue Zion from whatever opposes

her, even if that requires him to rescue Zion from herself. A sinner before
a just God has hope *only* in God's justice, which destroys flesh in order
somehow to rescue flesh.

WRATH NOW

John's message was urgent: the winnowing fork is *already* in the hand of the
winnower. So was Jesus': the kingdom of God is at hand. Judgment is coming,
and it is coming *now*. Jesus predicted a dire catastrophe, which he labeled
"the end," that would happen within "this generation" (Mt 24; Mk 13; Lk 21),
and this prophetic warning was integral to his entire mission to Israel.[13] John
writes that it is the "last hour" when "the world is passing away" (1 Jn 2:17-18).
Peter warns that the "end of all things is near" (1 Pet 4:7); James adds that
"the Lord is near," a "Judge" who is "standing right at the door" (Jas 5:8-9);
and Hebrews warns about the "day drawing near" (Heb 10:25). Revelation
begins with an assurance that the "time is near" (Rev 1:3) and ends with the
words of Jesus, "I am coming quickly" (Rev 22:20). There is a final judgment
yet to come, but the emphasis of the New Testament is on *imminent*
judgment. Wrath is coming against Israel, but not just Israel. Wrath is revealed from heaven against all the unrighteousness and ungodliness of humanity. God is preparing to judge the world, so that the "end of all things"
is just around the corner.

Such expressions are found often enough in Paul's letters to conclude that
he is as excitable as Peter, James, John and the writer to the Hebrews. Long
after the death and resurrection of Jesus, Paul can still speak of "salvation"
as something future, "nearer to us than when we believed" (Rom 13:11). At
the end of Romans, he assures the Romans that the "God of peace will soon
crush Satan under your feet" (Rom 16:20). Satan was defeated at the cross,
but there is apparently still a victory to win, and the feet that will trample
the serpent in the future are not those of Jesus but those of the saints. In
Philippians, he echoes James's claim that "the Lord is near" (Philippians 4:5).
After the cross and resurrection of Jesus, after Pentecost, still there is something called "salvation" that is still coming. Jesus cries, "It is finished," but
something is not yet finished even then. The justice of God will not fully
arrive until that something happens.

---

[13]The best treatment of this is in N. T. Wright, *Jesus and the Victory of God* (Minneapolis: Fortress,
  1997).

When faced with this significant evidence that early Christians believed there was a great catastrophe imminent, one that would end the world as they knew it, we have several options. We can, with much scholarship of the past two centuries, conclude that their expectations were mistaken, and that Jesus too was wrong about the future. The early Christians formed communities agitated by apocalyptic expectation. Jesus had promised to end it all, and they believed Jesus.[14] When it did not happen, they adjusted their expectations, along with their theology and church practice, to conform to the longer time perspective. Disappointed apocalyptic is the motivation behind the church's decision to settle for "early Catholicism," one of many mythical constructs of modern New Testament scholarship. We can, with some conservative scholarship, attempt to explain away the temporal indicators as atemporal propositions or as rhetorical devices. Or we can say that the temporal statements are indeed temporal, and that the expectations of the early Christians were *fulfilled*. That last option, though, requires us to understand "the end" quite differently.

In the Olivet Discourse, Jesus uses standard prophetic imagery to describe the collapse of a political universe. Stars, sun and moon were created to "govern" the day and night (Gen 1:14), and so they naturally become created symbols of rulers. When a prophet predicts that a star falls from heaven, or that the sun goes black and the moon turns to blood, he is not claiming that giant balls of burning gas will fall to earth.[15] He is saying that rulers will be "eclipsed," they will "fall" from their high positions, their time will be up. Jesus means the same thing. Whether we focus on the *oikoumenē* of the empire or the world of Judaism, Jesus means that the world order as it presently exists will come to an end.[16] When Paul says, "the Lord is near" and "salvation is nearer than when we believed," he refers to an event in the near future that

(the ruler of this world)

---

[14]Schweitzer famously said that Jesus himself expected the end, and in despair threw himself on the great wheel of history, giving it a turn, while being crushed underneath. Schweitzer's theory was ahistorical, but it did yield one of the great—one of the *few*—purple passages in the history of New Testament scholarship.

[15]Where would they all *go*? we want to know. Any single star is thousands of times larger than earth.

[16]I take it that the term *oikoumenē* has specific reference to the Gentile empires that were organized to shelter Israel during and after the exile. For defense of this claim, see James B. Jordan, *The Handwriting on the Wall: A Commentary on the Book of Daniel* (Atlanta: American Vision, 2007); Peter Leithart, *Between Babel and Beast: America and Empires in Biblical Perspective* (Eugene, OR: Wipf & Stock, 2012); Andrew Perriman, *The Future of the People of God: Reading Romans Before and After Western Christendom* (Eugene, OR: Cascade, 2010).

involved the Lord's advent, brought judgment on an old world and inaugurated something that can be described as "salvation" and the fulfillment of
the "hope of righteousness" (Gal 5:5). That event was a necessary conclusion
to the sequence of actions that brought an end to a world under sin and death,
a humanity living *kata sarka*. It was the final completion of the project of
delivering humanity from the curses of Eden and Babel, and the final dis-
mantling of the stoicheic order that governed Gentiles and Israel through the
Torah.[17] That judgment put an end to the old world, and the old humanity,
in order to bring a renewed humanity into being.

[handwritten margin note: u the Revelation?]

Throughout her history, Israel had broken covenant and turned from
Yahweh. She worshiped idols while in Egypt and during the time of the
judges. Jeroboam set up golden calves at what became the official shrines of
the northern kingdom, and Judah filled the land with high places and during
certain periods even set up idols in the temple of Yahweh. By the time of Jesus
that was all in the past. The temple of the first century contained no images
of Baal, and Josiah had long since destroyed the calf shrines of the north.

After all *that*, why is the final doom over the horizon? Why is the justice
of God about to strike once and for all? Why is *now* the fullness of time? Why
does Yahweh's war on flesh come to its climax in Jesus? *How* is Jesus' ministry
a continuation and climax of Yahweh's prosecution of flesh? How does he
deliver from bondage to the *stoicheia* and constitute a new human *physis*?

To answer these questions, we turn to the history of Jesus. To formulate
atonement theology successfully, we have to examine not only his death but
also the life that led to it and the resurrection that followed. Only by telling
the *whole* story of Jesus can we arrive at a fully evangelical theology of
atonement.

Spirit in Flesh

What would a human life look like if *not* dominated by flesh—if not ruled
by the vulnerabilities, weakness, fears, anxieties of flesh, if not driven by the
flesh's desire for pleasure or flesh's violent self-protectiveness? What would
a human life look like if it was lived *in* the flesh but not *according to* the flesh?

---

[17]Perriman has explained the way this "preterist" setting for Paul's letters affects our understanding of his basic themes. My use of this apparatus, however, takes a somewhat different direction.
For a summary of Perriman's thesis, see Peter Leithart, "The Future of the People of God," *First
Things* (blog), July 26, 2011, www.firstthings.com/blogs/leithart/2011/07/the-future-of-the
-people-of-god.

It would look like the life of Jesus.

In his advent, the Word assumed Israel's condition and operated under the conditions of Edenic and Babelic curse.[18] Jesus was truly human, and he came so fully under the conditions of weakness, mortality and vulnerability that John can say, "The Word *became* flesh." But he was not *controlled* by the fear of death and loss, by the desire for pleasure and protection, by the re-active and violent dynamics of flesh. Jesus' life was the embodiment of Torah-keeping that is not overwhelmed by flesh. He did not trade insult for insult, wound for wound. He neither attacked enemies nor recoiled from them, but loved them. He did not seek retribution, and he did not fear the suffering that others imposed on him.

In Jesus, God himself lived a human life *in* flesh that was not controlled *by* flesh. He came into flesh by an act of the Spirit, and so while in the flesh he lived the life of the Spirit. Thus Jesus is the true Israelite, the Davidic king, doing what Yahweh required every Israelite and every king of Israel to do, living according to Torah while in flesh. As Davidic king, Jesus embodies Israel; as just Davidic king, Jesus embodies the *just* Israel that Yahweh always wanted and promised. It is the kind of life that Torah's antisarkic regimen always aimed to produce.[19]

Jesus the Temple

What would the culture of Torah look like if Yahweh were to come out from his house, mingle with the crowd, eat with sinners without the safety-veil of temple barriers? What if purification were given directly by Yahweh rather than through the mediation of purity rites? What if sinners were made clean and holy by the sheer force of God's holy presence, the Holy Spirit? What if Yahweh made priests by the power of his indestructible life, rather than qualifying them according to flesh? What if Yahweh stepped down from the ark to touch unclean Israel and enacted his welcome of the unclean in

---

[18]Jesus comes in the "*likeness* of sinful flesh" (Rom 8), and Paul's slight qualification is critical. Jesus lives in flesh but does not live according to flesh under the dominance of flesh. His flesh has not been commandeered by sin so as to become *sinful* flesh.

[19]Even if Jesus is not Yahweh incarnate, or the eternal Word made flesh, it is difficult not to conclude that the Jesus of the Gospels is animated by a rare Spirit that makes his life a combi-nation of relentless boldness and overwhelming compassion, inspires him as a profound but clever teacher, makes him both cunning in his ability to keep religious professionals on their toes and guileless in his bluntness. He is a charismatic figure even for many who do not believe in charisma.

person? What would sacrifice look like if Israel were no longer outside Eden looking in, but had passed by the cherubim to stand in the presence of God? What would Torah-keeping look like once the Abrahamic promise came to pass and the nations were blessed through Abraham's seed? What would Torah-keeping look like if there was no more need for circumcision's gesture of separation from separation? What would Torah-keeping look like if it were carried out by Spirit rather than by flesh? What would human righteousness look like if human behavior were no longer instigated by the desires of flesh? What would Torah-keeping look like if the curses of Eden and Babel were lifted? What would poststoicheic life be?

Under those altered circumstances, the culture of Torah would look *just like* the life and ministry of Jesus, because that is what the life and ministry of Jesus *is*. In him Yahweh has indeed come down from his throne in heaven, in the Most Holy Place, to set up shop among human beings. In Jesus, Yahweh has stepped from behind the veil of the temple to live in the flesh among fleshly people. Jesus' ministry was a ministry of welcome, purification, access, communion, covenant festivity and delight, all that Torah was designed to do. There is, in this sense, complete continuity between Torah and Jesus: Jesus came not to destroy but to fulfill, to bring Torah's aims to their utmost completion. The one change—the single shift so massive that it changes *everything*—is that Yahweh is no longer hidden. At Sinai, Yahweh established his home in the midst of Israel, but with Jesus, Yahweh takes a further step into the world of flesh, beyond the tabernacle of curtains at Sinai. And then it becomes clear that the whole sanctuary apparatus, all the purity rules and rites of purification, all the sacrifices, the whole system was a complex type and shadow of Jesus' life and ministry.

As incarnate Yahweh, Jesus did what Yahweh had done through Torah, but did it more directly and intimately. He offered everything that the temple system, the stoicheic system, offered, but he enacted it himself.[20] Yahweh had refused to recoil at "unclean" and "sinners"; he refused to pronounce a divine "Ick!" On the contrary: he ate and drank with them. The entire

---

[20]Nicholas Perrin, *Jesus the Temple* (Grand Rapids: Baker Academic, 2010), argues that all of Jesus' practices are "essentially . . . temple practices" (79). Perrin argues, for instance, that Jesus' ministry of healing (154), his table fellowship (168-70) and his insistence that his disciples give up their wealth to support the poor (147) are all integrated parts of a new-temple program. Wright, *Jesus and the Victory of God*, develops the notion of Jesus' ministry as a "counter-temple" movement (e.g., 102, 108, 132), though less elaborately than Perrin.

sacrificial system was designed to bring Israel near so that divine Husband and human Bride could feast together at the house of Yahweh. Yahweh accommodated himself to the post-Edenic, fleshly situation of Israel. Israelites themselves did not approach Yahweh but drew near through animal mediators, animals whose flesh was destroyed so that they could be transfigured and ascend, as the worshiper could not, into Yahweh's presence. Israelite priests ate in the holy place, but only under controlled conditions; Israelites could eat and drink and rejoice before the Lord, but only at a distance from his fiery presence. Israelites could not go past the cherubic swords and live. Israelites could not become fire to join themselves to Yahweh's fire. But they could send animals past the cherubic swords, and Yahweh accepted the animals in place of the worshipers and Yahweh's fire "consumed" the flesh of animals so that their flesh was turned to smoke and fire, "divinized" into union with Yahweh.

When Yahweh came in the flesh, the need for that stoicheic apparatus began to end. In Jesus, Yahweh himself sat at human tables and ate food with them. This was what Torah aimed at from the outset. It was what Torah encouraged Israel to dream of. Jesus did what Torah always aimed to achieve, to make it possible for the Creator and his rebellious creatures to share space, to live and walk together in a common garden, to share a common table.[21] Yahweh's entire program in Torah was designed to make human beings his "companions" in the original sense of the word—God and humans as sharers of bread.[22] The ministry of Jesus is what the sacrificial system looks like after Eden's curse is overcome. Jesus qualified people to draw near to his table. He touched lepers and dead bodies, and instead of contracting their contagious miasma, his cleansing life flowed to them. Lepers were cleansed; a woman's defiling flow of blood was stopped.[23] The table fellowship of Jesus *is* the sacrificial system under poststoicheic conditions.[24]

---

[21]See Meyer, *Aims of Jesus*, 161, for a beautiful description of how Jesus' meal practices embody his message that the kingdom has come as a kingdom of grace, *free* and *now*.

[22]See Sam Wells, *God's Companions: Reimagining Christian Ethics* (Oxford: Wiley-Blackwell, 2006).

[23]Thomas Kazen argues that Jesus was "indifferent" to purity regulations in *Jesus and Purity Halakah: Was Jesus Indifferent to Impurity?* (Winona Lake, IN: Eisenbrauns, 2010). That misses the force of Jesus' actions. He is not indifferent, but he is deliberately challenging the purity regulations of the "expansionists" among the Jews, living out a fresh way of being Torah-observant. Theodore Jennings Jr. (*Transforming Atonement: A Political Theology of the Cross* [Minneapolis: Fortress, 2009], 90) rightly emphasizes that Jesus was not contaminated by touch because he was already living in the Spirit.

[24]John Dunnill nicely describes Jesus' ministry as "episacrificial," an apocalyptic intervention of

FULFILLED ISRAEL

What would Israel look like if flesh were overcome? What if a whole community began to operate according to Torah's antisarkic patterns? There would be feasting, that first of all. There would be ways for the unclean and excluded to draw near, that too. Gentiles would be invited to share in the goods, in some fashion. And this Israel would take up Yahweh and the king's war against flesh. A fulfilled (not merely restored) Israel would look like the band of twelve disciples that Jesus called, like the community of publicans, sinners and prostitutes, of Pharisees and Gentiles, that Jesus began to gather around him.

Even during his lifetime his disciples began to adopt poststoicheic patterns. Jesus taught his disciples not to wash their hands before meals, empowered them with authority to raise the dead, heal the sick and cast out demons. He taught his disciples not to be anxious about meeting the needs of this life, not to indulge fleshly fear of loss, weakness, lack or vulnerability. They should give generously, and then give again, without thought of return, knowing that their heavenly Father will make good on their gifts to the poor. By his example and teaching, he trained his disciples to mingle with the rejected and oppressed in order to deliver them. Torah established a pedagogy under conditions of flesh; Jesus, living Torah, established a fresh pedagogy and culture of the Spirit, a law of the Spirit of life. When Jesus said that the kingdom has come now, that it is freely offered here in Israel, he was talking about this real-life, concrete fulfillment of human destiny, the community that was beginning to gather around him, sharing goods and participating in the Father's own joy, the race of Adam fulfilled in a festive community in the Creator's presence. The kingdom had come because a culture of the Spirit, centered on the Spirit-filled Jesus, began to take form within the culture of flesh.

Jesus guided his disciples in a way of mature holiness that surpassed the righteousness of the scribes and Pharisees. The righteousness of Jesus and his disciples was not merely a negative. He did not simply *suppress* flesh-inspired behavior; he lived in a way so as to overcome the flesh and its

---

God to establish a table fellowship with his people. See Dunnill, *Sacrifice and the Body: Biblical Anthropology and Christian Self-Understanding* (Farnham, UK: Ashgate, 2013), 45. Dunnill is mistaken, I think, to set Jesus' ministry at odds with the Levitical system. He claims that Jesus revives an earlier, more holistic tradition of communal festivity and justice.

instincts, and he called his disciples to the same. He taught a way to overcome the dynamics of flesh in interpersonal, social and political situations—in other words, to overcome the flesh that dominates Babelic human society. He laid out a program of *redemptive* righteousness.[25] It is a description of his own life of Torah observance, and it is the script for an Israel formed by redemptive righteousness. Jesus' disciples were enlisted in Yahweh's war against fleshly violence, vengeance and reciprocity.

In Matthew 5:38, Jesus quoted from the "law of retribution" that is found several times in Torah (Ex 21:24; Lev 24:20).[26] Jesus did not attack Torah. The *lex talionis* was designed to limit violence. Lamech said he would take seventy-sevenfold vengeance on anyone who mistreated him, but Yahweh instructed Israel not to follow the example of Lamech. They could not take seventy-sevenfold vengeance, but only the limited vengeance the law permited. If someone strikes out one tooth, the victim cannot take out seventy-seven of his teeth. Under the control of flesh, though, the *lex talionis* that is given to limit vengeance can perpetuate rather than arrest violence. Jesus warned that applying this principle leads to cycles of violence, of insult and return insult, of vengeance and countervengeance. An insult leads to a response that is twice as bad, and that leads to a response, and that leads to a response that doubles the insult again. A cycle of vengeance, of eye for eye for eye for eye for eye, goes on forever until no one has any eyes left. As in *Hamlet*, it is life for life for life for life, and it ends only when everyone is dead on the floor or too exhausted to go on.

Jesus' instructions to his disciples detail a way of life that achieves what the *lex talionis* aimed at. Jesus' commands, though, go beyond an attempt to curb the effects of fleshly violence. Jesus taught a way to overcome flesh itself and to enact God's justice. The righteousness Jesus described surpasses that of the scribes insofar as it is designed to overcome flesh and to redeem human relationships. It seeks reconciliation and reunion in love, rather than simply trying to control the evil effects of sin and flesh. If enacted, the instructions of the Sermon would unravel the dynamics of flesh. Jesus did not dismiss the *lex talionis* so much as suggest a paradoxical,

---

[25]See Glen Stassen, "The Fourteen Triads of the Sermon on the Mount," *Journal of Biblical Literature* 122 (2003): 267-308, who uses the phrase "redemptive righteousness." The entire discussion that follows is inspired by Stassen's article.

[26]My discussion of the Sermon on the Mount is taken, with some revisions, from my *The Four: A Survey of the Gospels* (Moscow, ID: Canon, 2010).

surprising fulfillment of the law, a fulfillment that surpasses the fulfillment of the law by the scribes and Pharisees, a fulfillment that participates in the coming of the kingdom of God that brings harmony and peace and justice into the world. By following the Torah of Jesus, the disciples *are* that coming of the kingdom.

Jesus' first example—the slapping example—illustrates his point. The situation is about honor and dishonor, insult and shame. If I receive a slap on the right cheek, either the slapper has slapped me with his left hand or he is slapping me with his backhand. Either way, it is insulting. A slap on the *right* cheek with the *right* hand is probably a backhanded slap, an insulting slap rather than a danger to life and limb. The person who slaps you with the back of his hand is treating you as a slave, as an underling. He is sweeping you away like a flea. Instead of returning evil for evil, a slap for a slap, insult for insult, Jesus called his disciples to bear the burden of retribution *themselves* and offer to receive a second slap. Disciples of Jesus are to receive double harm rather than impose a harm on another. Jesus told his disciples to *accept* the second slap rather than *give* it. The "double restitution" comes back on the disciple, who not only bears the original insult but also bears the punishment on behalf of the one who assaults him. That "fulfills" Torah because it brings into concrete realization what Torah was aiming at from the outset.

Instead of a series of slaps and counterslaps, there are at most two slaps, both on the cheeks of the disciple, and then the contest is over. Instead of an ongoing cycle of escalating vengeance and retribution, the process is ended after two slaps, two miles, after the disciple strips off his undergarments and stands naked before his oppressor. Following these instructions also, subtly, restores the dignity of the person who gets slapped. The slapper wants to treat the slappee as a victim, the object of oppression. The slappee has no choice, no dignity. But when the slapped person turns the other cheek, he wrests initiative out of his opponent's hands. Instead of suffering the shame of being a victim, the disciple takes initiative into his own hands— disciples offer their cheek, remove their undershirt, go a second mile, give to whoever demands (Mt 5:40-42). In doing so, the disciple also exposes the bully for the brute that he is; turning the tables in a way brings shame on the oppressor. Slapping may make the slapper look virile, manly, in control.

Slapping someone who offers their cheek to be slapped makes the slapper look cruel.[27]

Jesus did not command turning the cheek because it is pragmatic, though it is. He commanded it because it was his *own* way that his disciples must follow. Jesus himself was the supreme embodiment of the righteousness he demanded of his disciples. Nearly everything Jesus mentioned in the Sermon happened to him in his passion: "Jesus himself was struck and slapped ([Mt] 26:67), and his garments (27:35) were taken from him."[28] As Suffering Servant, Jesus embodied this righteousness, as the prophet Isaiah already predicted.

> The Lord GOD has given Me
> The tongue of the learned,
> That I should know how to speak
> A word in season to him who is weary.
> He awakens Me morning by morning,
> He awakens My ear
> To hear as the learned.
> The Lord GOD has opened My ear;
> And I was not rebellious,
> Nor did I turn away.
> I gave My back to those who struck Me,
> And My cheeks to those who plucked out the beard;
> I did not hide My face from shame and spitting.
> For the Lord GOD will help Me;
> Therefore I will not be disgraced;

---

[27]Jesus says much the same when he describes our response to enemies. In Mt 5:43, the quotation is not from the Old Testament but summarizes a view that was held by some Jews, for instance at Qumran. The Old Testament doesn't endorse the view that we are free to hate enemies. The law tells us that we are to do good even to enemies—caring for his animals, for example (Ex 23:4). Proverbs tells us to feed and give a drink to our enemy (Prov 25:21-22). The stories of the Bible include many examples of people doing good to those who are persecuting them: Joseph doesn't take vengeance on his brothers but feeds them and robes them in glory. David has opportunity to pay Saul back but refuses. The prophets suffer for doing good and don't strike out in vengeance. Jesus particularly challenges the perversion of loving only those who love you (Mt 5:46-47). We are to love those near to us (see Gal 6:10), but if our love is restricted by blood, race, kinship, church membership or whatever, it is no better than the love of Gentiles and tax collectors. It is not the righteous love that surpasses that of the scribes and Pharisees. And notice again that Jesus doesn't tell us to leave our enemies alone. If N. T. Wright is correct that the "enemy" of the Sermon on the Mount is the Roman, perhaps specifically the Roman soldier, then love for enemies requires a breach of the barrier between Jew and Gentile.

[28]W. D. Davies and Dale Allison, *Matthew 1–7*, ICC (Edinburgh: T&T Clark, 1988), 546.

Therefore I have set My face like a flint,
And I know that I will not be ashamed. (Is 50:4-7 NKJV)

Through his Torah-keeping and teaching, Jesus was forming within the
flesh of Israel a new Israel that no longer lives *kata sarka*. Like Jesus, his
disciples are called not only to resist flesh in themselves but also to live in a
way that unravels the dynamics of fleshly rivalry, vengefulness and violence.
Jesus was not talking about nonresistance or nonintervention. He commanded resistance, but demanded that it be a redemptively just resistance
that takes the form of doing good. We might say that Jesus required resistance *not* to the enemy but to the *flesh* that motivates the enemy, and his
instructions were designed to target the flesh in a way that permits the
enemy to be reconciled as a friend. By following Jesus' instructions, disciples
are caught up in Yahweh's war against flesh, but in a way that targets flesh
and redeems rather than destroys the enemy.

Jesus' teaching brought to fulfillment Torah's assault on fleshly patterns
of life, and Jesus also enacted Yahweh's battle with flesh in his ministry of
exorcism and healing. By driving out unclean spirits, he delivered vulnerable
flesh from the dominating powers of the devil. The blind, deaf, mute, lame
are all living tokens of the weakness of flesh, the weakest of the weak, and
Jesus gave them strength in place of their weakness. Jesus raised the dead
and purified the unclean. He gave his disciples authority as apostles to carry
out the same ministry of proclamation, healing, exorcism and resurrection
(Mt 10). Long before Pentecost, the disciples were already carrying on the
mission of Jesus alongside him.

But this is only the surface meaning of Jesus' healing ministry, and
without qualification could lend itself to a "fleshly" interpretation. Jesus did
make the weak strong, bolster and heal the frail. More radically he began to
construct a new Israel, overseen by twelve new patriarchs, that *consists of*
the poor, weak, vulnerable. Scribes and Pharisees are outside looking in as
the kingdom comes among the despised, polluted sinners of Israel. *Children*
become model citizens of the kingdom, exemplifying mature human life.
The weak become exemplary, because in their desperate dependence and
neediness they display the reality that most human beings cover over with
a show of force and achievement, to make a good showing in the flesh.[29]

---

[29]On the exemplary character of the weak, see Meyer, *Aims of Jesus*, 172.

Conclusion

This *is* the justice of God operative through Jesus, the son of David, enacted in the society that follows Jesus around and keeps his commandments. God's justice is embodied in a representative Israelite and a community of charity, fellowship, peace, a community extended through the mission of the disciples, signified by a common table where goods are shared and enjoyed, a community whose life together constitutes a continuous critique of and assault on fleshly division and exclusion, phallic pride and bravado. The justice of God comes to social expression in a community of disciples who are beginning to live without *stoicheia*, as they enter a new world whose social physics comes from Spirit, not flesh. In Jesus we see the apocalypse of God's just kingdom, the beginning of the end of his case against flesh, his entry into the world to accomplish the work Torah could not do.

Jesus' kingdom campaign can only end in death. It can only continue by virtue of resurrection.

- seven -

THE FAITH OF JESUS CHRIST

✝

If Jesus' aim was to bring in God's kingdom of justice by leading Jews and Gentiles in the way of the Spirit, by fulfilling the fleshly institutions of *ta stoicheia tou kosmou* and by reversing the curses of Eden and Babel, why could he not be, as liberal theologians have long said, a teacher, teaching by word and example a way of compassion, justice, love and mercy? Why did he have to die if he simply wanted to change—to improve—the pattern of Israel's socioreligious life—to make them, in Augustine's terms, simpler, easier to understand, more potent? Why the cross and resurrection if Jesus came to inaugurate a new way of worship that flowed out in a new ethics and a new politics? Who would *not* want the justice of God? In dogmatic terms, why can we not be redeemed simply by the incarnation? What made him crucifiable? Why must he die? Why not tell them, "C'mon guys! We don't have to do all this anymore!"?[1]

The starting point for any historically plausible answer is: that was *exactly* what he *did*.

---

[1]The following is dependent on N. T. Wright, *Jesus and the Victory of God* (Minneapolis: Fortress, 1997); Marcus Borg, *Conflict, Holiness, and Politics in the Teachings of Jesus* (Edinburgh: T&T Clark, 1998). The term "crucifiable" comes from Wright, *Jesus and the Victory of God*, 86. In some ways the questions themselves betray an unbiblical anthropology that separates "external" patterns of ritual and life from the "internal nature" of the person. The questions assume that a change from complex and multiple sacraments to simpler and fewer ones does not touch the fundamental being of a person or a society. If, as I argued in chap. 2, cultural patterns give specification to human beings so that people of different cultures have different "natures," then a change in the "structures" and "patterns" of Israel's life is a change in the *nature* of Jews and Jewish society. Paul says that Gentiles are "uncircumcised by nature" (Rom 2:27); we ask, isn't *everyone*? But those who are uncircumcised by nature can be grafted into the tree of Israel, replacing natural branches, and so become "naturally" part of Israel (Rom 11:21, 24). By the cross, Jesus combined Jews and Gentiles into one new person, sharing a nature that they did not share before, precisely because they share a new pattern of liturgical and social life. He disrupts the social physics of the world by changing the arrangements of the social elements.

He called the Twelve out of the "Egypt" of Israel to be the foundation stones of a new temple that he himself was and the patriarchs of a new, freshly redeemed Israel. He taught the Twelve and other followers how to keep Torah in Yahweh's presence, how to enact Yahweh's war on flesh in their daily interactions with oppressors and enemies. He gathered the weak and called the strong to become like children, accepting their vulnerability and weakness and trusting the Father. He healed the frailties of flesh and drove away oppressive demons. He sparked sacrificial festivity wherever he went and brought the unclean near, cleansing them by the finger of his Spirit. As the greater Solomon, he built a new temple; as the new Moses, he formed a new priesthood, a new purity and sacrificial system in the middle of the old. During Jesus' life, this was only nascently achieved. Jesus' disciples kept purity rules, and Jesus sometimes instructed the people he healed to go through the requisite purification rites "for a testimony" to the priests (Mt 8:4). But something new was taking shape. Jesus began forming a poststoicheic community of the Spirit in the midst of a fleshly Israel still living under *ta stoicheia*.

Jesus died because his purposes and program for Israel clashed with the agenda of the Jewish leaders at every crucial point. The Jewish leaders considered Jesus a transgressor of Torah, who not only failed to keep Torah here and there but who overturned Torah altogether. To Jewish eyes, Jesus was a Sabbath-breaker. He flouted purity regulations, eating at defiled tables. He went freely among compromised Jews and prostitutes. He distributed bread in the wilderness as if he were Yahweh leading a new exodus, but the multitude who ate together was a mixed multitude packed with polluted Gentiles.[2] He spoke with Samaritans, even Samaritan women.

There were many faithful Jews in the first century, many who followed the humble faith of Abraham, renouncing flesh and trusting God. But many of the Jewish leaders had turned purity rules into mechanisms of exclusion, into expressions of disgust that increased rather than overcame distance.[3] Sacrifice was given to be a means of drawing near while remaining distant, but the Jews had made the temple and its sacrifices a protective cover for injustice and brigandage.[4] Sabbath was a sign of Yahweh's gift of rest to his enslaved

---

[2] Of course, the original exodus community was also a mixed multitude.

[3] It is common for historians of the first century to observe that holiness meant "separation" for the Pharisees and scribes. See, for instance, Borg, *Conflict, Holiness, and Politics*, 66-87: "Holiness was understood primarily as entailing separation" (67).

[4] N. T. Wright rightly points out that the phrase does not refer directly to what is happening in the

people—a ritual reminder of Israel's calling to be a rest-giving, redemptive people that, like Yahweh, breaks yokes and lifts burdens. The Jews had turned the Sabbath into yet another yoke. Jesus *enacted* Sabbath by giving relief to the suffering, and by healing on the Sabbath he provoked the Jews to reconsider their fleshly sabbatical observance. To the Jews, this was Sabbath-*breaking*. Circumcision, that great *renunciation* of flesh and phallic potency, had become a source of nationalist pride and fleshly boasting. Circumcision had become a source of absurd "boasting in the flesh" (Gal 6:13)—in flesh that was no longer there! Abraham trusted God and gave thanks for a future and a son that were sheer gift; Jews boasted in their fleshly achievements and status. Gentiles were considered unclean in themselves, something never contemplated by the Torah.[5] Herod's temple had a court of the Gentiles, dividing the "house of prayer for all nations," the house of the one God of all humanity, into a mirror of Babel. Instead of being a means for flesh to be transfigured to smoke to approach God, sacrifice was turned into a screen for injustice: the house of Yahweh had become a den of brigands, a safe house where the violent think they can get away with anything.[6] Israel's leaders turned the culture of Torah into another Egypt, a place of harsh bondage.

Israel's distortion of Torah was most egregious in the first-century temple and among the temple elites. Priests were household servants of Yahweh who performed a dangerous ministry on behalf of the people. They were called to be servants to the priestly people, servants of the servants of God, facilitating Israel's access to Yahweh from their median position, guarding Israel from wrath by protecting Yahweh's holy house. Instead, priests were notoriously greedy and used their status within Israel to trample the vulnerable. Designed to be a house of prayer for all nations, a place of festivity

---

temple but to the use of the temple as a "safe haven" for revolutionaries (Wright, *Jesus and the Victory of God*, 417-18). See the qualifications of Nicholas Perrin, *Jesus the Temple* (Grand Rapids: Baker Academic, 2010), 80-113.

[5]Though she is talking about later Mishnaic Judaism, Mira Balberg's description of the differences between biblical and rabbinic impurity is illuminating for the first century. The key differences are the intensification of impurity, the formation of a "world of impurity" and, on the other hand, the classification of Gentiles as both beyond the purity system and impure as such (Balberg, *Purity, Body, and Self in Early Rabbinic Literature* [Berkeley: University of California Press, 2014], 27-47, 122-47).

[6]*Here* is the place to plug in all that Girard and his followers say about sacrifice. Mark Heim is right to say that Torah is co-opted by sacrificial dynamics (Heim, *Saved from Sacrifice: A Theology of the Cross* [Grand Rapids: Eerdmans, 2006], 142), but fails to emphasize that those dynamics are a *corruption* of the original intention of sacrifice. Paul's theology may involve an indictment of sacrifice as practiced, but he does not indict sacrifice as intended by the law.

in Yahweh's presence, the temple had become a den of brigands, a center of extortion, embezzlement, sacrilege. It was almost axiomatic that the temple authorities robbed the temple treasury in various ways, and the priests set up credit schemes that enriched their coffers and extended their lands at the expense of the poor. The temple functioned as Israel's lending bank, and the priests used its mechanisms to their advantage. As Nicholas Perrin writes,

> The windfall income that would accrue to the temple leadership through illegal gain could then in turn be quickly turned around for punishingly high-interest-rate loans to the destitute. By being in a position to leverage usurious, high-risk loans, the temple financiers were then able to foreclose quickly and efficiently on landholders struggling to eke out an existence. Increased temple landholdings eventually meant more wealth for the priestly elite, more wealth meant even more high-interest loans, more high-interest loans meant more foreclosures on the land, and the cycle went on—crushingly so, for those at the bottom of the economic ladder.[7]

The rich got richer, the poor poorer. And the temple, the house that originally housed the tablets of Torah that revealed Yahweh's justice, was the chief promoter of economic injustice. The temple leaders turned stoicheic priestly hierarchy into a cover for fleshly lusts.

Jesus knew just where the pressure points were, and he courageously acted and spoke to provoke repentance, with the full realization that he would in fact provoke nothing but fury. His parables parodied Pharisaical pseudo-righteousness: they were the elder brother who complained glumly when his brother returned and brought his father joy; they were the vineyard keepers who plotted to kill the son of the vineyard owner—and they played to type by hatching a plot to seize Jesus (Mt 21:33-46). Jesus ate with sinners, calling the Jews to table fellowship, but his table practice became a point of controversy and one of the main charges against him. He charged that the Pharisees and scribes neglected the weightier matters of the law, focusing on trivialities, and by doing this they had made the law a burden rather than a liberation (Mt 23). In his temple "cleansing," he enacted the doom over the temple as he told greedy, violent temple elites that their house was going to be left desolate, their systematic brigandage dismantled within a generation. Jesus was Jeremiah, announcing

---

[7]Perrin, *Jesus the Temple*, 97. See also the various essays on the corruption of the temple in Craig A. Evans, *Jesus and His Contemporaries: Comparative Studies* (Leiden: Brill, 1995).

the temple's doom; he was Josiah, casting down the idols and building a purged human temple among his disciples. As Yahweh incarnate, he battered down binary oppositions that constitute the fundamental physics of Israel's world, but he also battered at the extra walls that flesh-dominated Torah had erected.

These were not breaches of etiquette. If Jesus' way became the way of Israel, then all the hopes and plans of the Pharisees and scribes were doomed, because their plans and hopes depended on maintaining and tightening the taste-not-touch-nots of stoicheic life. Maintaining purity, especially at the table, was central to the Pharisaical program for Israel's future. As Ben Meyer eloquently put it, "The distinctions of clean and unclean and of righteous and sinners shaped and permeated the self-understanding of Judaism. To subvert these distinctions was . . . a challenge to the social order."[8] Jewish leaders knew what was at stake. If Jesus' program were to catch on, if most Jews began sharing tables with sinners, if they all stopped washing their hands before meals, they would be undermining the divisions that structured the reality of Judaism. The physics of Israel's life would be disrupted; Jewish nature itself would unravel. If the *stoicheia* were dissolved, the only result would be utter chaos. If Jesus' way became *Israel's* way, then Israel as the Jewish leaders and teachers knew it would cease to exist. If Jesus was right, then the teachers and leaders of Israel must themselves have been transgressors of Torah. There was a stark choice: Torah or Jesus. For the Jewish leaders, it could not be both.

To the Jewish leaders, Jesus was an offender, a leper and pollutant, a transgressor. He was not cleansing the polluted but confusing the categories of pure and impure, and if he was successful Israel's order would collapse into a chaotic mash. When they saw Jesus' flesh flayed and his face disfigured by torture, when they saw him suffocating on the cross, they concluded that they had been right all along: he must be stricken, smitten *by God*, and afflicted.[9] They concluded they had been right to expel the

---

[8]Ben F. Meyer, *The Aims of Jesus* (1979; repr., Eugene, OR: Wipf & Stock, 2002), 159-60. See Perrin, *Jesus the Temple*, 171.

[9]These phrases from Is 53 are intended to emphasize that that chapter is a preview of the gospel *events*. Atonement theology is there in Is 53, but it is in dramatic, narrative form. The Suffering Servant's enemies regard him as an enemy of God, punished for transgressions. For discussions of Is 53 along these lines, see Darrin W. Snyder Belousek, *Atonement, Justice and Peace: The Message of the Cross and the Mission of the Church* (Grand Rapids: Eerdmans, 2012), 224-43; Bernd Janowski, "He Bore Our Sins: Isaiah 53 and the Drama of Taking Another's Place," in *The Suffering Servant: Isaiah 53 in Jewish and Christian Sources*, ed. Bernd Janowski and Peter Stuhlmacher (Grand Rapids: Eerdmans, 2004), 48-74.

dangerous poison that might have killed the body of Israel. Recoiling in fear at Jesus and the Israel he envisioned, the Jewish leaders defended the stoicheic system and defended it violently, zealous as Phinehas the priest for the purity of Israel.[10]

The Romans had their own reasons for opposing Jesus. Jesus was another Jewish irritant who disrupted Roman Judea and threatened the smooth flow of grain from Egypt to Rome. But Jesus was a more dangerous irritant than most. He announced the arrival of a *basileia* within a Roman world that already had a *basileus*, and that *political* challenge became a crucial point in Jesus' trial. Pilate in particular was faced with the dilemma of condemning an innocent man to maintain order and remaining on good terms with Caesar, or freeing Jesus and risking his post or his life. Naturally, he acted on fear rather than in the interests of justice.[11] He condemned the man of Spirit in order to cover his butt of flesh.

Insofar as the Romans knew anything about Jesus' program, they would find it impossible, an invitation to political chaos. Romans were *just* to their enemies; once they had defeated them, they invited some to share the blessings of Roman citizenship. But *loving* enemies, doing good to enemies, was absurd. Roman fear of death—that is, Roman fleshliness—drove them to dominate and control and suppress anything that might threaten loss; Rome's empire grew out of fear for security. Roman fear of death expressed itself as Roman honor-seeking, and Jesus' instructions to renounce honor posed a fundamental threat to the Roman way of life.[12] To give up phallic

---

[10]It is important to recognize a spectrum of responses here. While it is accurate to say, globally, that the leaders of Israel had distorted Torah, the experiences of individuals would have varied considerably. Some, like Paul, were "blameless with regard to Torah" (Phil 3), but provoked to blasphemy by the challenge of Jesus. When the Son and Spirit began bursting through the elements of the world, Paul "acted ignorantly in unbelief" (1 Tim 1:13), becoming a blasphemer of the Messiah and a violent, aggressive persecutor of the church. When Jesus came, his flesh lashed out to protect his inherited faith until Jesus visited him on the road to Damascus.

[11]The importance of the Roman imperial context for Jesus' ministry has been an important theme of recent work on the Gospels. See, for example, Richard A. Horsley, *Jesus and Empire: The Kingdom of God and the New World Disorder* (Minneapolis: Fortress, 2003). For a wisely cautious assessment of "empire studies" of the New Testament, see Scot McKnight and Joseph Modica, *Jesus Is Lord, Caesar Is Not: Evaluating Empire in New Testament Studies* (Downers Grove, IL: IVP Academic, 2013).

[12]Theodore Jennings Jr., *Transforming Atonement: A Political Theology of the Cross* (Minneapolis: Fortress, 2009) 35–40, describes how Jesus' life and practice provokes the powers. For the honor system of Rome, see Carlin A. Barton, *Roman Honor: The Fire in the Bones* (Berkeley: University of California Press, 2001). Augustine developed the same point with his emphasis on the "splendid vices" of the Romans.

displays and the fear of death would be to give up *Romanitas* itself. As the church expanded over the first century and beyond, confronting Rome and *Romanitas*, Romans began to fear for Roman *virtus* and protect it as violently as the Jews had protected their fleshly, stoicheic order. It would have been the same in Egypt or Babylon or Greece. Jesus was a man of Spirit, and so confronted Gentile *stoicheia* as decisively as he confronted Israel's fleshliness.

Before Yahweh delivered Israel from Egypt, he systematically demolished the world of Egypt. Israel had become all but Egyptian, worshiping Egyptian gods and adopting Egyptian ways (Josh 24). In delivering Israel, Yahweh had to uproot them from the alien world they had begun to inhabit, and to topple the Egyptian institutions and deities. He directed plagues against the Egyptian sky, the earth and the river; he attacked Egypt's gods, exposing them as no-gods. The exodus itself was the final demolition of the old world, and after passing through the sea Israel came to Sinai, where Yahweh established a new way of worship, which was also a new way of life.[13] Jesus came as a new Moses, and as such he brought "plagues" that destroyed "Egypt's" world of worship in order to make way for a new one. The plagues included eating with sinners; healing on the Sabbath; showing kindness to tax collectors and Gentiles; touching lepers, corpses and women with flows of blood. He instructed his followers to subvert the world order by returning kindness for harm, blessing for insult, by bearing others' burdens. Jesus came with plagues of mercy that subverted the perverse Torah-regime of the scribes and Pharisees and the brute force of the Romans.[14]

Even if Jews and Gentiles had accepted Jesus entirely, Jesus' ministry would have been a challenge to the status quo. He would have done things differently because things had changed: God was no longer distant, but near. While in the flesh, Jesus kept Torah in the fullness of the Spirit, something no other human had done before. If he spread his Spirit to others, a quite different Israel would begin to take form. Stoicheic order would become

---

[13]Thanks to Rev. Bill Smith for this way of summarizing the exodus, in a baptismal meditation delivered on December 14, 2014.

[14]The judgment that Jesus enacts against Jewish leaders is a judgment of mercy, compassion and kindness. It is similar to the "judgment" enacted by Elisha. When Elisha's name is first introduced, he is introduced as a destroyer (1 Kings 19), but his actual ministry involves feeding the hungry, providing for debtors, raising sons of widows. That mission of mercy *is* a judgment against the cruelty of Ahab's regime. It brings judgment by tearing Ahab's kingdom in two, with the sons of the prophets and their followers on one side and Ahab and his troops on the other. For more, see my *1 & 2 Kings*, Brazos Theological Commentary (Grand Rapids: Brazos, 2006).

obsolete and eventually would fall away. In the event, though, the Jews and
Romans did not accept Jesus' enactment of the justice of God's kingdom.
Jesus died because both Jews and Romans were under the dominion of flesh,
because they lashed out to protect their forms of stoicheic order against
Jesus. As Paul says in Romans 7, the spiritual Torah arouses and exposes
flesh. As living Torah, as the Torah-giver in flesh, Jesus aroused the fury of
flesh most of all.

This is not a "merely historical" account of the cross. It is an *evangelical*
account, one that takes in the whole of the gospel story. And it is a fully
theological account, taking the life of Jesus the God-man as its starting point,
as any historically plausible theology of atonement must.

JUDGMENT OF THIS WORLD

Because of the Jews' fleshly distortion of Torah, because they used Torah to
undermine Torah, they stood under imminent threat. God's kingdom was
coming—the kingdom of justice in which the curses of Eden and Babel
would be overcome. Because the kingdom *had* come in Jesus' person and
work, Israel was to repent and follow Jesus, the Lord who would lead Israel
from bondage and the king who would incorporate Israel into himself. Jesus
enacted this prophecy of doom with his provocative temple action at the
beginning of the final week of his life. He had walked a way of redemptive
righteousness and called Israel to follow. He had begun to establish a new
temple system within Israel, a temple system that fulfilled the aims of the
original temple system. That was itself a judgment on the mainstream
temple system. Jesus could have indicted the temple without saying a word
and called Israel's leaders to a new temple.

But the Jewish leaders rejected him. They preferred darkness to light,
childhood to maturity, elementary justice to the full realization of justice. In
his temple action, Jesus demonstrated the Lord's rejection of his house. It
was like the days of Noah: the culture of Torah had become so distorted, so
filled with fleshly violence, that it had to be swept away. But Jesus' enactment
of judgment, that final warning to fleshly Israel, became yet another ground
of accusation against Jesus. Instead of repenting and escaping the doom,
they raged against Jesus and sealed their doom. This was the climactic
moment of that trial because in first-century Judaism flesh had co-opted
God's good Torah and God's elect people.

This was the last plank in Yahweh's case against flesh: if flesh could turn the Torah he gave for Israel's life into an instrument of death, then the sinfulness of sinful flesh was proved. Yahweh's judicial case was sealed, and flesh was ready for the verdict of condemnation and the sentence of death. Given Israel's subjection to flesh, God had to act. If he did not kill flesh then, it would never be killed. If he does not act *now*, flesh may well win out. The Abrahamic promises to the nations would not be fulfilled because there would no longer be an antisarkic Israel to spread the justice of God.

It looked as if flesh did win. In Jesus' death, we see the climactic struggle of flesh and Spirit, enacted not internally in the Pharisees and Romans but publicly in the machinations of Jews and Romans to put the Spirit-anointed Messiah to death. In the cross, flesh seemed to triumph over Spirit, injustice over justice. And it looked as if Jesus' program for enacting the redemptive justice of God was stillborn. The toys of childhood stood. The one perfect, mature man was put to death.

In John's Gospel, Jesus' entire life is a series of trials. Yet the real trial is not the apparent trial. Not Jesus but the Jews who accused and "tried" Jesus are on trial. This becomes most evident in Jesus' trials and death. Speaking of his death after his entry into Jerusalem, Jesus referred to the coming hour of judgment on "this world" (Jn 12).[15] While the entire world was coming under judgment, that judgment began with the house of God, the people of Israel. Jesus' interpretation of his approaching death is in the background of the trial in John 18–19, where Pilate places Jesus on the judgment seat before the Jews, who renounce Jesus in favor of Caesar. Pilate too is on trial, but the trial centers on the people who claim to be sons of Abraham. By crucifying Jesus, the Jews and Romans ultimately condemned not Jesus but themselves. Flesh's apparent victory was flesh's defeat. By twisting Torah into an instrument to kill the living Word, by boiling the Torah-Giver in the milk of Torah, flesh is self-condemned. In Jesus' death, Yahweh's prosecution of flesh came to its climax.

Jesus was obedient to Torah even to the death. Even at the moment of crisis, in his arrest and trial, he did not succumb to flesh. He did not retaliate

---

[15]See Andrew T. Lincoln, *Truth on Trial: The Lawsuit Motif in the Fourth Gospel* (Peabody, MA: Hendrickson, 2000). Many commentaries on John stress the courtroom language and thematics of the Gospel. In many places in John, *kosmos* refers specifically to the world of Judaism, the world of those who are under the law. For argument to support this claim, see my *A House for My Name* (Moscow, ID: Canon, 2000).

against his accusers and enemies like an ancient hero. He did not return insult for insult or accusation for accusation. He did not turn violent. Even when all his disciples ran away, he did not flee self-protectively. Though he was mortal, though he feared death, he was not determined by the fear of death, did not live *kata sarka*. He went to death and laid down his life, giving it up in the Spirit to his Father, trusting that his Father would vindicate him in the end. As Jesus' death exposes the evils of flesh, it also answers to the brokenness of the human condition, the product of human frailty, vulnerability, mortality and the very sinful ways to stave off our weakness. It answers to our fleshly condition. We begin to have an account of atonement that captures the "inevitability" of the cross when we recognize that Jesus gave up the blood of his flesh so that he could enter fully into the life of the Spirit, and so he could share that Spirit with us.

This is what Paul means when he writes of *pistis Christou*.

The Faith of Christ

The grammatical/translation issue with the phrase *pistis Christou* has to do with the force of the genitive, "of Christ."[16] Is it an objective genitive, so that faith is directed to Christ as the object? Most English translations take the phrase in this fashion, using "faith in Christ."[17] To say one is justified by "faith in Christ" is to say that one is justified (whatever *that* means) by trusting in Jesus. On the other hand, the phrase could be taken as a sub-

---

[16]Matthew Easter provides a judicious and up-to-date discussion of the debate in "The *Pistis Christou* Debate: Main Arguments and Responses in Summary," *Currents in Biblical Research* 9 (2010): 33-34. Sigve Tonstad, "Πιστις Χριστου: Reading Paul in a New Paradigm," *Andrews University Seminary Studies* 40, no. 1 (2002): 37-59, not only provides a helpful summary of the arguments in favor of the subjective genitive reading, but also briefly sketches out the consequences for the overall reading of Paul's theology. See also Richard B. Hays, *The Faith of Jesus Christ: The Narrative Substructure of Galatians 3:1–4:11*, 2nd ed. (Grand Rapids: Eerdmans, 2002); James D. G. Dunn, "Εκ Πιστεως: A Key to the Meaning of Πιστις Χριστου," in *The Word Leaps the Gap: Essays on Scripture and Theology in Honor of Richard B. Hays*, ed. Ross Wagner, Kavin Rowe and Katherine Grieb (Grand Rapids: Eerdmans, 2008); Michael Bird and Preston Sprinkle, *The Faith of Jesus Christ: Exegetical, Biblical, and Theological Studies* (Peabody, MA: Hendrickson, 2009). N. T. Wright argues for a subjective genitive understanding of the phrase (*Paul and the Faithfulness of God* [Minneapolis: Fortress, 2013], 857; *Pauline Perspectives: Essays on Paul 1978–2013* [Minneapolis: Fortress, 2013], 201-2). An excellent bibliography on this question is available online at "Faith(fulness) in/of Christ Bibliography," *Paul's Epistle to the Galatians: All Galatians, All the Time* (blog), n.d., http://epistletothegalatians.wordpress.com/faithfulness-inof-christ -bibliography/.

[17]See Gal 2:16, translated as "by faith in Christ Jesus" in ASV, NASB, ESV, NIV, NKJV. Remarkably, the KJV translates both uses of the phrase in Gal 2:16 as "the faith of Jesus Christ."

jective genitive, translated as "faith of Christ." In that case, the faith named is not the faith of the believer in Christ but the faith of Christ himself. The objective genitive is an "anthropological" reading, and the subjective a "christological" one.[18]

The question is undecidable in the abstract, since the genitive can be used in either way, and in other ways.[19] The specific force of the genitive has to be determined in specific contexts, and even in specific texts the decision is not always obvious. In some passages, both appear to make equal sense. Contrary to some popular misconceptions, deciding that "faith of Christ" refers to Christ's own faithfulness does not negate the need for personal faith. Those who argue for a subjective genitive (the faith is Christ's own) still believe that Paul teaches that individuals must believe in Jesus (or trust in him) to be justified. Even if we take the phrase as a subjective genitive in Galatians 2:16, for instance, the passage affirms the necessity of believing: "Knowing that a man is not justified by the works of the law but by the faith that Jesus exercises, even *we have believed in Christ Jesus*, that we may be justified by the faith that Jesus exercises." Similarly, those who understand the phrase as an objective genitive would acknowledge that Jesus was faithfully obedient, even if they do not believe that Paul ever asserts it in precisely those terms.

This does not mean that the decision is trivial. It is not merely a question of what Paul means by this or that phrase, but ultimately a question of what Paul is talking about in general, the fundamental thrust of the gospel he proclaims, what is in the foreground and what is in the background. Is Paul's presentation of the gospel in Romans and Galatians mainly an answer to the question, how can sinners be saved? (Answer: Trust in Christ!) Or is it mainly an answer to the question, how did God reveal and manifest his justice in the world? (Answer: Through the faithful work of Christ.)[20]

---

[18]The terms come from Easter, "*Pistis Christou* Debate."

[19]See Preston Sprinkle, "Πίστις Χριστοῦ as an Eschatological Event," in Sprinkle and Bird, *Faith of Jesus Christ*, 165-84.

[20]The interpretation of the phrase affects the readings of specific passages. For example: In Gal 3:22, Paul writes that Scripture "shuts up everyone under sin" so that *hē epangelia ek pisteōs Iēsou Christou dothē*. Taking the genitive objectively, the NASB renders this "that the promise by faith in Jesus Christ might be given to those who believe." "By" is a potentially misleading translation of *ek*, which might point more to "source" than to "means." Thus the phrase could be "the promise [that comes or arises] out of faith in Jesus Christ." That means that the promise to Abraham is realized through the faith of those who believe in Jesus Christ. But that reading comes at the price of some redundancy, somewhat obscured by the use of different English words to translate

For every Greek scholar who says the subjective genitive would be the natural reading for a first-century Greek speaker, there is another scholar who says the opposite. Still we can resolve the grammatical question insofar as we *can* say *with certainty* that Paul is *capable* of using subjective genitives, and capable of using subjective genitives in phrases having to do with faith. We know this is possible because it is actual. Romans 4:16 is the proof. There, Paul correlates faith to grace, arguing that the promise is graciously given not to the seed who do the law but *to ek pisteōs Abraam,* to the one who is "from the faith of Abraham."[21] The question is, Is this describing faith *in* Abraham or the faith exercised *by* Abraham? Clearly Paul is not urging trust in Abraham, but rather presenting uncircumcised Abraham as the model of "Gentile" faith. Paul does use genitive phrases with *pistis* subjectively, phrases that mean "the faith exercised by *x.*" That is the very form of the phrase *pistis Christou,* and we must be open to the possibility, if no more, that it has a similar force to the phrase in Romans 4:16.

But we can say more. We do not need to leave this question within the realm of possibility. As we saw in chapter five, Paul's gospel is centrally concerned with the revelation of the justice of God, the fulfillment of his pledge to established justice among the nations. According to Romans 3, this justice is manifested through the *pistis Christou.* All we have said about *dikaiosynē* above applies here: Paul is announcing the good news of a Davidic king revealing, demonstrating and realizing the justice of God as a fulfillment of the hopes of Israel's prophets. In Romans 3, Paul makes clear *how* this Davidic king manifests this justice.

---

closely related Greek words. We might, more woodenly, translate the clause as "that the promise out of belief in Jesus Christ might be given to those who believe." That still makes sense: Paul is saying both that the faith of believers in Christ is the source of the fulfillment of the promise and that those who believe are the recipients of the promise. Though it makes sense grammatically, it is troubling theologically. In terms of Paul's argument in Gal 3, *is* it the case that the promise to Abraham has its *source* in the faith of believers? If that is the case, why could the promise not have been realized by Abraham himself, since *he* believed? If we translate the genitive subjectively, we come to this: "the promise [which springs] out of the faith exercised by Jesus was given to all those who believe." This makes excellent sense in itself: The promise comes to its fulfillment in the faithful work of Jesus himself, in his obedience to death; and that promise, offered to Abraham and now fulfilled by Abraham's seed, is given to those who have faith in the one who exercised faith. This reading eliminates the redundancy that was present in the previous reading. Instead of concluding that Paul describes two functions of human faith—as source and recipient of God's promise—Paul is talking about two different events, separated in time and subject: there is, on the one hand, the faithful act of Jesus, and then, later, there is the faith of those who hear and believe the gospel.

21 The simple genitive "faith of Abraham" is the all-but-universal translation. The *ek* is tantalizing, but not crucial to the argument.

The phrase *dikaiosynē theou* is more contextually determined in Romans 3 than in Romans 1. The full phrase appears in Romans 3:21, where Paul announces that the righteousness of God has been manifested (*pephanerōtai*; in Rom 1:17, the verb is *apokalyptō*), and Romans 3:22, where Paul describes this righteousness as coming *dia pisteōs Iēsou Christou*. In addition, *dikaiosynē* is used in Romans 3:25-26 without the genitive phrase, though in both verses it is modified by *autou*. In these latter verses, *dikaiosynē* includes the notion of just condemnation of evil. In a world disordered by idolatry, sexual confusions and social evils, the humble oppressed hope that God will come as Judge to destroy everything that sets itself against him and his good creation, and, having judged, to renew. This is what God does in Jesus as he displays Jesus as a *hilastērion* to demonstrate his righteousness. By setting Jesus out publicly as a *hilastērion*, God shows that his forbearance of evil has a limit.

Paul's point is not that God's righteousness is manifest in the belief of believers. Rather, he claims that God's righteousness is evident in what God *did* through Jesus. By Jesus' death, God manifests his seriousness in dealing with sin, a seriousness called into question by his past forbearance. What kind of God can allow the evils cataloged in Romans 1:18-32? The gospel's answer is that God is taking care of judicial business, and he does so in Jesus. In Jesus' death, God demonstrates that he is indeed Judge and will not sit idly by as sin and idolatry ruin his world and deface his image.[22] Romans 3:26 repeats the point, and again it includes God's action in dealing with sin more decisively than he had dealt with sin in the past. In Romans 3 there is little doubt that the "faith of Christ" refers to Jesus' trustful obedience unto death, his "obedience of faith" that drove him to be a *hilastērion*.

If *pistis Christou* describes the faithfulness of Jesus in his life and death, then even without the genitive phrase *pistis* might refer to Christ and his faithful work rather than to the belief or trust of those who hear the gospel. In two places in Galatians, *pistis* is a title, almost a name, for Jesus. "We" were kept in custody under the law "before faith came" (*pro tou de elthein tēn pistin*), Paul writes in Galatians 3:23. This cannot be a reference to faith as human belief, habit, action or attitude, since Paul began the chapter by commending the *pistis* of Abraham, who believed God (*episteusen tō theō*) and

---

[22]This strikes a Grotian, governmental note in Paul's atonement theology.

was reckoned righteous. The arrival of faith that Paul is talking about in Galatians 3:23 brings an end to the custody of the law; it comes *after* the law, while Paul is at pains to stress that Abraham came *before* the law (Gal 3:17). The only advent Paul could be talking about is the advent of Jesus, who is so much the faithful one that he can take the name or title "Faith." Galatians 3:22 has just referred to "the faith of Jesus Christ." In the following verse, Paul says that this Faith that arrives to deliver from the curse of the law is specifically the faithful work of Jesus. Paul uses the same expression, "the coming of faith," in Galatians 3:25, now describing what happens after faith comes.[23] The advent of faith is not the advent of belief, but of Jesus, the faithful one, who does Torah as it was meant to be done.

SACRIFICE ACCORDING TO THE GOSPEL

Jesus knew he would die,[24] and he taught his disciples what his death meant in many different ways.[25] Speaking to the mourning women along the *via dolorosa*, he linked his death to the coming crisis of Jerusalem and the temple (Lk 23:27-31).[26] At times Jesus borrowed terminology from the sacrificial system to explain what was happening. He claimed that his death

---

[23]This does not at all reduce the need for a response of faith—trust, assent, belief, loyalty. As Wright puts it, Christ's *pistis* evokes our *pistis*, so that the gospel moves from faith to faith (*Paul*, 967). Paul's usage here is linked with the Johannine naming of Jesus as *Pistis* in Rev 3:14 and Rev 19:11. If *pistis* can function as a name of Jesus, then we must be open to the possibility that "justification by faith" might refer *not* to an event that happens to an individual who believes and is forgiven of sin or put right before God but rather to the act of God in Christ by which justice is revealed and established. Justification by faith might mean: justification by the faithful work of faithful Jesus. Though the Gospels almost never use the term *dikaioō*, it might be the case that the entire gospel story is about nothing but justification by the faithful work of Jesus Christ. We will explore that possibility in the next chapter.

[24]Daniel Ullucci denies that early Christians generally equated animal sacrifice with the crucifixion. He acknowledges that the death of Jesus is given a sacrificial interpretation in Hebrews, but minimizes the sacrificial themes of Paul and the Gospels. To ancient people, he claims, death by crucifixion would not be considered in any way similar to animal sacrifice (Ullucci, *The Christian Rejection of Animal Sacrifice* [Oxford: Oxford University Press, 2011]). Ullucci is able to draw this conclusion only by ignoring the metaphorical uses of sacrificial language that were common in the ancient world, and also because he fails to see the elasticity of the notion of sacrifice. On the first point, see Martin Hengel, *The Atonement: The Origins of the Doctrine in the New Testament*, trans. John Bowden (1981; repr., Eugene, OR: Wipf & Stock, 2007); on the second, see John Dunnill, *Sacrifice and the Body: Biblical Anthropology and Christian Self-Understanding* (Farnham, UK: Ashgate, 2013), 126-27.

[25]An exhaustive and illuminating, though turgid, treatment of Jesus' death is Scot McKnight, *Jesus and His Death: Historiography, the Historical Jesus, and Atonement Theology* (Waco, TX: Baylor University Press, 2006).

[26]Ibid., 141-43.

would "ransom" many (Mk 10:45), paying the price of death to release them from bondage to sin, death and flesh (see 1 Pet 1:19). At the Last Supper, he offered his body and blood to his disciples, speaking of his death as a new liberating Passover event. His disciples "smeared" the blood of the Passover Lamb on themselves by drinking from Jesus' cup, and so were rescued from the angel of death abroad in the land, "cordoned" off from the doomed stoicheic system of Israel's temple. By accepting Jesus' bread and wine, they were incorporated into his death and called to take up their cross to follow him.[27] He went to the cross to offer his blood, the life of his flesh, as the blood of the covenant, as he offered himself as the founding sacrifice of a new covenantal order. We can add here all the other ways the New Testament describes the death of Jesus: as redemption, as cleansing for sin, as the basis for forgiveness; Jesus dies to bring us to God, to bring the distant near. Scripture gives a myriad of ways of understanding how Jesus' death affects sinners—as payment, cleansing, deliverance. All of these may be placed in the context of Levitical sacrifice, so that Jesus' death is seen as one moment in his sacrificial history that takes him into Eden, and us with him.

He could do all this because he was not a literal Passover lamb or the ram substituted for Isaac: blood from bulls and goats cannot take away sin. He fulfilled the sacrificial system because he did what all the sacrifices signified. Noah offered Yahweh an ascension offering that created a "Noahroma," a sweet-smelling savor that presented Noah's own righteous life. Every faithful Israelite worshiper offered himself, or the "son" of his herd or flock, to Yahweh at the altar. Jesus did this in fact when he offered *himself*, passing through death into union with God like an animal sacrifice. Jesus was not the first martyr to give his life to the God of Israel, but none of the earlier martyrs ended the stoicheic system or brought in a new covenant. What made Jesus' death different? The answer is, his *identity* and his *life*. Jesus was the "son of God" in the Old Testament sense: he was Israel's King, Israel embodied in a single person, and so his death, like the death of every king of Israel, was on behalf of his people. When he passed through death toward transfiguration, *Israel* went with him. More, Jesus was Israel's king and Israel's High King in one person, both David's Son and David's Lord. He poured out his blood, the life of his flesh, as Yahweh incarnate, and so his passage through death was Yahweh's own passion, God's own passage

---

[27]Ibid., 280, 326-28.

through human death. Besides, Jesus' entire life made his martyrdom unique. Heroic as they were, no other martyrs had lived a life of complete obedience to Torah. None had fully realized all that Torah required. Like every sacrificial animal, Jesus offered himself *"without blemish* to God" (Heb 9:14). Thus he fulfills the entire sacrificial system of Leviticus: those sacrifices were the shadows, but Christ's is the substance that cast the backward shadow.

Can we say more? Can we make this more concrete? Do the Gospels give any further clues to the "mechanism" of atonement?

LIFE FOR FRIENDS

Israel went through the death-and-transfiguration of sacrifice in the Old Testament: dismembered after Solomon, ultimately handed over to the grave of exile, finally raised from the dead in the restoration. The nascent Israel Jesus led went through a sacrificial sequence, disbursed at Gethsemane, then reunited in the Spirit after the resurrection of Jesus.

As head of the body, Jesus went to the cross for the body. Jesus died and rose again *for his disciples.* "Given for you" certainly means "given for all the people of God throughout the ages," but in the context of the Gospel it means, specifically and primarily, given *for the disciples.* When the Jewish leaders bore down on Jesus, the disciples were cowed by the pressure. Judas turned against Jesus, Peter denied him, the rest of the disciples scattered. Jesus called them to bear their crosses with him, but they were still too much in the flesh to do that. When the Romans and Jews struck the Shepherd, Jesus alone took the full fury of their fleshly vengeance. It was common for Romans to suppress Jewish rebellions by executing not only the leader but also the disciples of disruptive Jews.[28] When Roman soldiers and Jewish guards came to arrest Jesus in Gethsemane, he did not flee or cower. He stood between the soldiers and his friends and demanded that the soldiers let the disciples flee. He offered himself in their place. He went to the cross stripped not only of his clothing but also of the protective house of his friends. Quite literally, he laid down his life *for his friends.* He was put to death alone; the disciples were spectators, and distant ones at that.

This may seem a small gesture, but on *this* rests the salvation of the world. And this provides a historically plausible way of understanding the cross. Jesus was the incarnate Creator, come to bring the kingdom of justice by

---

[28]Wright, *Jesus and the Victory of God.*

establishing a fulfilled-Torah Israel. That mature Israel, growing up out of stoicheic childhood, would be the instrument for bringing the justice of God's reign to Gentiles. If Jesus' *disciples* died, that purpose would not be carried through. Yahweh's war on flesh would grind to a halt. Israel would not be restored, and if Israel were not restored, then Jesus' aims would fall to the ground and the Abrahamic promise would remain unfulfilled. If the disciples died along with Jesus, the redemption of the world would be stillborn. In laying down his life for *these* specific friends, Jesus preserved the new Israel, saving the twelve foundation stones on whom the new Israel would be built. In this sense at least (and there will be other senses), Jesus offered himself as a substitute in death for the life of the world. In that sense, he died to end the curses of Eden and Babel, died to bring in the justice of God. Jesus died to preserve the nucleus of a new social world that he had begun to form among his followers.

PENAL SUBSTITUTION

Jesus died not only for his friends but also as a penal substitute for *Israel*.[29]

---

[29]The theory of penal substitution has been controversial throughout the modern age. Faustus Socinius mounted the first and definitive critique in *De Iesu Christo Servatore, Hoc Est, Cur et qua ratione Iesus Christus noster seruator sit* (1595), whose arguments have been repeated regularly ever since. Socinius's arguments were embodied in the Racovian Catechism (see the English translation of Thomas Rees, *The Racovian Catechism* [London: Longman, Hurst, Rees, 1818], 297-319). Kant rejected penal substitution and worked out a Pelagian, moralistic alternative account of atonement (*Religion Within the Boundaries of Mere Reason* [1793], in *Religion and Rational Theology*, ed. and trans. Allen Wood and George Di Giovanni [Cambridge: Cambridge University Press, 1996], 112-17). John McLeod Campbell developed a theory of Christ's substitutionary confession and repentance in his 1856 treatise, *The Nature of the Atonement* (Haddington, UK: Handsel, 1996); on Campbell, see George M. Tuttle, *John McLeod Campbell on Christian Atonement: So Rich a Soil* (Haddington, UK: Handsel, 1986); Oliver Crisp, "Non-Penal Substitution," *International Journal for Systematic Theology* 9, no. 4 (2007): 415-33. For classic defenses of penal substitution, see Francis Turretin, *The Substitutionary Atonement of Christ*, ed. Matthew McMahon (n.p.: Puritan Publications, 2014); A. A. Hodge, *The Atonement* (Philadelphia: Presbyterian Board of Publication, 1867); more recently, J. I. Packer, "What Did the Cross Achieve? The Logic of Penal Substitution" (Tyndale Biblical Theology Lecture, 1973), www.the-highway.com/cross_Packer.html. Several movements in recent theology—feminism, the influence of René Girard, pacifism, the influence of Anabaptist theology—have converged to offer a severe challenge to this model of atonement. Among many books on the topic, see the critiques of penal substitution in Mark Baker and Joel B. Green, *Recovering the Scandal of the Cross: Atonement in New Testament and Contemporary Contexts*, 2nd ed. (Downers Grove, IL: IVP Academic, 2011); Darrin W. Snyder Belousek, *Atonement, Justice, and Peace: The Message of the Cross and the Mission of the Church* (Grand Rapids: Eerdmans, 2011); J. Denny Weaver, *The Nonviolent Atonement* (Grand Rapids: Eerdmans, 2001); Heim, *Saved from Sacrifice*. Timothy Gorringe traces what he considers the damaging effects of satisfaction and substitutionary theories of atonement on Western law in *God's Just Vengeance: Crime, Violence, and the Rhetoric*

Jesus died *because of* the sins of Israel. That is obvious enough, to believers at least. Jesus was not a transgressor of Torah, but the Jewish leaders pressured Romans to execute Jesus as a transgressor. In accusing and condemning Jesus, they committed a sin as they "nailed [him] to a cross by the hands of godless men and put Him to death" (Acts 2:23 NASB). It was not just any sin. It was the greatest atrocity ever committed, and it was committed in the name of Torah by the people who had been privileged as caretakers of the oracles of God.

We can be more precise. The charge against Jesus was that he was a Torah-breaker. He was accused of blasphemy (Mt 26:65; Mk 14:64), but not only because of the claims he made about himself, which were often murky with deliberate ambiguity. He described himself as one with the Father (Jn 10:33),

---

of Salvation (Cambridge: Cambridge University Press, 1996). On the other side of the debate, see Hans Boersma, *Violence, Hospitality, and the Cross: Reappropriating the Atonement Tradition* (Grand Rapids: Baker Academic, 2006); Garry Williams, "Penal Substitution: A Response to Recent Criticisms," *Journal of the Evangelical Theological Society* 50, no. 1 (2007): 71-86; Steve Jeffrey, Michael Ovey and Andrew Sach, *Pierced for Our Transgressions: Rediscovering the Glory of Penal Substitution* (Wheaton, IL: Crossway, 2007). My treatment of penal substitution owes much to that of Wolfhart Pannenberg, *Jesus—God and Man*, trans. Lewis L. Wilkins and Duane Priebe, 2nd ed. (Philadelphia: Westminster, 1977), 258-69, 278-80. Unlike some classic accounts of penal substitution, Pannenberg's flows out of the Gospel narratives and stresses the central importance of resurrection. Kevin Vanhoozer poses pointed questions to "relational" and "therapeutic" alternative explanations of the atonement, and charges that "both the penal substitution and the relational restorationist view . . . *abstract, to a greater or lesser extent, what God is doing in Christ's passion from the broader drama of redemption*" (Vanhoozer, *The Drama of Doctrine: A Canonical Linguistic Approach to Christian Doctrine* [Louisville, KY: Westminster John Knox, 2005], 384-85 [emphasis original]). Vanhoozer goes on to argue that a "postpropositionist" theology acknowledges that both penal substitution and relational restorationist views "have a foothold in certain biblical metaphors" but refuses to reduce the Bible to "a single conceptual scheme" (ibid., 385). Along similar lines, Stephen R. Holmes argues that penal substitution is one of the many legitimate but partial "metaphors" for grasping the significance of the cross (Holmes, *The Wondrous Cross: Atonement and Penal Substitution in the Bible and History* [Milton Keynes, UK: Paternoster, 2007]). The use of "metaphor" in discussing atonement theories is misleading. God is not "metaphorically" holding court at the cross: he really is Judge, and really is passing judgment. Jesus' death is not "metaphorically" sacrifice, but the first completely real sacrifice in human history. Rather than speaking of multiple metaphors, it is more accurate to say that this single event is subject to multiple complementary accounts.

I offer a version of penal substitution here, but I find some elements of recent critiques compelling. The Racovian Catechism is correct to emphasize that substitutionary death is not the *whole* of sacrifice, and to highlight the central importance of the *resurrection* in the accomplishment of salvation. Both of those points have been weaknesses in some accounts of penal substitution. It has also been common, as critics have insisted, for penal substitution to be isolated from Israel's history and from the gospel story, so that it becomes a logical structure with little relation to history. To be successful, an account of penal substitution must arise from the biblical story rather than being a paradigm imposed upon the story. Penal substitution survives these critiques, but only if its advocates first hear the critics and take them seriously.

and as Son of Man, but he blasphemed because he made himself equal with God by the free way he had with Torah and by habits and actions that subverted Torah. He was the rebellious son of Deuteronomy 21:18-21, a gluttonous man and a drunkard (Mt 11:19; Lk 7:34), who refused to listen to the traditions of the fathers or to Israel's Father, Yahweh.[30] He not only broke Torah here and there, but evidently renounced Torah entirely as well. It must have seemed deeply fitting to the Jews that this rebel ended up hanging from a tree, the fate of those who renounce Torah's demands.[31]

According to the gospel story, though, Jesus was completely innocent of all charges. He was not a blasphemer, not a Torah-breaker. Rather, the Jews who accused and condemned Jesus and had him killed—*they* are the blasphemers (Mk 3:28-29; cf. Rom 2:24). Indeed, they were committing blasphemy in the very act of accusing Jesus of blasphemy and putting him to death. The Jews accused Jesus of the very sin of which they were guilty. They condemned Jesus as the rebellious son when they were Yahweh's rebellious but beloved son, Israel (Ex 4:23). When they urged crucifixion and asked Pilate to put Jesus on a cross to display his cursedness, they were urging a punishment *they* deserved. The precision is exquisite: Jesus died as the penal substitute for Israel. This is not a piece of abstract theologizing, an inference from or an imposition on the Gospel narrative. It is a description of the gospel drama. It is there in the narrative. "Penal substitution" is a *plot* summary.[32]

How is this story of penal substitution *gospel*? How is it anything but a travesty of justice, happily overturned at the last moment by the *deus ex machina* of resurrection? When Sydney Carton takes Charles Darnay's place at the guillotine, Darnay goes free: Carton's "penal substitution" liberates. How did Jesus' willing suffering of the penalty Israel deserved make any difference to anyone?

Jesus' death at the hands of wicked men ransomed and redeemed because Jesus was the Davidic king, Israel embodied in one person. The Davidic king

---

[30]McKnight, *Death of Jesus*, 94, argues that Deut 21 provided the legal ground for the capital charge against Jesus.

[31]Tim Gallant notes that in Deut 21 the law about the rebellious son is immediately followed by the passage about the divine curse against those who hang on a tree (Gallant, *Paul's Travail: A Reintroduction to Galatians* [n.p.: Pactum Reformanda, 2013], 125-26). Perhaps this is one of the reasons the Jewish leaders demanded crucifixion rather than permission to stone Jesus. Of course, the Roman form of execution also means that Jesus dies as a rebel against the empire, and much of my argument can be adjusted to apply it to the Roman world.

[32]Thus falls one of the main charges against penal substitution—that it ignores the gospel story. On the contrary, penal substitution only makes sense *within* the gospel story.

was Yahweh's son, the representative of Israel (Ex 4:23). Between David and the Babylonian captivity, the fate of Israel turned on the faithfulness or unfaithfulness of her king. Jesus was the Son of David, declared and proved to be such by the resurrection.[33] The king lived for the people and died for the people. Jesus the King took on the penalty that Israel deserved, and so released Israel from the capital penalty for her blasphemy. If Jesus did not step in to take Israel's punishment, wrath would come to the uttermost, Israel would be scattered and die, the Abrahamic promise would not be fulfilled. Unless Jesus saved Israel, the world would not be saved, and he saved Israel by suffering the death she had earned.

Jesus' disciples betrayed him and scattered, yet he died for them, and in his resurrection forgave them and reconciled them to himself—a reconciliation signified by the resumption of table fellowship. In the aftermath of the resurrection, the Jews had two choices. They could acknowledge that they in fact crucified the Jesus who had been exalted as both Lord and Christ, and they could weep over the one they pierced and turn from their blasphemy. Like the penitent executioners of Isaiah 53, they could come to the painful recognition that "he was pierced for *our* transgressions," not his own, and was "crushed for *our* liabilities." They could entrust themselves to Jesus, and so be forgiven their blasphemy against Jesus as they joined the disciples who had been reassembled and reconciled to Jesus. Entrusting themselves to the Father of Jesus, they could adopt the way of Jesus.

Or they could stick with the charge of blasphemy, deny the resurrection and try to stamp out the expanding mission of the church. Either way, stoicheic order comes to an end. Those who followed Jesus the Risen voluntarily enter the Christian era and adopt the table practices and purity rules of Jesus the rebuilt temple. Those who opposed Jesus were heading, as Jesus repeatedly warned, to a disaster that would end with the destruction of the temple, and therefore an end to stoicheic order. By his death as a penal substitute, Jesus demolished the old order and inaugurated a new world. Jesus was a penal substitute for the world because he was first of all a penal substitute *for Israel*, because he ransomed Israel from the curse and constituted a new Israel to live by the *nomos* of the Spirit and to be sent on a mission to call the nations to share that culture. He was a penal substitute for the sins

---

[33]Rom 1:1-3. Note the quotation of Ps 2 in relation to the resurrection in Acts 13:33, Paul's first recorded sermon.

of the world insofar as he made a way of forgiveness and reconciliation with God through the new Israel.

As the priestly people, Israel represented the nations, and so her blasphemy represented the blasphemy of all nations. Insofar as Jesus died to pay the penalty of Israel's own blasphemy, he also suffered the punishment due to the nations for their blasphemy. Further, Romans joined with the Jews in putting Jesus to death, and so they too were guilty. The Romans condemned Jesus for making himself a king, a challenger to the true king. But he *was* the true King, the king of Romans as well as Jews. They executed Jesus for *lèse-majesté*, but their execution was the supreme act of *lèse-majesté*. In condemning the King in the name of their king, Caesar, the Romans, like the Jews, charged Jesus with the very crime they were committing. Jesus died as a penal substitute for Romans as well as for Jews.

Jesus was not only the true Israel and the world's king but also the Last Adam, the "Son of Man" who has come to tame the bestial empires that rise from the turbulent sea (Dan 7). This is something of an extrapolation from the gospel story, but it seems a legitimate one: Jews and Gentiles, which for the Bible constitute the sum of the human race, executed the Son of Man for the crimes they themselves committed. *They* punished him for their sins, and so made him their penal substitute for the sins of humanity.

None of this is accidental. As Peter said during his sermon at Pentecost, what the Jews did in nailing Jesus to a cross by the hands of godless Romans fulfilled "the predetermined plan and foreknowledge of God" (Acts 2:23 NASB). Jesus' becoming a penal substitute for Israel and the Romans was not a random accident, nor a deviation from the path he was sent to go. It *was* the path that the Father sent him to walk in the far country. It was the Father's pleasure to send his Son into this danger, into the valley of death, and it was the Son's pleasure to do his Father's pleasure. It was the Father's pleasure to deliver the Son to be crushed by godless hands; in delivering the Son to the godless the Father laid on the Son all of Israel's liability for punishment. The Son whose very being is to do his Father's will carried out this mission to the uttermost; he was crushed, and he suffered Israel's punishment for the joy set before him.[34] The Father sent the Son, and the Son

---

[34]For a general defense of substitution as a principle of all social order, see Pannenberg, *Jesus—God and Man*, 264-69. Pannenberg's discussion is one of the best brief treatments of atonement, including penal substitution, of the recent past. See also Pannenberg, *Systematic Theology*, trans.

willingly was sent, to take the burden of the sins of Israel, of Rome, of the human race. As true Israel, as the King, as Son of Man, Jesus bore our griefs and carried our sorrows, suffered for our liabilities, was chastened to make us well, so that by his stripes we may be healed.[35]

VINDICATED BY RESURRECTION

None of this was evident at the cross. There, everything was in question, even, it seems, Jesus' relationship with his Father. Entering into flesh, he suffered the Godforsakenness of flesh.

We know the end of the story, and its two-millennia-long sequel, so we miss the uncertainties of the events narrated by the Gospels. If we can come to the Gospels innocently, we encounter a story filled with drama. The Gospel writers are clearly on Jesus' side, and they tell us throughout that God is on his side too. Jesus is the hero. But if we were living through the events, it would be much more difficult to distinguish the good guys from the bad guys. Jesus seemed good, but he did and said unnecessarily provocative things. The charge that he broke Torah was a plausible one, and for many first-century Jews *more* than plausible. He certainly caused upheaval in Israel, and one can sympathize with the Pharisees and scribes who wanted to calm things, who wanted to protect the old ways. We certainly do not recognize that the Pharisees and scribes were blasphemers or enemies of

---

Geoffrey Bromiley (Grand Rapids: Eerdmans, 1991–2009), 2:397-453, which uses "reconciliation" as the key theme.

[35]Thus falls a second objection to penal substitution—that it violates trinitarian orthodoxy by putting the Son and Father in opposition. There are crude versions of penal substitution that are guilty of this charge, and it is both unbiblical and unorthodox to suggest that the kind Son pacifies his irascible Father. Both Father and Son are at war with sin, death and flesh; both Father and Son love creation and humanity and, with the Spirit, conspire to save. Even noncrude versions of penal substitution can fall afoul of trinitarian orthodoxy, especially when penal substitution is abstracted from the concrete events of the trial and death of Jesus. The Father *never* condemns the Son; he never counts him as a transgressor. He *cannot*, because Jesus is *not guilty*, because Jesus is his eternal, eternally beloved Son and because the work of the cross is the combined work of Father, Son and Spirit. The Father *never* makes common cause with Jesus' accusers. What the Father does instead is to hand Jesus over to be charged, falsely, by Jews and Romans, and then vindicate Jesus and condemn his accusers by raising Jesus in the Spirit. By his predetermined plan, God *parries* the accusations, condemnation and execution to overcome the sin of those who hate Jesus, including the very sin they commit in executing him. The Father counts Jesus' death as paying the penalty Israel deserved, but not because he counts Jesus guilty. Jesus takes responsibility for Israel's guilt, Israel's liability for punishment. *This* is the sense in which Jesus "becomes sin" and "bears the curse" for us. Jesus is *not for a moment* counted guilty in the divine court.

Torah; they seemed to be the only ones who upheld God's law. Even when reading the gospel story, we do not know what sort of story it is until the very end: Is it a story of a noble but doomed attempt to call the world back to God? Is it the story of a martyr to a good cause?

Only with the resurrection are these questions sorted. Because Jesus rose, we know that some power—perhaps the power he called "Father"—was on his side, and not on the side of his accusers. By the resurrection, we know that someone thought Jesus innocent and had undone the travesty of his trial. By the resurrection, the Jewish leaders stood condemned. The resurrection was judgment day—a favorable judgment day for Jesus, a terrifying condemnation of his enemies.

The Gospel writers tell us that the charges against Jesus were false, but we do not see with clarity just how deeply twisted the charges were. Once Jesus rose from the dead, and was revealed to be the true Son of the Father, the true Israel, the Lord of glory, the evil of his persecutors was fully revealed. In the light of the resurrection, it became clear that *they* were the blasphemers, the enemies of God. In the light of the resurrection, it became evident that the charges they brought against Jesus were the very charges that might have been brought, *justly*, against them. In short: it is *only* in the light of Jesus' resurrection that we can see the gospel story as a story of penal substitution. The resurrection was the act by which God turned the accusations against the accusers and condemned those who pronounced condemnation against Jesus. Those who acknowledge the justice of God's charges against them are saved; those who do not will be destroyed.[36]

By the same token, Jesus' courageous substitution for his disciples was *not* sufficient to save. Jesus' suffering and death also enacted Yahweh's final onslaught against flesh as he confronted fleshly Israel and fleshly Rome even at the cost of his life. By his death, flesh stood self-condemned: *now* is the judgment of this fleshly world. That was not enough either. If Jesus' death were not something more than an *exposure* of the brutality of flesh, it would not be a saving act. If flesh is merely *unveiled*, humanity may well

---

[36]Thus falls a final complaint against penal substitution—that it ignores the resurrection. On the contrary, if the gospel ended with Jesus' death, it would not be clear that he was an innocent substitute suffering the penalty his accusers deserved. To be consistent with trinitarian orthodoxy, penal substitution *requires* a strong emphasis on the resurrection. Without the resurrection, Jesus' death as a substitute *is* unjust and the whole theory does verge toward a bizarre form of divine child abuse.

be wiser, more sober, perhaps more modest about its self-exaltation. But it will still be flesh.

If Jesus remained dead, his program would not be realized. If he remained dead, then it would appear that the Jews were right after all: Jesus *was* a transgressor, stricken, smitten of God and afflicted. The way of Jesus *was* a pollution and a prescription for social and religious chaos. It was good that this man was put to death to save Israel from him. Jesus' order of sacrifice, purity and justice depended on Yahweh coming out from behind the veil and living among his people. If Jesus died and stayed in the grave, then he must never have been Yahweh incarnate to begin with. If Jesus died and stayed dead, then the Creator was still distant from his creatures, and the whole stoicheic system more firmly entrenched than ever. If Jesus died and stayed dead, flesh—*mortal* flesh—had the last word, and that means death and sin would continue to reign unscathed.

He did *not* stay dead. The Father he trusted and to whom he was utterly faithful raised Jesus, and in the aftermath of his resurrection he reassembled the broken body of his disciples. With the resurrection as proof that God approved Jesus, and filled by the Spirit that Jesus breathed at Pentecost, the Twelve became leaders and foundation stones for a renewed people of God. Thus, Jesus' death and resurrection formed the leadership of a new Israel.

Jesus' provocative action in the temple brought the conflict with Jewish leaders to a climax by concentrating central attention on the issue of authority: Who had the authority to teach in the temple and direct the future of Israel? In rage at Jesus, the chief priests and scribes put him to death. Once Jesus was raised, and especially after Pentecost, it became evident that the Jewish leaders had crucified the Lord of glory. They lost their divine legitimation, and the apostles were anointed by the Spirit as the leaders of the true Israel. This only increased their rage at Jesus and his followers, and they struck out at the church, but this further damaged their own status within Israel. In this way (and in many others), Jesus' death and resurrection formed a new Israel and fulfilled the promise of the prophets by setting a faithful Shepherd, and faithful undershepherds, over the people. Those who pass through this sacrificial sequence with Jesus are constituted as the new Israel, the just society, living by Spirit in the flesh.

This sacrificial "theory" of atonement depends *entirely* on the resurrection and exaltation of Jesus. If the Gospels ended with the *death* of Jesus,

Jesus' program was a failure, the sheep scattered, the project a noble but failed dream for the redemption of humanity. He challenged the stoicheic restrictions, lived a life beyond *stoicheia* as a mature adult and was stopped dead. At that point, Torah and its fleshly, Pharisaical interpreters were vindicated, and so were the temple authorities. A dead Jesus does not fulfill the Abrahamic promise; he does not reverse either the Edenic or the Babelic curse. If Jesus remained dead, his *way* was also dead, and we are *still* under the elementary things, still under the law, still under the Adamic curse. Jesus and his way are vindicated only if the Father reverses the judgments of the Roman and Jewish courts and raises Jesus.[37]

The sacrificial story *cannot* end with sacred violence, even *ultimate* sacred violence. Death must be swallowed up in victory, or there is no atonement, no release from the curse (1 Cor 15). Jesus must die *and rise* to be a sacrifice, because that is what sacrifices do: they are slaughtered in flesh in order to rise in smoke and Spirit. He must not only be slaughtered but also be translated to smoke and Spirit to pass by the cherubic guardians into the garden. He must be raised if he is going to be the ultimate, acceptable human self-sacrifice. Only a sacrifice that leads to resurrection and exaltation and union with God is a fully *Levitical* sacrifice. Only such a sacrifice can transform the physics of socioreligious life.

What made Jesus' martyrdom unique? His identity and his life, yes. And because of who Jesus is, he could not be captured by death. Ultimately what set Jesus' death apart was the fact that it was followed by resurrection. The resurrection was not merely confirmation of the efficacy or uniqueness of Jesus' death. Resurrection is what *made* his death unique and efficacious. For unless he was raised, we are still in our sins, still lingering outside Eden, still cursed with the curse of Babel. We are still in flesh, and still confined by the institutionalized fleshliness of *ta stoicheia*.

FLESH INTO SPIRIT

Even with the resurrection, Jesus' sacrificial progress was not finished. In Levitical sacrifice, a sacrifice was completed by the ascent of the animal in smoke to join the cloud of Yahweh's presence, and frequently by a meal. At the inauguration of the tabernacle, the glory of God descended and then

---

[37]Pannenberg, *Jesus—God and Man*, 251-58, emphasizes that the resurrection both proves Jesus right and condemns his accusers and opponents as transgressors of the law.

broke out to light the altar fire and consume the sacrifice (Lev 10:1-10). After Jesus was raised, he ascended to the cloud of the Father, like the Son of Man of Daniel 7, a sacrificial figure who also ascended to the Ancient of Days on the clouds of heaven. He poured out the fire of his Spirit at Pentecost to turn his disciples into living sacrifices, tongues of fire on their heads.[38] Jesus lived in flesh that had been created by the Spirit, and in the flesh he lived by the Spirit.[39] In his death, he died to fleshly life, died to what Paul calls his *psychikon* body (1 Cor 15), and by his resurrection entered fully into the life of the Spirit, with his *sōma pneumatikon*. He left his disciples behind, but he did not leave them fleshly. The Spirit that animated the life of Jesus—the life of welcome festivity, the life of breaking yokes, the life of cleansing sinners by the force and power of his Spirit and presence, the life of redemptive justice—*that* Spirit was poured out into the flesh of the disciples. The disciples devoted themselves to practicing Jesus' festivity, including Jews and Greeks, slaves and freemen, the unclean and the outcast. In preaching, generous almsgiving, hospitality, healing, they continued Jesus' war on flesh, which is Yahweh's war. They devoted themselves to the teaching of the apostles and to prayer. In the world of flesh, Jesus' death, resurrection and the outpouring of the Spirit created a "community called atonement."[40] That community will reach its final perfection in the final resurrection, but even now the Spirit of Jesus has formed and is forming a new humanity from the broken elements of the old. The atonement of Jesus—his formation of a new *kosmos* no longer operating by the ancient social physics or by the flesh—becomes a fact, a *social* fact.

The first generation of Christians was a world of transition. They continued to worship in the temple (Lk 24), Paul was willing to circumcise Timothy to pacify Jews, and late in his career as recorded in Acts, Paul fulfilled a Nazirite vow at the temple. Meanwhile, the disciples were enjoying sacrificial meals in homes, apart from the temple. They invited Jews, Gentiles and whoever would come to share their meals and their communal life.

---

[38]In John's Gospel, the whole sequence of cross, resurrection and departure is an ascent back to the Father, completed in Revelation, where the Lamb appears in heaven (Rev 5).

[39]Barth puts it this way: The Son takes the being of man that is in opposition to God, but the Son does *not* make common cause with humanity in its opposition to God (*Church Dogmatics*, IV/1, *The Doctrine of Reconciliation*, ed. Geoffrey W. Bromiley and T. F. Torrance, trans. Geoffrey W. Bromiley [Edinburgh: T&T Clark, 1956], 185).

[40]This is the neat phrase of Scot McKnight, *A Community Called Atonement: Living Theology* (Nashville: Abingdon, 2007).

They worshiped God without veils, Eden overcome, and embodied in their very social life the overturning of Babel's curse. The final destruction of the stoicheic order did not happen with the cross of Jesus. To be sure, from the death of Jesus stoicheic order is all but nullified, signified by the rending of the temple veil at the time of Jesus' death.[41] Woven with cherubim, the veil was a reminder that the gate into Eden was blocked and access to the Creator's presence severely restricted. The rending of the veil announced the end of the stoicheic order and of God's accommodation to flesh. As by one act of disobedience humanity was excluded from Eden and placed under a curse, so by one act of obedience humanity was offered a return to Eden. Stoicheic order was nullified by a final *sacrifice*, when Jesus offered his life to establish a new covenant that remits sins, when God put Jesus forth publicly as a *hilastērion* in blood (Rom 3),[42] when he brought Jesus as a sin offering to purify the people and temple once and for all (Rom 8:3).[43] Jesus became the first full human worshiper of Yahweh, the first Torah-keeper, who passed through death into Eden *as a man*. He died for the remission of sins, *so that* those who trust and follow him can enter Eden with him to feast without veils or barriers in the presence of God.

Stoicheic order did not end in social and religious reality until the end of the age, the last part of that generation, when the judgment that Jesus had

---

[41]N. T. Wright has suggested that the rending of the temple veil was a sign of the impending judgment on the temple, but if the temple is judged then the system that centers on the temple is also judged (Wright, *Jesus and the Victory of God*). Others have suggested that the rending of the veil indicates that a way of access has been opened by the death of Jesus. Humans are no longer excluded from the garden, as Jesus makes a way into the presence of the Father. That too implies that the entire stoicheic system is at an end, since the stoicheic system institutionalized humanity's exclusion from the presence of God. If there is free access, we are in a new religious and social world. It is also possible to think of the veil being rent from within, as if Yahweh were tearing through the barrier to step out onto the world stage. The veil, after all, is rent from above, ripping from heaven to earth. Yahweh, who had spent the old covenant behind tent curtains and then enthroned in a stone temple, now emerges into the open. Though John does not record the rending of the veil, we can put the point in Johannine terms: The rending of the veil is the final moment of the Word's becoming flesh to tabernacle among us, the moment when we do indeed see his glory, the glory of the only-begotten. For John, the glory of God shines especially through the crucified Jesus. When Jesus dies, the veil is torn because on the cross God's enfleshed glory is out in the open.

[42]I discuss this controverted term somewhat more fully in appendix 3. For now, it does not matter whether it means a place of expiation or an act of propitiation. It is clearly a sacrificial term, conjuring up specifically the sacrifices of the Day of Atonement, and my only point is that Jesus' death is indeed sacrificial.

[43]I take *peri hamartias* to mean "as a sin offering," not simply "for sin." Again, the choice does not matter much for my purpose here, since if Jesus were offered for sin, he is still a sacrifice. See appendix 3.

warned about with increasing urgency from the beginning of his ministry fell on the Jerusalem temple.[44] That epochal catastrophe occurred because the Holy City had become the harlot city; the city that had shed the blood of prophets (Mt 23) fell because she became drunk on the blood of the saints (Rev 17–18).[45] Followers of Jesus, filled with the Spirit and walking in the Spirit within a world of flesh, ended as Jesus did, dying a martyr's death. Faced with threats of death, they did not cower; they did not recoil or take vengeance, but marched to death in the power of the Spirit. As Jesus' death was followed by an earthquake that rent the temple veil, so the death of the martyrs produced a Roman earthquake that ended with the permanent fall of Jerusalem's temple. Jesus was the offering; on that offering the martyrs laid down their lives as firstfruits to God, so that their sacrifices filled up what was lacking in the sufferings of Christ (Col 1:24). Jesus died and rose to become the cornerstone of a new holy house, but prophets and apostles constituted the rest of the foundation (Eph 2:20). Jesus taught his disciples that the Old Testament was a typological account of Christ's sufferings and glory, *and* of the apostles' preaching of repentance and forgiveness to the nations (Lk 24:46-47). The first martyrs were not only *objects* and beneficiaries of Christ's atoning work; *because* they are beneficiaries, in Christ and by His Spirit, they are *subjects* of the actions by which God fulfills his promises and saves his creation.

We are tempted to flinch at the last moment. We are tempted to retreat from the ambiguities of history into an atonement theory whose mechanism works regardless of whether Torah had ever been given, one that does not depend on the events of Jesus' life or the faithful witness of the founding, firstfruits generation. We are tempted to conclude that Jesus' death and resurrection might effect salvation *without the church*, with all its failures and imperfections, obvious already to Peter, Paul, James and John. We are tempted to think we can have an atonement that needs no sacraments or an

---

[44]Ullucci is correct about this, though I do not believe it was a historical accident. I agree rather with the church fathers cited by Ullucci who argued that the elimination of the temple had been the plan all along. See Ullucci, *Christian Rejection*, 133-36. Hengel makes the arresting suggestion that the common root of the atonement tradition was the break with the temple, and that atonement theology was brought in to justify it (Hengel, *Atonement*, 47). I do not think that is accurate, but it highlights in a startling fashion how closely tied atonement theology was to the Christian formation of an alternative temple system in their communities.

[45]I will make a full case that the harlot city is Jerusalem in my commentary on Revelation, which will be published, *Deo volente*, in 2016.

atonement accomplished by the Son without the Spirit. We misconstrue Paul's claim to know nothing but Christ crucified and conclude that *everything* happened, the whole work of atonement occurred, during those three hours of suffering. And then we have to ponder how three hours of suffering can be adequate payment for an eternity in hell, and speculate on the infinite value of Christ's human life. Important truths have emerged from those ponderings and speculations, but detached from the history of Israel that climaxes with Jesus they can only leave us bewildered.

If we stick relentlessly, madly to the Christian confession that God saves humanity *within history*, those questions retreat to the background. What comes to the foreground is the fact that Jesus died to form a people, the church, his body and bride. He died to preserve his new temple movement; his death was a day of atonement where he bore the liabilities and punishments of Israel to give them a new past and a new future. His own sacrifice was part of his ordination, and he rose again to preside as an immortal high priest qualified not by flesh but by the power of indestructible resurrection life (see Eph 2:11-22; Heb 7:1-28). Jesus brought forgiveness because his death founded a forgiven people-temple where forgiveness continues to be freely offered: a temple where the single bath of baptism purifies and consecrates; where confession of sins *without* sacrifice cleanses from all unrighteousness; where the word of absolution is spoken with all the authority of the Son of God; where Jews and Gentiles, male and female, slave and free are invited to share a common sacrificial meal, eating Jesus' body and drinking his blood for the remission of sins. Salvation breaks into the world because God removes the veil, takes his gifts of word, bread and rod out of the treasure chest of the ark and hands them over to everyone everywhere who will receive them. Forgiveness comes to historical reality because by his death and resurrection Jesus establishes these simpler, fewer and above all more *effective* rites to unite us to God and one another.

By AD 70 Jesus had dealt a decisive blow to flesh and dismantled stoicheic order to produce a new Israel and a new creation. He had done it by living and teaching a redemptive justice by the Spirit; by dying a death that exposed and disempowered flesh, a death that saved his disciples from death to live and work another day; by being raised to the life of the Spirit and by pouring out that Spirit into the flesh of his disciples; by calling his disciples to take up their own crosses to follow him into martyrdom, a martyrdom that would complete the demolition of the scaffolding of *stoicheia* that Jesus had begun. When the scaffolding comes down, the human temple of God shines with the light of new creation. We have a historically plausible account of the atonement when we see it unfolding over the generation between the cross and the end of the Jewish temple system. Then we can see concretely how Jesus' death, resurrection, ascension and gathering of disciples through the Spirit altered the fundamental physics of social and religious life.

At the end of it all the temple was in ruins and all its elements melted and scattered like ash, the physics of socioreligious life had been transformed, and the disciples of Jesus, and also the world, had entered a new epoch of history. They had entered the era opened by Jesus, the Christian era, populated by humans of a new *physis*, neither Jew nor Greek but made Christians by the Spirit of Christ.

This entire sequence is the sacrifice of Jesus the eternal Son, and it is this *entire sequence* that saves the world.

A Concluding Travelogue

I am back in Jerusalem. I had thought that a return to my home country and the Holy City would bring peace, but I am not at peace. I am more agitated than ever.

In Egypt I found worshipers of the dead. In Babylon there were great temples to idols. In Greece they offer burnt offerings to demons on every street corner and dance lewd dances in their temples. I was sickened wherever I went, and I had hoped Jerusalem would make me well.

It has not. I visited the temple, and I have gathered with the men at the synagogue. But all they can talk about is this new sect. It is not the way of the Pharisees, they say, nor of the Essenes. There are followers of a Jesus, from Galilee of all places, and this Jesus has taught them to curse the temple and break all the commandments of Moses. I have heard that they commit abominable incest when they meet, and that they drink blood and commit all other detestable things. They say they can offer their sacrifices anywhere, and they do not need the temple. They do not wash their hands before meals and do not seem to observe any purity. They eat with Gentiles, and Jews and Gentiles join together as one people, as if Jews and Gentiles were not as different as heaven and earth. Just a few weeks ago, at Pentecost, they claimed the Spirit of God fell on them and gave them power to speak with foreign tongues. Thousands listened to them, from every corner of the world. Thousands more became their followers.

Egypt is half in love with death, half in terror. Babylonians boast, and Greeks worship their flesh. But at least in all those places they know how to honor their gods. They are false gods, but they know how to worship them. They know that sacred temples are inviolable, that only the pure can draw near to God, that we need priests to minister for us before him. They know that they need to offer gifts and sacrifices to make God favorable. They worship idols, but they do not insult their idols.

The spirit of these Nazarenes is a spirit of disorder. They are transgressors. They commit sacrilege and are filled with uncleanness. It grows, this horrible sect. They tear everything apart. They hate everything that keeps the world together. Things fall apart, and the center cannot hold. Chaos is out in the world.

I must do what I can to stop it.

There are shouts and the sound of a crowd outside. Someone rushed in to say that one of the Jesus followers is speaking to the Jews, and they are ready to kill him. I must go. Here is my chance to serve the God of Israel. I must be Phinehas.

—Saul of Tarsus

PART THREE

JUSTIFICATION

eight

JUSTIFIED BY THE FAITH OF JESUS

✝

In the cross of Jesus, God enacts a decisive judgment against flesh, sin and death. In the resurrection of Jesus, God vindicates his Son and the way of his Son. A temple is destroyed on the cross; a new temple, and a new temple system, is erected on the third day.

Paul's term for this act of judgment and vindication is *justification*.

To justify is to declare a verdict, but it is not merely a verbal act. In justifying, God *enacts* a judgment *against* evil and *in favor of* justice. God the Judge condemns by destroying the guilty and justifies by delivering the righteous. Justification takes the form of death and resurrection. Specifically, justification describes the judgment passed in the death and resurrection of *Jesus*. Justification in the death and resurrection of Jesus is the justification of God, his assertion of his rights over creation and the proof that he will not permit sin and death to have the last say in his world.[1]

Justification describes how God fulfills the prophetic promise to set the world right. In the life, death and resurrection of Jesus, God manifests and establishes justice by overcoming the curses of Eden and Babel. Jesus' obedient death and his justifying resurrection form a new regime that replaces the regime of sin and death inaugurated by Adam, a regime in which we participate by dying with Christ in baptism so that we can live out God's justice in our bodies. By his death and resurrection, Jesus has overcome flesh, and is overcoming flesh, for those joined to him. Because of the justification enacted in Jesus' death and resurrection, fleshly institutions give way to a pneumatic *paideia* and a pneumatic *nomos*. Humans born *ek*

---

[1]See Karl Barth, *Church Dogmatics*, IV/1, *The Doctrine of Reconciliation*, ed. Geoffrey W. Bromiley and T. F. Torrance, trans. Geoffrey W. Bromiley (Edinburgh: T&T Clark, 1956), 562.

tēs sarkos or *ek nomou* receive a new nature as those who have been born *ek tou pneumatos*. Human beings who have been living *kata sarka* are liberated to walk *kata pneuma*. By the justifying verdict of the cross and resurrection, God creates a new world and gives human beings a new *physis*. Twisting though the path may be, the cross and resurrection thus fulfill the original end of humanity, since Adam was from the beginning destined to ascend from flesh to Spirit: if there is a "natural" (*psychikos*) man, there will also eventually be a "spiritual" man (*pneumatikos*, 1 Cor 15:44).[2] *Cur Deus Homo*? Answer: To justify humanity from *ta stoicheia tou kosmou*, because only if humanity is brought out from these childhood restrictions can there be just, mature human societies, and only God can perform this deliverance.

Justification belongs with *redemption, atonement, reconciliation* and *propitiation* in the thesaurus of atonement theology.

DELIVERDICT

Admittedly, this is not how *justification* is normally used in systematic theology, where it refers to something that happens to individual sinners. Nor is it the way that *justification* is normally understood in Pauline studies. Even writers of "new perspective" or "post–new perspective" persuasion typically understand *dikaio-* as part of the *outworking* of the cross in the lives of individuals or the church. I argue instead that it is a way of naming the event of the cross and resurrection.

The account of justification that follows makes two notable adjustments to the standard view of justification, the first having to do with the *meaning* of the term and the second having to do with the *referent*, the real-life event that Paul describes as justification.[3] I argue below that *justify* is, as Protestant theology

---

[2] I agree with Richard Gaffin that this verse implies an eschatological trajectory for Adam (*Resurrection and Redemption: A Study in Paul's Soteriology* [Phillipsburg, NJ: P&R, 1987]). Regardless of sin, he would have been transfigured from soul and flesh to Spirit.

[3] This account of justification (1) is faithful to the Protestant insight that justification is a *forensic* act yet (2) makes good on Protestant claims to be consistent with the catholic tradition by emphasizing the life-transforming, *ontological* effect of that forensic act (see appendix 2 for more detail). Yet this proposal (3) helps resolve the tensions of Protestant soteriology and piety by making justification and sanctification truly inseparable, by consistently working out the decentered anthropology implicit in Protestant soteriology, and by stressing the corporate dimensions of justification and the Christian life. I affirm the classic Protestant slogans of justification—*sola gratia, sola fide, solo Christo*—and on my proposal one can affirm them *more* unashamedly than ever: if justification happens *extra nos* on the cross, then it is surely by grace and not by our works

has insisted, a juridical/legal term referring to the judgment of God in favor of a sinner. In contrast to some standard Protestant soteriologies, though, Paul treats this judgment not as a *mere* verdict of "righteous" that is the *basis* for liberation, but as *itself* an act of deliverance. The verdict of justification *does* change a person's status. A person is righteous before God because Christ shares his righteous standing with those who are united to him. Sinners have the righteous status of Jesus himself by faith, by trusting in Christ and entrusting themselves to the Father, by self-abandonment and loyalty to their Savior. Yet as a judicial act justification transforms a person's life-situation as well as their status. A justified person dies and rises in Christ, and so is delivered from sin, death and the domination of flesh. Justification is, to introduce my neologism, a "deliverdict," a forensic act, a judicial verdict that in its very forensic character is an act of deliverance.[4] It is a favorable judgment *in the form of resurrection.*

---

or a product of the law's operation; justification is the achievement of *the* Faith, Jesus himself—hence *sola fide* and *solo Christo.*

[4]I have introduced this term and concept, and defended it exegetically, in several places. See "Judge Me, O God: Biblical Perspectives on Justification," in *The Federal Vision*, ed. Steve Wilkins and John Barach (Monroe, LA: Athanasius Press, 2014); and "Justification as Verdict and Deliverance: A Biblical Perspective," *Pro Ecclesia* 16, no. 1 (2007): 56-72. The current chapter goes further than these earlier discussions in two respects: First, I am more convinced now that "deliverdict" expresses the characteristic meaning of Paul's *dikai-* terminology; it is not an occasional extension of meaning but part of the standard meaning of the terms. Second, here I link the notion of "deliverdict" to the claim that "justification" is a Pauline term to describe the atonement, not merely to describe the application of the fruit of the atonement to an individual person.

The view that justification is a "deliverdict" is reflected in ecumenical documents such as the "Joint Declaration on the Doctrine of Justification" produced by the Roman Catholic Church and the Lutheran World Federation: "In faith we together hold the conviction that justification is the work of the triune God. . . . By grace alone, in faith in Christ's saving work and not because of any merit on our part, we are accepted by God and receive the Holy Spirit, who renews our hearts while equipping and calling us to good works. . . . When persons come by faith to share in Christ, God no longer imputes to them their sin and through the Holy Spirit effects in them an active love. These two aspects of God's gracious action are not to be separated, for persons are by faith united with Christ, who in his person is our righteousness (1 Cor 1:30): both the forgiveness of sin and the saving presence of God himself" (Lutheran World Federation and Roman Catholic Church, *Joint Declaration on the Doctrine of Justification* [Grand Rapids: Eerdmans, 2000], 15, 18). A similar note is struck in "The Gift of Salvation," a statement produced by the American ecumenical group Evangelicals and Catholics Together, which hints at a transformational view of justification when it acknowledges that the gift of the Spirit is an aspect of justification and speaks of the "transformed life" that "issues from" faith. This document stops short of explicitly calling justification a transforming event: "In justification, God, on the basis of Christ's righteousness alone, declares us to be no longer his rebellious enemies but his forgiven friends, and by virtue of his declaration it is so"; "Faith is not merely intellectual assent but an act of the whole person, involving the mind, the will, and the affections, issuing in a changed life"; "In justification we receive the gift of the Holy Spirit, through whom the love of God is poured forth into our hearts (Romans 5:5)" ("The Gift of Salvation," *First Things*, January 1998,

Second, Paul uses the term not merely, or primarily, to describe what happens to sinners when they are accepted by God but to describe what happened once-for-all in the cross and resurrection of Jesus.[5] To use some

www.firstthings.com/article/1998/01/001-the-gift-of-salvation). For a summary, see Anthony N. S. Lane, *Justification by Faith in Catholic-Protestant Dialogue: An Evangelical Assessment* [London: T&T Clark, 2002], 152-58). See also Bruce L. McCormack, "What's at Stake in Current Debates over Justification? The Crisis of Protestantism in the West," in *Justification: What's at Stake in the Current Debates?*, ed. Mark Husbands and Daniel J. Treier (Downers Grove, IL: IVP Academic, 2004). I have summarized and critically interacted with McCormack's article on my website: "McCormack on Justification," *Leithart.com*, December 22, 2004, www.leithart.com/archives /001042.php. See also Eberhard Jüngel, *Justification: The Heart of the Christian Faith* (Edinburgh: T&T Clark, 2001). Historians of dogma have made similar arguments, especially Finnish scholars of Luther, whose views are superbly summarized in Tuomo Mannermaa, *Christ Present in Faith: Luther's View of Justification* (Minneapolis: Fortress, 2005). Some New Testament scholars have recognized that Paul sometimes uses "justify" to describe an act of liberation. See Elsa Tamez, *The Amnesty of Grace: Justification by Faith from a Latin American Perspective* (Nashville: Abingdon, 1993); more strongly and thoroughly, Douglas Campbell, *The Deliverance of God: An Apocalyptic Rereading of Justification in Paul* (Grand Rapids: Eerdmans, 2009); Campbell, "Reading Paul's Δικαιο-Language," in *Beyond Old and New Perspectives on Paul: Reflections on the Work of Douglas Campbell*, ed. Chris Tilling (Eugene, OR: Cascade, 2014), 196-213. Campbell quite rightly stresses that the distinction of judicial and executive is a modern one, unknown in the ancient world, where kings served both as chief judges and as chief executives. In that political setting, a "judgment" could not be a "mere" verdict. I have offered similar arguments in the essays cited above. See also Thomas Schreiner, *Romans*, Baker Exegetical Commentary on the New Testament (Grand Rapids: Baker, 1998), 399; Schreiner reversed his position on this issue in *Paul, Apostle of God's Glory in Christ* (Downers Grove, IL: IVP Academic, 2006), 192n2. Thanks to Dan Reid for alerting me to the change in Schreiner's views.

[5] This claim runs against much of the tradition, but it is not unprecedented. Barth and Barth's followers have taken justification as a description of God's No and Yes enacted in the cross and resurrection. See, for instance, Barth, *Doctrine of Reconciliation*, 553-65, where Barth argues that in the death and resurrection of Jesus the Son was justified as Lord and God, and that our justification involves reception of the Son and what happened in him. I avoid the universalist implications of Barth's theology of justification by stressing that the delivering verdict, though pronounced over all humanity and creation in the cross and resurrection, is realized in individuals and communities only by baptism and faith. That is to say, I avoid Barth's mistake by integrating justification-as-atonement with ecclesiology. The justifying event of the death and resurrection of Jesus creates a new world and a new epoch, but only those who trust and follow Jesus are fully participant in the Christian era. Michael Gorman, *Inhabiting the Cruciform God: Kenosis, Justification, and Theosis in Paul's Narrative Soteriology* (Grand Rapids: Eerdmans, 2009), 57-79, comes close to grasping the historical once-for-allness of justification, but at the cost of blurring its forensic character. Gorman claims that justification is "more than" forgiveness or acquittal, but includes the restoration of right covenant relations, reconciliation and even theosis. That formulation loses the specific *dik*-character of justification. Gorman's formulations seem to depend on a version of the dualisms of classic Protestantism: if justification is going to affect one's life and person, it must be *more than* a judicial act. It is more Pauline, I argue, to say that God's "judicial" acts are life- and world-transforming acts precisely in being judicial acts. For all the innovative brilliance of N. T. Wright's overall project, which puts justification into the context of God's purpose to restore and fulfill creation, he still defines justification as the advance sign for those who will share in the restored creation rather than as a description of God's act of judging and remaking creation per se (*Paul and the Faithfulness of God* [Minneapolis: Fortress, 2013], 925-66).

common Reformed terms, justification is not merely a matter of *ordo salutis* or application of redemption; it is also, and most fundamentally, an event in the *historia salutis*. "Justification" occurred two thousand years ago. Paul *does* use the term "justify" to describe what happens in the life of a sinful human being who is judged righteous, but this is not the only context in which Paul uses the term, and theologically it is not the most fundamental referent. The limitation of the concept of justification to the application of redemption distorts Paul's theology and confuses the interpretation of particular passages.

When we make these adjustments, we gain a fuller Pauline portrait of atonement, meeting one more of our criteria for a successful atonement theology. But those adjustments need to be defended.

VINDICATED BY THE SPIRIT

A glance at a passage that has played a minor role in debates about justification,[6] Paul's "mystery of godliness" poem in 1 Timothy 3:16, demonstrates the validity of both of these adjustments. Brief and neglected as it is, it is adequate to prove the possibility that (1) justification is a "deliverdict" and (2) justification is an event in the life story of Jesus.

By common confession, great is the mystery of godliness:

> He was revealed in the flesh
> Justified in the Spirit [*edikaiōthē en pneumati*]
> Beheld by angels
> Proclaimed among the nations
> Believed on in the world,
> Taken up in glory.

Though the grammatical antecedent of the clauses in this verse is unclear, the mystery is a catalog of events in the life of Jesus. Christ, or the Son of God, or the "living God" himself is the subject of the initial clause, "revealed in the flesh," and there can be no other moment of that revelation in flesh than the incarnation and life of Jesus. The final clause, stating that he was

---

That leaves Wright's theology and exegesis burdened by some of the same tensions that afflict classic Protestant soteriology, on which see appendixes 1–2.

[6]I learned of the significance of this passage from Richard B. Gaffin Jr. Most of what I have to say in this chapter is an extrapolation from things I learned from Gaffin, though he would not want to take the cab where I want to take it.

"taken up in glory," echoes accounts of the ascension (cf. Acts 1:9).[7] The movement of the mystery is from flesh to glory, a historical sequence from appearance to removal from sight (as emphasized in Acts). The four clauses in between fit within the frame of the first and final clauses: angels witness and announce his resurrection; Jesus is proclaimed to a large crowd of Jews and proselytes at Pentecost, and before we get very far in the book of Acts, the "world" of Gentiles is turning in faith to the risen Christ. However we decide the grammatical question of the antecedent, the passage is about Jesus and what happened to him.

The second clause, that Jesus (or Christ, or the Son, or God) was justified in (or "by") the Spirit, must take place within that frame as well. Before we specify what event Paul refers to by this phrase, we should pause to recognize that he is referring to an *event* in the history of Jesus, one recorded in the Gospels or, at the least, in the book of Acts. Here at least Paul uses the verb *dikaioō* not to refer to what happens to sinners when they believe in Jesus or to God's declaration that one is part of the Christian family. It refers instead to some historical event in the life story of Jesus. Whatever event it is, Paul believes that something that can be called "justification" happened between Christ's "revelation in the flesh" and his being "taken up in glory." That conclusion does not depend on specifying what event Paul is talking about. Even without going further, this raises the possibility that, for Paul, justification is *historia-salutis* language, not merely *ordo-salutis* language. Taking "justify" in the forensic sense of "favorable verdict," we can say that at some point between Jesus' appearance and his disappearance, someone, presumably God, rendered a favorable verdict on his behalf through the agency of the Spirit. Justification is at the heart of the mystery of godliness, but, perhaps surprisingly, the justification at the heart of the mystery of godliness is the justification *of Jesus*.[8]

What event is it?[9] It has to be an event that occurred between the incarnation and the ascension, an event that involved the work of the Spirit, and

---

[7]In both Acts 1:9 and 1 Tim 3:16, the verb "take up" is a compound of *lambanō*, *hypolambanō* in Acts and *analambanō* in 1 Timothy.

[8]In this sense, we can say that justification by faith *is* the gospel, since the gospel is a narrative of the story of Jesus. Because he defines justification exclusively as *ordo salutis*, Wright denies that justification is the gospel (*Pauline Perspectives: Essays on Paul 1978–2013* [Minneapolis: Fortress, 2013], 89).

[9]A number of options have been proposed, mainly by selecting among the prominent Spirit events in the gospel story: Jesus' baptism, the transfiguration, his triumph over Satan in the temptations. *in resurrection?*

an event that is justly described as a judicial act, an act of vindication or justification. The only event that fulfills all of these criteria is the resurrection of Jesus.[10] Jesus died in the flesh and rose before his ascension, and his "quickening" came by the Spirit (cf. 1 Pet 3:18). Though the resurrection is not explicitly characterized as a judicial act in the Gospels themselves, it does come at the conclusion of long narratives of (multiple) trials and a judicial execution, and that makes it plausible to see the resurrection as the Father's vindication of the Son who had been condemned by Jews and Romans. Carl Schmitt, Giorgio Agamben and Walter Benjamin argued that authority ultimately rests on the state of exception, the ability to act sovereignly, embodied in the power to kill. After state and religious authorities had exerted their most extreme authority against Jesus, after they had done *all* that they could do—which is to kill—the Father displays his strange judicial authority, reversing the verdicts of Jew and Gentile by raising Jesus from the dead. Resurrection is the state of divine exception that establishes his authority as Lord of the living and the dead.

Interpreting "justified in the Spirit" as a reference to Jesus' resurrection fits neatly with claims that Paul makes elsewhere about the resurrection of Jesus. If Jesus is dead, we are still in sin (1 Cor 15:17). Unless the resurrection follows the death of the Messiah, there is no remission or forgiveness, no deliverance from the domination of sin, no justification of sinners. As we will see more fully below, Paul links resurrection directly with justification in Romans 4:25: Jesus was "raised for our justification."[11]

---

[10]This is the view of Matthew Henry: "Whereas he was reproached as a sinner, and put to death as a malefactor, he was raised again by the Spirit, and so was justified from all the calumnies with which he was loaded" (*Commentary on 1 Timothy*, www.blueletterbible.org/Comm /mhc/1Ti/1Ti_003.cfm?a=1122016. Thomas Goodwin agrees that "Christ himself was justified, and that at his resurrection" (*Christ Set Forth*, www.blueletterbible.org/Comm/goodwin_thomas /ChristSetForth/ChristSetForth/CSF_305.cfm?a=1122016). Calvin thinks that the phrase has a broader reference to various manifestations of power but acknowledges, based on Rom 1:3, that one such manifestation is the resurrection (see *Calvin's Commentary on the Bible*, www.study light.org/commentaries/cal/view.cgi?bk=53&ch=3).

[11]Markus Barth suggests that the resurrection justifies because the victim reappears in court and proves that the murder has itself been reversed. That is quite vivid, but the relationship between resurrection and justification is much tighter if we recognize that the resurrection is Jesus' own justification, the Father's deliverdict pronounced in his dead Son. See Markus Barth, *Acquittal by Resurrection* (New York: Holt, Rinehart and Winston, 1964), 72-84. See Karl Barth, *Doctrine of Reconciliation*, 304-22. John Henry Newman also emphasized the significance of the resurrection for justification in his *Lectures on the Doctrine of Justification* (1874; repr., Eugene, OR: Wipf & Stock, 2001), 202-22.

Clearly, the resurrection is no mere verdict. The resurrection is a deliverance, a rescue from death for the dead Jesus. It is his transfer from the mortal flesh in which he appeared to the realm of the Spirit in which he now and ever lives, for he was sown flesh and raised in a spiritual body (1 Cor 15). Justification in this case *must* take the form of resurrection if it is to be a favorable verdict at all. If God pronounced Jesus "righteous" but left him in the grave, one could hardly speak of vindication or justification. If God reversed the verdict but did not reverse the sentence, the reversal of the verdict is impotent, pointless, a mockery of the innocent victim. If the resurrection is "justification," then resurrection is both a life-giving and a *judicial* act.[12] And if Paul can describe the resurrection as a justification, then it seems plausible to think he might be able to reverse that identification and see "justification" as a resurrection.[13] And if Jesus' justification takes the form of resurrection, then perhaps resurrection simply *is* the form of justification. The verdict of "justified," *whenever* it occurs, is a judgment of life from the dead.[14] Justification fulfills Yahweh's first global judgment, the flood, sweeping away in order to renew.

First Timothy 3:16 thus establishes the plausibility of both of my claims about justification: Justification is an event of redemptive history, a *once-for-all event* in the life of Jesus. If it also describes an event in my life history, it is because my life is somehow conformed to that of Jesus. Justification is not a bare verbal declaration about status. Justification is a deliverance from

---

[12]Cf. Wright, *Paul*, 943, 948-49, on the judicial character of resurrection. He does not, however, fully reckon with the consequences of this point. Referring to Gorman, he argues that we must "sharply distinguish" justification from personal renewal or theosis (ibid., 955) and insists that justification is a "divine declaration" rather than an act that changes the moral character of the person (ibid., 957). These formulations evidently share the status/person dualism that I critique in appendix 2.

[13]One might avoid this conclusion by suggesting that in using *dikaioō*, Paul is highlighting only *one* aspect of the resurrection, the judicial one, rather than claiming that the resurrection is itself the verdict of vindication. Though the resurrection is described in many ways in the New Testament, that seems to be splitting one too many hairs to protect a preconceived definition of "justification."

[14]This is implicit in even the strictest Protestant understanding of forensic justification. As Augustine said, human beings are justly delivered over to the power of sin because of their sins. In justification, God reverses the verdict and finds us not guilty, righteous in his court. It would be profoundly unjust if God then left those legally innocent human beings in the slavery that was the result of their guilt. Once the guilty verdict is reversed, the sentence of slavery and death must be reversed. Sometimes the deliverative element of justification comes out explicitly in traditional Protestant theology. When this point remains implicit and more or less ignored, Pauline theology is distorted.

death, a transition from flesh to Spirit, a release from bondage. Justification is not simply the basis or ground for forgiveness or for a new life.[15] The verdict takes the *form* of resurrection.

Elsewhere in Paul, justification is a deliverdict. In Romans, God's deliverdict takes on various dimensions. The justifying verdict of Jesus' resurrection is preceded by a condemnation of sin at the cross, a condemnation that proves God to be just. Justification comes by the faithful work of Christ, as God presents him as a public *hilastērion* at the cross (Rom 3:21-31). Abraham trusts the God who can raise the dead to give him the promised seed and land, and so Abraham becomes the father of all who trust the God who raised Jesus, whether Jews or Gentiles (Rom 4:1-25). Jesus' faithful obedience as Last Adam brings a regime change, ending the reign of sin and death and inaugurating the reign in life of those who receive God's justice (Rom 5:17). Paul calls this new situation, created by the obedience of Jesus, "justification," and it applies to everyone (Rom 5:16, 18). One man has been delivered fully from flesh, sin and death, and because that one man is the Last Man (*eschatos Adam*), justification has happened to the world. Justification happens to the world also because that Last Adam forms a new humanity that has been justified from sin by baptism into Jesus' death (Rom 6:7) so they can share already in the resurrection of the body, offering the members of their bodies as instruments of God's justice (Rom 6:12-23). Jesus' death also ends the old marriage covenant, freeing those who are in flesh

---

[15]Wright does not go far enough when he says that the cross is a prior event that "enables" justification (*Paul*, 951; cf. *Perspectives*, 310-11). He does not emphasize sufficiently the fact that Jesus *himself* is justified, and thus does not fully appreciate the fact that justification is a description of the once-for-all event of Jesus' death and resurrection. Wright resists this emphasis because he fears that if justification is a declaration made in the death and resurrection of Jesus and enjoyed by faith, then we are on our way to universalism: everyone is already justified, but many do not know it yet. Despite the slanders that are regularly hurled in his direction, Wright is quite traditionally Reformed in proposing instead that "regeneration" must precede justification (*Paul*, 954). It is not at all clear, however, that the consequences of saying that justification occurs in Jesus are quite so dire. On the one hand, Paul himself can sound quite universalist ("through one act of righteousness there resulted justification of life to all men," Rom 5:18 NASB). Yet Paul equally emphasizes that only those who are in Christ and trust him are justified from sin to walk in newness of life. To capture both, we have to say that justification occurs in the cross and resurrection in distinct senses: On the one hand, Jesus' death and resurrection affect the world *in general*, *all* humanity; but there is a specific, saving effect in those who are incorporated into Christ. Though stressing the subjective genitive in the phrase "faith of Christ," Gorman too sees justification as the application of the *non*justifying event of the cross and resurrection. Gorman helpfully argues that Jesus' death is a means, manner and mode of justification (*Inhabiting*, 59). He fails to see that it is all those things because it *is* justification.

from the bondage of Torah and binding them in a new marriage covenant with a risen Husband (Rom 7:1-6). Flesh had proved too powerful for Torah and turned it into an instrument of death (Rom 7:7-25), but at the same time Torah isolated flesh as the culprit so God could pass his verdict against sinful flesh in the sin offering of Jesus (Rom 8:1-4). God in Christ did what Torah could not do, and by completing his war against flesh God creates a new humanity of the Spirit, a people that enacts the justice of Torah.

In a broad sense, "justification" is a twofold movement, a No followed by a Yes, condemnation that yields to vindication. In a narrower sense, "justification" is the liberating verdict that takes the form of resurrection. It happens to Jesus in his death and resurrection: he is the first justified man, the only man justified because of his obedience. Every other deliverdict depends entirely on his vindication in the Spirit. Justification happens to the whole human race as God condemns sinful flesh and enables humans in flesh to live, as Jesus did, by the Spirit. Sin, death, flesh used to reign over the human race, but now there is a new regime of the Spirit. It happens to the church, and it happens to individuals in the church as they are justified from sin in baptism and raised to live lives of justice, as they keep *nomos* by living according to the *nomos* of the Spirit.[16]

With this in the background, we turn to a consideration of justification in Paul's letter to the Galatians.[17]

JUSTIFIED TO LIFE BY FAITH

According to Galatians, the good news is that the cross brings an end to an old era and old order, and introduces a new, Christian era.[18] It is an apocalyptic gospel, a message of "freedom" just because it is a message of justification.

---

[16]Justification as described here is *solo Christo*: justification happens in the interaction between Jesus and his Father, with the Spirit who raises Jesus. Justification enters *our* experience because of our union with Christ, the Justified Man. Justification is *sola gratia*: fundamentally, justification is *entirely extra nos*, and we are included in that liberating event not by works but by the grace of baptismal union with the Justified One. Justification is *sola fide*: justification is the Father's Yes to Jesus' *pistis*, his obedience of faith even to death on a cross. It is by the faith of Jesus Christ. As justification comes from faith, it is received by faith, as sinners hear and believe and so receive the Spirit of righteousness that liberates from flesh.

[17]The following discussion of Galatians refers occasionally to Romans. A fuller treatment of Romans would have slowed down the argument, so that has been shuttled off to appendix 3.

[18]John M. G. Barclay, *Obeying the Truth: Paul's Ethics in Galatians* (Minneapolis: Fortress, 1988), 206, citing Gal 2:19-20; 5:11; 6:14-15. Barclay's claim that the cross is a "symbol" of this shift is somewhat weak unless we acknowledge that it is an *effective* sign.

Freedom from what?

Paul's initial reference to justification occurs in his rebuke to Peter in Galatians 2:16. The verse is a dense cluster of the disputed phrases that we have begun to sort through in previous chapters: *dikaioō, pistis Christou, erga nomou.* We take our previously established definitions as given: "justify" as deliverdict, the faith of Christ as Christ's own faith, the works of the law as the condemnation and provocation catalyzed when Torah is mixed with flesh. We can now see that this makes very good sense of Paul's statement in Galatians 2.

The verse is arranged in a neat chiasm:

A Knowing that a man does not receive the delivering verdict by what the law does

    B but through the faithfulness of Jesus Christ

        C we have believed in Christ Jesus

    B′ so that we may receive the delivering verdict by the faithfulness of Christ

A′ and not by what the law does, since by what the law does no flesh shall receive the delivering verdict.

This structure indicates that the *pistis Christou* in the B and B′ sections is distinct from the act of faith by Paul and other believers, designated by the verb *episteusamen* (C). Paul does *not* say the same thing three times. He does not say, "We are justified by believing in Jesus, so we have believed in Jesus, so we can be justified by believing in Jesus." He repeats himself, but between the two statements about the faith of Christ he describes the appropriate human *response* to the faithful work of Jesus.[19] His rolling rebuke means this: "We are justified by the faithful work of Jesus, so we have trusted Christ Jesus, in order to be justified by his faithfulness."

The setup in Galatians 2:15 is crucial. Paul states a principle that he expects those who are "natural" (*physei*) Jews to agree with. Jews in general know that humankind is not justified by what the Torah achieves. He is speaking of Christian Jews, since he goes on to say, as something that Jews

---

[19]Though "faith" and "believe" have distinct referents, the repetition of different words built from the root *pist-* creates a complex conceptual pattern that Paul deploys again and again, especially in Romans and Galatians. If the justice of God is established by the *pistis* of Christ, then human beings share in that faithful work and in the spread of God's justice in a way that matches the work of Jesus, that is, by *pistis.* It might be too much to say that Paul's theology of justification turns on a pun, but it would not be altogether wrong.

by nature also know, that even Jews are justified by the faith of Jesus Christ. The word order suggests that "of works of law" (*ex ergōn nomou*) modifies "man" rather than "justify." It describes persons rather than an ineffective method of justification. Those who are "of the works of Torah" are those whose "nature" has been molded by circumcision, purity, temple, sacrifice and the moral demands of the law. Being "of Torah" is a specific way of living *kata sarka*. Further still, *ean mē* is best understood as concessive, meaning "except."[20] Galatians 2:15-16b may thus be paraphrased, "We Jews by nature . . . know that justification does not happen to human beings who are the product of the law's working except through the faith of Jesus Christ." Even Christian Jews, in other words, recognize that those who are "of law," who have their origin in the culture of Torah, still need to be "justified." And they recognize that the law does not render the liberating, justifying verdict that they need and desire. Torah *cannot* accomplish this, because Torah is designed for the condition of humanity during its exile from Eden and in its post-Babelic condition of division, and because Torah was co-opted by flesh. Natural Jews too need to be justified by the faithful Jesus, who loved us and gave himself up for us.

This means that in Galatians 2 *dikaioō* has a *liberative* connotation, specifically referring to liberation from Torah. As a Jew, Peter has been observing the rules of purity that are implied and imposed by circumcision. Beyond the strict requirement of Torah, he has been observing the Jewish custom of refraining from table fellowship with Gentiles.[21] Paul has to remind Peter of the good news of justification, the fact that Jesus died to justify Jews as well as Gentiles. The faithful work of Christ that justifies heals the post-Babel tears within the human race. As we have seen, the law cannot break the oppositions and obstacles of Babel because the law *assumes* the obstacles and oppositions of Babel *and* because Torah had been overtaken by flesh. Something new has happened in Jesus, though: the faith of Jesus breaks the barriers, condemning flesh, condemning the law as manipulated by flesh and thereby releasing Jews from the old covenant, and justifying

---

[20]This translation is indebted to Ardel Caneday, "The Faithfulness of Jesus Christ as a Theme in Paul's Theology in Galatians," in *The Faith of Jesus Christ: Exegetical, Biblical, and Theological Studies*, ed. Preston Sprinkle and Michael Bird (Grand Rapids: Baker Academic, 2010), 209-22.

[21]If that is not evident in Gal 2, it is in Acts 10. For all the difficulties of reading Acts and the Pauline epistles together, I remain convinced that they are harmonious. I have argued that this restriction is a distortion of Torah's intention, an example of the flesh's co-option of Torah to reinforce rather than overcome Babel's separations.

them by resurrection into a new covenant, a new order of worship and life. Paul reminds Peter that Jesus achieved a deliverdict in the cross and resurrection: he has liberated the world from the old age by his faithful death and his justifying resurrection.

Galatians 2:16 thus provides the background for Paul's autobiographical declaration in Galatians 2:20-21, where Paul describes the faith of Jesus: he "loved me and delivered himself up for me."[22] The fact that Jesus gave himself and "justified" Paul from the law means that Paul has a new self. Saul, the old Paul, died, joined to the cross of Jesus, crucified with Christ. Paul's death is specifically a death to Torah. He is *justified* from the law and from the law's deadly workings by participation in the faithful death of Jesus.[23] Paul says both that he "died to the law" and that he himself died. Saul's identity is outside himself, determined by his fleshly ancestry, his fleshly accomplishments, his circumcision in flesh, his most Hebrew Hebraicness. If he dies to Torah, he has no self left, since he is one of those who is *physei* a Jew. Saul's death to Torah occurs as he participates in the death of Jesus, as his flesh and fleshly accomplishments are condemned by the cross.[24]

---

[22]J. Louis Martyn (*Galatians*, Anchor Bible [New York: Doubleday, 1997], 271) points out how the parallel of Gal 2:16 and Gal 2:21 demonstrates that the subjective genitive is correct. Gal 2:16 begins with a denial that one is justified by *ta erga nomou*, and contrasts this with justification through the *pistis Christou*. Gal 2:21 makes the same contrast between righteousness *dia nomou*, but sets this in opposition to Christ's death.

[23]This is the point of Paul's marital allegory at the beginning of Rom 7. A woman is freed from the bond of the law of marriage by the death of her husband and free to marry another (Rom 7:2-3). The bride in the analogy is "you, the brethren" who died to the law through the body of Christ in order that they might be joined to Jesus who was raised from the dead. The "body of Christ" through which they have died might be a reference to the individual body of Jesus or to the corporate body of the church, which operates beyond the law, or, most plausibly, to both. Life in the flesh is linked with life under Torah, which provokes the passions of the flesh, and by the death of the man, the death of Adam, we are released from the law. We may ask how and when we died to the law, and the best contextual answer is that we died to the law when we died to the flesh, Adam, sin and death—that is, when we were "justified" from sin by participating in the death of Jesus. Justification is not mentioned at the beginning of Rom 7, but the treatment of release from the law is parallel to Paul's description in Rom 6. In baptismal union with the crucifixion of Jesus, the "body of sin is rendered inoperative" (*katargēthē*, Rom 6:6); just so, in the death of the husband the wife is liberated from the covenant of marriage that bound her—the law is "rendered inoperative" (Rom 7:6; *nyni de katērgēthēmen apo tou nomou*). On this verb and its use in these contexts, see Giorgio Agamben, *The Time that Remains: A Commentary on the Letter to the Romans*, trans. Patricia Dailey (Stanford: Stanford University Press, 2005), 97-98. In the death and resurrection of Jesus, he is "*justified* from Torah," and so are we when we die with him in baptism.

[24]This may explain, in concrete terms, how Paul died to the law *dia nomou*. Jesus was put to death by the Torah guardians, who used Torah to condemn him. They obviously did not use Torah properly, since the Torah could not be properly used to condemn the Word who gave Torah.

Paul, however, lives on after his own death, and his continuing life is radically ecstatic, ectopic. He comes to life with a new *physis*, no longer Jewish. He still lives in flesh—mortal, vulnerable, prone to defend himself violently; he remains the heir of all his fleshly inheritance as a Jew. But he does not regard himself, measure himself or judge himself by these fleshly standards and achievements. His self is outside himself, his life the life of another living in him. "I no longer live, but Christ lives in me." Insofar as Paul can talk about his own life, he has to say that he lives by faith in the Son of God: *ho de nyn zō en sarki, en pistei zō tē tou huiou tou theou*. Is this life in the flesh a life lived out of Paul's trust in the Son of God, who loved Paul and gave himself for Paul? Or is this life in the flesh a life lived out by the faithful Son of God *through* Paul's flesh? That it is difficult to decide is no accident. It is supposed to be difficult, even impossible, to decide. Paul lives a life in the flesh, but that life is no longer his own. Whatever life Paul lives, it is Christ's life lived out in Paul. And that life of Christ lived out in Paul is Christ's own faithfulness unto death recapitulated in the life story of the apostle, and life fulfilled in the life of the Spirit not the flesh. Justification happened in the cross and resurrection. In the apostle's own experience, justification is a deliverdict by which Saul is liberated from the law, accepted by God and incorporated into the life of Jesus the Son, so as to become Paul.

The condemnation of Jesus, though, exposes the weakness of Torah, shows that it is powerless to deliver from fleshly manipulation. Jesus dies through the fleshly misapplication of Torah, and insofar as Paul is crucified with Christ, he also died by the law.

nine

JUSTIFIED FROM THE ELEMENTS

✝

Paul recounts his rebuke of Peter in Galatians 2. Galatians 3 begins with another rebuke, this time to the Galatians, who have been acting like Peter. As with Peter, Paul's rebuke includes a reminder of their initial experience as disciples of Jesus.[1] The Galatians began by the Spirit, inaugurated into the culture of the Spirit by hearing and believing the gospel, but they have been bewitched into seeking maturity (*epiteleisthe*) by Torah, which is to say, by flesh. This is absurd, since Torah is designed for the *immature*. The Spirit rather than the law is the means to attain maturity, full sonship. Only the culture of the Spirit is suitable for grown-ups.

Paul phrases his question ("Did you receive the Spirit *ex ergōn nomou* or by hearing of faith [*ex akoēs pisteōs*]?" Gal 3:2) to imply a negative answer: The Spirit does *not* come by the "works of the law." The Spirit, like the Son, is sent forth in the fullness of time to redeem those who are under the law and to bring them into sonship (Gal 4:4-6). The Spirit comes along with the Son who redeems those who are under the law to bring them from the slavery of their minority, their "immaturity," into full sonship. Paul's denial that the Spirit comes from the works of the law is not primarily a denial that the Spirit is a reward for meritorious obedience. It is rather a denial that the Spirit comes through the mechanisms of Torah, under the conditions of the

---

[1] At the time of Paul's first visit to them, Christ was "publicly portrayed" before their eyes. Though often taken as a reference to the vivid rhetoric of Paul's preaching, it is best to see it instead as a description of Paul's own condition. He mentions in Gal 4:13 that he visited them in the weakness of his flesh, and Paul considers that significant. How could an apostle who was weak in flesh proclaim a gospel that encouraged confidence in flesh? Paul's sickness made his preaching Christoform and cruciform, as did the *stigmata* that he displayed before them, the scars of his apostolic commission.

operation of Torah. The Spirit does not spring up from what the law accomplishes. On the contrary, the Spirit comes from God "apocalyptically" to deliver those who have been in bondage to a law whose intentions they are powerless to fulfill. The Spirit comes to demolish Torah and to set up a new *nomos* where the requirements of Torah are actually fulfilled (cf. Rom 8:1-4). The Galatians received the Spirit, and should continue to seek the Spirit, by "hearing of faith." The Spirit broke into the experience of the Galatians when they heard the message about the Faithful One, the proclamation of the faithful work of Christ. They believed that message, and when they did, the Spirit was unleashed and immature slaves were delivered from their bondage and began the progress toward maturity. That is something the law did not and, as Paul will tell us, *could* not accomplish.

Flesh and Torah are, as we have seen in previous chapters, mutually defining (see Rom 7:1-6). Torah was given to human beings in a "fleshly" condition, and it accommodated to that condition. Subjection to Torah was perfectly legitimate—good and right and holy—for people who were in the flesh. Paul's rebuke implies that the Galatians who have already received the Spirit reverted to the flesh when they subjected themselves again to the Torah. They had been redeemed from flesh, like Israel coming from Egypt, but some have now returned to Egypt. Those who died to the law go back to live under the law, returning to the system that killed them in the first place. By Paul's lights, they *cannot* remain in the Spirit when they return to Torah. Reverting to fleshly *institutions*, they revert to *flesh*. Reversion to Torah suppresses the Spirit and undoes what Christ accomplished in his death. This logic shows, as I argued in chapter two, that Paul does not set "institutional" arrangements in opposition to "nature." That which is born of flesh is naturally flesh, and being "born" of *stoicheia* is being born of flesh. Humans whose lives are shaped by the elementary things cultivate a fleshly nature, even if they were once born by the Spirit into a new creation beyond *stoicheia*.

This is the apostasy of Galatianism. Paul indicates that it is possible to *leave* the Christian era, to reerect the boundaries and divisions of Torah, to leave Eden after being readmitted and to reestablish the dividing walls between nations that Jesus broke down. The world entered the Christian era by the justifying act of God in the death and resurrection of Jesus, but it is possible to renounce and leave it. That is insanity: if "justification to all men" describes the world epoch after the cross (see Rom 5:16, 18), to return to slavery is to leave reality behind. Outside the Christian era, outside the Spirit, there is nothing but death and the cursed life of the flesh. Nowhere is a grim place to be, but it is possible to go there. It is possible to die to Torah and then revert to life under Torah. It is possible to die to death, to be justified from Torah by the faith of Christ and then choose to return to the grave.

THE SPIRIT OF JUSTIFICATION

What Paul has to say about God's justice and how justification realizes that justice is intertwined with what he has to say about flesh and the Spirit. At the end of Galatians 2, he raises the question of whether *dikaiosynē* can come through Torah. If so, there was no need for Jesus to die. If Torah, or any other *nomos* other than the *nomos* of Christ and the Spirit, were adequate to establish the justice of God, the death of Jesus would not have been necessary as the means for bringing righteousness. In Galatians 3:6, he is right back talking about righteousness, citing Abraham's faith by which he was reckoned righteous. His discussion of reception of the Spirit by works of the law or by the message of the Faith, his charge that the Galatians began in the Spirit but are now trying, impossibly, to advance by flesh, is still part of a discussion of righteousness. The gift of the Spirit is crucial to the arrival of righteousness, the Spirit being the Spirit of righteousness. God's justice is established only by the Spirit. The question, how can there be justice? is identical to the question, How can humanity receive and be conformed to the Spirit? If justification comes by the faith of Jesus, then Jesus must be the source of the gift of the Spirit.

Paul supports his claim about the Spirit coming by faith with a quotation from Genesis 15:6: "Abraham believed God, and it was reckoned to him as righteousness" (NASB). Paul connects the citation to the previous question with an "even so" (*kathōs*). Neither the quotation from Genesis, nor Genesis 15, nor indeed the Abrahamic narrative as a whole, mentions the Spirit.[2]

---

[2]Though the Spirit is not mentioned in the Abrahamic narrative, Paul's pneumatological reading makes sense in the larger biblical context. Abraham is called from Ur in the aftermath of the fall of the postdiluvian world at Babel (Gen 11). That rebellion leads to a fragmenting of the nations, a splintering of humanity linguistically and religiously, both in lip and by tongue. The call of Abraham begins Yahweh's response. Instead of wiping out the nations as he did in the flood, Yahweh determines to bring the nations to himself by working from within. The call of Abraham is an "incarnational" move, an intervention into human flesh designed to redeem humanity. Ultimately, the curse of Babel is reversed by the outpouring of the Spirit at Pentecost, where a miracle of language unites divided nations into one body. So while the Spirit is not mentioned

Paul's argument works only if "Spirit" and "righteousness" are parallel, if not equivalent. The sequence of thought is: You received the Spirit who does acts of power by hearing the message, and *just in the same* way Abraham believed God and was reckoned righteous.[3] To be reckoned righteous is somehow to be an heir of the Spirit.[4] The blessing of Abraham *is* the gift of the Spirit.

There are a variety of ways to unpack this connection.

1. One might take a traditional Protestant view of Galatians 3:6 and reason this way: Abraham believed God's promise; God reckoned him righteous because of his faith (or declared him righteous, and he received the verdict by faith); and because he is reckoned righteous, he is an appropriate vessel of the Spirit. In this understanding, "righteousness" is not equivalent to the Spirit. Righteousness is strictly a status term describing Abraham's standing before God. But the righteous are the ones who become recipients of the Spirit.[5]

---

in the Abrahamic narrative, the Abrahamic promise is only fulfilled when the Spirit is poured out. Post-Pentecost, Paul can know that Pentecost fulfills the promise to Abraham, which is the promise to bring blessing to nations.

[3] As I discuss at length in appendix 3, n21, Paul avoids saying that Abraham was "justified." If we accept Douglas Campbell's interpretation of *logizesthai*, Paul is saying that Yahweh gave Abraham a promissory note to be paid at a future date (*The Deliverance of God: An Apocalyptic Reading of Justification in Paul* [Grand Rapids: Eerdmans, 2009], 730-32). That makes abundant sense in Gal 3: The justice that God credited to Abraham's account was the gift of the Spirit, which was not given to Abraham but unleashed only after the death and resurrection of Jesus had overcome flesh and made Torah unnecessary. What Abraham believed was God's promise that he would issue a deliverdict to the Gentiles by the Spirit (Gal 3:8), and because of his confidence in God's promise, God deposited the Spirit of justice in Abraham's account. As Heb 11 puts it, Abraham lived in faith, looking forward to a promise that was never realized. He died without receiving what was promised, and only "with us" does he come to enjoy the treasure that Yahweh credited to his account long before. The saints of the old covenant are made perfect together with believers in the new covenant (Heb 11:40).

[4] On the Spirit's role in justification generally, see Frank Macchia, *Justified in the Spirit: Creation, Redemption, and the Triune God* (Grand Rapids: Eerdmans, 2010). Note the chiastic structure of Gal 3:1-14:

    A Spirit comes through the message of faith (Gal 3:1-5)

        B Abraham believed God (Gal 3:6-9)

            C Those who are of law are cursed by law (Gal 3:10)

                D Law vs. faith (Gal 3:11-12)

            C′ Jesus becomes curse to remove curse (Gal 3:13)

        B′ So that the blessing of Abraham can come to Gentiles (Gal 3:14a)

    A′ So that we might receive the Spirit through faith (Gal 3:14b)

[5] This is the position defended by Chee-Chiew Lee, *The Blessing of Abraham, the Spirit, and Justification in Galatians: Their Relationship and Significance for Understanding Paul's Theology* (Eugene, OR: Pickwick, 2013).

2. One might take a "Finnish Lutheran" approach and reason as follows: Jesus is the righteousness of God in person; when the living Christ indwells a person, that person is reckoned righteous by the alien indwelling righteousness that is Jesus himself; Jesus indwells by the Spirit, and so the Spirit's indwelling is the indwelling of righteousness because the Spirit's indwelling is the indwelling of the Righteous One, Jesus. The Galatians believed God's message about Jesus and received the Spirit; Abraham believed God's promise and was reckoned righteous. These are two ways of describing the same indwelling righteousness.

3. From the new perspective, one might reason as follows: In Acts (Acts 10:44-48; 11:17), the gift of the Spirit to Gentiles is a sign that Gentiles are acceptable to God, or righteous; when the Galatians received the Spirit, and experienced the gifts of the Spirit, by believing the gospel, it was a public demonstration that God had accepted them as righteous, though they are not "of law." Thus the promises to Abraham concerning the justification of the Gentiles are fulfilled in the gift of the Spirit.

These various proposals have elements of truth in them, but none reckons with the deliverdict connotations of *dikaioō*. "Justify" refers not merely to a verdict but to a judicial act of deliverance or rescue. When Yahweh promised Abraham that he would "justify the Gentiles by faith," he was promising to judge sin and death, rescue the Gentiles and bring his blessing to them through the faith of the seed of Abraham. Abraham believed *that* promise concerning the Gentiles and was counted as just for that reason. What Galatians 3:6-14 describes, in a highly compressed and fragmentary fashion, is the process by which the promise to Abraham came to realization among the Gentiles. How does the faith of Christ enact God's deliverdict and free slaves? How does Christ overcome the curses of Eden and Babel?

Paul moves from a quotation of Genesis that informs us that Abraham was "reckoned righteous" (*elogisthē autō eis dikaiosynēn*, Gal 3:6) to declaring that those who share Abraham's faith are "sons of Abraham" (Gal 3:7) to speaking of the "blessing" on those who are *ek pisteōs* (Gal 3:9). Being reckoned righteous and being counted as sons are linked, if not identical, and those who are sons out of faith are recipients of the blessing promised to Abraham. We should recall our earlier conclusion that *pistis* is a title of Jesus, and also stress the "originative" force of the preposition *ek*. Paul says that those who have been born from the Faith—that is, from the faithful work of the Faithful One—are sons of God, heirs of the promise to Abraham. Paul returns to that promised blessing to sons at the end of Galatians 3, stressing that those who are sons of Abraham in the one seed that is Christ share in the inheritance of Abraham (Gal 3:28-29), an inheritance that Paul elsewhere describes as global in scope (Rom 4:13). Being reckoned as righteous is not *just* a matter of right standing before God, but qualifies one to be a recipient of the inheritance of Abraham. In the more immediate context, the blessing of Abraham is associated with the gift of the Spirit: Galatians 3:14 states that through Christ the blessing of Abraham comes to the Gentiles, so that "we might receive the promise of the Spirit through the faith."[6]

The good news was not only *to* Gentiles, but good news *about* the Gentiles. The *content* of the gospel is not how-to-be-saved but "all nations shall be blessed in you" (Gal 3:8). That is good news because the nations are in turmoil, filled with destructive violence, cursed, divided, far from God and separated from one another, dominated by sin and death because ruled by fleshly passions. The nations are formless, void and dark, but God promises to send out his hovering Spirit to nurture the world back to order and beauty. God promises to put the nations right when he pours out his Spirit on them, fulfilling his promise to Abraham. Referring to the beginning of Galatians 3, we can say that the perfection of the race depends on the Spirit, and since the Spirit's coming depends on Abraham, the perfection of the human race— the maturation of the human race to full humanity—depends on Abraham. Foreseeing that he would pass his delivering judgment through the faithful work of Jesus, God promised Abraham that he would bless the Gentiles (in context, by giving the Spirit, the Spirit who raises the dead).

This is the historical, geopolitical context in which Paul understands the work of the Faithful One. As N. T. Wright has stressed, there is an obstacle to the fulfillment of the Abrahamic promise, a dam that prevents the free flow of blessing (the Spirit of righteousness and life) through Abraham to the nations.[7] That obstacle is the curse on those who are "of the works of the law" (*hosoi . . . ex ergōn nomou*, Gal 3:10). Paul does not merely say that those

---

[6]Paul uses the image of a "down payment" (*arrabōn*) elsewhere (2 Cor 1), the Spirit as the initial installment of a gift that will be given in full later.

[7]N. T. Wright vividly describes it as a "traffic jam" (*Paul and the Faithfulness of God* [Minneapolis: Fortress, 2013], 865).

who received Torah are under a curse, though that is true enough. The curse comes on those whose existence and nature is shaped by the *working* of the law, by the way Torah operates (implicitly, among those who are in the flesh).[8] For reasons we have examined, Torah works death in Israel. It can *only curse, and if Israel* is cursed, then the blessing promised through Abraham will not come to the Gentiles. God's promises will be negated, and death and sin will have the last word.

The curse is not imposed on Israel because of Israel's efforts to obey Torah. They are *supposed* to obey. The curse is not exclusively because Israel became proud of her possession of Torah or because individual Israelites were proud of their meritorious law-keeping, though both of those attitudes are examples of how flesh perverts Torah. Paul's point is far more straightforward: the curse rests on Israel because she has *failed to obey the law* (Gal 3:10). A curse comes on everyone who does not abide by all that is written (quoting Lev 18:5). As he details in Romans 7, Paul delights in the law in the inner man, but finds that the law of flesh wars in his members and keeps him from embodying the justice of God's Torah. He does not, cannot, do the justice that Torah requires, and so comes under the Torah's curse. That is the case with *everyone* who receives the law in a condition of flesh, and it is the case for Israel *as a whole,* which received the law in a condition of flesh. Torah does not come from the Faith. Torah brings blessing only to those who practice the provisions of the law, and no one who is in the flesh can do so (Gal 3:11). That is one of the central charges in Paul's indictment against flesh, which is God's indictment: not only is flesh impotent but it also renders *Torah* impotent, and even turns God's good law into an instrument of torture. As in Romans, Paul refuses to blame the law directly. The law cannot accomplish the justice of God (Gal 3:21), and that does expose something of the limitation of Torah. More importantly, though, Torah simply highlights the impotence of those who attempt to keep the law.[9]

---

[8] I acknowledge that *ek* can have a number of different nuances, but it makes best sense of Paul's argument, I suggest, to take it as referring to source.

[9] Wright argues that Paul is merely stating that Israel is under a curse because, as a matter of fact, they did not keep the law. In Wright's reading, Paul draws on the whole narrative structure of Deut 27–33, which is a prediction that Israel will not be able to abide by the law and will therefore suffer the curse, preeminently the curse of exile. The remedy to this could not be to offer another sacrifice. The solution was for the nation to suffer exile and be restored: the solution was a kind of death and resurrection of Israel (though Wright doesn't use this last phrase). This is fine and helpful, but Paul *does* imply a suppressed premise that none of those who are "of the

God has chosen a narrow stream, the stream of Abraham, to bring blessing to the Gentiles but that stream is blocked by the curse that comes from the very law that marks the descendants of Abraham out from the rest of the nations, the law in which the Jews boasted, the Torah that it was Israel's privilege to receive and maintain. That law has turned into an enemy of the promise. If the blessing of Abraham is going to be brought to the Gentiles, then the curse has to be overcome. According to Paul, Jesus has broken through the curse "having become a curse for us." Hanging on the tree, he is a cursed one, and by bearing the curse he breaks through the curse. In Deuteronomy, this immediately follows a law demanding the execution of a son who has abandoned Torah.[10] Jesus is condemned as a rebellious son, though he is not. He is condemned as a rebellious son *by* the rebellious son, Israel in the flesh. In that precise sense, Jesus suffers the curse of Israel. Because Jesus the faithful Israelite bears the curse, he delivers/redeems (*exagorazō*) Israel from the curse (Gal 3:13). He takes the place of the Israel that should be cursed in order to remove cursing. And so the flow of blessing, the flow of the Spirit, begins.[11]

---

works of the law" have actually kept the law. This "old perspective" reading seems the most straightforward reading of the connection between Paul's assertion and the quotation of Gal 3:10. How does Paul know that no one keeps the law? The answer comes in Paul's quotation of Ps 143 in Gal 2:16: Paul knows from Scripture that no one is justified in the sight of God by the working of the law. The law has brought a curse on the very people that was to bring blessing because they failed to keep the law, as Moses had predicted they would.

[10]This is a crucial point made by Tim Gallant, *Paul's Travail: A Reintroduction to Galatians* (n.p.: Pactum Reformanda, 2013), 125-26.

[11]Paul describes the same sequence in somewhat different terms in Rom 3 and Rom 8. In Rom 3, Jesus is a public *hilastērion*, a propitiation that neutralizes wrath and a "place of atonement" where God takes Israel's sin to himself as he does on the Day of Atonement. In Rom 8, the target of God's condemnation is not Jesus but "sinful flesh," which has been flushed out of hiding by Torah's work and isolated as the cause of Israel's failure to keep Torah. Jesus is a sin offering by which flesh is condemned, and once flesh is condemned, God inaugurates a new *nomos* of the Spirit that embodies life and justice in actual human life, in the community of the Spirit that is the church. In all of these passages, the sequence is: Christ dies to bear the curse and wrath and to condemn sinful flesh, followed by the release of the Spirit, who forms a new social world.

These passages clarify how Jesus' death functions as a sin-bearing sacrifice that remakes the socioreligious terrain. Together they evoke the apparatus of sin offering and the Day of Atonement that we examined in chap. 5. The blood of a sin offering, which was the life of the animal's flesh given for covering, was placed on the sanctuary so that the sanctuary could "bear the burden" of sin and impurity. In most sin offerings, the priest bore the guilt of the worshiper by eating the flesh of the offering. Jesus' sin offering is for the whole people, and no human consumes the flesh of this type of sin offering. Only God can bear the iniquity of all Israel. On the Day of Atonement, these impurities were taken all the way into Yahweh's presence to be unloaded on him. Because Yahweh bore the iniquities of his people, the sanctuary could keep running and the priests could be reinvested. On the cross, God publicly displays (*protithēmi*,

Israel is the target of the curse and the beneficiary of Jesus' curse-busting curse-bearing. *Israel* is the only people who suffer the curse *of Torah*.[12] The curse that Paul describes does not come on everyone, but *only* those who are "of the works of the law," those whose lives have been formed by what the law does among a people who are in the flesh. If Israel is the people under curse, they are the ones who must be redeemed from the curse. Jesus' curse-bearing is for "us," that is, for Paul's people, Israel (Gal 3:14). Removing Israel from Paul's account of atonement distorts and dehistoricizes his argument. Jesus' death has universal effect, but it is an error, a profound and common one, to universalize the curse and the redemption from the curse prematurely. God's promise is universal, to "justify the Gentiles by faith," but that universal promise is realized only in the fulfillment of the particular promise that the blessing will come through Abraham's seed.[13] We gain a historically plausible atonement when we follow Paul in seeing that Jesus bears the curse for Israel, to form a new Israel enlisted by the Spirit to war against flesh.

Paul's story, then, goes like this: Abraham was chosen to be the conduit of blessing to the Gentiles. Abraham believed Yahweh's promise and so was reckoned righteous, God's covenant partner and future heir of the blessing. Israel, the Abrahamic people, was given the Torah, and Torah worked a curse. Unless that curse could be removed, the Gentiles would never receive the blessing of Abraham. Unless Israel could be repaired, the nations could not receive the delivering verdict of justification, could not be delivered from the reign of sin and death and flesh that undermined all striving for justice. Israel could not remove the curse on her own because in her flesh-

---

Rom 3:25) what has been going on in secret all along: God has been dealing with sin in his Most Holy Place since the tabernacle began, but now he reveals his righteousness by publicly taking the guilt of humanity to himself in the Son. If the exchanges of the Most Holy Place are now revealed in public, there is no further need for veils and priesthood and purity: when what has been whispered in secret is shouted from the hilltop of Calvary, the age of secrets is over. If the place of atonement is now "outside the gate" (Heb 13:10-12), out in the public square, the stoicheic system is negated. For further discussion of both passages, see appendix 3.

[12]N. T. Wright, *Pauline Perspectives: Essays on Paul, 1978–2013* (Minneapolis: Fortress, 2013), 307, speaks of the law's purpose as collecting sin and uncleanness into a single place so that it can be dealt with. See also Wright, *Climax of the Covenant: Christ and the Law in Pauline Theology* (Minneapolis: Fortress, 1993), 137-56. In that sense, Jesus' curse-bearing for Israel fulfills Israel's task of bearing sin and curse for the nations. I believe Wright is correct in principle, but in Gal 3 Paul's sights are narrowed to the issue of *Israel's* curse and its removal.

[13]Paul makes the same move from particular (Israel) to universal (Gentiles) in Gal 4, where "we" are held in bondage until the coming of the Son who redeems those who are under the law and brings them into full sonship (Gal 4:3-5). That cannot be universalized either without distorting Paul's argument.

liness she only created more occasions for cursing. The deliverance promised to the nations was accomplished because God sent the seed of Abraham, the true Israelite, to be a curse-bearing substitute *for his people*, to become the cursed Son that Israel was, so that the curse could be killed, buried and removed. Once that curse is removed, Israel is renewed; the removal of the curse implies a resurrection from the curse of death. Israel is delivered, receives the blessing of the Spirit, and from Israel that blessing flows to the nations. *That* is the justification of Israel by the faithful Messiah.

Once we recognize that Paul thinks of the atonement as a *historical* sequence, we can see how closely this matches the reading of the gospel story that we examined in chapter six: Jesus comes preaching the coming of the kingdom. When the kingdom comes, when Yahweh finally takes his throne, all that opposes him will be wiped out. That unfortunately includes Israel herself, and her temple and Torah, which have become centers of opposition to Israel's God. In Pauline terms, Jesus comes announcing that the curse against Israel is about to be carried out, a curse of death against all flesh. 'Tis another flood to wipe the world clean. Israel can be saved if she repents and keeps Torah in the way Jesus does, fulfilling the aims of Torah. Some do, and Jesus forms a faithful coterie of disciples, an Israel within Israel. Most of the Jewish leaders attack Jesus and his Torah-observance as a form of Torah-breaking.[14] They treat him as the rebellious Son, which is what *they* are. As the embodiment of the true Israel, as the seed of Abraham, the Son suffers death for Israel. So the Father and Son conspire together to destroy the curse by taking the curse to themselves. Israel curses God at the cross; instead of returning curse for curse, God turns his cheek to take the second slap in his Son, and thereby turns the human cursing of God against the curse. The Father sends the Son to let humanity do its worst—killing God. And when they have done their worst, the Father raises the Son by the Spirit to reconstitute his band of disciples and offer welcome and forgiveness to his murderers.

Jesus bears the curse, so there is no more curse on those who are with him. He rises from the dead *beyond* curse, and then he sends his Spirit to

---

[14]It might be better to say that it is too late for Israel to repent. Instead, she must simply accept the death sentence that is about to be carried out and trust Yahweh to raise her from the dead. For a stimulating account of Old Testament prophecy highlighting the point, see Donald Gowan, *Theology of the Prophetic Books: The Death and Resurrection of Israel* (Louisville, KY: Westminster John Knox, 1998).

his disciples. The new-Israel community that follows Jesus preaches the kingdom to the Gentiles, and Gentiles receive the Spirit that God had promised through Abraham from the beginning. A new form of human sociality begins to take form, one where Jews and Gentiles stand before God on equal terms, a body in which every member has a valued place. Receiving the Spirit, first Jesus' new Israel and then Gentiles are delivered from the curse of Eden; sharing the Spirit together, Jesus brings Jews and Gentiles together to overcome the curse of Babel. A just society becomes a human possibility and, given God's faithfulness to his promise, a human possibility that *will be* realized. God will not fail in his promise to Abraham. God has given his only Son to issue the deliverdict over the nations, and the God who gave his Son will also with him freely give all things. Through his judgment of sin and death by his death, through his curse-bearing, Jesus brings in the justice of God.[15]

Past guilt determines the present and the future. Adam's sin established a regime of spreading death that led to sin. Adam's flesh became sinful flesh, and sinful flesh filled the world with violence, pride, greed, injustice of every kind. Israel herself was overtaken by flesh and came under a curse. Guilt makes flesh behave even more badly, as the guilty scour the landscape for scapegoats who can bear the anguish of guilt. That past of rebellion and sin remained determinative for the future of humanity until the curse was removed. By bearing the curse for Israel, Jesus gave Israel, and humanity, a new lease on the future. The world's future would no longer be determined by Adam's sin but by the Last Adam's one act of obedience. Jesus' death brings a regime change: death no longer reigns; instead, those who receive the gift of righteousness reign in life (cf. Rom 5:17). Jesus' one act of obedience

---

[15]What role does Paul's quotation from Hab 2:4 play in the argument? Habakkuk's statement that the just live by faith comes against the background of an assessment of Israel's condition. The land is filled with violence, iniquity and destruction. The law cannot solve the problem; indeed, Torah is not merely ignored and disobeyed but has become impotent. It is "numbed," and is incapable of restraining the wickedness that the prophet faces. In this situation, Habakkuk is told that Yahweh's solution is to send the Chaldeans to punish Israel. This does not reassure the prophet, because the Chaldeans are perhaps even more wicked than Israel. How can a more wicked, more violent people be a solution to violence? Yahweh assures him that he will restore Israel in the end, and in the meantime those who wish to live must live by faith in the coming redemption of Israel, faith in Yahweh's promise to redeem his people. Here I am again dependent on Rikki Watts, "'For I Am Not Ashamed of the Gospel': Romans 1:16-17 and Habakkuk 2:4," in *Romans and the People of God: Essays in Honor of Gordon D. Fee on the Occasion of His Sixty-Fifth Birthday*, ed. Sven Soderlund and N. T. Wright (Grand Rapids: Eerdmans, 1999), 3-25.

broke through the curse to establish a new regime of life. Even those who do not respond to the faith of Jesus in faith live in a world under new management, under the Lordship of Christ and the reign of the saints. As Paul says in Romans 5, Jesus' obedience resulted in justification for all people (Rom 5:16, 18), a new regime of justice.

That new future is the future of the Spirit. Jesus bears the curse to offer hope for Spirit in flesh, and, at the end, Spirit that transforms flesh into itself, into spiritual bodies. The Spirit is the blessing promised to the Gentiles, and it is clear in Paul's argument that the gift of the Spirit to the Gentiles fulfills Yahweh's promise to justify the Gentiles by faith. Reception of the Spirit is justification for the nations. Since justification is the outpouring of the Power-Spirit of God, first in the resurrection of Jesus, then in the resurrection of fleshly human beings into new life, it cannot be mere words. Justification occurs for the Gentiles as the wind of the Spirit blows from Jesus' new Israel to the Gentile world, judging and delivering the Romans from their fleshly honor games, their *libido dominandi*, their culture of death.

Justification is what happened to Jesus: in his death, God condemned sin in the flesh, and by raising him the Father declared Jesus just by rescuing him from his death sentence. Justification is also what happens to Gentiles: they are justified (rescued from sin and death) by the outpouring of the Spirit.

JUSTIFIED FROM THE ELEMENTS

Somewhat surprisingly, the specific issue Paul focuses on in Galatians 3 seems to be very much a side issue: the *number* of the recipients of promise. Christ has borne the curse for Israel and released the blessing of Abraham to the Gentiles, and the result is "the one." The promises spoken to Abraham were to his seed—not seeds, Paul insists. That singular seed that is the recipient of the promise is, Paul says at the end of the verse, "Christ" (Gal 3:16). Paul asks, why is the law added? He answers that the law does not change the promise, because the promise goes to the one seed who is Christ. How does that explain *anything* about why the law was added? What does that have to do with Torah?

N. T. Wright has proposed the most convincing explanation of Paul's argument.[16] In Genesis, "seed" refers to a collectivity, a line of descent. To say that Abraham has a single "seed" does not mean that he has only one

---

[16]Wright, *Climax of the Covenant*, 157-74.

child but that he has a unified line of descent. The promise is given to that unified line of descent, and is not diffused over several different lines. Abraham had several children—not only Ishmael, but the later sons by Keturah, whom he married after Sarah's death. But the promise is given to one single line, to the covenant line that comes from Isaac. Nothing in the law can change that.

Torah regulates structures of separation.[17] After the law enters the world, there are still believing Gentiles, many of them, but they do not constitute part of Israel. Because Torah is accommodated to the conditions of Babelic humanity, under Torah there are two seeds, two of many different peoples, all of which may share the faith of Abraham but which are still separated from one another. This must be the case so long as flesh is the principle of social organization. So long as nations are divided by descent and ancestry they must remain divided, because a nation cannot unfather a father. If there is going to be one seed, another principle of social organization has to come into play, one that can knit people who do not share the same flesh into one body.

But God promised his blessing to a single "seed," and that means that the divided state of Israel and the Gentiles *cannot* be the final condition of humanity. If the Torah regulates Israel's separation from other worshipers of Yahweh, then Torah must be temporary. The promise came first, and the promise was given to a single people, and the Torah's work has to be a means for realizing the promise and not the realization itself.

Paul makes this explicit in Galatians 3:19-20, where he claims that Torah was given "until the seed should come to whom the promise had been made." This seed is the "one seed" of Galatians 3:16, the corporate seed that is in Christ, the unified people of God that comes into being through and in Christ's justifying death and resurrection.[18] As Wright has argued, Galatians

---

[17]I have come to disagree with Wright's claim that Torah *institutes* these separations. As I have noted repeatedly in the previous chapters, it is better to say that the law assumes separations among nations and regulates them in order to facilitate Israel's calling to bless the nations. Wright is correct that this requires some degree of quarantine: if Israel becomes a mirror image of the nations, devoted to idols and injustice, then Israel can hardly be God's light in the darkness. And Wright is correct too to emphasize that the point of whatever separations the Torah institutes is for the sake of the nations.

[18]That Paul identifies this single seed as "Christ" does not individualize the point. "Christ" in Paul's parlance had a body with many members. Indeed, in 1 Cor 12:12, He *is* a body with many members. The one seed is the one people that is unified by the Spirit in Christ, the same "one" that is "one in Christ Jesus" (Gal 3:28), one by baptism, those who belong to Christ and thus constitute Abraham's singular seed (Gal 3:29).

3:20 is not, as many translations imply, a statement about mediation in general. It is a statement about the specific mediator who mediated Torah, that is, about Moses. It means, "Now *this* mediator is not [mediator] of the one, but God is one!" (*ho de mesitēs henos ouk estin, ho de theos heis estin*). The "one" of which Moses is not mediator is the "one seed," the "one new man" that is constituted by the joining of Jew and Gentile. Moses is not the mediator of the one seed because the Torah he mediates is given to a "fleshly" people in the context of a divided humanity. If this mediator, Moses, is not a mediator of the one seed, but God *is* one, then Moses *cannot* be the mediator of a seed that resembles God. Torah cannot be the final stage of God's dealings with humanity because God intends to make humanity into the image of his oneness. As Wright puts it, Paul appeals to the Shema to relativize Torah.

The Abrahamic promise of blessing to the "one seed" does what the one God ought to do. The creation of the "one" is one aspect of the "justification of the Gentiles." By the faithful work of the Son and the gift of the Spirit, God has judged fleshly division and rescued humanity from all the evils of that division. As the blessing and inheritance promised to Abraham, the Spirit is a power of unity broader and stronger than flesh. As soon as he comes at Pentecost he begins to form a new sort of social body, not organized by flesh but unified by being animated by a single Spirit, the Spirit of the Creator God.[19] While human beings continue to live in flesh, God in Christ has

---

[19]Paul says Torah was added "for the sake of transgressions" (Gal 3:19: *tōn parabaseōn charin prosetethē*). Given its ambiguity, this does not seem to help much. It has often been taken as a reference to the public uses of the law as a restraint on evil and sin. That is hard to square with Paul's clear discussions of the actual effect of the law, including the discussion earlier in this chapter. Paul has insisted that the law brought a curse instead of blessing to Israel because Israel did not obey the law, and, implicitly, could not do so. If the law was added to inhibit transgressions, it failed miserably in its stated purpose. Paul's claim could, however, be taken to mean that the law was added to provoke transgressions or to "define" transgressions. That is the argument of Rom 5, where Paul claims that there is no transgression where there is no law. There is certainly moral wrong, and certainly sin, without law, but those sins do not rise to the level of transgressions in the absence of law. Law raises the profile of generic sin, and so exposes sin for what it is. Paul makes a related point in Rom 7, as we have seen, where the evil of sin is evident in the fact that it can even turn the Law, holy, righteous and good, into an instrument of death. Paul does have positive things to say about the role of the law here. The image of the law as a *paidagōgos* might be taken in a negative direction, emphasizing the sternness, the disciplinary harshness or the cruelty of the child-conductor. If Paul had emphasized such negative features of the pedagogue, he would not have been the first in the ancient world to do so. Such implications, though, have to be read into Paul's use of the image because Paul emphasizes none of this. Instead, he emphasizes the law's function in conducting Israel to Christ (*gegonen eis Christon*)

inserted Spirit into flesh, into the flesh of Jesus, into the flesh of the church, so that human beings can begin to live by the Spirit while in flesh. Emphasizing the ecclesial dimensions and effects of the atonement enables us to formulate a historically plausible theory of atonement, a model that also explains how Christ's death fixes what is broken in the human race.

OUT FROM UNDER ELEMENTS

At the beginning of Galatians 4, we finally come to *ta stoicheia tou kosmou*. I argued in chapter two that the phrase refers to the institutions and life patterns of Israel's and the nations' childhood, expressed in a "ranking" of the world in fundamentally binary patterns: pure/impure and holy/profane. Paul uses the phrase partly because of its scientific connotations, but here as elsewhere Paul "socializes" Greek philosophical and scientific terms. Stoicheic patterns and institutions constitute the "fundamental physics" of human *social* life. Those who live *hypo ta stoicheia* have a fleshly human nature. Jews and Gentiles share much of this stoicheic apparatus, but Torah is a powerful subversion of the fleshly assumptions of Gentile *stoicheia*. To that extent, Jews were humans of a different "nature" from Gentiles. So fundamental are these stoicheic institutions that human beings who are "of" different cultures are different in "nature." For Paul there was no unified human nature prior to the Last Adam: there were Jews *ek physei* shaped by their birth and training *ek tou nomou*; Gentile life has a different fundamental physics and thus a different *physis*. If the human race is going to be put together again, it is somehow going to have to acquire a common *physis*, operate by the same *stoicheia* and come to occupy the same *kosmos*.

Living under *stoicheia* meant living in a socioreligious world mapped by a fundamentally binary structure of holy/profane, clean/unclean, priest/nonpriest. To say that a premise is an "element" is to name not only the premise but also its immediate implicate; to identify an object as *stoicheion* is to imply that it casts a shadow that is its image. The *taxis* of ranked objects

---

so that Israel could receive God's delivering judgment through the faithful work of Jesus (Gal 3:24). Paul uses the two images at the beginning of Gal 4, the law's function as *epitropos* and *oikonomos*, in the same neutral or positive fashion. The law is useful for Israel while it is in its childhood and prepares Israel for the coming redemption that is in Christ. As noted in previous chapters, Jesus brings into effect precisely what the Torah always aimed at. In doing that, he necessary bursts through the *stoicheia* that pertained to the life of the flesh. But this is not a nullification of Torah. Jesus fulfills Torah; he does not destroy it.

is often a binary order, a set of ones and zeros. In the context of ancient cosmology and religion, it names the binary structures that form the fundament of ancient religious and social life. For nearly all ancient peoples, this binary structure involved, in practice, the construction of temples as sanctified spaces within a profane world, the consecration and purification of priests and worshipers to enable them to make limited, dangerous passages across the boundaries into the realm of the god(s). This sacred topography constituted the physics of the social world.

Stoicheic order includes mediating rituals and persons who cross dangerous boundaries to connect gods and people. Sacrifice in some form, whether it involved killing and burning or not, was a central rite that connected worshipers with their gods across the binary divide but also reinforced the distance between them. The binary order of the elements of religious life remained stable and secure only so long as the boundaries were maintained. The boundaries being ritual and symbolic boundaries, they are maintained by the symbolic avoidances of pollution and cleansings effected by purification rites. The elements of the world remain in harmony only by observance of the elemental rites. In this way the *stoicheia tou kosmou* form a system, a unified whole of dependent parts.

Stoicheic worship was worship under the Edenic curse of distance. Stoicheic social life assumed the divisions of Babel. Stoicheic binary patterns within Israel provided means of access to God under postfall conditions; they regulated Israel's worship and life for an Israel of flesh or, to use Paul's imagery in Galatians 4, regulations for a childlike Israel. Stoicheic order institutionalized flesh, institutionalized humanity's exile from Eden and Babelic division in a set of habits, concepts and practices. *Stoicheia* form the customs and patterns of religious and social life among humans who live *kata sarka*.

Paul considers *ta stoicheia* as a form of governance for children (*nēpios*, Gal 4:1; cf. Gal 3:23-24).[20] Whatever else Paul might have in mind, the

---

[20]There is an exodus motif in the background: Israel is Yahweh's child, whom he delivers from slavery to Pharaoh. Paul, however, describes a postexodus slavery to the law, from which the children of God must also be redeemed (see Wright, *Paul*, 876). See James Scott, *Adoption as Sons of God* (Tübingen: Mohr Siebeck, 1992), 181-86. As the structure indicates, Paul's analogy is quite precise:

    Heir as child (*nēpios*)
        no better than slave (*ouden diapherei doulou*)
            under guardians and managers (*hypo epitropous . . . kai oikonomous*)

association with childhood highlights the fact that the elements are elementary. They are the basic constituents or components of something, suitable for children. By the same token, the *stoicheia* are designed to be temporary. What is right for children is not suitable to adults. Children can be excused for believing in Father Christmas; adults cannot. Continuing under their tutelage after the faith has arrived, after God has sent the Son and Spirit (Gal 4:4, 6), is to lengthen childhood beyond what is fitting. By resubmitting to *ta stoicheia*, the Galatians place themselves in a state of arrested development and extended immaturity. The immaturity has to do particularly with the command and use of the inheritance that the father promises when his children are grown. Children who have not received inheritance are fully heirs (Gal 4:1; cf. Gal 3:29), and with inheritance comes rule. In minority, children are like slaves though they are lords of all (*kyrios pantōn*); now, no longer minors, they are in fact what they have always been in principle.[21] If we place Paul's argument in its fullest biblical framework, he is describing the advancement of humanity from Adamic service to full Adamic dominion through the coming of the Last Adam. Like Adam in the garden, Israel was heir of all things but treated as no better than a slave during her childhood. In earlier chapters, we have seen that Jesus' justifying death and resurrection delivers from flesh, and if that is so, it must also deliver from the institutions and practices accommodated to flesh.

The elements are identical to the guardians and managers. Both "guardians

---

> When we were children (*nēpioi*)
>   held in bondage (*dedoulōmenoi*)
>   under *ta stoicheia tou kosmou*

[21]The term *stoicheia* is part of a prepositional phrase with a modifying genitive, *hypo ta stoicheia tou kosmou*. Galatians uses the preposition *hypo* twice as often as any other book of the New Testament. Matthew and Romans are tied for second, with five uses each. The preposition is clustered in the central portion of Paul's argument in Gal 3–4. All are "under" sin (Gal 3:22), but Jews were kept in custody under the law (Gal 3:23), under a tutor (Gal 3:25), until faith came. Paul shifts the imagery slightly at the beginning of Gal 4, but the preposition continues to express subjection, under "guardians and managers" (Gal 4:2), under the elements (Gal 4:3), until the time when the Father determined to redeem those "under the law" (Gal 4:4-5). The phrases are certainly not equivalent, nor do the descriptions all apply to the same people. All are under sin, but only Jews are under the tutelage of the law. My point is a straightforward one: whatever *ta stoicheia* might be, they are something that has the capacity to exercise authority, to subject, to take a high place and put human beings "under." This is not necessarily an indictment of the elements. Children, as Paul says, are rightly "under" guardians to curb the folly of their youth. Still, it is clear that being "under" is not the ideal position for human beings. Existence under the law, under guardians, under the elements are all described as forms of slavery from which the Son and Spirit come to deliver.

and managers" and "elements" describe something that children are "under" (*hypo*), and both are described as imposing a kind of bondage. The guardians keep the child in a condition of slavery (*doulos*), and life under the elements is a form of slavery: *hypo ta stoicheia tou kosmou ēmetha dedoulōmenoi*. Paul connects child-under-guardians and we-under-elements with *houtōs kai*, "so also." The structure of the two sentences creates a cross-echo: we = minors; guardians = elements; date set by father = fullness of time (Gal 4:4). If we press the analogy, we might conclude that the elements are beings (note the plural) who guard and manage children in their minority. Prior to the coming of the Son and Spirit, some guardians, perhaps angelic or demonic, trained and prepared the sons who were to become lords. Jews received the Torah, Paul has just indicated, through angels; and Gentiles too were under beings that are "by nature no gods" (Gal 4:8; cf. 1 Cor 10:19-22, where Paul claims that Gentiles sacrifice to demons).[22] In Galatians 3–4, Paul describes the childhood of the race as a set of bondages. The parallels are evident from the repeated use of the preposition *hypo*.

Before faith, we were *hypo nomon*.

The *nomos* functioned as a *paidagōgos* (a tutor or guide for children).

A child is *hypo epitropous kai oikonomous* until his majority.

As children, we were bound *hypo ta stoicheia tou kosmou*.[23]

---

[22]Some have suggested that Paul portrays the pedagogue and the managers negatively. Clinton E. Arnold ("Returning to the Domain of the Powers: 'Stoicheia' as Evil Spirits in Galatians 4:3, 9," *Novum Testamentum* 38 [1996]: 65) characterizes the managers as "taskmasters," but the imagery is paternal and familial: Would a father subject his minor children to brutes? Arnold runs into difficulties when he recognizes the parallel between the law and the elements in Gal 4, saying, "It is doubtful Paul would have made the Torah coextensive with demonic powers," and claims, contrary to his own analysis of the text, that there is an "association" rather than identity between the two (ibid., 68). Martinus de Boer asks whether the pedagogue and guardians are "positive" or "negative" portraits of the law ("The Meaning of the Phrase τα Στοιχεια του Κοσμου in Galatians," *New Testament Studies* 53 [2007]: 212n37), but the question is overly simplistic. One might as well ask whether sleeping in a crib is "positive" or "negative." For an infant, it is necessary, however much it might frustrate the little one's desire to roam. A teenager confined to a crib, however, is either neurotic or a victim of abuse.

[23]This is reinforced by the chiastic structure of Gal 3–4:

A Faith of Abraham (Gal 3:1-14)
   B Faith and law (Gal 3:15-22)
      C Law as pedagogue (Gal 3:23-25)
         D Baptism into the seed (Gal 3:26-29)
      C' Childhood under guardians and managers (Gal 4:1-11)
   B' Weakness of Paul's flesh/Paul's first visit (Gal 4:12-20)
A' Allegory of Abraham and Sarah (Gal 4:21-31)

Law, pedagogue, guardians and managers, elements of the world—all these are ways of describing the same reality, namely, those things that kept "us" in bondage during our childhood.

Since both the "pedagogue" and the "guardians and managers" are personal categories, it is possible that Paul has in mind angelic overseers. That would fit generally with biblical descriptions of humanity's condition under the old order ("a little while lower than angels"), and with the childhood order designed for Adam in the garden. It has some contextual weight as well, since Paul claims that the law was delivered to Israel through the mediation of angels (Gal 3:19). It would make sense for angels to serve as the enforcers of the Torah that they delivered by hand. The Angel of Yahweh oversees Israel to ensure that she stays within the bounds. As N. T. Wright has put it, the term *stoicheia* conjures up the notion of tutelary deities that governed each tribe and tongue and nation.[24]

While there is a personal dimension to the *stoicheia*, I have argued that Paul's accent lies elsewhere.[25] After all, the guardians and managers of Galatians 4:2 continue and expand the analogy of the pedagogue that Paul begins in Galatians 3:24. In real life, both managers and the pedagogues are persons, but in Galatians 3 Paul uses the pedagogue to describe *Torah*, not a human or angelic guide or guardian. In the end, there does not seem any need to choose between an exclusively personal and impersonal interpretation of the various images that Paul employs. Torah is not a person, but Torah came through the agency of angels (Gal 3:19; cf. Acts 7:53), so that submission to Torah involves submission to Torah's angelic mediators. This is the issue in the opening chapters of Hebrews. Though Jewish speculation

---

The C and C′ sections both describe children who are under authority during their childhood. In Gal 3:23-25, the image is explicitly applied to the law (*nomos*), and while Paul does not explicitly identify the guardians and managers of Gal 4:1 with the law, that is certainly the import of the analogy.

[24]See N. T. Wright, *Colossians and Philemon*, Tyndale New Testament Commentaries (Downers Grove, IL: InterVarsity Press, 2008).

[25]Similarly, despite the overlap between the elements and Paul's theology of flesh, sin and death, I do not think they are equivalent (as does P. Vielhauer, "Gesetzesdienst und Stoicheiadienst im Galaterbrief," in *Rechtfertigung. Festschrift fur Ernst Kasemann zum 70. Geburtstag*, ed. J. Friedrich [Tübingen: Mohr Siebeck, 1976], 553). Rather, the elements are institutions and practices for human beings who exist under conditions of flesh, sin and death. See above, chap. 4, for my extended analysis of "flesh." I agree with Stanislas Breton that flesh, death and sin are "potencies," but I do not believe "elements" has the same connotation (Breton, *A Radical Philosophy of Saint Paul*, trans. Joseph N. Ballan [New York: Columbia University Press, 2011], 112-15).

had led into overt worship of angels, the contrast in Hebrews has rather to do with the contrast between persistence in the order established by Torah and faithfulness to the Son, who is superior to angels and angelic Torah. For Jews, stoicheic life involves both childish subjection to beings who are not God *and* subjection to a certain pattern of life and worship laid out in the written law. For Gentiles too, *ta stoicheia* involved both subjection to demons or angels and a pattern of life and worship somehow analogous to Torah.[26] Egyptians had their temples, priests, purity rules and sacrifices, and so did the Babylonians—Paleo and Neo—the Greeks and the Romans. For all of these, stoicheic order was an order of flesh: It arose from a strange love-hate relationship with mortality (Egypt); from compensatory displays of power (Babylon); from hero culture that attempted, impossibly, to transcend flesh by fleshly violence, fleshly indulgence, fleshly combat and triumph.

Stoicheic institutions and practices are accommodated to fleshly existence, designed to regulate the human race during the time of minority, during the period of exclusion from Eden and the division of nation from nation. Indeed, stoicheic structures and the associated practices were fundamentally intertwined with fleshly life. While regulating humanity's contact with God and with one another, the stoicheic regulations are easily susceptible to fleshly manipulation. Israel receives Torah from God, and thus is given a privileged position as the priestly people, the temple-keepers of the ancient world. That is a good gift, but it can easily turn to a national boast. At the same time, the privilege of Israel can rouse the envy of other nations. The binary oppositions of holy/profane and clean/unclean are designed in Torah to give controlled access to God, but they can become structures of exclusion and tyranny. Stoicheic regulations are a form of benevolent bondage for children, but they can become instruments of very unbenevolent slavery. In overcoming flesh and sin, then, the Faith must also overcome the stoicheic regulations. The hierarchies, separations and

---

[26]This is close to the view of the Reformers, who equated the elementary principles with the institutions of the law, particularly the ceremonies of the law. Hugo Grotius noted that Paul uses the phrase to denote practices shared by both Jews and Gentiles. See David Bundrick, "*Ta Stoicheia tou Kosmou* (Gal 4:3)," *Journal of the Evangelical Theological Society* 34 (1991): 357; and John Riches, *Galatians Through the Centuries* (Oxford: Wiley-Blackwell, 2013), 218-21. Grotius cites Erasmus to the effect that the phrase refers to *ritibus illis qui nobis cum mundo erant communes: qualia sunt templa, area, victimae, liba,* and so on. He knows the etymology of the term and suggests that Paul is talking about the *elementa . . . in re pietatis,* by analogy with the rudiments of *rerum natura,* also called *elementa* (Grotius, *Annotationes in Novum Testamentum* [1646], 532).

exclusions that are inherent in stoicheic order make it particularly susceptible to rivalry, strife, ostracism and division. At best, *stoicheia* can achieve
only a simulacrum of just social order. It cannot achieve justice itself.

Even if stoicheic institutions had not been abused, they would become
useless once the promise of the Spirit was realized, once the Abrahamic
promise came to fruition. Once the gate of Eden is opened again, there is no
need for sacrifice; the cherubim lay down their flaming swords and let those
who are in Christ enter freely. Once Jesus has borne the curse for Israel and
opened up the flood of the Spirit to the Gentiles, thus creating "the one" that
Moses did not mediate, the structures that distinguish Jew from Gentile are
pointless. Maintaining such structures is, by Paul's lights, worse than
pointless. Anyone who sets up barriers at Eden's gate is trying to reverse the
work of Jesus. Anyone who reerects stoicheic barriers between Jew and
Gentile is trying to split "the one" that was formed by the Son and Spirit, and
implicitly denying the Shema, denying that God is one by denying that his
people is one. Galatianism is the heresy of heresies because it is denying the
fundamental truth of the gospel: that in the fullness of time God sent his
Son to die and rise to justify humanity from sin, to redeem from *stoicheia*,
to bring children to maturity.

If Jesus' death is a justifying verdict against sin and flesh and in favor of
Jesus, then it must also be a verdict against *stoicheia*. By the faithful work of
Christ and the surging power of his Spirit, God breaks the chains of the elements and brings children to maturity. This is the new creation that Jesus
brings, a new pattern of human life liberated from slavery to elements, a
world beyond binaries of circumcision and uncircumcision.[27] The justice of

---

[27]Paul's declaration at the end of Gal 3 is that in Christ there is no more Jew or Greek, slave or
free, male or female. This has been taken as a slogan for Christian feminists and appropriately
so. A declaration affirming the dignity, gifts and status of women is inherent in the gospel and,
despite missteps, Christianity has expanded the freedom and status of women wherever it has
taken cultural hold. See, for instance, Rodney Stark, *The Rise of Christianity* (San Francisco:
HarperSanFrancisco, 1997), 95-128. For women in Judaism and the New Testament, see Ben
Witherington III, *Women and the Genesis of Christianity* (Cambridge: Cambridge University
Press, 1990). Yet Paul's slogan is not grounds for an anachronistic egalitarianism. Slaves and slave
owners were "one" in a specific sense. Paul did not think the gospel made them interchangeable.
He addresses slaves *as slaves* in his letters, giving them instruction about how to enact the gospel
while in slavery, and he addresses Philemon as a master. If observed, his instructions to Philemon would have transformed master-slave relations, but Paul did not demand or expect that
hierarchies be dissolved. Even in the church, there were leaders to be obeyed and followers called
to obey. So too, Paul does not dissolve the created order of male-female (see 1 Cor 11:1-16), much
less male-female difference as such. It would be desperate to enlist Paul as an advocate of

God cannot be realized so long as stoicheic order prevails because the justice of God requires the death of flesh, and the elements follow and in some ways reinforce the contours of flesh. Justice requires oneness, between God and humanity and among humans; stoicheic order accepts the divisions and separations of Eden and Babel, and so cannot mediate the one. This is how the justice of God is realized, how the "one seed" can take form: Jesus has borne the curse, died to the flesh and unleashed the Spirit of resurrection. A just society can emerge only after the physics of social life has been transformed, after the apparatus of stoicheic order is abolished, and *that* happens only by the justifying death and resurrection of Jesus, the "justification by the faithful one" that God accomplished in his Son.

Conclusion

Over the past several chapters, we have developed an account of atonement that is historically plausible—rooted in the history of Israel among the nations; Levitical—showing how Jesus' death and resurrection follows and so fulfills the contours of Levitical sacrifice; evangelical—taking account of the whole gospel history; inevitable—explaining how the cross is the obvious solution to the damage of human social life; and Pauline—able to account for the actual statements and arguments that Paul makes about the cross. It remains to show that this account is fruitful, that the allegory of sacrifice fulfilled by Jesus can unfold in a tropology. It *must* be fruitful, since it has a pneumatological core: it is about the release of the Spirit, the Spirit who bears his fruit in flesh. And so Paul goes on from describing how the "one" comes into being to providing a sketch of life in the Spirit, a community no longer structured by *stoicheia* but coagulated into the one seed by the fewer, simpler, more potent rites and practices and signs of the church. It remains to show that the theology of atonement outlined here can contribute to a theology of mission.

---

transgender freedom; on the contrary, "let each man remain in that condition in which he was called" (1 Cor 7:11). The point can be made from Gal 3. Galatians 3:28-29 is not a standalone slogan, but the hinge of a chiastic argument, and the terms of the argument (one, heir, Abraham's seed, promise) are repeated here. "One" has already been defined in terms of the "one seed" that is not mediated by Torah; the blessing promised to Abraham has already been explained as the gift of the Spirit. In *that* sense there is no male or female: they are all equally engrafted into the one, and not even the Torah's male-only sign remains in effect; all receive the same Spirit and are clothed by baptism in the one clothing that is Christ. This doesn't make them simply interchangeable or equal in every respect.

PART FOUR

CONTRIBUTIONS
TO A THEOLOGY
OF MISSION

ten

IN RANKS WITH THE SPIRIT

✝

The works that flesh does are "immorality, impurity, sensuality, idolatry, sorcery, enmities, strife, jealousy, outbursts of anger, disputes, dissensions, factions, envying, drunkenness, carousing and things like these" (Gal 5:20-21 NASB). So long as flesh rules, there is no hope for human society. Families will be torn apart by sexual indulgence, adultery, jealousy, anger. Neighborhoods are rent by anger, cycles of vengeful dispute, factions that stare across the barricades. Laborers who labor in flesh are not content with wages, full of envy. If human groups are going to function peaceably and justly, if the justice of God is to take root in creation and humanity, flesh must be defeated. And since the elements of the socioreligious world institutionalize flesh and are taken over by flesh, these institutions must be dismantled and/or transformed if human society is going to flourish.

Jesus died and rose again to condemn flesh and to open the flow of the Spirit to the nations, to justify human beings by the Spirit who raised him from the dead. In delivering Israel and then the nations from flesh, he delivered them from the elements of the ancient socioreligious cosmos. By his death and resurrection, he became a new kind of human being, a *pneumatikos* man, and by the gift of his Spirit he enables those who receive him to live the life of the Spirit while still in the flesh. By dying and rising to justify us from the flesh and from the elements, Jesus made possible the formation of "the one," the unified, harmonious humanity that Yahweh promised to Abraham.

This is the social gospel of Jesus.

At the heart of this good news is the good news that Jesus has formed, is forming and will ultimately form a new human race. He has brought children to full sonship, and the one who began the good work will bring it to perfection at the last. The atonement is nothing unless it forms a new humanity with a renewed socioreligious *physis*. To avoid the peculiar jargon of this book: there must be a *church* if there is to be social transformation, if the damage of flesh is going to be overcome. The church *is*, in fact, the first form of transformed human society. This is why the God-man must die and rise: if society is to be saved, there must be a church; if there is going to be a church, there must be a Messiah dead and risen.

If the world is to be saved, atonement must become a social fact. If it is going to be plausible, atonement theology must be social theory. And if atonement theology *is* social science, then a theology concerning the social mission of the church is inherent in the theology of the atonement.

In this and the following two chapters, I offer sketchy reflections on the theology of mission that flows out of the atonement theology developed in the rest of this book. What I offer in these chapters is, first, an outline of what the atonement implies about the aims, goals and means of missions; second, a typology of religions based on adherence to *ta stoicheia tou kosmou*—a theology of atonement as comparative religion; and, third, a map of the mission field of the supposedly "secular" West—a theology of atonement as a theory of secularization.

WALK IN THE SPIRIT

Jesus threw the world into a crisis: How can the human race continue after Jesus and the Spirit have tampered with the physics of religion and society? If earth is no longer earthy, fire no longer fiery, air no longer aerial, water no longer wet and heavy, then the world as we know it no longer exists. If you destroy the elements of the socioreligious cosmos, then can there be a cosmos at all? If you rearrange the elements, how will the world stay together? Will not things fall apart? Will not chaos engulf us all?

We do not need to *imagine* that this is what people thought. We know. Saul of Tarsus believed that without Torah, Pharisaically interpreted, Israel would dissolve, and so he devoted himself to purging the pollution from the holy people. Saul's persecution was an effort to contain the damage by reasserting the boundaries of purity and holiness that kept social chaos at bay. After Damascus, Paul joined in, and the Romans began to accuse him of being one of the rabble-rousers who wanted to turn the world upside down.

It is hardly surprising that the Galatians were tempted to slip back into that older, simpler, childlike world. Any pious Gentile knew that their own health, and the health of their people, depended on maintaining good relations with the gods, and that required pure sacrifices. For Jews, being under the elements and being under Torah were one and the same.[1] Without Torah-observance, the world would spin out of control. Maintaining the binary boundaries of holy and profane, clean and unclean, offering regular sacrifice to satisfy the Creator Yahweh—all this was necessary to hold the world together. Doing Torah constituted the physics of social life. For Jews, the distinction of Jew/Gentile, circumcision/uncircumcision is the fundamental groundwork of reality. Anyone who tampered with Torah was threatening all order, casting the world back into chaos.

Paul's answer to that challenge is straightforward: the *Spirit* is the new fundamental element of social life, and he is a God of order, not confusion.[2] The Spirit is the quintessence of a new world. By the Spirit, human beings can share in the deliverdict that the Father enacted in the Son's death and resurrection. By the Spirit, humans are delivered from death and the fear of death. The Spirit forms the "one" out of the binary fragments of stoicheicized humanity.

BAPTIZED INTO THE ONE

The Spirit is the quintessence of the new humanity, but the Spirit, like the Son, works in and through the creation. Jesus touched lepers and spoke to the dead, and the world leapt back to life. The Spirit too touches and speaks, using the creation as his language and medium as the Son used the flesh of his human nature. The new rites of the church point to the sort of society that is to take form among us, and by the power of the Spirit they form that society out of us.

And so the Spirit forms the one, but he forms the one through *water*. As in Romans 6, so in Galatians 3: baptism is the key point of transition from

---

[1]Martinus de Boer, "The Meaning of the Phrase τα Στοιχεια του Κοσμου in Galatians," *New Testament Studies* 53 (2007): 215.

[2]John M. G. Barclay emphasizes the disorienting character of Paul's "Torah-free" gospel and highlights the role of the Spirit. See Barclay, *Obeying the Truth: Paul's Ethics in Galatians* (Minneapolis: Fortress, 1988), 107. In a recent essay, Barclay discusses Paul's ethics in Galatians under the heading of "gift": see Barclay, "Under Grace: The Christ-Gift and the Construction of a Christian *Habitus*," in *Apocalyptic Paul: Cosmos and Anthropos in Romans 5-8*, ed. Beverly Roberts Gaventa (Waco, TX: Baylor University Press, 2013), 59-76; and now Barclay, *Paul and the Gift* (Grand Rapids: Eerdmans, 2015).

the world of flesh to the world of Spirit, from stoicheic immaturity to full sonship.[3] Those who are baptized into Christ are clothed with Christ (Gal 3:27). Wearing this common priestly clothing, they are all "one," no matter what their "fleshly," social or stoicheic status.[4] Jew and Greek, separated under stoicheic order, are baptized, and don the same Christ-garments. In the ancient world, the free are free because they are well-born or because they have achieved free status; in either case their freedom is a fleshly achievement. And slavery too is a fleshly status, a result of defeat in war, of low birth, of poverty and low achievement. But these fleshly distinctions are erased by baptism, as both free person and slave assume the same status of being in Christ.

Sexual difference remains. Paul does not teach that the created male-female distinction is undone in every respect. But at the root, he announces the union of male and female in Christ, that the division of the socioreligious world into "male and female" has become as obsolete as the arrangement of the world into circumcision and uncircumcision (Gal 3:28). Fleshly society is society under phallic control. Torah was an antisarkic pedagogy, beginning with the cutting off of the flesh of the phallus in circumcision, but Torah could and did become a bludgeon to suppress women. Circumcision made men more womanly, but some Jewish men used their *absence* of virile flesh to vaunt themselves over women. Biblical sanctuaries had no separate courts of women, but the temple of Herod included such a court. In Christ, those distinctions are gone. Women are no longer excluded from the sanctuary, even if they are unclean by the standards of Torah. A woman can draw near during her menstrual period or a day after childbirth and receive the touch of Jesus. Females wear the same baptismal clothes as males, as Jew and Greek, as slave and free, because all are clothed in Christ. They have the same privileges as all the baptized, are as gifted by the Spirit as males, are as much members of the one body as any man.

Through baptism, the "one" that was promised to Abraham comes into existence.[5] God told Abraham that he would be father of many nations.

---

[3] On baptism in Paul generally, and specifically in Galatians, see the superb discussion of N. T. Wright, *Paul and the Faithfulness of God* (Minneapolis: Fortress, 2013), 417-27, 962-64. See also the illuminating discussion in Stephen Richard Turley, *The Ritualized Revelation of the Messianic Age: Washings and Meals in Galatians and 1 Corinthians* (London: Bloomsbury, 2015).

[4] I have treated the priestly significance of baptism in my *Priesthood of the Plebs: A Theology of Baptism* (Eugene, OR: Wipf & Stock, 2003).

[5] Martinus C. de Boer, *Galatians: A Commentary*, New Testament Library (Louisville, KY:

Israel was to be the conduit of blessing to the post-Babelic world, but the curse prevented that, and the "one seed" that had been promised to Abraham could not be realized until the curse was removed. In his death as the rebellious son on the tree, Jesus bore the curse, unblocked the logjam, released the flow of blessing and made it possible for the "one" to become a real-life social form, in the church of the baptized. The "one" of the baptized is the "one seed" that is Christ (Gal 3:16, 20). As Paul makes clear in Galatians 3:29, the baptized are children of Abraham, heirs of the promise.[6]

The Spirit is the promised blessing, and the Spirit is the bond of union that knits together the diverse orders of humanity into the one as he breaks through the binary oppositions of stoicheic order. That Spirit is the gift to the baptized, and baptism is the Spirit's watery instrument for forming a single human race, united in Christ and so united to God, joined in unity with one another.

By the Spirit, baptism forms the church as the society of the atonement. It does not instantly change the hierarchies of the surrounding society. By forming the church, it plants within the cities of this world a new form of the city; the church stages an eschatological form of social life before the nations and before the principalities and powers. Baptism announces that fleshly society is not the only form of human society, announces not merely the possibility but the reality of a communion that is constituted by the Spirit.

Each baptism is a little Pentecost; and given the way Paul has set up his argument, that means each baptism is also an echo of the justifying event of the cross.[7] Gentiles are justified—that is, delivered from flesh, sin and death; pronounced righteous before God by sharing Jesus' resurrection—when they receive the Spirit. That fulfills the Abrahamic promise to justify the Gentiles by the faith of Jesus. The Spirit gives them a share in the resurrection power of Christ, and the Spirit's invasion of their lives is a "justifying" act. If baptism is the rite by which one receives the promised Spirit, then it is equally the act by which the Spirit reenacts the deliverdict of the resurrection in the experience of an individual.[8] Because it is the rite of

---

Westminster John Knox, 2011), 244.

[6]Emphasized in ibid., 247. De Boer points out that Paul shifts from speaking of Christians as sons of Abraham to speaking of them as sons of God.

[7]This point is not as explicit in Gal 3 as in Rom 6, where Paul actually uses *dikaioō* when speaking about baptismal incorporation into the death and resurrection of Jesus.

[8]This should not be taken to imply that baptism is the sole site of this justifying act, or taken to

Spirit-reception, baptism is also the rite of justification. Justification happens once for all in the cross and resurrection of Jesus, but that event of justification by death and resurrection happens repeatedly, in a series of nonidentical repetitions, in the sacraments of the new society. It happens in the life of each person who is justified (*dikaioō*) from the Egypt of sin and death, from the cursed realm of Adam, in the name Jesus (Rom 6:7). Baptism is one of those more effective rites that come in with the new covenant. The fact that baptism takes the place of the multiple, complicated cleansing rites of stoicheic order is itself a sign that salvation has come to the world. And the fact that baptism does the miraculous work of binding diverse flesh into one body means that baptism is one of the rites that *effects* the social salvation of humanity. When we grasp what baptism means for Paul, we discern a truth that initially seems ludicrous: Jesus died and rose again to end the purity system of circumcision and Torah, and to introduce the rite of Christian baptism. When we understand baptism rightly, saying *that* is simply to say: Jesus died and rose again to unite divided, Babelic humanity in one new humanity brought near to God.

Though Paul does not explicitly mention the Lord's Supper in Galatians, table fellowship is a key issue in Galatians 2. Whether or not the issue in Antioch concerned the Lord's Supper or common meals, the principle holds. What baptism declares and effects—that there is no more Jew nor Greek, male nor female, slave nor free—is reenacted repeatedly, daily or weekly or (horror of horrors!) monthly or quarterly, at the table. Like baptism, the sheer fact that Christians eat and drink Christ's own body and blood; that we drink blood at all;[9] that we drink wine in the presence of God (see Lev 10); that all eat and drink the same food, without a graded distribution among priests and people, between slaves and freemen, between male and female—all that signifies the arrival of salvation in the form of a poststoicheic

---

minimize the Spirit's work through preaching. After all, Paul begins Gal 3 with a reminder that the Galatians received the Spirit by hearing with faith, or by hearing the message of the Faith. When they heard and believed the gospel, the Spirit invaded their lives and "justified" them from sin, flesh and *ta stoicheia*. Paul is not entirely clear about how justification by trusting the message is to be reconciled with justification by baptism. But he says both, and we must at least do that.

[9]Here the emphasis placed on flesh in the phrase "the life of flesh is in the blood" becomes most significant. Israel was prohibited from eating blood because they were not to get life from *flesh*. The "blood taboo" was part of God's antisarkic campaign. But the blood of Jesus is not the blood of flesh; it is the blood of the spiritual person, the blood of the person who has risen from flesh to Spirit. We are not drinking the "life of the flesh" at the Eucharist but the lifeblood of the Spirit. Drinking Jesus' blood thus means precisely the opposite of drinking animal blood.

community. And, like baptism, the Supper *effects* what it signifies: It signifies communion with God in Christ by the Spirit because that is what it *is*; it signifies fellowship among all people in Christ because that is what *happens* (or ought to) at every celebration; it signifies remission of sins, and *grants* remission, because it *is* God's hospitable welcome of sinners; it signifies fellowship in holy things because it gives holy things to holy people. Once we see what the Supper signifies, we can see the truth in this: Jesus died and rose again so that we could celebrate the Lord's Supper together. *That* is simply to say: Jesus died and rose again to enact the kingdom, the feast of all humanity before the face of God, the aim of the entire ceremonial system of the Torah. No wonder Paul went into a rage at Peter. By withdrawing from table fellowship, by avoiding Gentile impurities at the table, Peter was undoing the cross, leading part of the host of Israel back toward Egypt.

As people are incorporated into Christ by the Spirit, the *nomos* of the Spirit spreads in the world. As the Spirit spreads, the "one" grows, stoicheic divisions and hierarchies are transposed into the order of the Spirit, and a social body replaces a pyramid society, founded on slaves.[10] Speaking of his own experience, Paul describes himself as living "in flesh" (*en sarki*, Gal 2:20). He is still limited, vulnerable, weak, mortal. He has not wholly passed, as Jesus has, from flesh to Spirit, and he will not be entirely *pneumatikos* until he is raised in body as Jesus was. The church will not be entirely *pneumatikos* until the eschaton. That means that Paul (and we) will continue to be pulled toward the flesh, toward rivalry, strife, sensuality, to all the evils that he describes in Romans 1 and Galatians 5. Yet, while living in flesh, we live by faith in the Son who gave himself to destroy flesh.

To say the same thing, those who are baptized live on *in* flesh but live *by* the Spirit. We still have ancestry and parentage, but our ancestry and parentage no longer determine the limits of our love and concern. We are still citizens of nations and fall into different social and economic classes, but we are no longer Americans *physei*, or Koreans or Peruvians or Hutu, or part of the 1 percent or the 99 percent by nature. Our nature is determined instead by the Son and Spirit, by water, word and feast. We will die, but the Spirit overcomes the fear of death and impels us to follow Jesus

---

[10]For this particular way of putting things, I am indebted to Pastor Rich Lusk, who contrasted a "pyramid" to a "body" model of social life in a sermon delivered at Trinity Presbyterian Church, December 21, 2014.

into suffering service, to follow Jesus to the cross. We are still tempted to all the reactionary violence that flesh is heir to, but the Spirit labors to form the patient endurance of Christ in us. The Spirit enables us to rejoice in the weakness and vulnerability of flesh, to exult when we are counted worthy to suffer for his name.

All this to say that when Jesus delivers us from flesh by the Spirit, we are also justified from the elements. And that means we must learn to live as sons, no longer children.

LIFE AFTER *STOICHEIA*

Stoicheic *order* has been completely dismantled by the advent of the Son and Spirit. Flesh has been killed in Jesus, and is being killed in those who are in Christ, but until the consummation of all things there is warfare between flesh and Spirit (Gal 5:17). Flesh desires to re-erect and maintain the exclusions of fleshly society, and to rebuild the binary order of the *stoicheia*. Within the church too, flesh continues to fight back, and the fact that there is war between flesh and Spirit is as clear an indication as we could want that Paul considers the current condition of the church a subeschatological one. In the resurrection, the Spirit will triumph at last, and the war will end with the Spirit's utter victory. In the meantime, the Spirit's desire wars against this fleshly desire, for the Spirit's desire is the desire of Jesus, which is the fulfillment of the promise to Abraham: the Spirit's desire is to form "the one," the community of peace and justice. To live by the Spirit is to live a *militant* life, a life of warfare against flesh, having been enlisted into Yahweh's millennia-long war.

The fruits of the Spirit are direct assaults on fleshly life: In place of enmity, the Spirit produces love; in place of strife, patience and kindness; in place of envy, contentment and thankfulness; in place of the unrestrained passions of flesh, self-control. The fruits of the Spirit are the fruits needed to make society Edenic. Flesh has its own stoicheic ranking, but those who are in the Spirit keep in ranks with the Spirit. Paul deliberately echoes the language of *stoicheia* when he talks about the Spirit's leadership of the church. As we saw in chapter two above, the noun form comes from a verb that means "to arrange in ranks" or "to classify in contrasting pairs." Troops are stoicheicized when they are mustered, and bricks form a stoicheic pattern when built into a wall. This is the verb Paul uses when he speaks of "keeping in step with the

Spirit"; it could be translated, "If we live by the Spirit, with the Spirit also keep in ranks" (*Ei zōmen pneumati, pneumati kai stoichōmen,* Gal 5:25).[11] Stoicheic order involves a ranking and arrangement of things, and the Spirit too is a source of order, not of chaos. Stoicheic order involves the erection of binary oppositions, and though the Spirit breaks through those binary structures, the Spirit establishes an absolute "binary" opposition to life according to the flesh.

Contrary to the fears of those who defend stoicheic order, the society of the Spirit is not permissive but strictly disciplined; it does not tolerate evil but restores the offender with gentleness. Fulfilling the *nomos* of Jesus, disciples bear one another's burdens (Gal 6:1-2). Now at last, in the release of the Spirit, God has formed the fully trained army that began with Israel, the army trained to fight with weapons of weakness and spiritual power, an army that stands in the ranks of the Spirit in his war with flesh. Not only do Jesus and the Spirit form a just community but they also send us out on a mission of justice.

The Spirit transforms stoicheic liturgy, but the spiritual transformation is not limited to the liturgy. Even under the order of Torah, ritual and life were inseparable. The sacrifices of a hard-dealing businessman were *not* pleasing to God, no matter how precisely they were performed. Sacrifice was not designed to provide a protective screen for injustice. When the boundaries between temple and exterior are broken down in the atonement, life and liturgy become even more fully integrated. Christian rites express, embody and enact the way of Jesus that should encompass the whole life of the community. Not only at the font and table, but everywhere, Christians are to live as the one. Having been baptized into the one, we are to walk worthy of our calling and practice the virtues of unity, harmony and peace (Eph 4:1–6:4). The Spirit transgresses stoicheic boundaries not only to establish a new

---

[11]The play between the noun *stoicheia* and the verb *stoicheō* cannot be accidental. J. Louis Martyn calls the fresh oppositions of the age of the Spirit "apocalyptic antinomies" (*Galatians,* Anchor Bible [New York: Doubleday, 1997]; see Martyn, "Apocalyptic Antinomies in Paul's Letter to the Galatians," *New Testament Studies* 31, no. 3 (1985): 410-24. That we "keep in ranks" with the Spirit indicates that life in the Spirit is a life of warfare and, as Barclay emphasizes, this is part of Paul's response to the charge that his gospel of freedom leads to libertinism: if life in the Spirit is war, it must be a life of resolute discipline. Those who walk by the Spirit are "caught up into this conflict," and therefore "they are not free to do whatever they want" (*Obeying the Truth,* 112, on the phrase "they do not do what they wish" in Gal 5:17, often taken as a concession to the power of flesh).

liturgy and a new way of life but also to establish a liturgy *of* life, a sacred dance of daily practice in which we offer our bodies as living sacrifices in a *logikē latreia* (Rom 12:1).

Thus all the patterns and categories of stoicheic order are translated into the Spirit, renewed and made conducive to justice and peace, to the life of salvation and the redemption of human society.[12] The order of *ta stoicheia* comes to fulfillment, maturity, in the practices and life of the church.

This is evident within Galatians, where Paul rehabilitates the "negative" terms of the first part of the letter by placing them in the new context of Christ and his body. Torah has brought curse, but Christians are under the "law of Christ" (Gal 6:1-2). Paul lists "ten commandments" that pertain to the Spirit (Gal 5:16, 25, 26; 6:1, 2, 4, 6, 7, 9, 10). He describes the freedom of believers as "slavery" to one another (Gal 5:13). "Works," associated with the law earlier in the letter, become an essential aspect of faith and love (Gal 5:6; 6:10).

More abstractly, we can infer a profound and profoundly clever inversion in Paul's theology of flesh and Spirit. Flesh is weak; Paul himself preached to the Galatians in "weakness of flesh" (Gal 4:13). But the works that flesh produces are all expressions of strength. We have been toying with that paradox throughout this book: Weak flesh compensates for weakness by displays of strength; fearful flesh deflects fear by acts of bravado, by exhibitions of the *libido dominandi*. Flesh becomes *rebellious* flesh when it rebels against creatureliness and seeks to be as God. Flesh is sinful flesh, we can say, because it refuses to accept its own fleshliness. The Spirit permits flesh to be flesh, and in that sense those who are *ek tou pneumatos* are *more* fleshly than those who walk *kata sarka*. In the Spirit, people who are in flesh can boast of their weakness, their afflictions, their wounds, because those who are in the Spirit know that their power is not from flesh but from God. Mimicking the faith of Abraham, those who walk by the Spirit look to the God who raises the dead and speaks of things that are not as though they were. Like Solomon in Ecclesiastes, those who walk by the Spirit *rejoice* in a world of vapor, exult in their wispy weakness, where every achievement is

---

[12]For Paul's continuing use of purity motifs, see Michael Newton, *The Concept of Purity at Qumran and in the Letters of Paul* (Cambridge: Cambridge University Press, 1985). Walter Houston (*Purity and Monotheism: Clean and Unclean Animals in Biblical Law*, Journal for the Study of the Old Testament Supplement 140 [Sheffield: JSOT Press, 1993]) closes his book with some challenging reflections on the sustainability of monotheism in the *absence* of ritualized purity.

temporary and every life ends in death. The Spirit came so human beings can become comfortable in our own flesh.

SPIRITUAL ALCHEMY

This suggests that the institutional patterns of the church are, in a sense, *more* weak and beggarly than the elements were. When Christians started meeting to break bread from house to house, they could look up the hill and see the impressive temple complex, gleaming on the Temple Mount, apparently immovable for all eternity. It took an act of faith to say that the temple was childish and the little gatherings of disciples were mature. It took an act of spiritual bravado to say that the little gatherings of disciples were the *thing* of which the temple was only a shadowy figure.

But that was the bravado of the early church. They claimed that the base metals of the old world had, by the spiritual alchemy of Easter and Pentecost, been translated into the gold of the new. All the elements were still there, but they had been altered beyond recognition.

We see this pattern of thought everywhere in Paul's letters: the patterns of stoicheic life are not lost but transposed into a new key. Early Jewish Christians continued to worship in the temple, but the sanctity of the temple was packing up and moving elsewhere. The only holy space that Paul acknowledges is the holy space of human beings and human communities, those that are consecrated as temples by the indwelling Spirit of Jesus.

- "Do you not know that you are a temple of God [*naos theou*] and that the Spirit of God dwells [*oikei*] in [or among] you. . . . The temple of God is holy [*hagios*], and that is what you are" (1 Cor 3:16-17 NASB).

- The body of the Christian is a "temple of the Holy Spirit" (*to sōma hymōn naos tou en hymin hagiou pneumatos estin*), claimed by God as his property (1 Cor 6:19). Because it is holy space, the Christian's body must not be defiled by *porneia* (1 Cor 6:18), lest the Spirit abandon its place.

- By his death, Jesus has broken the dividing wall between Jew and Gentile, forming the two into one new man, a building that is a holy temple (*naon hagion*, Eph 2:21).

- Not only persons but things are sanctified, not by a consecration ritual involving washing, oil and blood but by the simple act of thanksgiving (1 Tim 4:4).

The predominant use of the adjective *hagios* is, of course, in the title that is given to all Christians, that they are "saints," holy ones in the Holy One Jesus, holy ones by reception of the Spirit and by sharing in the holy things of the Spirit.

Jewish believers might continue to observe purity rites, so long as they did not interfere with fellowship with Gentiles and "unclean" Jews. But, like the language of temple and holiness, purity is being reformulated and rereferenced.

- In the new world after *ta stoicheia*, "all things are clean" (*panta . . . kathara*, Rom 14:20), and "nothing is unclean in itself" (*ouden koinon di' heautou*). In context this has special reference to foods. Dietary decisions are no longer guided by the binary opposition of clean and unclean but by the demand of love (Rom 14:15).

- For those who are clean, everything is clean (*panta kathara tois katharois*, Tit 1:15). Those who have been cleansed by being joined to the death and resurrection of Jesus no longer defile or are defiled. The unbelieving are defiled because their mind and conscience is defiled (*miainō*).

- The new covenant's cleansing penetrates beyond flesh to the conscience (*syneidēsis*), which is sprinkled (*rhantizō*) by the blood of Jesus, and opens an entry into the holy place. Bodies too have access to the holy place through a washing with pure water (*lelousmenoi to sōma hydati katharō*, Heb 10:22). Because they have been cleansed by Jesus, the whole world is pure (see Tit 1:15).

- Impurity does not come from bodily emissions but from covetousness, which is idolatry (Eph 5:5).

- God gives idolaters over to their own impure desires (*eis akatharsian*, Rom 1:24). That impurity is expressed in sexual sin, and in injustice, wickedness, greed, envy, murder, strife, malice, deceit, slander, arrogance (Rom 1:28-30). In Levitical categories, these are "land" defilements.

- Before the justifying liberation of baptism, in the weakness of flesh, the Romans "presented [their] members as slaves to impurity" (*akatharsia*, Rom 6:19 NASB). Now they are to offer their bodies as tools and weapons of justice.

- Impurity is linked with greed and sensuality, and all three are to be excluded from the Christian community (Eph 4:19-20).

Sacrifice is no longer confined to the offering of an animal to God at the temple. Sacrifice can be performed anywhere there is a temple—that is, any-where where there is a person or community sanctified by the indwelling Spirit. Any action devoted to God is a sacrifice, a true *human* sacrifice, beside which the sacrifices of the law are pale bestial figures. Suffering in service to Christ and the people of God is one of the key forms of sacrifice.

- Paul urges the Romans to offer their bodies as a holy sacrifice (*thysian zōsan hagian*), an act of worship (Rom 12:1). As Paul continues, it becomes clear that the living sacrifice of the Christian is not confined to acts of worship but includes using one's gifts to build the body, love, devotion to one an-other, mutual honor, joy and hope, perseverance in tribulation, prayer, hospitality, refusal of retribution, doing good to enemies. All these are li-turgical forms of the sacrificial *leitourgia* performed by the body of Christ. These are sacrifices not because they involve loss but because, like Levitical sacrifice and the sacrifice of Jesus, they are means of drawing near to God. We offer this sacrificial liturgy through Jesus, our heavenly high priest.

- Paul's sees his ministry as a drink offering poured out on the sacrificial service performed by the Philippians (Phil 2:17), and acknowledges their gifts as "an acceptable sacrifice, well-pleasing to God" (*euōdias thysian dektēn euareston tō theō*, Phil 4:18 NASB).

- Christian sacrifice includes a sacrifice of praise and thanksgiving, and the overflow of praise that takes the form of sharing goods (Heb 13:15-16). Hebrews too regards this form of sacrifice as a liturgy-in-life (Heb 12:28), a priestly service that includes hospitality to strangers, visitation of pris-oners, sexual purity, contentment and avoidance of greed (Heb 13:1-7).

- Paul describes his mission to the Gentiles as a priestly ministry (*hierourgeō*) of offering sacrifice, as he cuts up the nations by the sword of the Word, carves off the flesh and transfigures them to smoke in the power of the Spirit (Rom 15:16).[13]

Thysia refers primarily to the peace offering, the festive, bridal offering of the Levitical system. If the whole Christian life has become *thysia*, it has

---

[13]In his *Reply to Faustus the Manichean*, Augustine gives classic expression to this Pauline trans-figuration of Torah. According to Augustine, Christians announce the fulfillment of the sym-bolic ordinances of the old covenant precisely by their *non*observance of rites once commanded, and he insists that Christian sacraments *are* the rites of the old law in fulfilled form. What unites these two responses is the conviction that in Christ and his body Israel's future-tense sacraments are conjugated into the joyous perfect tense of the gospel.

become bridal food, a continuous anticipation of the Marriage Feast of the Lamb that is yet to come.

As Augustine knew, this translation of the Levitical system brings that system to fulfillment, to *reality*.[14] It is not that animal sacrifice was *real* sacrifice and Christian sacrifice is *metaphorical* sacrifice; nor is Christian purity, priesthood or holy space a "spiritualization" of the real thing. The fulfillment in Christ and the Spirit is not *figura* but *res*: End reveals essence, and what comes last indicates what the first was about all along. Christian practices constitute the *paideia* and *nomos* of the Spirit, a pattern of life that itself wages constant war against the flesh and sweeps the participants up by and in the Wind of God to carry on Jesus' kingdom mission to the nations, to a human race still largely enslaved to the weak, beggarly, childish elements of the world.

From all this we can draw a fundamental conclusion about the mission of the church: the church fulfills and advances the justice of God by keeping in the ranks of the Spirit. The church *is* the people delivered from slavery to flesh; the church *is* the poststoicheic communion, the socioreligious entity that operates by matured forms of purity and holiness, that performs genuine sacrifices. The Spirit is at war with flesh, outside and within the church, and it is the duty of the church's members and leaders to stay in the ranks of the Spirit as he carries out that warfare and not abandon the Spirit to join forces with the flesh. The church's first mission is to be the church, to embody the justice of God in her own life together in the Spirit.

For the fruits of the Spirit are love, joy, peace, patience, kindness, goodness, faithfulness, gentleness and self-control. Against such there is no *nomos*. This is a socioreligious order that only the *nomos* of the Spirit can achieve.

SOCIETY AFTER *STOICHEIA*

But the church is not alone in the world. Jesus is Lord of all, and Paul even speaks of a universal "justification" (Rom 5:18). Insofar as God has issued his delivering verdict in the resurrection of Jesus, and insofar as those who are in Christ are justified from sin and flesh, just in this way justification is a reality for the race as a whole. The fact that justification has actually taken place for One Man, and in him for many, means that the world is no longer simply under the reign of sin, death and flesh. In the resurrection of Jesus,

---

[14]E.g., Augustine, *Contra Faustum* 6.9.1.

God has established a new state for humanity, since within humanity there is a state of exception.

Universal though the gospel's scope is, it is self-evident that the church arose and continues to exist, wherever it exists, in the midst of other socio-religious communities. And the church's mission is not merely to maintain herself an outpost exhibiting heavenly justice and the life of the Spirit; the church is not a dim desk lamp in the midst of the howling darkness. The church claims to be heir of the promises to Abraham, and the promise that Abraham believed and was reckoned righteous was that "all nations shall be blessed in you" (Gal 3:8). Isaiah's promises (see chapter six) indicate that the light of God's justice will shine like dawn through Zion to illumine the nations. Zion will become not a hill or a minor mountain, but the *chief* of the mountains, prominent enough to draw the attention of the nations, who stream there because Zion is the place where military technology can be put to agricultural uses (Is 2:2-4).

That is to say: while *being* the church, the poststoicheic communion of the Spirit, is the first mission of the church, it is not the *last* mission. The church is and remains the first form of mature social order, but God has promised that other socioreligious entities will exhibit his justice in some degree. The question is, how does that happen? How does the church, as the community called atonement, fulfill the globally transformative mission of God?

We have a paradigm case in the New Testament—in fact, two paradigmatic cases: first the mission of Jesus, and second the mission of the apostles. The pattern is the same in both cases, a fact especially evident in the parallels between Luke and Acts. Jesus comes in the power of the Spirit, proclaiming liberty to captives and sight to the blind and the favorable year of the Father's Jubilee. He preaches, teaches, heals, drives out demons. He gathers twelve disciples to form the nucleus of a new Israel, an Israel that will live by the Spirit as he does, even while they remain in flesh. He welcomes sinners to his table, sharing the joy that he claims is the joy of the Father himself over one sinner who repents (Lk 15). In the midst of an Israel still organized by stoicheic institutions, still patterned by binary oppositions of purity/ impurity and holy/profane, still living under the curses of Eden and Babel— in the midst of that world he begins to form a communion of disciples who can live beyond the elements, who will outgrow the childhood managers and guardians to reach maturity.

The early church carries on the *same* mission in what amount to the same circumstances. They too are filled with the Spirit, given new life by the risen and ascended Lord, so that they can carry on his work. They too preach and teach, heal and drive out demons and raise the dead. They too proclaim the favorable year of the Lord. In Jerusalem, they form an Israel within Israel, led first by the Twelve and then by others in addition, devoted to the apostolic teaching—which is the teaching of Jesus—to sharing goods and gifts, to breaking bread in fellowship meals, to prayer. They form a sizable poststoicheic platoon in the midst of the capital city, in the shadow of the temple, that monument to the elements, that monument to Herodian flesh. The communion of disciples announces to the world and to the powers that the universal reign of death has ended and the seed of life has been planted.

And they grow. First three thousand are baptized on Pentecost, then thousands here and hundreds there, and individuals as well who hear the gospel in chariots and in prison cells and from a perch in a second-story window. Everyone who hears, believes and is baptized leaves the old *kosmos* behind, begins to share in the fewer, simpler, more efficacious rites of the new Israel. Everyone who hears, believes and is baptized takes on a new *physis* that is neither Jewish nor Gentile but something else: Christic nature. They take up the calling to devote their baptized bodies as instruments of justice (Rom 6), and to stay with the Spirit in combating flesh and its desires. And so the community devoted to God's justice grows. Nations stream in. Abrahamic promises are fulfilled.

Of course, it was not so smooth for Jesus, nor for the apostles. Jesus declared Jubilee and promised to extend mercy to Gentiles, and the people of his hometown wanted to toss him from a cliff (Lk 4). Jesus formed a mature Israel within the womb of mother Israel, but many Jews preferred childhood and defended the old physics and its elements. They insisted that Jesus be put on a Roman cross, and there an end—so they hoped. But the Father raised his faithful Son, justified him from death, sin and flesh. In the light of the resurrection, the point of the cross becomes clear: in it, God, Father and Son, condemned sin in the flesh of the Son. What looked like a noble but tragic failure turned out instead to be a genuinely new beginning, as the poststoicheic Israel of the Spirit survived the death of the head by sharing in his resurrection.

For the apostolic generation, the pattern was similar. When Gentiles started entering the church, purified in all their uncircumcised glory by baptism, Jewish Christians balked. When Peter sat down to eat and drink with Gentiles at a common table, flouting food laws, men came from James to pressure Peter to withdraw from fellowship. Stoicheic barriers that Jesus had brought down were hastily reerected. Those who did not believe in Jesus at all became violent in their opposition, stoning Stephen, executing James, beating and stoning and pursuing Paul, arresting him and plotting his death, hounding him to Jerusalem and from Jerusalem to Rome. The apostles shared in the sufferings of Jesus, Paul boasting that he bore the brand-marks of Jesus (Gal 6:17). And they suffered for the same reasons Jesus suffered: Stephen was stoned on the charge that he had spoken against the temple and had told everyone to ignore the law (Acts 6:13). Paul faced similar charges. And the Romans accused the Christians of undermining Roman order. Both Jesus and the apostles faced murderous opposition from the guardians of stoicheic order because they were forming a community whose primary element, the one thing that constituted the communal physics, was the free Spirit of God.

It was not just that Jesus and the apostles proposed something new. That would have been controversial enough. It is possible that, given Torah's venerable status, an effort to change the way things were done would have been enough to arouse the fury of the Jewish leaders. Perhaps the simple fact that Christians caused disruptions was enough to worry Roman governors.

But it was *what* they proposed that ensured that traditionalists would be hostile. The church was born in a Jerusalem where a temple still stood, a holy place buffered by rules of purity and consecration. Jews already had the world mapped out, from the sacred center of the Temple Mount and radiating out to the ends of the earth.

Then along came the Christians claiming that they were the temple of God, the holy space inhabited by the Spirit. In a sense, as we have seen, they rejected the holy/profane binary of stoicheic order but they replaced it with what J. Louis Martyn calls an "apocalyptic antinomy," the binary opposition of flesh and Spirit, or of church and world. And they claimed that their little communities constituted true holy space. In a sense, they renounced purity regulations. There are no more forbidden foods; everything is clean, and all foods are to be received. But they did have food laws. To be received rightly, food has to be "consecrated" eucharistically—by giving thanks (1 Tim 4:4-5). Once it was wrong to eat unclean food; now it is wrong to refuse unclean food (Acts 10–11; Gal 2), especially if that food is being shared by Jew and Gentile. On the other hand, their purity demands were all-encompassing. Disciples were to renounce all forms of sexual indulgence, including lust; greed and envy defiled; murderous thoughts and angry words condemned one to hellfire. They even maintained food laws: The only unclean food becomes food sacrificed to idols; the meal to avoid is the divisive meal that excludes some of those who know and confess Jesus as Lord. No sacrificial smoke rises from Christian assemblies, but they claim to be offering the true, spiritual sacrifice of praise, worship and holy living (see Rom 12:1-2).

For a time, Christian Jews continue to frequent the temple and offer sacrifice, but eventually that too fades out of Christian practice.[15] They still sacrifice, but they renounce killing and burning animals. In short, in a world where the curses of Eden and Babel have been institutionalized in *stoicheia*, right in the face of the *stoicheia* the church forms a community with post-stoicheic patterns of holiness and purity, of sacrifice and priesthood, of temple and sacred space.

That is what leads to the clash between Jesus and the Jewish leaders, between the apostles and the Jews and eventually between the Christians and the Romans. In each case the church is a standing challenge and rebuke to an existing socioreligious system. In each case the leaders of that system consider the church a dangerous intrusion, a pollution, a confusing and defiling mixture of classes, sexes, nationalities. Christians are incestuous for the love between brothers and sisters; their cannibalistic feasts are abominations; their refusal to serve the gods puts everyone in danger.

What happens in these paradigmatic cases in the New Testament is what happens every time the church sets up shop within a new society. As we will see in the next chapters, there are different sorts of socioreligious entities, with different relationships to the stoicheic order and social physics of the old creation. But the church always comes as a socioreligious community into another socioreligious community. Sometimes the existing society welcomes the church, unaware of what it will have to give up to accommodate this strange new society. More often there is resistance, a struggle, perhaps

---

[15]See Daniel Ullucci, *The Christian Rejection of Animal Sacrifice* (Oxford: Oxford University Press, 2011).

to the death. Sometimes the church is driven back. Sometimes the church is killed and rises again on the bloodied ground. Sometimes the church is grudgingly accepted. Sometimes the society comes to admire the church and to begin to remodel itself, over long slow centuries, into something like the body politic, the somatic polity, of the church (see Rom 12; 1 Cor 12).

MISSION AS SOCIAL REFORM

Let me slow down and think through one or two of these possibilities more methodically.[16] Let me start with a scenario of welcome. Jesuit missionaries arrive on a remote Pacific island and begin to celebrate daily Mass. They study and pray together, get to know the villagers, find ways to serve and help with mundane chores. The island is populated by several related tribes that have been locked time out of mind in a cycle of uneasy peace, attack, vengeance, countervengeance, negotiation, trading of hostages and uneasy peace. After months of listening and learning the language of the tribe where they have established their base, they discover that the inhabitants have been expecting them. They have preserved a prophecy that white-skinned missionaries would visit and teach them about the true God. The chief is eager to hear what the Jesuits have to say, and within a year he has been baptized, and his household—the entire tribe—with him.

They begin attending Mass, learning Christian truth, learning to pray. Slowly, selectively, wisely the Jesuits instruct them on what customs they can retain and which are incompatible with Christian life. They are told they must no longer worship their traditional gods, and must give up their images. They are told that they no longer have to put menstruating or pregnant women into isolation, nor fear the burial ground of their ancestors. "Honor your fathers," the Jesuits tell them, "but do not fear their spirits." Parts of the island once taboo are opened; foods once rejected become common fare; rejected table companions are welcome at Mass, eventually at common tables. The mountain is no longer the holiest place on the island, the Jesuits tell them; the holiest place is the altar where Jesus' sacrifice is re-presented in an unbloody manner. Men are told they must love their wives and care for them, and the pattern and atmosphere of family life begins to change.

---

[16]I begin to repeat myself, a common enough occurrence for someone of my advanced age. For similar arguments, see my *Defending Constantine: The Twilight of an Empire and the Dawn of Christendom* (Downers Grove, IL: IVP Academic, 2010), 14; Leithart, *Against Christianity* (Moscow, ID: Canon, 2003), chap. 5.

Lazy men are rebuked and taught useful skills. Beggars and blind people are no longer scorned but cared for. The Jesuits begin to discuss the possibility of providing a translation of the Bible in the tribal language and talk of starting a school for the children of the tribe.

A year or two into the mission, an incident puts the converted tribe into conflict with a tribe on the other side of the mountain. The chief summons the men of the tribe and they prepare for war. The Jesuits intervene, reminding them that Jesus and Paul teach that Christians must reject vengeance, seek peace and leave things to the Father. Keep ranks with the Spirit, they urge. Instead of renewed conflict, the two tribes negotiate their disagreement and arrive at a mutually agreeable solution. The Jesuits encourage the baptized chief to tell his rival counterpart about Jesus. The rival chief listens raptly, for his tribe too has heard a prophecy about white-skinned messengers from heaven. Within a year, the second chief is baptized along with his tribe, and the tribes that were once rival brothers share one faith, one baptism, one Mass, one Lord.

Two tribes, living in flesh, living under stoicheic order, come out of the old world into the Christian era, and in the process the socioreligious life of each tribe, and of the tribes together, is transformed. Swords are beaten to plows; spears to pruning hooks.

This is rosy, of course, and hypothetical. I have smoothed and cleaned and brightened the picture to make a point. But it is not entirely a fairy tale, for rougher, messier versions of this scenario have been repeated all over the planet since the first Christian century.

Let me sketch another, more contested scenario, this one more directly rooted in reality. In the New Testament, the Romans frequently defend the church against her enemies, but in the mid-60s AD the first Roman persecution breaks out under Nero. Periodically over the following three centuries, Romans sporadically, unsystematically persecute Christians. Sometimes emperors issue decrees that cover the entire empire; other persecutions are more localized. Motives vary, but a recurrent theme is that the presence of Christians endangers Roman order. Christians refuse to worship the traditional gods and steer clear of some rites and celebrations of Roman civic life. The Christians recognize that the Roman world is a religio-political order, the *pax Romana* dependent on the *pax deorum*, and the latter dependent on a regular supply of sacrifices. When the gods seem angry—when earthquakes shake or volcanoes erupt or the Roman army is humiliated on the field—Christians become scapegoats. They are the ones who have made the gods angry. Their "atheism" is a pollutant, and they are abominations that need to be cleansed from the Roman world, if necessary by sword and fire. Their political and social effects are judged pernicious: they are peaceable to everyone, including Rome's enemies, and their blithe indifference to social caste encourages slaves and other subordinates to become uppity. All in all, persecution is a rational response, a commonsensical defense of Roman order.

So Roman authorities order Christians to sacrifice to the emperor. They refuse. They threaten, and the Christians continue to refuse. They torture, but the apparently masochistic Christians take delight in their pain. The Romans make an example of one, then another of the ringleaders, designing vicious, deliciously theatrical forms of execution. Some Christians give in, but many, instead of cowering or conforming, honor the dead as heroes of faith and look for opportunities to follow their example. And the church is growing. Christians seem to be everywhere, even in the Roman army, even in the court of the emperor. They are a contagion, and sterner measures are needed. But the sterner measures do not work.

The Romans have few choices, none good. They can keep intensifying the pressure and the pain, but that plan has self-evidently failed to contain things. They can try to ignore the Christians, but that means making space within the Roman Empire for a community that mocks and despises many of Rome's dearest values. Christians claim that their communities are holy spaces, but the boundaries of these holy spaces are fluid, shifting. Romans would be happy to accommodate. Some emperors would even be willing to incorporate Jesus into the Roman pantheon and build the Christians a temple. Then they could have their sacred space, on Roman terms. Christians politely (or rudely) refuse. Christians claim that the Roman gods are no gods at all, and the bolder and more vocal ones call the Roman gods wicked demons. How can such a sect be tolerated? The very act of toleration would involve an adjustment of Roman order, a curbing and qualification of Roman claims.

At the end of a long and complicated history, the Roman Empire admitted defeat, as the emperor himself became a Christian and later emperors turned Rome into a Christian empire. Without getting into the pluses and minuses of what is, inevitably, a mixed outcome, we can say that in the conflict between the church and the empire, the church won. It is, after all, still *here*; and the Roman Empire?

Conclusion

In these hypothetical/real-life scenarios, the church carries out its mission first by simply being the poststoicheic community it is, by proclaiming the gospel of Jesus that invites all listeners to be justified from sin in the waters of baptism, by staying in the ranks of the Spirit. By virtue of the simple fact of setting up a sacred space—the church itself—*different* from the sacred space of the existing order, the church poses a challenge to preexisting socioreligious arrangements. By insisting on purity regulations different from those of the surrounding society, the church rebukes the surrounding society. Even if tolerated, it might create a bipolarity in a monolithic system of sacredness; or, in a polytheistic setting, it establishes a monotheistic sacred community that lays an exclusive claim to holiness, and so disrupts the existing system from another direction. Just by *being present* as the setting of the poststoicheic purity, holiness and sacrifice of the Spirit, the church leaves its mark. It cannot help but meddle, cannot leave well enough alone. And often its effects, for those who want to protect the status quo, are far more than merely meddlesome. Often the effect will be to topple the great from their high places and raise the poor from the dust heap to sit with princes.

eleven

OUTSIDE THE CHRISTIAN ERA

✝

Like the last chapter, this is a contribution to the theology of mission, but under the guise of a contribution to the study of comparative religions, or comparative anthropology.

In the last chapter, we tested the fruitfulness of the theology of atonement presented in this book. We discovered, I trust, that this view of atonement opens out with some ease, without any grinding of gears, into a theology of mission. Since ecclesiology is inherent in atonement as I have explained it, mission is also inherent. Since this atonement theology is social theory, it lends itself to explication of a social gospel and a mission of socioreligious transformation.

In this chapter and the next, I tropologize and schematize the theology of atonement in another direction. Instead of discussing the aims and methods of missions, I examine the terrain of missions. Using the concept of *ta stoicheia tou kosmou* explained in earlier chapters, I map out the mission field and pause to examine three regions in slightly more detail. Outside the church and civilizations affected by the church, much of the world is still under stoicheic order. In the first part of this chapter, I examine tribal cultures that exhibit many of the features of ancient socioreligious order. This is a fairly easy case to make, and I will not spend undue time on it, offering only a brief summary of religious customs and practices of tribes in different parts of the world.[1]

---

[1]It is common among students of comparative religion to *define* religion in stoicheic terms, as if they were the permanent and inevitable forms of religious life. The influential Mircea Eliade is one scholar who has ontologized the distinctions of sacred/profane and pure/impure. See, for instance, *The Sacred and the Profane: The Nature of Religion* (New York: Harcourt, Brace, Jovanovich, 1987). If this is true, then we should say emphatically, with Bonhoeffer and others (including,

But the terrain is not uniform, and the gospel has had its effect even on religions and societies that have never been, in any meaningful sense, Christian. Some socioreligious groups are on the borderlands of the Christian era, one foot in the realm of *stoicheia* and one in the new world, half in the flesh and half in the Spirit. Judaism provides one example, which I examine all too briefly. I have chosen to focus on an example where the impact of the gospel and the church is easy to establish. Sri Lankan Buddhism is on the borderland of the Christian era because of the influence of an apostate Christian, the lapsed American Presbyterian Henry Steel Olcott, the "white Buddhist," who did his level best to form a Presbybuddhist church in Ceylon. In different ways and certainly to different degrees, Judaism and Sri Lankan Buddhism straddle the boundary of the Christian era. Olcott hints at a third sort of socioreligious order: those that have once been liberated from the stoicheic order, entered the Christian era and then reverted. These are "Galatianist" societies, and I contend in the next chapter that we in the modern West are living in such a society.

The fruitfulness of the theology of atonement is partly intellectual. That there are still "archaic" societies in the world, that there are religious groups who are not Christian but who have taken on Christian features: such exotica are worthwhile, and delightful, to study for their own sake. And the paradigm of atonement laid out here gives us a scheme by which we can make some sense of these monsters. Ultimately the theology has to prove itself fruitful in practice, in actual mission. Given my own instincts, inclinations and gifts, I have less to say about the practical fruit of my theory than I would like. Along the way, I offer some admittedly armchair reflections on what all this means for those who are on the ground. Perhaps mapping out the territory will be considered service enough, and others can take it from there: I have my work, they have theirs.[2]

STOICHEIC SOCIETIES IN THE CHRISTIAN ERA

It would be easy to assemble several volumes illustrating how tribal peoples continue to live *hypo ta stoicheia tou kosmou*, guided by archaic binary

---

remarkably, Alexander Schmemann) that Christianity is *not* a religion. It is preferable to conclude that Eliade is not correct, and his thesis is a signal of adherence to intellectual *stoicheia*.

[2]For a much more extensive and detailed treatment of religions from an angle similar to mine, see Daniel Strange, *Their Rock Is Not Like Our Rock: A Theology of Religions* (Grand Rapids: Zondervan, 2015).

distinctions of sacred/profane, clean/unclean, often worshiping by slaughtering animals in sacrifice or at least by doing table service for the god. Some form of priesthood or shamanic authority is also common. We have plenty of richly observed supporting evidence: ethnographers have long recorded the religious and social customs of tribal peoples, and before them we have extensive accounts from missionaries. I have chosen three brief illustrative examples.

The Toda people live in the Nilgiri Plateau of south India, and were the subject of a classic 1906 ethnographic study by W. H. R. Rivers.[3] A small people (less than 1,500 during most of the past century), the Todas attracted the attention of anthropologists because of their unique customs, many of which cluster around their main product, buffalo milk. Buffalo are sacred among the Toda, and "each kind of buffalo is tended at its own kind of grade of dairy by its own special grade of priesthood." The dairies themselves are graded according their degree of holiness, and the more sacred the dairy the more complex the rituals regarding milking and the disposal of milk, and the holier the person of the "dairyman-priest." The most holy of the priests are under stricter rules of daily conduct, designed to protect their sanctified status.[4]

Each village has its own dairy, but five of the clans "possess dairies where are kept herds of great sanctity, the herds of the *ti* or the *tiir.*" At these dairies, the ritual performed by the *palol*, the dairy priest, is extremely complicated. The complications begin with the *palol* himself, who "must be celibate, and if married, he must leave his wife, who is in most cases also the wife of his brother or brothers." He is permitted to visit his wife in the woods every week. Lower-ranking priests are free to cavort with their wives at will, but because sex pollutes, the higher-ranking priests have to be abstemious. Death is also polluting: "If a death occurs in the clan of a *palol*, he cannot attend any of the funeral ceremonies unless he gives up his office. If he resigns he is not again eligible for the office till the second funeral ceremonies have been completed."[5] A *palol* is not under food prohibitions, except that he is forbidden to eat chilies. During the time of his office, he is forbidden to cut his hair or nails. He wears dark gray clothing known as a *tuni*, but only

---

[3] W. H. R. Rivers, *The Todas* (London: Macmillan, 1906).
[4] Ibid., 38-39.
[5] Ibid., 99.

when "definitely engaged in dairy-work and on certain ceremonial occasions."[6] He is ordained to his priesthood in a ceremony that begins on a Saturday and ends a week after the following Monday with a ritual bath. Rivers writes that "the essential feature of the various ordination ceremonies is purification by drinking water from certain leaves and rubbing the body with the juice of certain plants or the bark of a tree mixed with water from a dairy stream or spring."[7]

Once ordained, the *palol* is devoted to a round of daily and occasional rituals performed at his *ti*—ceremonies performed with the milk itself, over a calving buffalo, ceremonies of giving salt to the buffalo. In the *ponup* ritual, the normal salt ceremony is expanded into a ceremony of "festival salt." When the churning is finished but before the buffalo are milked, the *palol*

> brings six sprigs of the shrub called *puthimul*, each sprig having on it five or six leaves. Three of these sprigs are put on one side, and the other three are used as follows:—Rice has been previously prepared and placed either on the leaf called *kakuders* or on that called *katers*. The *palol* makes a hole in this food in which he puts butter, and, taking the first sprig of *puthimul*, he plucks from it one leaf and, using it as a spoon, takes up some of the food and puts it on the fire in the fireplace . . . saying the name of the chief *teu* or god of the *ti*. He then takes some of the butter, and holds it over the fire til it drops, when he utters the name of the same god. He repeats this with a second leaf of the *puthimul*, saying the name of the second most important god of the *ti*, and so on with the other leaves.[8]

The *palol* is also an officiant at the sacrifices of the *ti*, which are offered on either Wednesday or Sunday. The day before the sacrifice, the *palol* takes wood to the sacrificial spot. He performs the sacrifice in the morning or evening, during the daily dairy ceremony. When his assistant has arranged the firewood, the *palol* "lights the wood with fire brought from his dairy. The calf is then killed and cut up" into a dozen or more specific parts. The priest places the flesh on the fire, and the roasting is tended by assistants. When the priest returns, he eats a specific portion of the animal and the assistant receives part of the liver, while other portions are set aside for the *palol* and his assistant to consume in the future.[9]

---

[6]Ibid., 103.
[7]Ibid., 164.
[8]Ibid., 177-78.
[9]Ibid., 285-86.

We leave the Todas for New Guinea and a briefer but remarkable example of the role of purity regulations among the Hua people. Pollution regulations for the Hua revolve around food and sex, as they do for many peoples. Food is considered a congealed form of *nu*, the life force, and even in the most normal domestic situations it must be handled with care. Anna Meigs describes the tight restrictions on contact with food:

> In the community of her birth, an *abade* "girl" may produce or prepare food for all but the newest *kakora* "initiates." Her food, like the girl herself, is fully accepted in her natal village. After marriage, the girl is a *hauva a'* "new woman" in the community of her husband where her stock plummets. No initiated person of this community, including her husband, can eat any food that she has produced, prepared, or served. Nor may any initiate eat from an earth oven into which she has placed leafy green vegetables. Once the new woman has borne a child, her alienation from her husband's community diminishes; it continues to diminish with every subsequent child she bears. So too does the danger of pollution from her hands. By the time she has had three children, she may assume the honorable status of a *ropa a'* "mature or venerable woman." Leafy green vegetables that she has picked may then be freely eaten by an older initiate, though still not by new initiates or her own husband. After about fifteen years of marriage, the proscriptions on eating leafy green vegetables picked by the wife are informally terminated. The wife gives her husband some leafy greens, and his classificatory elder brother (that is, any older man from his village) tells him to eat them freely, as if they came from the hand of his own mother, who is not only a woman he has always trusted but also a totally desexed being to him. The final transfiguration of a woman occurs after menopause.[10]

Sacrifices and offerings are pervasive in traditional Hawaiian religion,[11] offered at the commencement and at the conclusion of many daily activities. Dancing students begin their training by placing an offering on an altar, and are initiated into the company of performers by eating the brains of a sacrificial victim. Sacrifices are offered before fishing to ensure a successful catch. Sacrifices are offered to separate a person from any wrongdoing and to make

---

[10]Anna Meigs, *Food, Sex, and Pollution: A New Guinea Religion* (New Brunswick, NJ: Rutgers University Press, 1995), 21.

[11]Here I draw on Valerio Valeri, *Kingship and Sacrifice: Ritual and Society in Ancient Hawaii* (Chicago: University of Chicago Press, 1985).

the gods favorable. From the viewpoint of the Hawaiian worshiper, the sacrificial object embodies some feature or attribute of the gods, or symbolizes the result that the worshiper aims to achieve by sacrifice. An offering of shrimp is given to "peel" off something that clings to the worshiper like a shrimp skin. Some sacrifices embody an aspect of the worshiper that is mortified in the killing of the animal: "The pig may represent the sacrifice as transgressor, as well as the very idea of transgression. In expiatory sacrifices, its death thus represents the destruction of what is false human in the sacrificer because it is connected with his transgression of the terms that make him human." He kills the animal to destroy his animality.[12]

Hawaiian religion also includes purity rules. Menstruation pollutes a woman, as does an excessive oozing of "grease" from the pores. Any food that spoils is unclean. "All these are impure," Valerio Valeri concludes, "because they manifest a loss of integrity, of life . . . or the nonachievement of a normal form, of a perfectly functioning life."[13] Sacrifice and purity practices together reinforce the hierarchical order of Hawaiian society. Some food, including sacrificial food, is reserved for men, some for women, and the distribution of the food separates "the species into two: one is sacred and reserved for men; the other, which is profane, goes to the women." Even among men, sacrificial meals divide by rank: "Only people of the same rank and sex are proper commensals."[14] The social hierarchy is reflective of a cosmic hierarchy, since "one can sacrifice only to the gods that correspond to one's hierarchical position in society. . . . Sacrifice ensures that the hierarchy of the gods is translated into a social hierarchy and reproduces it."[15]

These fairly randomly chosen examples could be greatly extended, but enough has been said to make the point. Tribal cultures continue to function under a version of stoicheic order. Not only are the practices and institutions of ancient *stoicheia* operative—purity, sacrifice, priesthood (to a lesser extent) and holy space—but they function to exclude and separate. That is, these stoicheic patterns of life institutionalize flesh, and hence institutionalize injustice.[16]

---

[12]Ibid., 48.

[13]Ibid., 85.

[14]Ibid., 120, 124.

[15]Ibid., 109.

[16]It seems a giant leap to move from these small tribal religions to Hinduism. Toda, Hua and traditional Hawaiian religion are practiced by only a few hundred or thousand people in the

world; Hinduism is the third largest religion, practiced by nearly a billion people. For a breezy overview of some of its main themes, see Stephen Prothero, *God Is Not One* (San Francisco: HarperOne, 2010), 131-68. See also John Stratton Hawley, "Hinduism," in *Britannica Encyclopedia of World Religions* (Chicago: Encyclopedia Britannica, 2006), 433-63.

It is notoriously difficult to generalize about Hinduism. Yet the family resemblances are plain enough. For many Hindus, the puja is the center of devotion, consisting of the offering of goods to the gods at a temple or in a shrine at the home. Though the puja involves no slaughter, it reflects ancient sacrificial procedures, as a gift is offered to the god as an honored guest and then shared by the worshipers. Devout Hindus offer daily rituals—a gift of food to the gods at meals, a ritual offered to "all beings," a libation of water and sesame to the spirits of the dead, hospitality and recitation of the Veda. At Hindu weddings, offerings are made of roasted grain, and the bridegroom leads the bride around a sacrificial fire. The most dramatic similarity between tribal religions and Hinduism has to do with the role of purity. The caste system of India distinguishes groups by status, provides detailed rules for maintaining the separation and insists that the divisions of castes facilitate the contribution of each caste to the whole society. At base, as Louis Dumont observes, the caste system is reducible to the single opposition between pure and impure: "This opposition underlies hierarchy, which is the superiority of the pure to the impure, underlies separation because the pure and impure must be kept separate, and underlies the division of labor because pure and impure occupations must likewise be kept separate" (Dumont, *Homo Hierarchicus: The Caste System and Its Implications*, trans. Mark Sainsbury, Louis Dumont and Basia Gulati [Oxford: Oxford University Press, 1998], 43). The subdivisions within castes are also based on purity criteria. Certain occupations, like barbering or washing, are professions of impurity. Only Untouchables may hold such occupations, since their vocation and purity status correspond. Diet, marriage customs and other aspects of life continuously mark off the difference between the pure and impure (ibid., 56). Every Hindu can become unclean, and the uncleanness is spread by bodily processes, by objects and by family connections. Effluvia—saliva, urine, feces, other emissions from the body—create occasional, temporary impurity. The death of one member of a family affects not only those who are present with the body, or in the same house, but also all those who are related by birth. Yet the virulence of death impurity depends on the caste of the person. Brahmins are affected only by the deaths of close relatives, while the death of an Untouchable has much wider effects (ibid., 50-51). Social life is affected by the purity condition of the person: "A menstruating (or pre-pubertal) woman may not mount her husband's funeral pyre, she must wait for four days and the final bath (she would have to bathe in any case before burning herself alive). A marriage ceremony must be postponed if a fairly close death occurs during the preparations for it, or if the mother is menstruating. It is sometimes said that one should not come near the fire nor breathe on the fire with one's mouth if one is impure. A verse of Manu (II, 27) clearly shows the nature of impurity: 'The pollution of semen and of the womb [that is to say, birth] is effaced for the twice-born by the sacrament of pregnancy, birth, tonsure and initiation.' (The 'twice-born' are the members of the categories who are entitled to initiation, a second birth.) It can be seen that impurity corresponds to the organic aspect of man" (ibid., 50). Purification usually takes place by water, not only because water has natural cleansing properties but because water is often thought to contain a spiritual presence. Hindu festivals take place on "holy" ground. The four locations of the Kumbh Mela are the places where, according to legend, divine nectar fell from heaven to earth. Washing in the rivers at those places cleanses karma and makes the purified person eligible for nirvana. The impurity that attaches temporarily to those who have certain physical conditions attaches permanently to the Untouchables. In Hinduism we have an entire, large, complex civilization whose social principles are stoicheic. Pure and impure are established by birth, by direct fleshly descent, and they are kept in separate categories by purity boundaries and regulations. For more on purity in Hinduism, see Alexis Sanderson, "Purity and Power Among the Brahmans of Kashmir," in *The Category of the Person: Anthropology, Philosophy,*

The church would necessarily confront and subvert these stoicheic patterns. It is not politically correct to say so, but traditional cultures cannot be preserved intact if they enter the Christian era, the new creation. As members of these groups are baptized, they will need to reorder certain aspects of their social lives. The complicated purity regulations governing Hua sexual relations would be dismantled; a woman who marries into a new clan would not be classified by the "flesh" she received from her clan of origin. She would be one with her husband, able to cook for and eat with him. Hawaiian table exclusions that follow social and sexual divisions would be overturned at the Lord's table, set for members of every tribe and tongue and nation. Over time, if these tribes are converted en masse, Christian patterns of social relation will become more prominent. In place of life *kata sarka*, the gospel promises Spirit in flesh. It *must* be the case that things will fall apart, the center will not hold and the old world will die under God's justifying judgment as it is baptized into the death and life of Jesus.

Missionaries have to be cautious and wise in dealing with these customs, of course. They need to be aware of the danger of snuffing out a smoldering wick, the danger of killing openness to the gospel by impatience and ignorance. But some of what these cultures hold most dear cannot survive if the cultures are to enter the Christian era. And, of course, as missionaries since Pope Gregory and Augustine have known, elements of traditional culture may persist. The Todas will continue to produce buffalo milk and run dairies; traditional Hawaiians will still eat pigs. But even these traditional cultural features will be transformed, made new by the Spirit. The ranking of Toda dairies and dairy priests might remain, but the basis for the ranking would change. Once baptized, a priest could not think himself more holy than another priest; their ranking would be dissolved in baptismal water. Again, missionaries must be selective and careful about what remains. Whatever is retained, the fundamental physics of stoicheic culture will be transformed. They will not become identical to the missionaries. They will continue to be recognizably Toda, Hua and Hawaiian. But they will come to

---

History, ed. Michael Carrithers, Steven Collins and Steven Lukes (Cambridge: Cambridge University Press, 1985), 190-216. A similar point could be made by examining the sacrificial practices of Hinduism. For overviews, see Kathryn McClymond, *Beyond Sacred Violence: A Comparative Study of Sacrifice* (Baltimore: Johns Hopkins University Press, 2008), 35-38 and passim; Henri Hubert and Marcel Mauss, *Sacrifice: Its Nature and Functions*, trans. W. D. Halls (Chicago: University of Chicago Press, 1964).

share a new nature: their societies will become *Christian* Toda, Hua and Hawaiian.

BORDERLAND OF THE CHRISTIAN ERA

Many socioreligious orders in the world have a more complicated relationship to the Christian era than the Todas, Huas or traditional Hawaiians. Instead of being simply outside the poststoicheic cosmos of Christianity, they have been influenced, in one degree or another, by Christian social habits and patterns of life.

Judaism is the paradigmatic example of a faith that straddles the border of the Christian era, half in and half out. On the one hand, the destruction of the temple that led to the church's final break with stoicheic worship also forced a widespread reformation of Judaism. It would be too much to say that the destruction of the Second Temple initiated this redefinition. Already in the exilic and postexilic period, Jews had learned to make do without a temple. Categories and structures that originated in the temple—the very term "temple" and the idea of a sacred space—were transferred to the synagogue.[17] Worshipers entering synagogues were expected to purify themselves as if entering the temple courts, and writers like Philo spoke of synagogue prayer as *thysia*.[18] Much like Paul and the other apostolic writers, the terminology of stoicheic order was translated to meet the challenges associated with the interruption of stoicheic institutions. Christian and Jewish translations differ in many details. In the New Testament the many cleansings

---

[17]Josephus writes, "Although Antiochus surnamed Epiphanes sacked Jerusalem and plundered the temple, his successors on the throne restored to the Jews of Antioch all such votive offerings as were made of brass, to be laid up in their synagogue, and, moreover, granted them citizenship rights on an equality with the Greeks. Continuing to receive similar treatment from later monarchs, the Jewish colony grew in numbers, and their richly designed and costly offerings formed a splendid ornament to the holy place [τὸ ἱερόν]" (*Jewish War* 7.44-45; quoted in Lee I. Levine, *The Ancient Synagogue: The First Thousand Years* [New Haven, CT: Yale University Press, 2000], 125). See Donald D. Binder, *Into the Temple Courts: The Place of the Synagogue in the Second Temple Period*, Society of Biblical Literature Dissertation Series 169 (Atlanta: Society of Biblical Literature, 1997), who argues that Josephus writes here about the synagogue at Antioch.

[18]"A woman, then, should not be a busybody, meddling with matters outside her household concerns, but should seek a life of seclusion. She should not show herself off like a vagrant in the streets before the eyes of other men, except when she has to go to the *hieron*, and even then she should take pains to go, not when the market is full, but when most people have gone home, and so like a free-born lady worthy of the name, with everything quiet around her, make her oblations [*thysia*] and offer her prayers to avert the evil and gain the good" (Philo, *De specialibus legibus* 3.171-72; quoted in Marianne Bjelland Kartzow, *Gossip and Gender: Othering of Speech in the Pastoral Epistles* [Berlin: Walter de Gruyter, 2009], 99).

of the old order become the single bath of baptism, but they are transferred into the multiple washings of synagogue entrance by Philo. Still, the fact that Jews have lived for nearly two millennia without a temple, without sacrifice, with purity and holiness regulations transformed and humanized, means that they have entered, to that degree, the Christian era.[19]

On the other hand, Jews from the first century to the present insist that the stoicheic order of Torah provides the permanent order of Jewish life. In a penetrating discussion, David Gelernter summarizes Judaism in a series of metaphors, one of which is the "veil": "The veil that separates God and man—like a bridal veil, or the curtain that hangs before the holy ark in synagogue. The veil itself is important because it is God-given, but its ultimate importance attaches not to the veil but to what lies beyond it."[20] This apophatic image symbolizes God's transcendence.

> What the world calls "Judaism" is only a reflection in a window. You cannot see through the window, because the far side is black (or at any rate, invisible). But you must grasp that it is a window, there is a far side—and the far side is God. God is transcendent: cannot be seen, described, imagined. All you can imagine is the windowpane. All you can know is that it is a windowpane. . . . Yet the God of Judaism is no cold, remote abstraction—because of the windowpane, the "veil" itself, which might be the most remarkable religious device ever conceived. Jews believe in a transcendent God Who does not part the veil and become human but does invite (indeed, implore) man to approach. The veil proclaims that God's ineffable, transcendent presence can be closer to you if it is separated from you. You cannot see or know God but you can see, know, and approach the veil, knowing that God is on the other side. The veil symbolizes God's inconceivableness and (simultaneously, paradoxically) draws God and man close. In my theme-picture, the veil is the *tallis* worn at prayer, the mask Moses wears after encountering God; the two

---

[19]The parallel with the poststoicheic way of life in the church is often uncanny. Jacob Neusner writes, "The question taken up by the Mishnah, in the aftermath of the destruction of the Temple, is whether and how Israel is still holy. And the self-evidently valid answer is that Israel indeed is holy, and so far as the media of sanctification persist beyond the destruction of the holy place—and they do endure—the task of holy Israel is to continue to conduct that life of sanctification that had centered upon the Temple. Where now does holiness reside? It is in the life of the people, Israel—there above all. So the Mishnah may speak of the holiness of the Temple, but the premise is that the people—that kingdom of priests and holy people of Leviticus—constitute the center and focus of the sacred" (Jacob Neusner, Bruce Chilton and William Graham, *Three Faiths, One God: The Formative Faith and Practice of Judaism, Christianity, and Islam* [Leiden: Brill, 2002], 169).

[20]David Gelernter, *Judaism: A Way of Being* (New Haven, CT: Yale University Press, 2011), chap. 3.

curtains of the Holy of Holies, the curtains before the holy ark in any synagogue; the opaque *tefillin* boxes or the mezuzah hiding biblical texts; the ark
of the covenant, screened by cherubs' wings, hiding the tablets of Sinai. The
veil is present in the wordless, tuneless sound of the shofar, the overpowering
blank of the Western Wall, a Jew's refusal to pronounce God's name.[21]

The veil is perhaps the best single symbol to express the unavoidable, head-
on and mutually exclusive claims of Christianity and Judaism.[22] For Paul the
veil in all its senses is precisely what is removed: The veil that separates
Yahweh from his people has been breached in the coming of the Word in
flesh; the veil has been rent at the cross, and in the resurrection Jesus appears
in glory unveiled to his disciples; the veil that protected Israel from the
glorious face of Moses has been removed so that it can transform believers
from glory to glory. The veil crystallizes stoicheic order. The gospel is the
good news that the veil has been lifted. In nearly a direct inversion of Paul
(2 Cor 3), Gelernter defines Judaism as the religion of the *permanent* veil.

I do not expect to resolve the fraught, centuries-long theological and
political struggle between the church and Judaism in these two paragraphs.
But perhaps these brief notes open up a path for interchange between Jews
and Christians, one that focuses on practical stoicheic concerns that have
been central to the religion of Israel from the beginning, and a path whereby
Christians can recognize that, for all the reality of an impasse between the
two, Judaism is not merely *outside* the Christian era but at the doorway of
the Christian era.[23]

INVENTING WORLD RELIGIONS

Judaism is genetically linked with Christianity, and so we expect the family
resemblances noted above (divergent though the members of the family may

---

[21]Ibid., 180.

[22]See the generous, thoughtful discussion of David Novak's theology of supersessionism in Matthew Levering, *Jewish-Christian Dialogue and the Life of Wisdom: Engagements with the Theology
of David Novak* (London: Bloomsbury, 2011), chap. 1. Levering writes, "Teleologically one can only
ask, 'Which is the best way to and from the Lord God of Israel: the Torah or Christ?' The answer
cannot be both. Judaism does not accept Jesus of Nazareth to be the Messiah, and Christians, who
do accept Jesus as Messiah, believe that he has reconstituted the Torah around himself" (ibid., 22).

[23]I acknowledge that this way of stating the issue is a Christian way of stating the issue. I make no
apologies for that, but I do acknowledge it. And I also acknowledge that this will, perhaps inevitably, be taken as a kind of triumphalism, whereby Christianity is permitted to define the
terms of the debate between Christianity and Judaism. I know no other way to proceed: there
must be *some* framework to define the debate, and no possible framework is neutral.

be in their specific features). We are not entirely surprised to find a fascinating combination of stoicheic and poststoicheic motifs, not shocked to discover that the rabbis, like Rabbi Paul, transposed old covenant concepts, practices and values into new keys. It seems far less plausible to suggest that *other* world religions might also straddle the boundary that divides the inside from the outside of the Christian era. Yet by both direct and indirect influences, Christianity transformed the world's great religions. It is too much to say that Christianity invented the world religions by giving the world the concept of a world religion. But it is not wholly false.[24]

For a variety of reasons, partly in response to aggressive Christian missions, Judaism, Islam, Hinduism and Buddhism remade themselves during the nineteenth century, each asserting a quasi-Christian claim to be a global religion. Hinduism and Buddhism became more unified and structured,

---

[24]My aim is, more narrowly, to highlight specific ways that Christians and the poststoicheic life of Christianity affected the development of specific world religions in specific times and places. But I am inclined to think that the concept of "religion" used in comparative religious studies, and the concept of world religions as it is popularly understood, is an echo of Christianity. The notion that there is a single entity, "religion," that takes a variety of specific forms, is not universal. Until the modern era, "religion" did not have this universalizing force. Arguably Christianity lent the word this significance. It certainly has been the case that the specific shape of what counts as "religion" in early scholarship of religion takes Christianity as a paradigm case, though scholars have recently become aware of the parochial character of that definition. For the claim that the category of world religions is itself a European invention, see Tomoko Masuzawa, *The Invention of World Religions: Or, How European Universalism Was Preserved in the Language of Pluralism* (Chicago: University of Chicago Press, 2005). If I wished to develop a larger theory, the comments of C. A. Bayly would provide a useful starting point: "The nineteenth century, for instance, has been seen preeminently as the high point of nationalism and capitalism. But equally it was a period when 'religion' in the sense that we now use the term came into being across much of the world. Priests, jurists and lay people created more authoritative sources of power and bodies of doctrine. Pilgrimage expanded along the new lines of communication. The world religions began to look more like each other as Buddhists and Hindus adopted the methods of control and evangelisation that had long been common among Christians and Muslims. The new 'imagined communities' of the world religions vastly outpaced the growth of national communities based on the printed word. The rise of 'world religions' was above all a set of multi-centred transformations in which events in the regions impacted on the centre and the non-West influenced the West. The consolidation of domestic Christian churches in Europe and North America resulted in important cases from the needs of missionary activities overseas. But Christian churches were often themselves reacting to the prior expansion of Islam in Africa or Asia. Religious building shows how modernity was diffused from several cultural centres. This was certainly an era when the neo-gothic church style of northern Europe spread across the world. But the period also saw Middle Eastern styles of mosque building and the tenth century Hindu temple style appear in places as distant as the Caribbean and Fiji, displacing local forms of religious architecture. A growing uniformity of aspirations, styles of behaviour, ideology and bodily practice—the way people dressed, ate and deported themselves could be seen across the world. Yet this uniformity had origins in the non-European world as well as in the West, even at the high point of colonial domination" (Bayly, "Writing World History," *History Today* 54, no. 2 [2004]: 40).

and gave more definition to a core of belief and practice. As C. A. Bayly has argued, "Hinduism in 1780 was a huge extended family of systems of belief, philosophies, rituals, and techniques for harnessing esoteric power, which were recognized by insiders and outsiders as having something in common." During the eighteenth century, "authority tended to be localized and specific to certain Indian communities, while only a tiny minority read, and even fewer understood, the Vedas." Most Hindus at the time worshiped Brahman or one of his particular forms, Vishnu or Shiva, but many scattered throughout India "would have worshipped divinities who had only the most distant relationship to these great gods." Over the course of the nineteenth century, Hinduism "took on a much more closely defined form." Pressured by missionary attacks on the falseness of traditional Indian beliefs, Indians banded together and recognized their commonality. Standing together, they become Hindus. Hinduism allied with anti-English nationalist sentiment, again giving a cohesion to Indian religion that it had lacked. Ideas of sin, salvation, goodness and philanthropy shaped what might be called a "Hindu church" that "reflected the impact of Christianity."[25]

This is all very general. A more detailed and specific example will put flesh on these bones.

WHITE BUDDHIST

To this day, schoolchildren in Sri Lanka learn about the "doctrine" of Theravada Buddhism from a *Buddhist Catechism* first published in English and Sinhalese in 1881.[26] Described by its author as an "antidote to Christianity" and as a bulwark against Christian missionaries invading the East, the catechism begins with these questions:

Q. Of what religion are you?

A. The Buddhist.

Q. What is Buddhism?

A. It is a body of teachings given out by a great personage known as the Buddha.[27]

---

[25]C. A. Bayly, *The Birth of the Modern World, 1780–1914* (Oxford: Wiley-Blackwell, 2003), 342.
[26]That they learn "doctrine" at all is itself a sign of Christianity's mark.
[27]Quoted in Stephen Prothero, *The White Buddhist: The Asian Odyssey of Henry Steel Olcott*, Bibliotheca Indo-Buddhica Series 182 (Delhi, India: Sri Satguru Publications, 1996), 102.

Other questions are framed to highlight the differences between Buddhism and Christianity.

Q. Was the Buddha God?

A. No. Buddha Dharma teaches no "divine" incarnation.

Q. Do Buddhists accept the theory that everything has been formed out of nothing by a Creator?

A. . . . We do not believe in miracles; hence we deny creation, and cannot conceive of a creation of something out of nothing.[28]

Elsewhere the catechism discusses the merit of good works, insisting that "there is no great merit in any merely outward act; all depends upon the inward motive that provokes the deed." Questions 179-82 raise the issue of idol worship. Though Buddhist monks "make reverence before the statue to the Buddha, his relics, and the monuments enshrining them," they are not engaged in either crass pagan idolatry or the refined idolatry of other religions. Instead, the "Buddhist reverences the Buddha's statue and the other things . . . only as mementos of the greatest, wisest, most benevolent and compassionate man in this world-period." As for "the worship of gods, demons, trees, etc." this was "condemned by the Buddha" as a mere "external worship" that binds the worshiper like a "fetter that one has to break if he is to advance higher." Question 184 claims that Buddha "condemned the observance of ceremonies and other external practices, which only tend to increase our spiritual blindness and our clinging to mere lifeless forms."[29] Before they finish learning the catechism, Sinhalese schoolchildren have been instructed in the evils of slavery and the virtues of "temperance . . . gun control, chastity, and women's rights."[30]

In its catechetical form, apologetic content, moralistic tone and polemic against ceremony and ritual, the *Buddhist Catechism* suspiciously echoes nineteenth-century Protestant polemics against Roman Catholicism. As Stephen Prothero, Henry Steel Olcott's biographer, has written, the "lexicon" of the catechism was Buddhist, but the "grammar or deep structure was Christian."[31] This is no accident, for Olcott, not unlike the guru Arhat in

---

[28]Quoted in ibid., 101-2.
[29]Citations from Henry Steel Olcott's *Buddhist Catechism* are found in Donald S. Lopez, ed., *A Modern Buddhist Bible: Essential Readings from East and West* (Boston: Beacon, 2002), 16-18.
[30]Prothero, *White Buddhist*, 104.
[31]Ibid., 103.

John Updike's novel *S.*, was a New Jersey–born convert, a lapsed Presbyterian reformer, journalist and spiritualist.

Olcott's catechism was one of his main contributions to the late nineteenth-century revival of Sinhalese Buddhism,[32] a revival that significantly shaped the form and emphases of modern Buddhism. Olcott's efforts to reform Buddhism in Ceylon and to organize a unified Buddhism were inspired by the teachings and personal influence of his friend and collaborator the Russian émigré spiritualist Helena Petrovna Blavatsky. Together Olcott and Blavatsky founded the Theosophical Society in 1875 to reform the spiritualist movement, and after 1880 they moved their headquarters to India and devoted much of their considerable energy, talent and charisma to developing connections between Buddhism and Theosophy and learning from Hindu and Buddhist teachers. Once in the Far East, despite his earlier professions that he was ignorant of Eastern religions, Olcott rapidly turned reformer, describing his arrival in Asia as an inverted Puritan errand into the wilderness: "Just as I have left my home, and business, and friends, to come to India to worship the Parabrahm of primitive religions, so, in 1635, one of my ancestors left his home in England to seek in the wilderness of America that freedom to worship the Jewish Jehovah which he could not have at home."[33]

Before Olcott arrived in Ceylon, Christian missionaries had had considerable success in Christianizing the island, particularly in its educational system. A number of reforming Buddhist monks resisted the Christianization effort, and Buddhist reform movements continued after Olcott's time.[34] Olcott's influence was decisive; if others led the First Great Awakening

---

[32]"Scholars identify the Theravāda form of Buddhism that grew in Sri Lanka as Sinhala Buddhism. The adjective Sinhala is both a reference to an ethnic group: Sinhala people, the majority population in Sri Lanka, and to an Indo-European language: Sinhala spoken by the Sinhala public. Thus, Sinhala Buddhism has two meanings—Buddhism in the Sinhala language and Buddhism practiced by the Sinhala people" (Mahinda Deegalle, "A Bibliography on Sinhala Buddhism," *Journal of Buddhist Ethics* 4 (1997): 218, http://blogs.dickinson.edu/buddhistethics/files/2010/04 /deeg1.pdf).

[33]Quoted in Prothero, *White Buddhist*, 77.

[34]The best known was Miggettuwatte Gunananda, who became famous following an 1873 debate with the missionary Reverend David de Silva. Gunananda has been described as a "fiery orator, pamphleteer and a fighter who led the challenge to Christianity and the missionaries" (Stanley Jeyaraja Tambiah, *Buddhism Betrayed? Religion, Politics and Violence in Sri Lanka* [Chicago: University of Chicago Press, 1992], 6). Tambiah notes that Gunananda later became a member of the Theosophical Society. In 1862, he founded the Society for the Propagation of Buddhism and had been printing anti-Christian pamphlets. The "true founding father" of what has been called

in Ceylonese Buddhism, Olcott was the Finney responsible for directing the Second Great Awakening. It took a former Presbyterian to save Buddhism on the island.

Olcott instructed and inspired Dharmapala, the "Homeless Protector of the Dharma,"[35] described by some scholars as "the founder of international Buddhism, both in the sense of making Buddhists in different Asian countries aware of each other and in starting propaganda for Buddhism."[36] More generally Olcott had the Yankee ingenuity and organizational skills to unify Ceylonese Buddhism and ensure its transmission to future generations. Taking a page from itinerant revivalists,[37] he traveled the country on several lecture and healing tours, and he organized schools and voluntary associations. According to one summary of his contributions,

> he invented a Buddhist flag (that in due course became the emblem of the international Buddhist movement),[38] formulated a Buddhist catechism in terms to which he felt (wrongly) all Buddhists could assent, persuaded the government to declare Vesak a public holiday,[39] and encouraged Buddhists to celebrate it

"Protestant Buddhism" was a protégé of Olcott's, who adopted the name Anagarika Dharmapala. His Maha Bodhi Society, founded in 1891 to recover the sight of Buddha's enlightenment for Buddhists, still sponsors all Sinhala Buddhist monasteries outside Sri Lanka (Richard Gombrich and Gananath Obeyesekere, *Buddhism Transformed: Religious Change in Sri Lanka* [Princeton, NJ: Princeton University Press, 1988], 206).

[35] As Gombrich and Obeyesekere write, Dharmapala met Olcott and Blavatsky in 1880, "When [Dharmapala] was only sixteen, and when they returned to Sri Lanka in 1884 he persuaded Olcott to initiate him into the Theosophical Society. Despite paternal objections he went with Olcott and Madame Blavatsky to the Theosophist headquarters in Adyar near Madras. Here he wanted to study occultism with Madame Blavatsky, but she persuaded him instead to study Buddhism and to learn Pali, the classical language of its scriptures. Returning the same year to Sri Lanka, he became manager of the Buddhist Theosophical Society and worked for it, with some interruptions, till 1890. He also edited and produced the society's newspaper, *Sandarasa*. By then Madame Blavatsky had died, and he and Olcott were drifting apart; they finally separated in the early 1900s, when Olcott claimed that the tooth relic in Kandy was an animal bone. ... Olcott's rationalistic (Protestant) view of relics was too much for Dharmapala's Sinhala Buddhist sentiment" (Gombrich and Obeyesekere, *Buddhism Transformed*, 206).

[36] Ibid., 206. Between 1889 and 1906, Dharmapala traveled to Japan, India, Burma, Thailand, Europe and the United States, representing Buddhism in Chicago at the 1893 World Parliament of Religions. Through these travels and activities Dharmapala not only consolidated Buddhism in Sri Lanka but also helped to revive Buddhism elsewhere. Lopez describes Dharmapala's friendship with Yang Wen-hui, a Chinese engineer who was instrumental in reviving Buddhism in China and spreading Buddhist ideas in the West (Lopez, *Modern Buddhist Bible*, xviii-xix).

[37] Olcott was sometimes quite open about combating Christian missions with their own weapons: "As the Christians have their Society for the diffusion of Christian knowledge, so this should be a society for the diffusion of Buddhist knowledge" (quoted by Prothero, *White Buddhist*, 97).

[38] And which Olcott compared to the cross in Christianity.

[39] Vesak commemorates the birth and enlightenment of Buddha, celebrated in May.

with songs modeled on Christmas carols—whence further developed the custom of sending Vesak cards on the analogy of Christmas cards. But besides imparting a Christian style to Buddhist civil religion, he founded institutions that had a more solid impact. Probably the most important function of the Buddhist Theosophical society was that it founded and ran Buddhist schools to emulate those founded by Christian missions. It was clearly Olcott's inspiration that led to the founding of the Young Men's and Young Women's Buddhist Associations and the Buddhist Sunday schools, which came to be held in almost every village and were supplied with textbooks and an examination structure by the Young Men's Buddhist Association.[40]

According to Donald S. Lopez, Olcott was "the first to try to unite the various Asian forms of Buddhism into a single organization, an effort that bore fruit long after his death when the first world Buddhist organization, the World Fellowship of Buddhists, was founded in 1950."[41]

Not only organizationally, but also conceptually, Olcott's work was less a revival of Buddhism than a recasting of traditional Buddhism into a modernist shape inspired by liberal Protestantism. Olcott attacked the Buddhist practice of veneration, and made the distinctively Western and Protestant claim that the essence of Buddhism did not lie in the rituals of the Buddhist monks but in the philosophy and texts of Buddhism, which functions as "sacred Scripture."[42] The modern Buddhism that Olcott helped to form included only those elements that were "most compatible with the ideals of the European Enlightenment that occurred so many centuries later [than the Buddha], ideals embodied in such concepts as reason, empiricism, science, universalism, individualism, tolerance, freedom, and the rejection of religious orthodoxy."[43]

---

[40]Gombrich and Obeyesekere, *Buddhism Transformed*, 204-5. The authors add that "the society's schools were taken over by the government in 1961, but they still exist and so do the Sunday schools." Prothero claims that there were 1,200 state-sponsored schools in Ceylon when Olcott arrived, only four of which were Buddhist (*White Buddhist*, 86). By 1897, 47 Buddhist schools had been founded, and there were 427 by 1940 (Heinrich Dumoulin, ed., *Buddhism in the Modern World* [New York: Macmillan, 1976], 78).

[41]Lopez, *Modern Buddhist Bible*, xvi.

[42]Olcott, in Lopez' words, "allowed modern Buddhism generally to dismiss the rituals of consecration, purification, expiation and exorcism so common throughout Asia as extraneous elements that had crept into the tradition" (quoted by Peter Steinfels, "The Roots of Today's Buddhism," *Urban Dharma: Buddhism in America*, www.urbandharma.org/udharma5/roots.html).

[43]Lopez, *Modern Buddhist Bible*, ix-x. Prothero agrees: "Olcott's ostensibly non-Christian Buddhism sounded like liberal Protestantism. More than an antidote to Christianity, Olcott's Catechism was a homeopathic cure, treating the scourge of Christianity with a dose of the same. His critique of Christianity shared many elements with liberal Protestants' critique of Christian

Beginning in the late nineteenth century, thus, the "essence" of Buddhism was distilled from its regional and local particularities, "to create something simply called Buddhism." Through this process, Buddhism came to see itself, and to be seen, as a universal religion.[44] And this distillation was achieved in significant measure by a former Calvinist who throughout his career articulated Buddhism according to what Prothero has called a "liberal Protestant grammar"[45] and advocated Protestantized Buddhist practices.

CONCLUSION

The ironies of this story are legion: the church equipped a leading opponent of Christian missions, one of the great antimission missionaries of the nineteenth century, who deployed the methods and even the concepts of modern American Protestantism in his battle against missionaries. Westerners who convert to Buddhism are frequently attracted to a form of Buddhism that, for all its claims to antiquity, is a modern creation, and includes much of the Christianity that Western converts are attempting to escape. Western converts, indeed, are often attracted to *precisely* those features of Buddhism that owe most to liberal Protestantism—tolerance, the elevation of reason, the hostility to elitism and hierarchy. The unified Buddhism that Christianity confronts in Asia is, in some measure at least, a product of Christianity itself. Christianity helped create its own rivals. In a farcical enactment of G. K. Chesterton's story of a traveler who circumnavigates the world only to rediscover Britain, missionaries now go halfway around the world and discover they have to fight theological modernists.

Theologically, the example of Sri Lankan Buddhism shows in concrete detail how a religion other than Christianity can partially enter the Christian era and be formed by Christianity. Christ's justifying death and resurrection had real, universal, objective effects on the world (Rom 5:16, 18). By forming a community that lives beyond *stoicheia* and sending it on a mission to call the nations from childhood to maturity, Jesus created the possibility of

---

orthodoxy, including a distrust of miracles, an emphasis on reason and experience, a tendency toward self-reliance, and a disdain for hell. Like their Jesus, his Buddha was a quintessential Christian gentleman: sweet and convincing, the very personification of 'self-culture and universal love'" (*White Buddhist*, 104).

[44]Lopez, *Modern Buddhist Bible*, xxxvii.

[45]Even the notion that a religion could be distilled to an "essence" betrays the liberal Protestant provenance. Olcott's was a Harnackian Buddhism.

Olcott's Presbybuddhism. In terms of mission, the Christian elements do not make Sri Lankan Buddhism another form of Christianity. It is not an alternative way to the one God who is the Father of Jesus. But the Christian elements are there, and important. Since it has been partially brought into the Christian era by lapsed Christians who taught Buddhists to regard their religion as if they were Protestants and to conform their practices, Buddhism is not *simply* other to Christianity. It participates to some degree in the poststoicheic world of the Protestant church.

If the church is going to carry on effective missionary efforts in areas dominated by Buddhism, she will need to know that she is in some degree and in some places confronting her own offspring. We have met the enemy, and he is us.

twelve

GALATIAN CHURCH, GALATIAN AGE

✝

Deep in the pit of hell, the pilgrim Dante comes across yet another chilling sight—a man walking with his torso split open from chin to groin, so that "his guts spilled out, with the heart / and other vital parts, and the dirty sack / that turns to shit [*merda*] whatever the mouth gulps down."[1] Like a motorist rubbernecking at an accident, Dante stares in fascinated horror, and the man begins to speak.

> See how I tear myself!
> See how Mahomet is deformed and torn!
> In front of me, and weeping, Ali walks,
> his face cleft from his chin to the crown. (*Inferno* 28.22-33)

The surprise in this scene is not the gruesomeness of Muhammad's punishment. A descendant of Crusaders, Dante would not have given a second thought to the sensitivities of Muslims, nor did he regard Muslims as fellow worshipers of the God of Abraham. The surprise is the place where this scene occurs, in the ninth bolgia of Malebolgia, in the subcircle of hell reserved for *schismatics*. Muhammad is not among the idolaters or the pagans, but among sinners being punished for tearing the Christian church, all of whom, appropriately enough, have their bodies rent as retribution for rending the body of Christ.

In treating Muhammad as a Christian schismatic, Dante gave poetic expression to views widespread in his time. Many in the Western medieval world believed that Muhammad himself had apostatized from Christianity,

---

[1] The opening paragraphs of this chapter are taken from my "Mirror of Christendom," available at marshillaudio.org.

and some even believed he had once been a cardinal.[2] Centuries before Dante, John of Damascus (675–749) treated Islam in the final section of his treatise *de Haeresibus*, calling it the "heresy of the Ishmaelites." John wrote that Muhammad was influenced by an Arian monk named Bahira, who encouraged the spread of Islam by predicting that Muhammad would become a prophet.[3]

These medieval treatments of Islam find little favor today, even among Christians, yet as a purely historical matter the medieval accounts have some points in their favor. That Muhammad had contact with a Syrian monk is mentioned in the *hadith*, the collections of Muhammad's words and actions that serve for most Muslims as a second source of authority alongside the Qur'an.[4] And it is clear that Muhammad had wider contact with Christians. One of the key themes of the Qur'an is a denial of the Trinity, since it is "far from his glory" for Allah "to beget a son" (sura 4:171; cf. 2:115; 5:73, 116; 6:101; 9:30-31; 18:4-5; 25:2; 112:3). More generally, Nestorian Christianity had by Muhammad's time spread through Arabia, Syria, Iraq, Persia and eastward as far as China,[5] and monophysite Christians had founded churches in Syria

---

[2]Dante Alighieri, *The Divine Comedy: Translation and Commentary*, trans. Charles A. Singleton (Princeton, NJ: Princeton University Press, 1980), 2:503.

[3]Daniel J. Sahas, *John of Damascus on Islam: The "Heresy of the Ishmaelites"* (Leiden: Brill, 1972), 73. Sahas discusses the disputed authenticity of the section of John's treatise devoted to Islam (60-66), but even if the section is not from John, it was added to his treatise at an early date and thus provides important evidence of early Christian views of Islam. Peter the Venerable, abbot of the famed abbey of Cluny during the twelfth century, hesitated over whether to call Islam a heresy or a form of paganism, "for I see them, now in the manner of heretics, take certain things from the Christian faith and reject other things; then—a thing which no heresy is described as ever having done—acting as well as teaching according to pagan custom." Yet Peter wrote treatises with titles like *Summa totius haeresis Saracenorum* (Summary of all the heresies of the Saracens) and *Liber contra sectam sive haeresim Saracenorum* (A book against the sect or heresy of the Saracens), and he viewed Islam as a sum of all Christian heresies. According to Peter, Muhammad himself had been taught by a Nestorian monk named Sergius who "made him a Nestorian Christian," and Muhammad's teaching was a mishmash of Sabellianism, Nestorianism, Manicheanism and Judaism. False teaching was bad enough, but Peter was equally concerned with Muslim practice. Even if, as Peter concedes, the Qur'an records truths about the prophets and Jesus, Muslims reject the sacraments, which is something that "no one besides these heretics ever did." James Kritzeck, *Peter the Venerable and Islam* (Princeton, NJ: Princeton University Press, 1964), 129-36, 144-45.

[4]Sahas, *John of Damascus*, 73. As Sahas points out, the monk's prophecy was frequently used by Muslim apologists to rebut the claim that Muhammad's prophetic ministry had not been announced. For transliterations of Islamic technical terms, I have relied throughout on Ian Richard Netton, *A Popular Dictionary of Islam* (London: Curzon, 1992).

[5]Laurence E. Browne, *The Eclipse of Christianity in Asia: From the Time of Muhammad Till the Fourteenth Century* (New York: Howard Fertig, 1967), 5, 50; Kenneth Cragg, *The Arab Christian: A History in the Middle East* (Louisville, KY: Westminster John Knox, 1991), 22, 40, 55-56;

and Egypt. Prior to the Islamic conquest of the Middle East and North Africa, those areas were predominantly Christian, if often heretically Christian. It is, furthermore, a vast oversimplification to suggest that these Christians submitted to the superior force of the Islamic sword, since many Christians greeted the Arabian conquest as a liberation and willingly converted to Islam. Whatever the experience of individuals, as a region and as a culture the Middle East and North Africa became Islamic by abandoning Christendom. The medieval perspective is true to this extent: the Islamic world is not pagan but apostate. Islam exists in a world *once* Christian, which a millennium ago removed itself from the Christian era and returned to *ta stoicheia tou kosmou*.[6] Islam is a product of Galatianism.

In the previous chapter, we glanced at Henry Steel Olcott's efforts to organize and revise Buddhism in Ceylon. To the degree that Olcott influenced the development of modern Buddhism—and he did—Buddhism is the product of an intersection of Christianity and older forms of Buddhist devotion. It is not "pure." Here as elsewhere, Christianity deals in mixtures. But Olcott was not alone. He was not the first, or last, individual to leave

---

J. Spencer Trimingham, *Christianity Among the Arabs in Pre-Islamic Times* (London: Longman, 1979), 159-62, 280-82.

[6] A handful of Western scholars now think there is historical truth to this medieval view of Islamic origins. According to the standard Muslim account, the Qur'an contains revelations that Allah delivered to Muhammad through the angel Jibril between 609 and 632. They were fixed in written form under the third caliph in the mid-seventh century. Christoph Luxenberg doubts most of this. In 2000, he published the German edition of *The Syro-Aramaic Reading of the Koran* (New York: Prometheus, 2009), arguing that that the Qur'an is an Arabic translation of an original Syriac/Aramaic Christian lectionary. The contributors to Karl-Heinz Ohlig and Gerd Puin, eds., *The Hidden Origins of Islam: New Research into Its Early History* (New York: Prometheus, 2009), develop similar revisionist accounts. It is not until the ninth century that Muslim writers claim that the Qur'an contains the revelations given to Muhammad. The year 622—which Muslims mark as the year Muhammad and his followers made the *hijra*, a fateful journey from Mecca to Medina—was not originally connected with Muhammad at all. Before there is any record of Muslims dating time from the *hijra*, Arabic Christians dated the beginning of the Arabic era to 622, when they gained independence from Persia's Sassanian Empire. Other early Islamic texts support the notion that Islam emerged not as a new religion but as a novel development within a Syriac-Christian milieu. In his contribution to *Hidden Origins*, Luxenberg applies his method to the inscription on the Dome of the Rock, which seems to contain a straightforward Islamic confession: "There is no god but God alone . . . Mohammed the servant of God and his messenger." Luxenberg points out that Muhammad, usually understood as a proper name, means "exalted be" or "praised be," and also notes that Syriac Christians, who were skeptical of the Nicene doctrine of Jesus' divine sonship, preferred Isaiah's title "Servant" for Jesus. He contends that the inscription should read: "There is no god but God alone. . . . Praised be the servant of God and his messenger." This makes better sense of the sequel, which explicitly identifies "Messiah Jesus, son of Mary" as "the messenger of God and his Word."

Christianity for another religion. Long before Olcott, the Galatians entered the Christian world by the Spirit, and then retreated back to the old world of shadows and elements.

Societies, like individuals, have dabbled with Galatianism. Churches have reverted to stoicheic patterns of worship and sociality, reintroducing veils and barriers and divisions that Jesus and the Spirit had torn down. Entire civilizations have become Christian and then retreated, forming an odd post-Christian, post-poststoicheic socioreligious entity. I argue in this chapter that we are living in just such a civilization: one that was once Christian but has returned to the obsolete life under the elements of the world. This chapter thus provides a tidy-bow conclusion to my typology of socioreligious orders. There is the Christian order of the church that exists (not always faithfully) in the Christian era. And beyond the church there are socioreligious groups that more or less completely remain under the elements, groups that straddle the border of the Christian era and groups that have entered the Christian era, spent the night or a millennium, settled in and gotten comfortable, and then decided to move on out the other side.

Modernity is known for its scientific, rational mindset, its superior scoffs at primitive taboos and fears, its *de*sacralization of all and everything. Modernity is a boundary-busting power, not a boundary-erecting one; if anything, it looks hyper-Christian, hyper-poststoicheic rather than stoicheic. We no longer erect settled boundaries between male and female, much less between slave and free, Jew and Gentile. We will tolerate no distinctions at all. I concede below that this is *part* of the story, but it is a superficial part. An exclusive focus on *de*sacralization is blind to all the ways modernity brings a *re*sacralization. If the premise stated at the very outset of this book is right—the premise that has lurked around the corner of every period and paragraph, the premise that societies are inevitably, inescapably organized by purity and holiness and sacrifice—if that is true, then modernity's claim to escape these habits and forms of life must be a diversion. I propose that we not go for the head fake. Keep your eye on the ball.

My argument could be spun out along several lines. We might, for instance, examine the role of purity concepts in modern philosophy along the lines suggested by J. G. Hamann.[7] The modern rave for systems, scientific

---

[7]A representative quotation will, alas, have to do. Hamann summarizes the progress of modern philosophy as a series of "purifications": "The **first** purification (*Reinigung*) of philosophy

and philosophical, could provide another line of evidence. Systems can be expressions of flesh: fearing loss, leakage, decay or disorder, thinkers gain control by finding a place for everything, getting everything in its rank. Human knowing is inevitably partial, vulnerable; we chance on critical bits of information, stumble on the truth. For some that is too risky, and so they invent *methods* to eliminate change, predetermine the steps to truth and master all the bits of information without remainder. Systematizing is the heroism of ideas, an inverted expression of the weakness and vulnerability of flesh. Modern philosophy, systematizing to stave off the dangers of intellectual and cultural disorders, employs separations that resemble the holiness and purity separations of stoicheic order. Reason is not to be contaminated by mere probable fact; philosophical language is not to be profaned by metaphor or poetry.[8] Systematizing is the "civilizing process" applied to thought, the philosophical equivalent of not farting at a dinner party.[9] Philosophy in step with the Spirit, by contrast, would be quite at home with the limits of fleshly intelligence, untroubled by untied threads and undotted *i*'s. It would make much of the Logos of reason but would not neglect the rhetorical breath and music of the Spirit of poetry. Spiritual thinkers would be impure thinkers.

---

consisted in the partly ill-conceived, partly unsuccessful attempt to make reason independent of all custom, tradition, and belief in the latter. The second is still more transcendental and aims at nothing less than an independence from experience and its everyday induction—for, after reason sought who knows what? **beyond** experience for 2000 years, it suddenly not merely despairs of the progressive course of its ancestors, but also promises its impatient contemporaries, with so much **defiance**, and this in a short time, that universal and infallible **Philosopher's Stone**, so indispensable for Catholicism and despotism, to which **religion** with its **sanctity** and **legislation** with its **majesty** are swiftly subjected, especially in the wane of a critical age, where empiricism on both sides, struck with blindness, makes its own nakedness more suspicious and ridiculous day by day. The **third**, most sublime and as it were **empirical** purism therefore concerns language, the single, first and last *organon* and criterion of reason, without any other credentials than **tradition** and **use**" (from Gwen Griffith Dickson, *Johann Georg Hamann's Relational Metacriticism*, Theologische Bibliothek Topelmann 67 [Berlin: de Gruyter, 1995], 520; bold in original). Hamann charges that this can only end in nihilism; Kant's purgations turn "the straightforwardness of language into such a senseless, ruttish, unsteady, indefinite something = x that nothing remains but the soughing of the wind, a magical phantasmagoria, or at best, as the wise Helvetius says, the talisman and rosary of a superstitious transcendental belief in *entia rationis*." Kant, on Hamann's reading, is a sophisticated Pharisee pursuing a program of intellectual purification.

[8]There is a countermovement within modernity that revels in mixtures and impurities. See Wolfram Schmidgen, *Exquisite Mixture: The Virtues of Impurity in Early Modern England* (Philadelphia: University of Pennsylvania Press, 2012).

[9]The phrase "civilizing process" comes from Norbert Elias, *The Civilizing Process: Sociogenetic and Psychological Investigations* (London: Blackwell, 2000).

Purity concerns are not constant in the modern age. Remakes of Shakespeare during the early modern period smooth out the Bard's jagged edges, correcting his "impure aesthetics."[10] Classicists aim for purity; romantics revel in mixtures. Modernist architecture is an architecture of pure lines, uncluttered shiny surfaces; modernist music strips off the ornamentations of romanticism; modernist painting includes Mondrian's geometry and the impressionist aim to render the objective play of light in paint. The arts, literature and music raise another thread of evidence: modern *sacralizations*. The distinction between "high" and "low" culture forms a sacred boundary that is also a social boundary. The concert hall, theater and museum are treated with the hushed reverence of sacred space, and certain protocols of dress, gesture, posture and movement were, until recently, expected, protocols appropriate to the sacred actions and objects within.[11] Here the operative principle is not the binary of pure/impure but of holy/profane. Clearly the logic here is not identical to that of ancient stoicheic order. No one literally believes that the pianist or the composer is divine or that the concern hall is a temple inhabited by the goddess Art. But the rhetoric is there, and the patterns of behavior, and the hierarchies and exclusions, so it is not difficult to see in it a post-Christian afterglow of stoicheic life.

Gadamer once remarked that we need a history of the idea of purity, and to that one might add the need for a history of the concept of the sacred in modernity. This chapter is neither, but to make it something more (if only

---

[10]See Hugh Grady, *Shakespeare and Impure Aesthetics* (Cambridge: Cambridge University Press, 2009). On the adaptations, see Hazelton Spencer, *Shakespeare Improved: The Restoration Versions in Quarto and on the Stage* (Cambridge, MA: Harvard University Press, 1927); Allardyce Nicoll, *Dryden as an Adapter of Shakespeare* (London: Shakespeare Association, 1922); George C. Barnam, *Eighteenth-Century Adaptations of Shakespearean Tragedy*, University of California English Studies 14 (Berkeley: University of California Press, 1956); Jean I. Marsden, *The Re-Imagined Text: Shakespeare, Adaptation, and Eighteenth-Century Literary Theory* (Lexington: University Press of Kentucky, 1995). Collections of adaptations include Christopher Spencer, ed., *Five Restoration Adaptations of Shakespeare* (Urbana: University of Illinois Press, 1965); and Sandra Clark, ed., *Shakespeare Made Fit: Restoration Adaptations of Shakespeare* (New York: Everyman's Library, 1993).

[11]Peter Stallybrass and Allon White (*The Politics and Poetics of Transgression* [Ithaca, NY: Cornell University Press, 1986], 2-3) argue that categories of "high" and "low" cut across various spheres of cultural life, and that the classification of high and low in one sphere is inseparable from the same classification in another sphere. Thus, "The ranking of literary genres or authors in a hierarchy analogous to social classes is a particularly clear example of a much broader and more complex cultural process whereby the human body, psychic forms, geographic space, and the social formation are all constructed within interrelating and dependent hierarchies of high and low." "High" literary works, which appeal to the higher faculties and the upper classes, are those that eschew concerns for "lower" bodily functions.

slightly more) than merely suggestive, I will focus in some detail on a central feature of modernity that betrays the Galatianist substructure that holds up modern secular order. That is modern politics.

SECULARIZATION OR GALATIANISM?

Charles Taylor is only the most recent to tell us that ours is a secular age.[12] Our "buffered" selves, no longer believed to be open to external spiritual forces, are disembedded from cosmic order and now live in a disenchanted world. Large numbers of people now live as "exclusive" humanists without a second thought to religious concerns. More drastically, even believers hold their beliefs differently than religious people of earlier ages. Believers' faith is not instinctive and taken for granted but "reflective," because we are aware that our beliefs are chosen and that many around us hold very different beliefs.

It is a familiar story, though a contested one.[13] Both secularization and its denial seem equally obvious today. On the affirmative side, there is one massive fact: the near absence of throne-and-altar regimes in the contemporary West. They hung on long past their use-by date, and vestiges linger still. Billy Graham or Rick Warren or Jesse Jackson may still visit the White House, but none is a Richelieu. When terrorists toppled the twin towers, we gathered in the National Cathedral to pray to our pantheon. Throne and

---

[12]Charles Taylor, *A Secular Age* (Cambridge, MA: Belknap Press of Harvard University Press, 2007). For a lucid introduction to Taylor's argument, see James K. A. Smith, *How (Not) To Be Secular: Reading Charles Taylor* (Grand Rapids: Eerdmans, 2014).

[13]Of the many, many works on secularization, see Steve Bruce, *Secularization: In Defense of an Unfashionable Theory* (Oxford: Oxford University Press, 2011); Bruce, *God Is Dead: Secularization in the West* (Oxford: Wiley-Blackwell, 2002); David Martin, *On Secularization: Towards A Revised General Theory* (Farnham, UK: Ashgate, 2006); Mary Eberstadt, *How the West Really Lost God: A New Theory of Secularization* (Philadelphia: Templeton Press, 2014). Peter Berger has been a useful bellwether for the theory. See Berger, *A Rumor of Angels: Modern Society and the Recovery of the Supernatural* (New York: Anchor, 1970); and *The Desecularization of the World: Resurgent Religion and World Politics* (Grand Rapids: Eerdmans, 1999). The issue is not merely about whether religion is in decline but the *causal* connections between modernization (consisting of technological development, urbanization, democratic politics, capitalist economics, the rise of science) and the decline of religious authority and practice. I entirely agree with John Milbank's claim that "once there was no secular," and his additional claim that the secular was not some "natural" form of human life waiting to be revealed when the veils of religious faith were stripped away, but rather a regime that had to be intellectually and politically *constructed*. Milbank, *Theology and Social Theory: Beyond Secular Reason*, 2nd ed. (Oxford: Wiley-Blackwell, 2006); Milbank, *Beyond Secular Order: The Representation of Being and the Representation of the People* (Oxford: Wiley-Blackwell, 2014).

altars, perhaps, but that is still a far cry from Christendom. On the denial side: religiously infused politics dominates the Islamic world, complex alliances of power and faith are emerging in what Philip Jenkins calls "the next Christendom," and one of the most thoroughly "modernized" nations on earth, the United States, stubbornly refuses to trade in its Bible belt for something more elastically comfortable.

From one angle, the secularization thesis fits cozily into the concerns of this book. As Taylor and others have argued, the Reformers did "rationalize" and "disenchant" space, people and things. They shattered images that had been objects of devotion for many during the medieval period; mocked the notion that relics possessed some sacred charge by connection with a saint; gave holy bread and wine back to the holy people, thus abolishing or radically altering the line between sacred priest and profane laity; removed altar rails and other signs of exclusion of the laity from sacred space and holy things. Most of the Reformers retained the office of minister and a structure of authority in the church, but on a very different basis than the medieval Catholic Church had done. In his early treatises, Luther spoke of baptism as an ordination to priestly office and insisted that all Christians are clerics. All this reflects the anti-Galatianist program of the Reformers, and this anti-Galatianism is near the heart of the Reformer's agenda.[14] In this sense, the Reformation was a major advance in the formation of a poststoicheic church that keeps in rank with the Spirit. It was a major battle, and a partial victory, for the Spirit in his warfare against flesh and institutionalized flesh. Modern civilization is in part the triumph of the Christian era.

Yet "secularization" is, in my judgment, not the best category to employ to assess the gains and losses of the modern age. That is true in part because no purely secular society has ever existed. As I will describe below, modern political regimes have been deeply religious, even if not constrained by traditionally religious concepts, institutions or practices. This is not a *devastating* critique of secularization theory because every careful sociologist

---

[14]Historically, this form of apostasy has been described as "Judaizing." I think that an unfortunate usage, partly because it does not match Paul's usage of *ioudaizein*, which he uses only once and specifically to describe the imposition of Jewish patterns of life on Gentiles. The term is unfortunate too because the historical figures who use the term often join it to vicious anti-Jewish rhetoric and theology. In what follows, I adopt the term "Galatianism" to describe the more general heresy of abandoning the Christian era, and use forms of the word *Judaize* only when talking about or quoting writers who themselves use the term.

admits that no social type ever exists in a pure form. Still, it is important to remember that in important respects "we have never been modern."[15]

More penetratingly, the contrarian French anthropologist Bruno Latour has described modernity in terms of a dual process of "purification" and "hybridization." Purification involves the construction of a clean zone of nature (and science) separated off from society and the self, while hybridization involves mixtures of nature and culture. Moderns conceive of the world divided between the realms of the real and the artificial, the natural and the social, separated from each other, each a pure form. At the same time, modernity produces all sorts of nature-culture hybrids (most recently and dramatically, an "Internet of Things," by which your house plants call you on the phone to tell you they need watering!). For moderns the purification process is overt, while hybrids are denied, even though they proliferate in modern societies. Modernity both purifies and hybridizes, but can never admit to doing both. Modernity can never admit that there is anything going on along the interstices between nature and society, since these two realms encompass all reality. The realm of the hybrid is the "middle kingdom" that modernity cannot acknowledge without ceasing to be modern, because as soon as modernity acknowledges the middle kingdom it collapses back into "premodern" indifferentiation. Yet the collapse into indifferentiated hybrids is going on all the time; indeed, modernity is about *nothing else* than the production of such mixtures.

We moderns *have* to maintain the pretense of purity, the boundary between nature and culture, because that alone separates us from premoderns. Premoderns smush everything together. For a tribal fisherman, preparing to fish requires not only technical skill to inspect and repair the net but also religious activities—perhaps only a prayer, perhaps a small token sacrifice—to ensure the success of his expedition. He has not learned to differentiate between religious and economic activity. Many tribal cultures do not develop separate institutions for schooling; instead, education takes place in the home, at work, at clan or tribal events. In some cultures the division of labor is blurry. Each clan or family produces and prepares its own food,

---

[15] I am summarizing the argument of Bruno Latour's difficult, essential book, *We Have Never Been Modern* (Cambridge, MA: Harvard University Press, 1993). Anthropologists have been telling us for a long time we are not so different from "primitives." It is perhaps the raison d'être of anthropology. See, among many examples, Mary Douglas's analysis of the "bog Irish" in *Natural Symbols: Explorations in Cosmology*, 3rd ed. (London: Routledge, 2003).

makes its own vessels and tools, and so on. Modern society differentiates between various spheres of social life.[16]

We moderns have given up every sacred boundary except *one*: the quasi-temporal boundary between Us and Them. And if we do not police that boundary, we will not remain modern.

"We have never been modern" because the act that forms what we call modernity is a *premodern*, indeed a *stoicheic*, gesture. Latour hints toward this with his use of the term *purification*: he uses a stoicheic term to describe the founding act of modernity and the continuous process of maintaining the pretense of modernity. When we survey the modern world, we see the same gesture repeated everywhere. A region of "secular" social life can exist only if it is differentiated from the "sacred." A boundary has to be constructed between the sacred and the profane, and that boundary has to be policed to ensure that the secular remains free of the contamination of the sacred. Guardians on the other side of the boundary want to protect the sacred from the bleeding of the secular. Forming and maintaining boundaries between the sacred and profane is the work of a "priesthood." Plato said that purification is the "science of division," and modernity has specialized in precisely *this* science. The very formation of secular space requires the *sacred* act of purification. And so, once again and fundamentally: we have *never* been modern; we have *never* been secular.

Yet the modern age *is* distinct from what preceded it. How is it different? It is different not because it is secular, or because its pretense of secularity is a pretense. It is different in that it is a *Galatianist* culture and social order, an order once Christian that has reverted to stoicheic patterns of social life. In using this category, I admit to a degree of "metaphorization" of "Galatianism." The process I review is not *literally* a turning back to the elementary things; modern political orders do not literally reimpose the exclusions of Eden or the separations of Babel (though in the latter case it is nearly literal). They do not return to Old Testament circumcision or purity rules or animal sacrifice or houses of gods (though they have their sacred spaces and

---

[16]This has even been worked into a theoretical model of "sphere sovereignty" by Christian theologians in the Kuyperian tradition. Each "sphere" operates by different principles, possessing its own responsibility, competence, and structures and sources of authority. The church is not to rule the sphere of the state, nor the state rule the church, and neither has authority over the family or the school. Kuyperian sphere sovereignty appears to depend on acceptance of social "differentiation" as universal and normative, a highly questionable assumption.

demand their sacrificial victims). Yet it is a useful category, not only because the metaphorical Galatianism does in fact resemble the Galatianism of the Galatians but also because it arises from a *literal* Galatianism, a tragic reversion of the church to the stoicheic order of flesh.

ARCHETYPAL HERESY

Though the church was undoubtedly right to honor the Old Testament as authoritative Scripture and simultaneously to refuse to observe its ceremonies, the resulting dance has not always been graceful. For many church fathers, heresy was nearly defined by failure to maintain the rhythm of this two-step. Some heretics like Faustus, and Marcion before him, renounced the Old Testament entirely, but more commonly the fathers judged that heretics tipped in the other direction. "Arianism" has been called the "archetypal heresy," but Athanasius and others had a preexisting label to attach to the Arians—that of "Judaizer." Patristic genealogists of heresy nearly always start with Simon Magus or another Jewish figure from the New Testament.[17]

Today such claims are viewed as boilerplate invective: Jews are vicious and bad, so calling heretics Jews creates a noxious cloud around Arians, Apollinarians and even, strangely enough, Marcionites and Manicheans. Others today see patristic polemics against Judaizers as mechanisms for Christian self-definition or as part of a Christian struggle for market share.[18] I believe, on the contrary, that the church fathers had substantive reasons for using the label.

Paul used the word *ioudaizein* (Gal 2:14) to describe Gentiles who, under pressure from Jewish believers, adopted Jewish customs: Why, Paul asked in exasperation, do you who are free from the Torah force Gentiles to Judaize? For Paul, "Judaizing" violated the gospel because it undermined in action what the church confessed in word: the finality of Jesus' death and resurrection, and the fact that new creation broke out through and in him.

---

[17]Alison Salvesen finds a tilt toward "Hebraization" in Origen's and Jerome's reliance on Jewish tools and Hebrew texts in their biblical work. See Salvesen, "A Convergence of the Ways? The Judaizing of Christian Scripture by Origen and Jerome," in *The Ways That Never Parted: Jews and Christians in Late Antiquity and the Early Middle Ages*, ed. Adam H. Becker and Annette Yoshiko Reeds (Minneapolis: Fortress, 2007), 233-57.

[18]See, e.g., Averil Cameron, "Jews and Heretics—A Category Error?," in Becker and Reed, *Ways That Never Parted*, 345-60; Judith Lieu, *Neither Jew Nor Greek? Constructing Early Christianity* (London: T&T Clark, 2005); Lieu, *Image and Reality: The Jews in the World of Christians in the Second Century* (London: T&T Clark, 2003).

Following Paul's lead, patristic authors leveled the charge of "Judaizer" against Christians who kept Old Testament food laws, attended Jewish feasts and fasts, frequented the synagogue, or literally became Jews by circumcision. During the early centuries the term took on wider connotations. In some texts a "Judaizer" was a Christian who was guilty of nothing more than showing kindness to Jews. More substantively, Arians were "Judaizers" because they denied the divinity of the Son, as first-century Jews had done before them. On the assumption that the Jews interpreted Scripture literally, Christian literalism was denounced as "Judaizing."[19] How far this instinct to sniff out Galatianism in every heresy persisted through the Middle Ages is a topic that demands more attention. Jewish and Judaizing influences are detectable in Catharism, among the Waldensians and among the Passagii in twelfth-century Lombardy.[20] Jan Hus was denounced as a Judaizer, and the early Reformers, influenced by the Humanist drive *ad fontes*, earned the moniker by studying Hebrew, Jewish commentaries and the Kabbalah.

REFORMATION GALATIANISM

Whatever their departures from tradition, the Reformers were fully part of the church's tradition in their rhetoric of Judaizing.[21] When the Reformers condemned their Roman Catholic opponents as Judaizers—as they *often* did—they added a new dimension to the term. In his treatise *The Necessity of Reforming the Church*, Calvin described Catholicism as a *novus iudaismus* because, though Catholics rightly discontinued Jewish ceremonies, "which God had distinctly abrogated," they did so only to replace them with "numerous

---

[19]See Shaye J. D. Cohen, *The Beginnings of Jewishness: Boundaries, Varieties, Uncertainties* (Berkeley: University of California Press, 1999), 175-97; Robert L. Wilken, *John Chrysostom and the Jews: Rhetoric and Reality in the Late Fourth Century* (Berkeley: University of California Press, 1983). On Cyril of Alexandria's attempt to keep the rhythm of the two-step, see Robert L. Wilken, *Judaism and the Early Christian Mind: A Study of Cyril of Alexandria's Exegesis and Theology* (1971; repr., Eugene, OR: Wipf & Stock, 2004), esp. chaps. 3-4. Wilken concludes that in the end Cyril leans to the side of discontinuity.

[20]See Louis Israel Newman, *Jewish Influence on Christian Reform Movements* (New York: Columbia University Press, 1925), parts 1-2. Intriguingly, Camilla Adang explores the "Judaizing" tendencies in medieval Islam in "Ibn Hazm's Criticism of some 'Judaizing' Tendencies Among the Malikites," in *Medieval and Modern Perspectives on Muslim-Jewish Relations*, ed. Ronald Nettler (Luxembourg: Harwood Academic, 1995). See the paragraph on "Judaizing" heresies in medieval Spain in Norman Roth, ed., *Medieval Jewish Civilization: An Encyclopedia* (New York: Taylor & Francis, 2003), 199. The author comments that "the subject deserves a complete investigation."

[21]I have argued elsewhere that the "Judaizing" tendency began in the late patristic period, with shifts in the understanding of priesthood, changes in liturgical rituals and architecture. See Leithart, *The Priesthood of the Plebs* (Eugene, OR: Wipf & Stock, 2003), chap. 5.

puerile extravagances, collected from different quarters." Calvin complained about the "immense number" of Catholic ceremonies, arguing that the Roman church had revived a ceremonial religion that God had "abrogated." In the background is Augustine's repeated claim that the rites of the New Testament are *fewer*, simpler, better and more potent than the rites of the Old, a thesis that led Calvin to conclude that any proliferation of rites is, almost by definition, a reversion to the old order. He cites Paul's claim in Galatians 4 that the elementary principles of the world were "weak and beggarly" and warns that the turn to "abstinences, vigils, and other things" shows a preference of "shadow" over the "substance," which is Christ. Calvin also charged that the forms of worship in the Catholic Church are treated perfunctorily, so that "they think they have fulfilled their duty as admirably as if these ceremonies included in them the whole essence of piety and divine worship." The dislodging of externals from the inner state of the soul is the "most deadly evil of all."[22]

For the Reformers, the central instance of Catholic "Judaizing" was the belief that the Mass was a sacrificial rite, repeating (so Protestants understood) the slaying of Christ in a manner that resembled the repeated burnt offerings of Israelite worship. In his 1548 *Treatise on the Sacrament of the Body and Blood of Christ*, Miles Coverdale pointed out the difference between the Old Testament figural ceremonies and the sacrificial meal of the church: "By the institution of Christ we are not commanded to offer a sacrifice, but to take and eat the thing that is already offered and sacrificed." In

---

[22]John Calvin, "The Necessity of Reforming the Church," 1543, available at www.swrb.com/news lett/actualNLs/NRC_cho2.htm. Calvin makes the same argument in his reply to Sadoleto. Catholics have "more than enough" ceremonies, but they are childish, superstitious and have little power to preserve and sustain the church. The Reformers aimed to "to restore the native purity from which they had degenerated, and so enable them to resume their dignity." Many ceremonies have been abolished, but Calvin almost seems apologetic about the extent of the purge: "We were compelled to do so." Ceremonies had filled the minds of the laity with superstition, and these "could not possibly remain without doing the greatest injury to the piety which it was their office to promote." But the purgation was also needed because the complexity of the Catholic church's liturgical life "had degenerated into a kind of Judaism." Calvin's assault was not on ceremonies per se, which he considered not only divinely instituted but also necessary to communal religious life. But for pastoral reasons, the Reformers believed they could retain only "those which seemed sufficient for the circumstances of the times" ("Reply to Sadoleto," 1539, available at http://rels365fa10.pbworks.com/w/page/33320860/Calvin's%20%E2%80%9CReply% 20to%20Sadoleto%E2%80%9D). Calvin was not alone in these sorts of arguments. In his letter to Emperor Charles on the *fidei ratio*, Zwingli condemns as "Judaism" *variis unctionibus, ungentis, oblationibus, victimis, ac epulis* (Ulrich Zwingli, *Huldrici Zwinglii opera: Completa editio* [Turici: Ex officina Schulthessiana, 1841], 11).

Catholic theology, Coverdale argues, what was unique to the death of Christ has been transferred to the Mass, which Catholics offer believing that it will "satisfy God for our offences, and that we might be reconciled by it." The Reformed Supper, by contrast, is compatible with the new covenant because it brings "no new sacrifice" but is "the application of that only sacrifice whereof I have spoken."[23]

Catholics did not take the charge lightly, and answered strenuously. One Catholic writer objected to the Protestant characterization of Catholic unction, quoting Innocent III's insistence that "the sacrament of unction (or anointing) doth figure and work an other thing in the new testament than it did in the old" and Innocent's sharp conclusion that therefore "they lie who charge the church with Judaizing . . . in that it celebrateth the sacrament of unction." Some Catholics acknowledged the continuity of Jewish and Catholic worship, but simultaneously denied they were reverting to the old covenant. In his *Rejoinder to M. Jewels Reply Against the Sacrifice of the Mass* (1567), Catholic Thomas Harding claimed that "the Sabbath, Pasche, Pentecost, Sacerdos, Altare, Sacrificium all admit of two uses, old and new, legal and evangelical." He agreed that old Jewish observances expired with Christ, because Christ himself died with the *Consummatum est* on his lips. Still, "faithful Christians now keep, use, and celebrate their Sabboth, that is to say, their restingtide, their Parasceve, or preparingtide, commonly called Goodfriday, their Pascha, or Easter, their Pentecost, or Whitsontide, their Priesthod, their Aulter, their Sacrifice, in suche manner, order, sense, and meaning, as the new state and condition of the Church succeding the Jewish Synagoge, requireth: that is, not according to the figure, shadow, letter, or signification, but according to the truth, the body, the spirite, and the very things." Harding's paradigm for dealing with the old and new was quite close to Augustine's views in *Contra Faustum*.

Reformers shortly turned on each other, making sure to redeploy the "Judaizing" rhetoric in intramural Protestant battles. For the Lutheran Aegidius Hunnius, Calvin's "literal," nonmessianic treatment of the Psalms smacked of Judaizing.[24] Not to be outdone, Catholics charged one another

---

[23]Miles Coverdale, *Writings and Translations*, ed. George Pearson (Cambridge: Cambridge University Press, 1844), 452.

[24]See G. Sujun Pak, *Judaizing Calvin: Sixteenth-Century Debates Over the Messianic Psalms* (Oxford: Oxford University Press, 2009).

with Judaizing too. Ambrosius Catharinus Politi accused Cajetan of Judaizing when the latter denied that Elohim refers to the Trinity.[25]

The charge of "Judaizing" suggests that visceral Protestant responses to Catholic "abominations" may have been overlaid with an equally visceral anti-Semitism. More centrally, it indicates that the Reformation was a battle over Christian practice as much as it was over formulations concerning grace, works and justification. For most Christians of the sixteenth century, the most evident effect of the Reformation was liturgical, and the Reformers aimed to convince their congregations that the changes represented an evangelical purgation of Judaizing corruptions. The Reformers perceived medieval Catholicism as a partial reversion to stoicheic worship and piety, and labored to bring the church back to the gospel.

UNIVERSAL GALATIANISM

While the Reformers had plausible reasons for charging the Roman Catholic Church with Judaizing, their polemical stance hid the Galatianism of their own efforts. Far more fateful than the intramural squabbling over which church was more the Judaizer was the global Galatianism involved in the very division of Catholics from Protestants, and their avoidance of their respective Eucharists. The Galatianism is glaring in the very notion that separate churches might have their own "respective Eucharists."

Protestants denounced the Mass as such a perversion that it was no longer the Supper given by Jesus. It was not merely a flawed Eucharist but a completely different rite, blasphemy and idolatry rather than an act of worship. Even if Catholics had not excluded Protestants from the Mass, no Protestants would have wanted to participate.[26] Refusal to join Catholics in the Mass was inherent in the Reformers' opposition to Rome. However, the Reformers could have denounced and avoided the Mass but invited and welcomed Catholics to the Protestant Supper. The mainstream Reformation view of Catholic baptism provided sufficient ground for this policy. Apart

---

[25]See Magna Saebo, *Hebrew Bible/Old Testament: The History of Its Interpretation* (Göttingen: Vandenhoeck & Ruprecht, 2008), 623; Jared Wicks, "Cajetan, Tommaso de Vio," in *Dictionary of Major Biblical Interpreters*, ed. Donald K. McKim (Downers Grove, IL: IVP Academic, 2007), 286. Thanks to my colleague Ben Merkle for these references.

[26]For an example of an admittedly extreme Protestant denunciation of the Mass, see Mack P. Holt, "Divisions Within French Calvinism: Philippe Duplessis-Mornay and the Eucharist," in *Adaptations of Calvinism in Reformation Europe: Essays in Honour of Brian G. Armstrong*, ed. Mack P. Holt (Farnham, UK: Ashgate, 2007), 165-77.

from the Anabaptists, the Reformers accepted Catholic baptisms as valid baptisms, and thus might have reasoned that baptized Catholics, wearing the name of Jesus, should be welcomed at the table of Jesus. Even the most hardcore Protestants could have reasoned that any Catholic who wanted to share in the Protestant feast was already showing appropriate signs of suspicion toward Catholic idolatry and moving toward Protestantism. In practice the issue seems not to have come up. Protestants could be disciplined for attending Mass, and fervent Protestant pastors would not have been likely to allow Catholic idolaters to pollute the Lord's table.[27] Catholics considered Protestants to be heretics. The two churches more or less went their separate ways, each with a table they claimed was the Lord's table. Within Protestantism, some churches lay exclusive claim to the table. To this day, some Lutherans banish non-Lutherans from the Eucharist.

The notion that the wars of the sixteenth and seventeenth century were "religious wars" is overly simplistic, but there is no doubt that armed Christian faced down armed Christian, each trying to kill the other. From a Pauline perspective, it is an obvious, if horrifying, effect of the churches' refusal to break bread together. If they divided the body at the center, in the holy assembly, why not break each other's heads on the field of battle?

The cultural impact of the mutual condemnations and manifest hatred between Catholic and Protestant was staggering, and is still with us.[28] Early modern political thinkers and philosophers concluded that theology must be a game of private judgment because Christians were clearly incapable of agreeing about the basic claims of their faith. There seemed to be no way to adjudicate differences between Calvinists and Lutherans, much less Protestants and Catholics. Many concluded that theological claims must be sheerly subjective because interminable post-Reformation debates made theological claims *appear* to be sheerly subjective. Galatian divisions of post-Reformation Europe bore epistemological and philosophical fruit.

Economic life was reshaped as well. The Weber thesis that Calvinist predestinarianism was responsible for the rise of capitalism has a surface

---

[27]Elena Brambilla, "Ways of Exclusion in Catholic and Protestant Communities," in *Religion and Power in Europe: Conflict and Convergence*, ed. Joaquim Carvalho (Pisa, Italy: Edizioni, 2007), 111-29; Scott M. Manetsch, *Calvin's Company of Pastors: Pastoral Care and the Emerging Reformed Church, 1536–1609* (Oxford: Oxford University Press, 2013), 203-4.

[28]The most complete exploration of these effects, and it is a damning one, is Brad Gregory, *The Unintended Reformation: How a Religious Revolution Secularized Society* (Cambridge, MA: Belknap Press of Harvard University Press, 2012).

plausibility, since some of the most fully capitalist systems arose in the most thoroughly Reformed regions of Europe. But Weber did not understand Calvin very well, and the link between predestination and "inner-worldly asceticism" is tenuous. Besides, both Catholics and Protestants approved of some capitalist practices and techniques. Neither was consistently antitrade, antimarket or antibusiness. The thrust of their teaching was to nudge economics toward the aims of the kingdom, the glory of God, the common good, and away from greed, abuse, the idolatry of luxury goods. Despite these commonalities and intentions, the economic result of the Reformation was the "disembedding" of economics from ethics. Economic activity was freed from moral constraints. Brad Gregory writes that the ultimate cause lay in the unintended divisions and fragmentation that resulted from the Reformation:

> Their doctrinal disagreements, confessional intransigence, and mutual hostility understandably contributed to a reactive proliferation of social behaviors, the formation of institutes, and an articulation of ideologies that together created modern Western capitalism and consumption. Discord about the Bible subverted biblical teachings about human desires and material things. Antagonisms between Christian moral communities liberated market practices from traditional Christian morality and produced a market society. Competing confessional empires prompted countervailing nationalist assimilations of providence that viewed wealth, power, and prosperity as signs of God's favor, thus recasting mercantile avarice as politically and religiously sanctioned duty.[29]

Gregory's arguments have proved controversial, but we do not need to accept his every conclusion to see the thrust, or to acknowledge its justice. Nor do we have to range so grandly over the history of the "modern West" or look at the course of civilization to see the effects. It is well known to everyone who has even glancing acquaintance with the church that it has been riven by rivalry, strife and mutual hostility. Churches are set up in conscious opposition to churches from other traditions. Pastors preach *against* other churches as much as from the text of Scripture. Theologians put their weight gladly into the Galatian effort, as they magnify slight divergences in formulation and shape entire theological systems to reinforce

---

[29]Ibid., 272.

the fact that *we* are not *them*.[30] And, as we shall see, ecclesial divisions played their role in the development of zealous nationalisms that have left a trail of blood and destruction for the past two centuries. Having grieved the Spirit who makes us "the one," is it any surprise that he has left us to the destructive and self-destructive deeds of flesh?

THE MIGRATION OF THE HOLY

The French Revolution is often presented as the dawn of modern, secular politics.[31] Before the revolution the French state was deeply allied and aligned with the French church, in a symbiosis that went back to the Merovingians. After the revolution, the ancien régime was gone. It was a supreme act of boundary-marking: state and church, which once constituted a single, undifferentiated France, had been cut asunder, and a secular state emerged.

Nothing could be further from reality. Natural, secular France did not emerge in its purity when the artificial garments of Christendom were removed. France *itself* had to be constructed from a crazy quilt of villages, towns and regions that had long had their own structures of authority, customs, rituals and identities.[32] During the revolution, the construction of a unified France was largely the work of public festivals. Led by the painter Jacques-Louis David, the revolution's festivals were efforts, in the view of the French historian Jules Michelet, to erase the boundaries of time and space in order to forge a nation: "Time and space, those material conditions to which life is subject, are no more. A strange *vita nuova*, one eminently spiritual, and making her whole Revolution a sort of dream, at one time delightful, at another terrible, is now beginning for France. It knew neither time nor space."[33] Out of the festivals, the revolutionaries hoped that a single,

---

[30]As one seminary professor put it, the older Protestant dogmatics texts had a three-point format: First, the Catholic error; then the Lutheran (or Reformed) error; then the Reformed (or Lutheran) truth. Whatever insights are to be gained from these works, and they are legion, the structure of the project is heresy because the structure is Galatian.

[31]I take the term "migration of the holy" from William Cavanaugh, *Migrations of the Holy: God, State, and the Political Meaning of the Church* (Grand Rapids: Eerdmans, 2011).

[32]On the slow and often deliberate process of constructing national identity, see Benedict Anderson, *Imagined Communities: Reflections on the Origins and Spread of Nationalism*, rev. ed. (London: Verso, 2006).

[33]Quoted by Michael Burleigh, *Earthly Powers: Religion and Politics in Europe from the Enlightenment to the Great War* (San Francisco: HarperOne, 2007), 76.

unified, sacred nation would emerge. The French state was separated from the French church. It was not separated from the sacred.

Though an innovation of the eighteenth century, sacred France was in another sense the end of a centuries-long development. In early medieval theology, "holiness" or "sacredness" had been attached to the eucharistic elements, the sacramental body of Christ; but over time, sacrality migrated to the church itself, newly christened the *corpus mysticum*. Earlier it had been understood that the church was made holy by its communion in food made holy by the Spirit; later it was understood that the elements were made holy by the holy church. In a final stage of development, the terminology of holiness migrated to political communities. By the end of the Middle Ages, it was already possible to speak of "holy France."[34]

The religious fervor of the festivals was not an isolated factor in the revolution. Revolutionary speeches were filled with the language of "catechism, credo, fanatical, gospel, martyr, missionary, propaganda, sacrament, sermon, zealot," transferred from a religious to a political context. Mirabeau described the Declaration of the Rights of Man to be the "gospel" of France, "a religion for which people are prepared to die." In place of the yoke of superstition and theocracy, Marie-Joseph Chenier urged revolutionary leaders to adopt "the single universal religion . . . which has neither sects nor mysteries." It was a religion in which "our law-makers are the preachers, the magistrates the pontiffs, and in which the family burns its incense only at the altar of the *Patrie*, common mother and divinity." Early attempts to ally the revolution with the church had failed, so the leaders elevated "the Revolution itself into the religion."[35]

It was to be a regenerating religion, one that remade not only the political order but also the human spirit. By ceaseless participation in the laws, games and festivities of the Fatherland, citizens were to fall ever more ardently in love with their nation. Their inclinations were, as the Committee of Public Safety declared in 1793, to be directed "toward this single passion" until they acquired "a national physiognomy" and the "monarchical spirit" was transformed into "a republican spirit."[36]

[34]For this development, see Henri de Lubac, *Corpus Mysticum: The Eucharist and the Church in the Middle Ages*, trans. Gemma Simmonds (Notre Dame, IN: University of Notre Dame Press, 2007).
[35]Quotations in this paragraph from Burleigh, *Earthly Powers*, 16.
[36]Quoted in ibid., 16.

Theorists of the revolution recognized that they could establish a unified, sacred France only with an assault on the divided authorities of Christendom. Thomas Hobbes had already condemned the "double worship" of Christendom, its loyalties divided between church and nation. As Michael Burleigh observes, Jean-Jacques Rousseau recognized the same problem and appealed to the example of Islam to support the revolutionary ideal:

> In his more extended political writings, Rousseau discussed what he dubbed "civil religion." He revealed himself more admiring of Islam's blurring of the sacred and temporal than of Christianity. He sought to transcend the potentially divisive duality of spiritual and secular powers inherent in Christianity (with hindsight its major saving grace), by separating each citizen's right to an individual opinion on the afterlife from his duties as a citizen and moral actor in society. The latter was to have as much weight as the former.[37]

France spread this regenerative nationalist spirituality throughout Europe, both deliberately and inadvertently: deliberately through the spread of Enlightenment and post-Enlightenment philosophy; inadvertently by arousing nationalist opposition to Napoleon's conquests. Germany's war against Napoleon made the first German nationalist martyrs. In the aftermath of the Napoleonic wars the anniversary of the Reformation provided an opportunity for Germany to celebrate its contribution to the development of freedom. As Burleigh puts it, "Patriotic piety had been transformed into religious patriotism, with the nation itself elevated into something sacred."[38] National Socialism was drawing on this tradition when it roused Germans to a peak of nationalist zeal with appeals framed in terms of creed, confession, faith, sacrifice. Nazism produced by the thousands the kinds of priests that one German had hoped for already in the 1920s, "priests who slaughter." Only in this way could the Aryan race purge itself of the contamination of foreign blood that, according to Hitler, had resulted from the Aryan mixtures with the populations they conquered. Only by this purging sacrifice could Aryans overturn their expulsion from paradise.[39]

The Young Italy movement traded in the same set of values. Their manifesto "was saturated with words like apostolate, belief, creed, crusade,

---

[37]Ibid., 78.

[38]Ibid., 155, 162.

[39]Michael Burleigh, *Sacred Causes: The Clash of Religion and Politics, from the Great War to the War on Terror* (San Francisco: HarperOne, 2008), vii, 103, 107-8.

enthusiasm, faith, incarnation, martyrs, mission, purification, regeneration, religion, sacred, sacrifice, salvation." "Our religion of today," the manifesto declared, "is still that of martyrdom." This was not simple Christian martyrdom. As Giuseppe Mazzini put it, "I am a Christian plus something more." That something more was his sacred Italianness. Young Italy promised to regenerate the nation itself.

> Both initiators and initiated must never forget that the moral application of every principle is the first and the most essential; that without morality there is no true citizen; that the first step towards the achievement of a holy enterprise is the purification of the soul by virtue; that, where the daily life of the individual is not in harmony with the principles he preaches, the inculcation of those principles is an infamous profanation and hypocrisy; that it is only by virtue that the members of Young Italy can win over others to their belief; that if we do not show ourselves far superior to those who deny our principles, we are but miserable sectarians; and that Young Italy must be neither a sect nor a party, but a faith and an apostolate. As the precursors of Italian regeneration, it is our duty to lay the first stone of its religion.[40]

Fascism and Communism are variations of this quasi-stoicheic politics, a politics of sacred/profane, clean/unclean, a political order that redraws and maintains sacred boundaries and cleanses out pollutions. A stoicheic order, inevitably, encourages fleshly violence, the sacred violence of sacrifice. The Russian émigré philosopher Semyon Frank observed that Russian nihilists in the late nineteenth century were preeminently priestly figures, eager for sacrifice.

> Sacrificing himself for the sake of this idea, he does not hesitate to sacrifice other people for it. Among his contemporaries he sees either merely the victims of the world's evil he dreams of eradicating or the perpetrators of that evil.... This feeling of hatred for the enemies of the people forms the concrete and active psychological foundation of his life. Thus the great love of mankind of the future gives birth to a great hatred for people; the passion for organizing an earthly paradise becomes a passion for destruction.[41]

The cause of sacred nations was advanced not only by philosophes and secularists but by Christians, including Christian clergy. It was a rare

---

[40]Quoted in Burleigh, *Earthly Powers*, 187-88.
[41]Quoted in Burleigh, *Sacred Causes*, 39.

German theologian (read: Barth) who was able to sort through the "hopeless muddle" of patriotism and faith, a muddle evident in the outlook of Barth's lifelong frenemy and interlocutor Friedrich Schleiermacher. In France of the Third Republic, Catholic clergy fostered the nationalist spirit. Alfred Loisy observed that the "feeling for France" was more profound and widespread than any Christian faith: "This feeling for French humanity . . . is our common religion," a feeling sustained by sacrifice.[42] The divisions between France and Germany were partly the result of political struggles, but they were overlaid with post-Reformation theological divergences. To be German was to be Lutheran, and thus hostile to Catholic France. Splintered by the Reformation, the church was co-opted quite literally by fleshly politics, that is to say, by the politics of blood. During the Civil War in the United States, preachers on both sides of the conflict called for Americans to sacrifice themselves on the altar of the nation.[43]

The fact that armed Christian could face down armed Christian on a battlefield was already a sign that something had gone awry. By New Testament standards, the two were brothers, sharing a common *physis* because they shared a common baptism and common loaf. Though they lived on in the flesh, and lived in the midst of fleshly nations, they had been justified from the elements, from the flesh and from the fleshly divisions of Babel. They were members of the same body, and could no more kill one another than a person could randomly amputate a limb. A Christian willing to take up arms against another Christian is a Christian who has traded in his membership in the post-Babel communion of saints for membership in a nation governed by refurbished stoicheic values. They have traded in their loyalty to the temple of the Spirit for loyalty to the flesh. Christians who make war against other Christians are Galatians, bewitched by the lure of patriotism, which is simply the lure of the flesh. They are no longer in the ranks of the Spirit.

Christian martyrdom was enacted in imitation of Christ, in resistance to established regimes of oppression. It was a blow against the principalities and powers. Modern politics co-opted Christian martyrdom and sacrifice

---

[42]Ivan Strenski, *Contesting Sacrifice: Religion, Nationalism, and Social Thought in France* (Chicago: University of Chicago Press, 2002), 59-60.

[43]Harry S. Stout, *Upon the Altar of the Nation: A Moral History of the Civil War* (New York: Penguin, 2007).

for its own uses, transferring these concepts into the new sacred realm of the holy nation. This is most starkly evident in totalitarian regimes of left and right, but it is equally descriptive of liberal order. Paul W. Kahn has described liberal politics as "a distinctive form of religious experience" since "popular sovereignty was experienced as a claim of ultimate meaning on the individual citizen." This is nothing else but a demand for sacrifice, a demand that citizens be willing to make the ultimate self-sacrifice for the sake of the nation. Thus "the domain of sacrifice shifted from that of religious resistance to that of political patriotism."[44]

Modern European politics is not *secular* politics. It is *Galatian* politics. The once-Christian nations of the West have reverted to a quasi-stoicheic system in which nations are considered sacred entities, sacred nations are divided from one another, and citizens are expected to give and take lives for the sacred cause of liberty, of union, of Holy Mother Russia, of *das Vaterland*. Christians have enthusiastically cooperated in this exodus out of the Christian era. As Paul could have predicted, this apostasy from the gospel produces a resurgence of flesh—of regimes defined by race and descent, of rivalry, of self-protective violence, glory-regimes that become machines manufacturing nationalist heroism. Why the violence of modern politics? Why does flesh still reign? One answer is: because Christians returned to life under the *stoicheia*. Because we went back to Babel. Having begun in the Spirit, we sought perfection in national flesh.

Conclusion

We are not what we think we are. We think we are new, shiny, modern, sleek, very different from all that came before. Looking at our world through the lens of fleshly *stoicheia* and their destruction by the Spirit, we see ourselves differently. Alongside the novelty of modern culture—and there is novelty aplenty—there is much that is very, very old. There is much that we have borrowed from pre-Christian stoicheic order and reestablished in the Christian era. A Galatianist church has formed a Galatianist age.

The churches of the West face a rare, if not unprecedented, task: we confront a civilization once deeply Christian that has attempted to leave the

---

[44]Paul W. Kahn, *Putting Liberalism in Its Place* (Princeton, NJ: Princeton University Press, 2005), 91. See also Kahn, *Sacred Violence: Torture, Terror, and Sovereignty* (Ann Arbor: University of Michigan Press, 2008).

Christian era. Its effort to progress beyond the Christian era has been—perhaps inevitably—a retreat, a turn back to the things of childhood, bright lines separating nations and races, sacred boundaries around the religious institutions of art, systems of pure reason. We confront a world that follows stoicheic patterns, but stoicheic patterns that have been modified by the influence of the gospel. In attempting to transcend the ambiguities of Spirit in flesh, it has reverted to flesh, with often horrific consequences.

Like Jesus, we need to identify the pressure points, the sacred boundaries on which the modern cosmos is built, and then find ways to transgress those boundaries. We need places to eat with sinners, to eat *with one another*. We need to identify the sacred dens where the brigands gather, so we can enact God's indignation at sinful flesh. I suspect we will find many in that splendid temple-pocked capital city of ours. We need to follow J. G. Hamann's lead in telling parables at the expense of intellectual, political and cultural Pharisees. Above all we need to remonstrate with each other. For we have all become timid Peters, in desperate need of a shock from Paul.

thirteen

CUR DEUS HOMO?

✝

Here is my story of atonement:

Adam and Eve were created good, and were given abundant life with access to God's earthly house, the garden in the east of Eden. They were created flesh, weak, vulnerable, dependent. Adam was a child-servant in the garden, forbidden to eat from the tree of knowledge, which signified mature kingship and participation in God's judicial rule of the creation. Someday he and Eve would be transformed from flesh to Spirit, receive their full inheritance as son and daughter, and enter more fully into communion with their Creator. For the time being, as good creatures, they were under *ta stoicheia tou kosmou* until the time set by the Father.

Out of fleshly impatience to transcend flesh, Adam sinned. In the jealous wrath that expresses his wounded love, Yahweh delivered Adam's flesh over to death. Created flesh became mortal flesh, and the fear of mortality, vulnerability and loss drove human beings to sin—sins of weakness but also sins of self-protective violence and retaliation. As Paul puts it in Romans 5: When sin entered the world, death began to reign, and under the reign of death, sin spread to fleshly humanity. After the fall, the Creator no longer met with human beings to feast with them in his garden. His house became off-limits, a holy place from which sinful, unclean humans were excluded. "Taste not, touch not," originally a program for children, expanded to become a restrictive pedagogy for *rebellious* children. All humanity operated under these restrictions. All ancient civilizations cultivated habits and imposed rules governing sacred space, purity, sacrifice and priesthood. Under these circumstances no fully just social order could take hold. Until the exile from Eden was overcome, human life could not flourish. Shadowy justice, force to limit violence, confinement of flesh—that is the best humans could hope for.

God *is* just, and is determined to establish just order, peace and abundant life in his creation. He is determined not to let humans despoil themselves or his world. If justice is to reign, if humanity is to be rescued/saved from sin, death, flesh and itself, then flesh has to be remade, and so does the stoicheic system that is ordered to flesh. From the moment of the fall, he began his ages-long war against and prosecution of flesh. In the flood, Yahweh waged war against flesh by destroying humanity, but even after the flood human beings were *still* in the grip of flesh. Babel introduced yet another division within human life: After Babel, humans were not only excluded from God's presence but also divided from one another. Flesh was divided not only from Spirit, but also flesh from other flesh. Egypt, Babylon, Greece and Rome—all the great civilizations of the ancient world developed fleshly culture, hero systems founded on the fear of death, on phallic display, on violence, honor and vengeance. All set up systems of blood and ancestry; the privileged were those who had the right sort of flesh. These systems and structures were the basic physics of antique social life.

After the curse of Babel, Yahweh continued his war on flesh by beginning an antisarkic pedagogy within one family, cutting off and discarding flesh from *within* the human race, enlisting one nation among the nations to join him in his antisarkic campaign. The sign of circumcision indicated that God was at work to kill flesh *without* killing fleshly humans. Within a world operating by elementary principles, Yahweh introduced a new form of *ta stoicheia tou kosmou*, which, while being accommodated to fleshly conditions, still targeted flesh. By circumcision, Yahweh formed a new kind of human being—those who were Jewish *physei*. Circumcision is a *parody* of a tribal tattoo in that it discards flesh instead of enhancing it. Circumcision separated Israel from the Babelic world of division; by circumcision, Israel died to the culture of death that surrounded it.

Torah expanded the Abrahamic campaign against flesh. Torah introduced norms of behavior, a pedagogy in story, liturgy, institutional structures and song, an order for Israel's life as a people. Torah functioned as a written constitution for Israel, so that life *hypo nomon* meant inhabiting the material, ritual and symbolic world that the written Torah laid out. Torah was delivered in postfall, post-Babel conditions and set Israel apart as a new

Adamic people, with real though limited access to an Edenic sanctuary and real though limited means for overcoming the divisions that sundered the nations after Babel. Torah enlisted Israel into Yahweh's campaign against flesh, for justice.

Torah established a system of holiness and purity, temple and sacrifice, that enabled Israel to draw near to the Creator during the time of their childhood, while they existed in flesh. Yahweh set up his holy space within Israel, a house of prayer for all nations, where he called the nations to worship the one God. Yahweh invited Israel to visit, to eat, drink and rejoice in his presence. Entering the garden again was dangerous; one could draw near only by passing through the sword and fire of the cherubim. Under Torah the curse of Edenic exile was partially overcome as priests entered holy space to minister on Israel's, and the nations', behalf, and as the sacrifices of Israelites were turned to smoke to slip past the cherubim into Yahweh's presence. The purity rules were rules of *access*, setting the conditions under which fleshly Israel could draw near to God. Sacrifice involved the substitutionary death of the animal, but that was only a step on the path toward transfiguration into Yahweh's fire. Neither Israel nor the Gentiles were yet sufficiently grown up to have full access to his house or its treasures. But they were allowed to draw near. Torah was a pedagogy for Israel, a pedagogy of approach, a pedagogy of welcome, a pedagogy that inculcated the protocols for life in the presence of God.

Torah was a campaign in Yahweh's war against flesh, but Torah itself was powerless to overcome flesh. It checked the worst effects of flesh, but it was accommodated to Adamic conditions and was susceptible to co-optation by fleshly instincts and aims. Gentiles employed their stoicheic order to support claims of "racial" superiority and to dominate other nations. Though many faithful Jews kept the humble faith of Abraham, teachers in Judaism turned Torah itself into a weapon of bondage. Jews came to boast in the absent flesh of circumcision; they used purity rules to exclude other Israelites and Gentiles; they imposed burdens rather than relieving them. Torah was good and spiritual, but in the hands of fleshly Israel it became an instrument of oppressive injustice. In practice Torah did not control flesh but intensified its desires and its violence. Instead of combating and overcoming the Edenic and Babelic curses, Israel sharpened those divisions and so came under the curse of the Torah.

Since Israel was to be God's instrument for bringing life and righteousness to the nations, the curse on Israel created what N. T. Wright describes as a "traffic jam" that prevented the blessing of Abraham from flowing to the nations. Since Israel was supposed to be advancing Yahweh's antisarkic campaign, their submission to flesh meant that flesh reigned supreme not only in the nations but also in Israel itself. If Yahweh was to save his creation, he had to deal with this complex of problems: Adam's fall into death, the reign of flesh and sin, the stoicheic pattern of life that intensified the reign of sin and now the fall of Israel into flesh.

Jesus came announcing that God was going to establish his kingdom through the son of David, Jesus himself. Through Christ, God would deal a death-wound to flesh and demolish stoicheic order, and bring in his reign of justice among all nations. What Torah proved incapable of doing, God was about to do—condemning sin in the flesh but at the same time transforming flesh to make it susceptible to the life of the Spirit. God did not send another flood: instead of destroying flesh by destroying humanity, God in Christ targeted flesh and condemned it to death. Jesus brought God's warfare, his prosecution of flesh, to its climax and sealed the case against it.

Jesus enacted all that the Torah had aimed at. Jesus was conceived by the Spirit, filled with the Spirit, driven by the Spirit, empowered by the Spirit. In flesh he lived by the Spirit. As Yahweh he came out from behind the temple curtains into Israel's flesh, and like Yahweh at the tabernacle Jesus offered access, welcome, festivity and hospitality. To draw near Jesus was tantamount to drawing near to the temple. Anyone who ate with Jesus at the table was closer to Yahweh than any priest had ever been. Those who drew near to Jesus were purified by the finger of God, the touch of the king that communicated the purifying and sanctifying power of the Spirit. Wherever Jesus went, Eden was realized again, an Eden of open access and abundance, the very thing that Torah aimed at and partially achieved. Jesus welcomed Gentiles, and healed and ate with them too, thus fulfilling the promise to Abraham. Babel was being overcome at the table of Jesus. Jesus taught the way of justice, a righteousness that surpassed the scribes', and so around Jesus a community of followers formed, living by the Torah of Jesus. A nucleus of a just human society was taking form around Jesus, a community beyond the stoicheic restrictions of fleshly humanity, a community animated by Jesus and his Spirit. In Jesus' ministry, the day set by the Father was fulfilled, the day when the children were released from their bondage to *ta stoicheia tou kosmou*. Since the Lord of the house himself had appeared, since the elder Brother had been sent, the minor children were ready to enter into full sonship and to inherit the Spirit that Jesus himself bore.

Why wasn't that enough? Why could Jesus not simply come and introduce a new way of life, *teach* people to offer a new form of sacrifice in loving self-gift, tell people that they needed only to live in moral purity, instruct them that the restricted access of the temple and priestly order was over? Why could he not be another Moses, and simply bring in the new covenant from a pulpit? Why did he have to die to realize this new order of things? Why did he have to die to release the children from their bondage to the elements, to bring in a new human *physis* and to introduce a new social physics of salvation?

We can answer these questions counterfactually. What if Jesus *had* only taught Israel a different way of worship and life? What if he had convinced Israel to adopt the pattern of life that he taught and lived? Even then stoicheic order would have been doomed. Stoicheic order presumes the curses of Eden and Babel. It is an order accommodated to a human race *outside* Eden, a human race divided by flesh. If Jesus had convinced Israel to live as if they had reentered Eden, the structures of *ta stoicheia* would have become useless.

But it could not have worked, because if Jesus had not died, no human would have reentered Eden. Eden could be reentered *only* by passing through the cherubic sword and fire, only through death and transfiguration. If Jesus had been nothing but a teacher, if he had died a peaceful death in bed, he would not have fulfilled the sacrifices of Israel. Without death and resurrection, he could not have made a way into the presence of the God who is a consuming fire. Apart from his death and resurrection there is no transfiguration of human nature from flesh to Spirit.

Jesus could have taught Israel that "taste not, touch not" prohibitions were no longer valid, that God was no longer going to meet with them from behind a curtain, that all of them would be priests with access to holy food and holy places, that the people themselves were a temple, that the whole stoicheic order had been transposed into the key of the Spirit; but without his death and resurrection, that new order would have been imposed on a *fleshly* human race. Without the cross, flesh would not have been condemned for derailing Torah; there would have been no judgment passed on flesh;

there would have been no liberating verdict of resurrection; Jesus himself would not have passed from flesh to Spirit; and if Jesus did not, no one else would have either. Without the death and resurrection of Jesus, humanity would still be outside Eden looking in, still under the wrath of expulsion, too afraid of the cherubic swords to get close. Jesus had to take the curse of Eden and of Israel to himself, to suffer the death of reentry, so that he could make a way for others to follow. Without the death and resurrection of Jesus, there would be no Spirit in flesh.

The "institutional" reconfiguration brought about by the atonement can be effective only if human nature is transformed from flesh to Spirit. By the same token, the transformation of human nature takes hold in social life only if institutional changes, changes of practice and symbol, accompany it. For Paul, in fact, this very distinction makes little sense. For him, *physis*, nature, and *nomos*, cultural order, are intertwined. To live by a certain *nomos* is to have a certain *physis*, and vice versa. To be delivered from one socio-religious world to another is to undergo a change of nature. According to Paul the cross and resurrection transfigured human life, translating those who receive Christ from flesh to Spirit, from the *nomos* of condemnation to the justifying *nomos* of the Spirit, from the pedagogy of elementary things to the *paideia* of Christ. By the cross and resurrection, Jesus takes the two *physeis* of Jew and Gentile, mixes the elements and comes out with a new chemical combination: Christian *physis*, a spiritual community made up of those born by Spirit.

In fact, Jesus spent most of his public ministry teaching and enacting a new way, but the rulers and authorities of this world, those who were part of the civilization of Torah and those who were not, would not let him get away with it. Flesh had taken over Torah, and because Torah was employed for the sake of flesh it could not allow Jesus to bring the law of the Spirit of life. Jesus was killed because he was considered a rebel against Torah, because he claimed authority to purify and heal, because of his lordly act in the temple. Jews wanted Jesus dead because he threatened the elemental system they considered the unchanging physics of religion and society. Romans wanted Jesus dead in order to protect the peace and calm of a bit of the Eastern empire, and to vindicate Roman power and Roman honor. Torah and Roman justice were both commandeered by flesh into a *supreme* act of injustice—killing the One who enacted the justice that Torah and

Roman law always aimed to achieve. Jesus lived by the Spirit in the midst of the flesh, and the guardians of stoicheic life could not tolerate the transgression of the Spirit who blows where he will. They put Jesus to death, a son sacrificed to the interests of the slaves, a mature man slaughtered by children content to remain children. Jesus was killed by Torah-breakers for breaking Torah, taking *their* penalty as his own. Because he was Israel's king, and the true Israel, his death was the death of Israel herself. He was Israel's penal substitute. Because he offered his lifeblood in devotion to God, in complete obedience to the Father, he was a true sacrifice that remits the sins of his people and therefore of the world. By his death he passed by the cherubim and rose again in Eden, in the presence of God. Because Jesus has suffered the sacrificial passage through death to new life, those who are joined to him also die and rise to take a place at the table of their Father.

This account meets several of our criteria of success: It describes Jesus' sacrifice in Levitical terms, emphasizing not only his atoning death but also his resurrection and ascent to the Father. Jesus lives and dies and rises as a sacrifice, and *must* move through the whole sequence to overcome the curses of Eden and Babel and Israel. This account takes the whole of the gospel narrative into account, showing how Jesus' ministry leads inexorably to his death and how his resurrection is essential to the achievement of atonement. It is a fully *evangelical* account because it takes the gospel narratives as atonement theology. And because it connects Jesus' atoning death and resurrection with his position as a leader of a reform movement within Israel, because it integrates "ecclesiology" into the heart of the atonement, it is a historically plausible atonement theology. We have not transcended the historical Jesus to see how the atonement works; we have seen how the atonement works *as a historical process.*

This is what Paul describes as the condemnation of sin in the flesh (Rom 8:1-4). In the death of Jesus the elementary things were exposed as the flesh's instruments of torture; Torah is used as a pretext to murder God incarnate. *Torah* is not judged, and neither is Jesus, but sinful flesh *is*. And so the death of Jesus, an act of supreme injustice, becomes the final piece of evidence in God's prosecution of flesh: if flesh can go this far, if flesh seeks to kill God, if flesh turns Torah into a grounds for condemning the eternal Torah of God, then the case against flesh is closed. Flesh stands naked and condemned. So the cross is the judgment of this fleshly world.

If the story of Jesus ended there, there would be no atonement, there would be no overcoming of the curses of Eden and Babel. There is no sacrifice if an animal is slaughtered without being transformed into smoke, and *and ascension* there is no human sacrifice unless death is followed by resurrection. Without the resurrection, human beings would not yet be invited into the inner sanctuary; Jew and Gentile, slave and free, male and female would still be estranged and separated from one another. But the Son born under the law, slain under the law, was raised by his Father in the Spirit. In that resurrection the Father put his seal on the justice of Jesus. Jesus' way of sacrifice, his way of purity and temple service, was not contrary to Torah, but Torah's *fulfillment*, the way approved by the God who raises the dead—the God who gave promises to Abraham. Jesus had been faithful to his Father, and his Father passed judgment in his favor by raising him from the dead. The resurrection vindicated Jesus as the Father's beloved Son, and in vindicating Jesus it condemned the way of flesh. By virtue of the resurrection it becomes clear that Jesus was innocently suffering, dying not for his own sins but as One sinned against, taking the curse for those who cursed him. In the resurrection, not only Jesus was vindicated: the Way of Jesus was vindicated; Jesus *as the Way* was vindicated. After the resurrection, because of the resurrection, the new physics of social and political life that began to take form in Jesus' ministry persisted among his disciples, a community beyond elements, beyond stoicheic order, a community that combines all nations to call all the nations to die to flesh and join the ranks of the Spirit. This twofold movement of death-and-resurrection, of condemnation and vindication, is God's act of justification through the faith of Jesus Christ. It is God's act that establishes a just human society on earth. It dismantles the vulnerable, childish institutions of Torah, and it remakes humanity. Now at last the life of Spirit in flesh is a reality among humankind.

Jesus' death fulfilled Torah and the Prophets. You meant it for evil, Joseph told his brothers, but God meant it for good. There is a double agency, a double will at work in the cross. To grasp the cross, we have to look at the event "stereoscopically." There is the evil will of Jesus' enemies, who abused the best of God's gifts to condemn God himself to death. But the purpose of God triumphed over, indeed *through*, that *in*justice, and so Jesus' death was the supreme act of sacrifice, the supreme purification, the supreme atonement, the destruction of the temple of God and its raising-again after three days. Jesus' murderers were *not* priests at his sacrifice. Jesus was his own priest, laying down his life of his own volition so that he could take it up again. Jesus offered the sacrifice that Torah aimed at but could not achieve, a human sacrifice of obedience that could travel past the cherubic sword and enter Eden again. This triumph over human injustice, this establishment of the structures of justice through a supreme act of injustice, is what God had intended and purposed all along. Everything in Israel's history recorded in Scripture pointed to the suffering and glory of the Christ, to the cross and resurrection where God issued his deliverdict, where sin and death and flesh were condemned and Jesus was declared righteous in being rescued from the dead. The death and resurrection of Jesus are God's act of justification, the delivering judgment that releases from sin, flesh and the elementary principles of the world.

Individuals who are united to Jesus experience this justification in death and resurrection in their own lives. Baptized into Jesus' death, they are justified from sin (Rom 6:7), called to live in faith that they *have* died to sin and to offer their bodies as instruments in God's continuing campaign for justice, his continuing war against flesh. But what happened in Jesus does not only affect those who are joined to him. In the aftermath of Jesus' death and resurrection the world enters a new epoch with a new future. By the obedience of the Last Adam, justification comes to all people (Rom 5:18). The world has a future of life rather than death because it is a future determined by the Last rather than by the First Adam. Not all are in step with that future. Not all share now in the Christian era, and even Christians share in the Christian era only in part. For the time being, the Spirit is *in* flesh; the transformation of flesh into a spiritual body is yet to come. Yet the sheer fact that a new form of individual and social life takes root in the world changes the world as objectively and as universally as you would wish, and *permanently*. The wrath of God, congealed as stoicheic exclusions and separations, has been overcome by the sacrificial death and exaltation of the Son of Man. Thus Jesus is the propitiation for our sins, and not ours only, but for the sins of the whole world.

Paradoxically, the life of the Spirit is more fully fleshly than the life of the flesh. Flesh is weak, limited, mortal, but life according to flesh is a massive effort to deny weakness, overcome limitation, escape death. Flesh vaunts itself on its potency, sexual and otherwise. Flesh covers its fearfulness by protecting against vulnerabilities, protecting with violence, protecting by fomenting enmities, strife, jealousy, anger, disputes, factions. In all these ways flesh refuses to be flesh. The last thing flesh wants is to be itself.

Flesh desires to return to stoicheic order, which is an infantile return to childhood. A return to stoicheic life is, Paul says, *itself* a return to the flesh. That, we have seen, is the force of his charge in Galatians 3:1-5: The Galatians received the Spirit who forms "the one," the one new humanity made up of Jews and Gentiles. The Spirit who is the blessing of God to the nations came to them as they heard the good news of the Faith with faith. Then they began to seek progress in the flesh by returning to the order of stoicheic purity, exclusion, sacrifice. Flesh can operate more freely under *stoicheia* than it can under the Spirit because the Spirit is at war with the flesh, and because by design stoicheic order coheres with fleshly habits and aspirations. Flesh seeks privilege, and stoicheic order provides ready-made structures of privilege; flesh seeks to exclude and marginalize whoever is not of the right flesh, and stoicheic order includes practices that can be easily turned to exclusions; flesh lives in fear of death and harm, and stoicheic order can be used as a fortress against mortality, a hero system. The *nomos* of the Spirit militates against all of these habits: by insisting that all are clothed in Christ at baptism, that all are saints by the indwelling Spirit, that all share the same food at a common table, that every member of the social body contributes to the edification of every other member, and of the whole body.

We have found that the category of Galatianism offers a fruitful perspective from which to survey the goals and the fields of the church's mission. It helps us grasp both the successes of the church in transforming culture and the failures of the church as it is pulled back into stoicheic structures that encourage the life of the flesh. This account of atonement has also proved fruitful in formulating a typology of non-Christian religions, some of which are more or less thoroughly stoicheic, some at the borderlands of the Christian era, some the product of Galatian apostasy. It gives us a more accurate grasp of modernity than secularization theory does because it highlights how "primitive" modernity actually is. Quasi-stoicheic structures have been established in a world once Christian—sacred politics, sacred art, purity regulations that protect elites from commoners, Pharisaical philosophical systems. The Babelic church that emerged in the West after the Reformation is an ecclesial reversion to the *stoicheia*, a Galatianist apostasy that leaves space for Christians to ally with fleshly holy nations. A Galatian church produces a Galatian age of blood and tyranny, full of the works of the flesh.

Life by the Spirit is an embrace of weakness, limitation, even a ready acceptance of suffering and death for the other. Life by the Spirit is humility, meekness, gentleness, kindness. Flesh unloads burdens, which can be uncomfortable; the Spirit makes the baptized like Christ, burden-bearers for one another. Flesh exalts itself, striving to be lord rather than servant; Spirit works itself out as *mutual* slavery (Gal 5:13). For flesh, distinctions of flesh, of circumcision versus uncircumcision, mean *everything*. For the Spirit, these are *nothing*, and the only thing that matters is the Faith working through love (Gal 5:6).[1] Paradoxically, those who insist on Torah fail to keep Torah, while those who follow the direction of the Spirit fulfill Torah as it was meant to be fulfilled, fulfilling it as Jesus exemplified and taught.[2]

The paradox is intensified eschatologically: the flesh seeks mastery and life and immortality, but those who sow to flesh receive only corruption; the Spirit sows in weakness and humility, and receives what flesh seeks—eternal life (Gal 6:7-8). Flesh is supremely, boastfully self-confident despite its frailty; whoever lives by the Spirit is self-critical, aware of their susceptibility to temptation (Gal 6:1). Flesh is the condition of humanity as created, the condition of pre-eschatological humanity. Only a life that acknowledges this createdness with gladness is a truly human life. What Paul calls life *kata sarka* attempts the opposite. Since Adam's fall, flesh attempts to transcend its createdness, and in striving to be superhuman it becomes inhuman and bestial. Only the Spirit enables a person to live comfortably *en sarki* without being dominated by the desires, fears and passions of *sarx*. Only the Spirit enables genuinely human life. Only the Spirit enables people to present the members of their bodies as instruments of God's justice.

A just society must acknowledge human limitations. A just society must extend mercy and forgiving reconciliation to the outcast; flesh casts out and

---

[1] My capitalization is meant to suggest that the *pistis* that works through love is not human belief but the *pistis* that comes to deliver Israel from slavery to the tutelage of Torah, the *pistis* that comes to deliver the delivering verdict. If I am correct in my suspicion that Paul is still personalizing and Christologizing *pistis* in Gal 5:6, then much of the historical debate about this verse is quite beside the point, however critical the debate may be as a theological question.

[2] I follow Barclay in taking *nomos Christou* (Gal 6:2) in this sense (John M. G. Barclay, *Obeying the Truth: Paul's Ethics in Galatians* [Minneapolis: Fortress, 1988], 133-34). Galatians 6:2 dovetails nicely with Rom 8:4: In both, the Spirit is the one who ensures that Torah will be fulfilled.

does not recover, but the Spirit moves us to seek outcasts and to restore them. A just society is ordered to acknowledge the equal humanity of all its members and to celebrate each member's unique contribution to the whole; flesh seeks mastery and dominance. Fleshly societies are rigidly hierarchical, while the society of the Spirit is a society of mutual service in which each member is gifted for the sake of the common good.

It would be too weak to say that the Spirit through the Son's curse-bearing, justifying death and resurrection creates a new human *possibility*,[3] because God in Christ has achieved more than a possibility. For Paul the formation of "the one," the one seed of Abraham that lives by the Spirit, fulfills God's own covenant promise to Abraham, a promise upheld not only by God's truthfulness but also by his oath. The fulfillment of this promise comes through the Father's gift of his only Son for us all, and having given his Son, he will also with him freely give us all things. The gift of the Son and Spirit is the self-gift of God, and God will not deny himself. He will not fail to achieve his aim to establish a just human community in the world.

This society is possible, and actual, not only because the Spirit has been unleashed in the death and resurrection of Jesus but also because the structure of life after *stoicheia* does not lend itself to the deeds of the flesh. Poststoicheic worship is worship in the presence of God, without a veil, and so there is no room for veil-keepers to keep others at a distance. The Spirit purifies and sanctifies, and so those who have received the Spirit are not excluded by fleshly marks, blemishes, flows or issues. The blemished and lame are no longer excluded from the service of God's house. Eunuchs are made priests; sacrifice becomes what it truly is: any act that aims at communion with God in holy society. Alms and good deeds become forms of sacrifice, the sacrifices to which the slaying and burning of animals dimly pointed. Because Jesus has been slain and has ascended in Spirit, because we are joined with him in his sacrifice, our lives become living sacrifices, sweet savor of the fruit of the Spirit.

The sheer reality of the church poses a challenge to the principalities and powers of the stoicheic world. Here is a religion that no longer looks religious, and it has the imprimatur of heaven on it—the resurrection of Jesus. Here is a socioreligious order that changes the meaning of sacrifice, and purity, and priesthood, and temple, and makes them all descriptions of

---

[3]As Barclay points out, it is an actuality (ibid., 212-15).

human beings and the way of charity and peace. Other societies and religions can ignore or suppress; political powers can ignore or suppress. Others can persist in stoicheic immaturity. But they cannot remain unmarked by the challenge that this new form of life proposes. By being the community of the Spirit, living out of the new *physis* of the Son, the church carries out its mission. By living out of the liberty won for her by the justifying death and resurrection of Jesus, the church offers an alternative to fleshly systems. And in the proclamation of the word the church calls the nations to enter into the new era, the Christian era, and adopt the way of Jesus appropriate to full-grown humans, slaves who have grown up to be sons and lords of all.

And this *is* salvation, a salvation already a reality and destined to be fulfilled at the final resurrection. The community that keeps Torah in *this* way, indwelt by the Spirit, following the redemptive justice of Jesus, *is* salvation in social form. Salvation comes to human society when stoicheic, fleshly structures of exclusion and division are abolished and when human beings grow up out of their minority through the work of the Son and Spirit, when human beings are translated from Adam's flesh to Spirit in Christ. Salvation becomes an actuality in the world when God welcomes human beings to enter his very life by entry into the life of the Son by the Spirit. Justice is realized when the divisions of Babel are broken down in the death and resurrection of the Son of God, when a new order of life and worship is established in which the distinction of Jew and Gentile has become utterly inconsequential, where the division between circumcision and uncircumcision means nothing. Justice is established in the world when God takes flesh to deliver human beings from the tyranny of flesh, and to bring them to live by the Spirit while in flesh.

Spirit in flesh: *that* is new creation.

THE METAPHYSICS OF ATONEMENT

Natural and Supernatural

✝

In this and the next appendix, I examine the metaphysical and anthropological underpinnings of medieval and Protestant soteriology, paying special attention to the ways natural/supernatural schemes interfere with the biblical understanding of atonement and justification. These appendixes highlight the need for something like the revisionary account of soteriology I offer in the body of this book.

Gift, Grace and Pure Nature

During the twelfth century, theologians began to make more precise distinctions among various gifts from God. Natural gifts (*datum*, "given") were distinguished from gifts added to gifts of nature (*donum*, "gift"). Reason, will and other capacities shared by all humans are in the category of *datum*, while justifying grace is in the category of *donum*. Being made in the image of God is *datum*, while being renewed in the image of God is *donum*. Building on this distinction, John Scotus Eriugena formulated a systematic distinction between natural (*datum*) and supernatural (*donum*), using the explicit language of "supernatural grace" (*gratia supernaturalis*).[1] In the following centuries, theologians increasingly employed phrases like "above nature" (*supra naturam*) or "beyond nature" (*ultra naturam*), and defined the boundaries between what is natural and what is more than natural with increasing precision.[2]

---

[1]*Donum gratiae neque intra terminos conditae naturae continetur neque secundum naturalem virtutem operatur, sed superessentialiter et ultra omnes creatas naturales rationes effectus suos peragit.* Quoted in Alister McGrath, *Iustitia Dei: A History of the Christian Doctrine of Justification*, 3rd ed. (Cambridge: Cambridge University Press, 2005), 129n310.

[2]Simon of Tournai argued that *datum* is natural, while *donum* is spiritual: *Datis autem subsistit*

As theologians refined this paradigm, they developed the theoretical idea of "pure nature." Though the full development of this notion did not occur until the sixteenth and seventeenth centuries,[3] medieval theologians already toyed with it.[4] Here "pure" does not mean the opposite of "impure"; with these terms theologians were not claiming that Adam was created innocent, though they believed that. Rather, "pure nature" means "nature and nothing but nature" or "undiluted nature." The concept provided a way of speculating about the capacities of human beings *as such*—capacities for reason, will, moral decision and action—while bracketing the question of humans' religious life, their communion with God. "Pure nature" was human nature wholly untouched by grace, a human nature that has received no revelation; it is nature unaffected by the special presence and gifts of God. Initially theologians considered "pure nature" a pure hypothesis, since they all believed that in reality Adam the natural man was also endowed by his Creator with some sort of supernatural gifts as well, gifts that would enable him to reach his ultimate destination.

The problem of "pure nature" comes into play especially in connection with the issues of desire and end (or purpose). On Aristotelian assumptions, every nature aspires and desires to reach the perfection of its nature. What do humans aim for and desire as their highest perfection? If they are considered as purely *natural* beings, then their highest aim, desire and perfection is also natural. A nature cannot, by Aristotelian definition, transcend its nature; a nature *is* a principle of action and life that is limited by the capacities of that nature. As pure nature, humans aspire only to employ their reason and will within the

---

homo, quod est et qualis est naturaliter; donis vero qualis est spiritualiter. Ex datis ergo contrahit naturalem; ex donis, spiritualem. Peter of Poitiers suggested that *naturalia* were what originated in man, while *gratuita* originated from God: *Naturalia dicunt illa quae habet homo a nativitate sua,* and this included *ratio, ingenium, memoria,* etc. Grace is *illa quae naturalibus superaddita sunt,* such as *virtutes et scientiae,* and it is called *gratuita* because *a Deo homini per gratiam conferuntur.* Early in the thirteenth century, Praepositinus of Cremona (who deserves to be remembered if only for his name) argued that there must be an order beyond nature. Reason, he claimed, is the highest of natural human qualities, yet faith is higher; therefore, faith must belong to a realm beyond the natural: *Fides mea est supra rationem et ratione nullum naturale bonum est homine excellentius. Ergo fides supra omnia naturalia.* Similarly, Philip the Chancellor, in McGrath's summary, "distinguishes the natural order from the 'more noble' supernatural order: to the former belong reason and natural love, to the latter faith and charity." All of these from ibid., 129-32.

[3] For this later development, see, in English, Henri de Lubac, *Augustinianism and Modern Theology,* Milestones in Catholic Theology (New York: Crossroad, 2000), especially chap. 6.

[4] Gabriel Biel, for example. See Heiko Oberman, *The Harvest of Medieval Theology* (Grand Rapids: Baker, 2000), 47-50, 139-41.

natural world. As pure nature, humans may be interested in scanning the heavens, but they have no desire for the Love that moves the sun and all the other stars; they may use their reason to manipulate numbers, but they will have no desire to know the God who is one and three. They may *in fact* aspire to commune with their Creator, but on this paradigm this desire must be *added* to their nature. It is not part of their "natural" being. A theologian operating on a strict natural/supernatural dichotomy would say that humanity has a double desire and a double end. There is no necessary relation between the two, though in practice the two ends may be somehow connected. Human beings can, theoretically, reach their natural end without union with God, and can bypass their natural ends in their progress toward the beatific vision.

This dualistic conception of human existence does not reflect the views of the church fathers or the best of the medieval scholastics, whose "focus was on one, sole order: the concrete order of grace in which humans were made for God and human nature could be intelligible only by reason of its sole finality, divinization."[5] On this earlier view, there is no such thing as "pure nature," since humans are created with a desire to seek their fulfillment in communion with God. Aquinas's notion of a "natural desire" for God was an Aristotelianized version of Augustine's "unquiet heart" seeking rest in God. Despite his Aristotelianism, Thomas remained in continuity with Augustine and maintained two propositions in tension: human beings have a natural desire to enjoy the vision of God, and yet this natural desire is only fulfilled by an act of *pure grace* on God's part. The fact that humans have a natural desire for God does not in any way *obligate* God to fulfill it, and the "supernatural" fulfillment "fits" humanity's character as created. Supernatural grace is not a crown on a canary; it crowns a creature created to be a king, a being made a king only by the favor of the High King.

Later Scholasticism failed to maintain this tension, and the notion of a natural desire for God was qualified out of existence. Nor is Thomas wholly free from culpability for this development, largely because his attempt to combine the patristic/biblical emphasis on humanity as image of God with an Aristotelian view of nature was not entirely successful: "Aristotelian transposition of the patristic heritage" in Thomas "paved the way for later misrepresentations of his thought by those paleo-Thomists who betrayed

---

[5]Stephen J. Duffy, *The Dynamics of Grace: Perspectives in Theological Anthropology* (Collegeville, MN: Liturgical, 1993), 296.

the nourishing soil of the tradition with their over-rationalized theology." Thomas rightly asserts that humanity is created, as a "natural" being, for communion with God. But he errs in too readily accepting the Aristotelian conception of nature: "Thomas transformed Augustinianism and ended by allowing an autonomous philosophy to take up residence in the Christian house of intellect. . . . In time his position came to be read as menacing orthodoxy and provoking the extrinsicism that sealed off the supernatural from nature and welcomed in all the demons of dualism that have come to haunt the Catholic household."[6]

The natural/supernatural system was introduced, in part, to protect the gratuity of grace.[7] If humans have *no* inherent natural capacity, and not even any natural inclination or desire for reaching the final end for which they are created, then that end must be a sheer gift from God. On the other hand, if human beings have a natural desire for God, then it appears that they might have some capacity *in themselves* to seek for and perhaps to achieve communion with God. If God created human beings with a natural desire for communion, then it seems that communion ceases to be a gift *from* God and becomes an obligation imposed *on* God. One must keep nature and grace separate to make sure that grace remains purely gracious.

This way of staving off Pelagianism, however, comes at significant costs, since it suggests that the realm of the supernatural is "extrinsic" to what humanity *is* by virtue of creation. Grace appears not so much to elevate or perfect human creatures as to *replace* nature with a different (super)nature. Supernatural grace does not bring to fulfillment the natural inclinations, goals and capacities of human life; rather, it cancels them in favor of *other* inclinations, goals and capacities. In this scheme, grace is seen as truly gracious—but this gratuitous grace is not the fulfillment of created humanity: grace bestows a crown, but it is like a crown on a canary. Because they treated nature as a semiautonomous region, nature/grace schemes distorted notions of causation, which in turn created pressures toward the idea of preparation for and cooperation with grace.

---

[6]Ibid., 299. Duffy is summarizing the work of Henri de Lubac.
[7]This is the argument of E. L. Mascall in *The Openness of Being: Natural Theology Today* (Philadelphia: Westminster, 1971). Henri de Lubac makes the same point in various places; see *The Mystery of the Supernatural*, Milestones in Catholic Theology (New York: Crossroad, 1998). For a powerful exposition and extension of de Lubac, see John Milbank, *The Suspended Middle: Henri de Lubac and the Debate Concerning the Supernatural* (Grand Rapids: Eerdmans, 2005).

The more fundamental mistake was in imagining that there was something that could be called "humanity in itself." Since human beings exist only by, in and through God's call and command, we are *never* independent of God in even the slightest degree. Even "natural" desire must be entirely a gift. The solution to the dilemmas created by the natural/supernatural scheme is not to strive for more precision in relating the natural and supernatural but to reject the whole paradigm. The natural is always already infused with the gifts and graces of God, always already the arena of revelation; humans always already, in every action, are aiming for communion with God or alienating themselves from that communion. There is no way to draw the line between the two. Dislodging nature from grace distorts the whole system, and medieval soteriology is a particular expression of this fundamental dualism. In the end the effort to protect grace inverts. Nature takes on a life of its own and compromises the gratuity of grace that the whole paradigm was designed to defend.[8]

PROTESTANTS ON PURE NATURE

In their attacks on medieval soteriology, early Protestant theologians at times recognized that they were taking on the natural-supernatural schemes of the medieval and post-Reformation Catholic theologians. Francis Turretin defines "natural" as "what constituted nature and is its essential or integral part," and what is natural is "what immediately and necessarily follows the constituted nature." If "pure" is taken as the opposite of "impure," Turretin agrees that humans were created with a "pure" nature, that is, one unstained by sin. But he recognizes that for Catholic theologians "pure nature" is set in "opposition to gifts and spiritual habits of righteousness and holiness." A man is in "pure naturals" if he "consists of his own parts and essential properties without the gift of original righteousness and without any superadded qualities of habits (good or evil)." To say humanity was created in a state of pure nature thus raises the question "whether man, as he came from the hand of God, was created in such a state" that he was neither good nor depraved.[9]

---

[8]This is obviously a schematic description of medieval theology, stated starkly to bring out the issues more clearly.

[9]Francis Turretin, *Institutes of Elenctic Theology*, trans. George Musgrave Giger, ed. James T. Dennison (Phillipsburg, NJ: P&R, 1992), 1:462-64.

According to Turretin, Pelagius argued that "man at the beginning was created (and even every day is born) in a state of pure nature." Augustine quotes Pelagius to the effect that "we are born capable both of good and evil, but not in possession of these qualities; for in our birth we are equally destitute of virtue and vice."[10] Latter-day Pelagians[11] follow Pelagius "that they may the more easily prove original righteousness to have been a supernatural gift, superadded to nature." Thus "a pure and fallen nature differs in no other way than a 'naked' from a 'despoiled'" nature (Bellarmine's image). Humans are created without any clothing of good or evil; they were robed with superadded, supernatural graces. But at the fall, they lost this covering and reverted to his original state of nakedness. Unfallen Adam differs from fallen Adam "only in that the one has lost what the other never had."[12]

Turretin reflects a common position of the Protestant Scholastics.[13]

---

[10]Augustine, *De Gratia et Libero Arbitrio*, quoted in ibid.

[11]Turretin recognizes that not all Catholics accept the notion of pure nature, but some define "pure naturals" simply as "innocence." Turretin mentions Bellarmine, Alexander of Hales, Bonaventure and Jesuits, as well as Socinians and Remonstrants.

[12]Turretin develops two overtly biblical arguments against the notion of pure nature: First, humans are made in the image of God, and that must mean they were morally upright; second, they were made to glorify God, and they could not have fulfilled this duty without wisdom and holiness, which are gifts of God. In addition, he offers an argument from logic: "Where two things immediately opposed belong to any subject, one or other of the two must necessarily be in it. Now righteousness and sin are predicated of man as their fit . . . subject and are directly . . . opposed to each other. Therefore one or the other must necessarily be in him; nor can there be a man who is not either righteous or a sinner." Even infants, though they are not righteous or sinners by any actual righteousness or sin, may still be righteous or sinners by virtue of "habitual and congenital" features, as an infant is described as rational without having exercised reason. Adam was not in fact created in a state of pure nature, and Turretin argues that God *could* not have created humanity in a state of pure nature. Humans are physically dependent on God their Creator, and by the same token they must be "ethically" dependent. Once God determined to create, "he could not have created him lawless and not imposed a law upon him when created." The reason "Romanists" hold to a doctrine of pure nature is "for the purpose of patronizing the integrity of free will and to make concupiscence natural in the first man" (*Institutes of Elenctic Theology*, 464).

[13]According to Polanus, "The original wisdom in man's soul was that excellence and perfection of knowledge, by which unimpaired man rightly knew God and God's work and himself and wisely understood all things unifold, singular, and universal, and rightly compounded or divided them and reasoned from the composites rightly and without error—in sum: knowledge, judgment, foresight not only sufficed to govern the animal life, but also ascended with them to God" (quoted in Heinrich Heppe, *Reformed Dogmatics*, ed. Ernst Bizer, trans. G. T. Thomson [London: Wakeman Trust, 1950], 238). Cocceius said that "the image of God was natural to man, not because it flows from the actual substance and faculties, but because it would have been unbecoming in God not to make man upright" (ibid., 239). Rissen is careful to distinguish the senses in which the image of God is "natural" to humans: "This image may be called natural to man, not as though it were an essential part of his nature, but (1) because it was created along

Humanity, according to this view, was created with various gifts—wisdom, righteousness, free will and the capacity to do good, dominion over the lower creation and earthly blessedness. Adam, to be sure, was destined to grow in knowledge, wisdom and righteousness, but all this growth would be a maturation of capacities and virtues he possessed from the moment of creation in the image of God. These gifts, a complexly interwoven set of gifts related to humanity's role in creation and gifts necessary for communion with God, are all "natural" to humanity. Covenant theologians of the Reformed tradition often claim that even the covenant relation between God and humans is "natural" in some sense.[14] Frequently the natural covenantal relationship between the Creator and the creature is seen as the foundation for the specific arrangements of the covenant of works.[15]

In some Reformed theologians, however, the distinction between the natural covenant and the covenant of works comes close to positing a kind

---

with the nature; (2) because it was not contrary to it; (3) it was necessary to the end of created man; (4) it would have had to be propagated along with the nature" (ibid., 239). Hottinger agrees that the "original righteousness and immortality of the first man were natural gifts, not supernatural, so far as that is natural which the first man received with his actual nature; while supernatural is what is above the intact nature and its condition." These gifts are "supernatural" only when they are considered in contrast to the corrupted nature of fallen man, but not when considered as part of the being of Adam as created (ibid., 239).

[14]Johannes Heidegger wrote: "It may also be recognized naturally, that there is a covenant intervening between God and man. Man's conscience keeps asserting that to God the Creator and Lord of man obedience on his part as a creature is bound to be enjoined and He must be loved singly as the most excellent and the Author of all good. In such obedience and love moreover consists the duty which God requires of man. . . . Then too man is naturally not ignorant of the promise of God in promising good to the obedient. Indeed he knows that God as the most excellent is not sought, looked up to, loved in vain, in fact that he who loves enjoys by love the God whom he loves; in which enjoyment of God man's blessedness consists. And since man is not unaware of being God's creature and dependent (*cliens*), he is equally not unaware of the necessary requirement, that there should be friendship between himself and God, who offers it on terms. And no one can doubt the parallel requirement, that he in turn should expect from God the reward promised to the obedience and should be able to receive it because of God's truthfulness and faithfulness known by nature" (quoted in ibid., 284-85).

[15]Cocceius suggests that the covenant of works "rests upon the law of nature" and therefore "may be called the covenant of nature." Robert Rollock writes that the covenant of works "is founded in nature" since "after God had created man after his own image, pure and holy, and had written his law in his mind, he made a covenant with man." This natural goodness "thus beautified with holiness and righteousness, and the light of God's law, is the foundation of the covenant of works" since "a covenant on condition of good works and perfect obedience to God's law could not well stand with the justice of God unless he had first created him pure and holy, and had engraved his law in his heart, from whence those good works might proceed" (quoted in Rowland S. Ward, *God and Adam: Reformed Theology and the Creation Covenant* [Wantirna, Australia: New Melbourne Press, 2003], 100-101).

of pure nature and a natural/supernatural dualism.[16] It is true that Adam was created "imperfect," but only in the sense that "perfection" is an eschatological concept. He was created "immature," destined for glorification and maturity. But his "imperfection" does not consist of his reliance on senses, or the fact that he had a body, or the necessity that he communicated by symbols. An overtly natural/supernatural scheme appears in the work of Francis Junius. Like the medieval theologians, he employs the natural/supernatural scheme in an effort to protect the gratuity of grace, but in so doing significantly alters the federal scheme.[17]

---

[16]William Ames describes the need for a covenant of works this way: "Since man is less perfect than the angels and needs more instruction and practice, something positive was added to (though on the same basis as) the law of nature . . . [and] because man in this animal life understands by the senses and is led by the hand, as it were, from sensible to intelligible and spiritual things, outward symbols and sacraments were added to the spiritual law to illustrate and confirm it. These symbols contained a special and positive law, a profession of general obedience to the law of nature put in man before, and a solemn confirmation of promises and threats as sanctions" (quoted in ibid., 101). Ames's formulation is flawed on many counts. The notion that knowledge should progress from "sensible" to "intelligible" employs Platonic terminology to make essentially a Platonic point. How this fits with the Christian confession that the highest knowledge comes through our union with the *incarnate* (and hence "sensible") Son is difficult to see. Ames also implies that the symbolic form of communication is an accommodation to the "imperfection" of man, necessary but somewhat unfortunate. William Strong implies something similar: "God dealt with man in a Covenant-way in his Creation. Man stands bound to God by a double bond of Creation and stipulation; the one is natural and necessary, and the other voluntary. Thus God binds the Creature to himself by all imaginable engagements, to prevent future apostasy. By the one we are bound to God, and by the other God is bound to us" (quoted in ibid., 102). Strong thus claims that the bond of creation is a "natural" bond, necessitated by the sheer fact of being created, but the covenant bond is a "voluntary" one, freely chosen by God. But this distinction breaks down in several ways: Creation is as much a voluntary act as the covenant is. If one insists on maintaining the distinction, it remains the case that humanity even "before" the covenant is already created in the image of God, which is a voluntary determination on God's part, not necessary to the fact of creation as such. It is not at all clear how a creature made *ex nihilo* is in any kind of "natural" relation to anything.

[17]In Mark Karlberg's summary, "The covenant, according to Junius, was established with our first parents by God the Father in the love of his Son. It held out the promise of supernatural life for obedience and the curse of death and separation from God for disobedience. . . . Although Adam was obliged to render complete and perfect obedience to the law of God by virtue of his debt as a creature (*ex puris naturalibus*), the covenantal reward of life eternal was strictly one of grace and mercy (*ex pacto*)" (Mark W. Karlberg, *Covenant Theology in Reformed Perspective* [Eugene, OR: Wipf & Stock, 2000], 98). This was, Karlberg says, the first "significant revision of Calvinistic doctrine regarding creation and God's covenant with Adam. No longer was the covenant concept organically related to the order of creation. The result was a logical, if not temporal, abstraction of a natural order from a supernatural, covenantal order in creation. On this interpretation the covenantal order was perceived to be superimposed upon the natural. Junius' view of supernatural grace offered in the way of covenant was virtually equivalent to the scholastic notion of the *donum superadditum*." Johannes Cloppenburg followed the same line of reasoning. Again Karlberg's summary: "Whereas God's revelation to Adam was both natural and super-

Reformed theology has had no Henri de Lubac to sort through the history of the Reformed use of the natural/supernatural scheme, but these citations are sufficient to suggest that Protestant orthodoxy was willing to employ the terminology and sometimes the concepts of medieval theology, no doubt partially under the influence of Aristotle. Since Reformed Scholastics worked out their theology of justification in the context of a theology of covenant, it seems likely that this natural/supernatural paradigm would have some effect on Reformed soteriology.

NATURE, SUPERNATURE AND ATONEMENT

The distinction between nature and the supernatural is evident in both atonement theologies and accounts of justification, though in distinct ways. In atonement theology, natural/supernatural dualism appears in the detachment of atonement theology from the historical events and circumstances of Jesus' life and in the way the effects of the atonement are conceived in "supernatural" rather than natural (sociopolitical) terms. In theologies of justification the natural/supernatural dualism appears in medieval accounts of causation, and thus of notions of cooperation with grace, both of which the Reformers rejected. Within Protestant soteriology, however, nature/supernatural dualisms reappear insofar as justification becomes detached from historical concerns for social and political justice. Nature is isolated from social and institutional factors; society is treated as a loose-fitting garment on an unchanging nature. By contrast, as has been emphasized throughout this book, the Bible treats social arrangements as internal to human nature.

In this appendix, I examine the effects of natural/supernatural schemes in atonement theory, focusing on the elision of political concerns from soteriology. In the following appendix, I offer a more detailed account of how natural/supernatural schemes infect both medieval and, in a different way, Protestant teaching on justification.

---

natural, Adam's ability to know God and to trust him required the supernatural communication of grace. The covenantal relationship—*personal* communion and fellowship with God—was not natural to Adam's original state in creation, but rather rested upon a special act of condescension on God's part. Although the covenantal reward of eternal life was contingent upon Adam's compliance with the law of God, the actual granting of eternal life was itself purely a matter of God's grace. Cloppenburg made use of the distinction between the reward based on "strict justice" (intrinsic merit) and reward granted in the way of covenant. As image-bearer of God, Adam was a servant of the Creator; his elevation from the status of servanthood to sonship was contingent upon God's covenantal love and condescension" (ibid., 99).

Social atonement. That Jesus' death has a direct "social" and even "institutional" impact is evident from Paul's argument in the latter part of Ephesians 2. "By the blood of Christ," those who have been far off and excluded from the covenant—uncircumcised Gentiles—have been brought near to God (Eph 2:11-13). Once strangers, they are now sons and saints, citizens and family members of God's house. Since God's house is a temple, they are holy ones, priests serving in the presence of God (Eph 2:19-22). Access to God is linked with union among human beings. The fact that distant Gentiles are brought near, and strangers made saints, implies that the division of Jews and Gentiles is overcome. The text does not, however, leave that to inference. After affirming that the far off have been brought near by the blood of Jesus' sacrifice (Eph 2:13), Paul immediately adds that Christ broke down the dividing wall that separated the two halves of the human race, Jews and Gentiles, and incorporated them into one new humanity, reconciling them in "one body to God through the cross" (Eph 2:16). The death of Jesus is not only the means for overcoming the Edenic curse that separates human beings from God, but it is simultaneously a removal of the Babelic curse and a fulfillment of the promise that all nations will be blessed in Abraham's seed. The atonement accomplishes both, reconciling us to God "vertically" and "horizontally" to one another, ripping up not only the veil that separated Yahweh and humanity but also the "wall" that separated Jew and Gentile. Ephesians 2 summarizes the point of this entire volume.

In many patristic treatments of the atonement, the psycho-social effects of the death of Jesus are front and center, and even when atonement theologies become more formalized and systematized in the Middle Ages, these dimensions are not entirely lost. In some theologians, however, they play a very marginal role. In the brief survey of atonement theologies here, I attempt to discern whether social and political, or ecclesial, concerns are integrated into atonement theory. This approach suggests the possibility that atonement theologies might be distinguished not as "objective" versus "subjective"[18] but as those that integrate soteriology and ecclesiology and

---

[18]This distinction should be dispensed with entirely. It is hard to imagine an account of the atonement accomplished in Jesus that is purely objective—that is, purely a matter of historical event, without any account of how the death and resurrection of Jesus is aimed at changing people. It is equally difficult to imagine a purely subjective atonement, one in which Jesus' death makes an appeal to human observers and hearers without anything being actually accomplished by him. What sort of appeal is that?

those that do not. We might put it this way: atonement theologies differ in the proximity of soteriology and ecclesiology, in the degree to which the formation of the church as a historical community is explicitly set out as the aim of Christ's redeeming work. We could describe a spectrum of atonement theologies by asking to what degree the atonement is considered a part of *political* theology.

Such a typology reveals some interesting alliances, such as that between Aquinas and Abelard, or between Aquinas and Reformed covenant theologians. It also reveals some intriguing divergences, such as that between Anselm and Thomas. Here I first examine two atonement theologies (Anselm and Calvin) in which soteriology and ecclesiology are quite "distant," and follow with a brief summary of two atonement theologies (Athanasius and Aquinas) that unite soteriology and ecclesiology, and hence soteriology and politics, more intimately. My contention is that atonement theology and formulations of justification are distorted by the metaphysical problems attending to the natural/supernatural paradigm.

Anselm. *Cur Deus Homo?* is typically viewed as the classic statement of the "satisfaction" theory of atonement,[19] and *satisfactio* is a central term and satisfaction a central concept in the treatise. Anselm seems to use the term in much the same way as it was understood in Roman law, where *satisfacere* meant in general "to fulfill another's wish, to gratify the desire of a person; when used of a debtor = to carry out an obligation whatever its origin."[20] *Satisfacere* was sometimes opposed to *solutio* (payment) to refer to "other kinds of extinction of an obligation": *satisfactio pro solutione*, satisfaction in lieu of payment of a debt. The surface of Anselm's argument fits neatly into these categories. He describes the problem of sin as a problem of indebtedness. Humans are indebted to God by virtue of creation. We owe him everything, specifically a debt of obedience and honor. Sin dishonors God, and therefore sinners are in default. Besides, we willingly incurred the debt of sin; we have stolen his honor, and we add further to our debt thereby. What do we have to make up the deficit? We already owe everything; how

---

[19] I am relying on the English text found in Anselm, *The Major Works*, ed. Brian Davies (Oxford: Oxford University Press, 2008). A Latin edition is available online at the Internet Archive, *S. Anselmi Cantuariensis : libri duo Cur Deus homo* (Berolini: Sumptibus: G. Schlawitz, 1857), https://archive.org/details/sanselmicantuaro4laemgoog.

[20] Adolf Berger, *Encyclopedic Dictionary of Roman Law*, Transactions of the American Philosophical Society, New Series, 43, part 2 (Philadelphia: American Philosophical Society, 1953), 690.

can we pay back *more* than everything? We need a Redeemer who can take our debt, who can pay *satisfactio pro solutione* on our behalf.

Beneath the surface the question is why God cannot merely forgive the debt, as the king does in Matthew 18. In trying to answer that question, Anselm moves away from *satisfactio* toward *dispositio*. In the dialogue (1.19), Boso (Anselm's dialogue partner) refers to the petition of the Lord's Prayer *dimitte nobis debita nostra* and asks why we pray in that way. If we are already paying the debt, there is no reason why we should ask for it to be forgiven. If we are not paying, it is "pointless" to pray (*cur frustra oramus*) that it be remitted. Why? Because God cannot remit an unpaid debt. And why is that? Because it is not "convenient," not fitting (*quia non convenit*). Why unfitting? Anselm (1.24) explains that it is impossible for God to remit debt simply on the "ground that [the sinner] is incapable of making repayment."

In fact, he claims that it is logically impossible for God to do so. Anselm examines two possibilities. If God forgives a debt that the debtor is willing but unable to repay, he is remitting what he is not able to get anyway (*dimittit Deus quod habere non potest*). Anselm considers this a "mockery" (*derisio*) and not true *misericordia*. It is difficult to know what Anselm means here. It is perhaps something along these lines: My parents gave me life, fed and clothed and sheltered me, ensured that I got an education, and so on. Since it is a debt I can never repay, it would be foolish for my parents to say, "We forgive your debt." They were never going to get repayment in the first place, so their forgiveness is empty. If this is what Anselm means, there is perhaps some force in it (it implies that release from such a debt is more psychological than financial). But not much force. Is not forgiveness of a debt *by definition* a remission of a debt that the creditor is not going to receive anyway? Is not that precisely what the king (representing the heavenly Father) does in Matthew 18? Forgiving a debt that cannot be paid certainly is not self-contradictory (*contrarium*), as Anselm claims.

On the other hand, God might intend to exact "repayment" involuntarily through punishment. In this scenario too it is not fitting for God simply to forgive debts because such mercy would relax punishment and leave persons happy in their sin. The debtors' incapacity to repay is their own fault, and is sin. God would condone sin if he allowed the incapacity to pass. Again, this is not true *misericordia*, since it is a travesty of God's justice. This is a more convincing explanation than the first, but it is important to note that we have moved out of the realm of debt and repayment into the realm of government. What prevents God from exercising "pure" mercy is his justice, expressed in punishment. The claim that God demands *satisfactio* rests on the more fundamental claim about God's *dispositio* of the world's order.

In understanding why Anselm thinks "pure" mercy unfitting to God, the key passage is in 1.15: Once humans have sinned, there are two alternatives—"voluntary recompense for wrongdoing, or the exaction of punishment from someone who does not give recompense." In light of the common view that Anselm teaches a "penal substitution" view of the atonement, it is worth noting that the two options of satisfaction and punishment are *opposed*: *either* a criminal can be punished, *or* he or someone else can make satisfaction on his behalf. Anselm does *not* claim that the other can be *punished* on behalf of the criminal. But the question is, Why not a third alternative, forgiveness *without* recompense? Anselm answers:

> If the divine Wisdom did not impose these forms of recompense in cases where wrongdoing is endeavouring to upset the right order of things, there would be in the universe, which God ought to be regulating, a certain ugliness, resulting from the violation of the beauty of order, and God would appear to be failing in his governance (*in sua dispositione*). Since these two consequences are impossible as they are unfitting (*inconvenientia*), it is inevitable that recompense or punishment follows every sin.

God would damage the beauty of creation, would fail in his governance, if he indulged in the false mercy of pure forgiveness. *Satisfactio* is necessary for governmental and aesthetic reasons, which in this passage are virtually identical: it would not be beautiful for God, the judge and ruler, to forgive sin without some form of payment for the wrongs done.

In all of this, Anselm's focus is on the way the cross of Jesus provides for the reconciliation of individual human beings with God.[21] Individuals owe a debt of obedience and have incurred a further debt by their disobedience.

---

[21] Adam Kotsko makes the important point that Anselm's entire theory depends on the assumption of a "relational ontology" according to which a single human being is capable of acting for all humanity. In general he sees Anselm as marking a departure from the more relational ontologies of patristic theologians (Kotsko, *The Politics of Redemption: The Social Logic of Salvation* [London: T&T Clark, 2010], 126, 129. To clarify, Kotsko's book has a different focus from my discussion in this chapter, though our concerns are connected. Kotsko's interest is in the ontology and anthropology underlying atonement theology. What I am examining is not "relational ontology" but the sociopolitical aim and effect of the atonement.

They must either be punished or make adequate satisfaction. Punishment would mean the end of the human race, and God will not allow his creatures to be destroyed. Anselm's theory is a piece of political theology in one sense, since the crux of his argument is that God the judge must demonstrate his judicial governance of the world. But there is no indication how the church, much less extra-ecclesial polities, are created or even affected by the death of Jesus.

Calvin and the wall of separation. Anselm's treatise makes no reference to Ephesians 2. Even the more biblically oriented atonement theology of Calvin, however, marginalizes the horizontal effects of the cross. Calvin of course is aware of Ephesians 2, and in his commentary on the passage recognizes that Paul is speaking of the union of Jews and Gentiles into the one body of the church. Jews were "separated, for a certain time, from the Gentiles, by the appointment of God," and the ceremonies of the law "were the open and avowed symbols of that separation." Enmity between Jews and Gentiles arose because there were boundaries placed between the two. In the gospel, though, the "privilege of adoption" is extended to the Gentiles, and "Christ has now made us all to be brethren."[22]

Despite this emphasis on the union of Jews and Gentiles in the cross, Calvin is strangely hesitant to connect the cross *directly* with the breakdown of the dividing wall between Jews and Gentiles. He traces the abolition of enmity not to the cross but to the incarnation: "The Son of God, by assuming a nature common to all, has formed in his own body a perfect unity." And he employs political analogies. When two contending nations are brought under the same ruler, he insists that the two "remove the badges and marks of their former enmity." Hence, Jews are instructed to abandon circumcision and the other marks of Jewish identity as they submit to the universal kingship of Jesus.[23] He acknowledges that Paul speaks of reconciliation among human beings, but immediately turns the argument back to the fact that "we have been brought back into favor with God." The phrase "by the cross" does not refer directly to the death of Jesus as the source of human reconciliation, but rather points to the "propitiatory sacrifice" that restores us to God's favor. Through the cross, the ceremonies have been abolished, but the cross's relation to this change in covenantal adminis-

---

[22]John Calvin, *Commentary on Ephesians* 2:14, trans. William Pringle, Christian Classics Ethereal Library, www.ccel.org/ccel/calvin/calcom41.html.

[23]Calvin, *Commentary on Ephesians* 2:15.

tration is indirect: "Having redeemed both Jews and Gentiles, he has brought them back into one flock." The proclamation of peace is not an announcement of peace among humans but the proclamation of peace with God, "indiscriminately available to Jews and Gentiles." The gospel is a message of peace because in it "God declares himself to be reconciled to us, and makes known his paternal love."[24] The gospel is *not* a proclamation of peace between Jew and Gentile. Because it reconciles both Jews and Gentiles to God, the partition between the two is removed. But that horizontal result is not a direct aim of the atonement. The "social life" of the church is not, apparently, a direct concern of the atonement. Jesus' death has to do with the individual's relation to God, not with historical communities of believers. At best, the "natural" concerns of uniting Jew and Gentile are secondary to the atonement's primary aims.

Calvin rarely appeals to the latter half of Ephesians 2 in his systematic treatment of doctrine in the *Institutes of the Christian Religion*.[25] When he does, the text supports arguments that have little to do with the reconciliation of Jews and Gentiles. He uses Ephesians 2:11-12 in arguments regarding sacramental theology. When Paul says that the Gentiles were strangers and aliens to God prior to Christ, he is using a metonymy in which the lack of circumcision is taken as a lack of the thing that circumcision signifies.[26] In the same verses, Paul "interprets circumcision imprinted upon infants as a testimony of that communion which they have with Christ."[27] Calvin appeals to Paul's use of *atheoi* when he argues that worship outside of Christ is nothing more than idolatry and atheism.[28] Twice he refers to Ephesians 2:14 as proof that in the cross God has destroyed enmity between himself and human beings, arguing, as he does in his Ephesians commentary, that Christ is our "peace" insofar as he is "the bond whereby God may be found to us in fatherly faithfulness."[29] In a number of places, Calvin uses Ephesians

---

[24]Calvin, *Commentary on Ephesians* 2:16-17.

[25]On Calvin's atonement theology, see Adonis Vidu, *Atonement, Law, and Justice: The Cross in Historical and Cultural Contexts* (Grand Rapids: Baker Academic, 2014); Paul van Buren, *Christ In Our Place: The Substitutionary Character of Calvin's Doctrine of Reconciliation* (Eugene, OR: Wipf & Stock, 2002).

[26]Calvin, *Institutes* 4.14.12; cf. 4.16.3. All quotations from the *Institutes* are from John Calvin, *Institutes of the Christian Religion*, ed. John T. McNeill, trans. Ford Lewis Battles, 2 vols. (Philadelphia: Westminster, 1960).

[27]Calvin, *Institutes* 4.16.15.

[28]Calvin, *Institutes* 1.4.3; cf. 1.5.13; 2.6.1; 3.24.10; 4.16.24.

[29]Calvin, *Institutes* 3.2.28; 3.2.32.

2:20 in anti-Catholic polemics designed to show that the church is founded on the teaching of the prophets and apostles.[30]

In two places, he refers to the breakdown of the dividing wall between Jews and Gentiles in Christ. Arguing that Abraham is father of both Jewish and Gentile believers, he observes that this undermines the boasting of the Jews.[31] The division between Jew and Gentile is one of the features of the "administration" of the old covenant, but in the fullness of time this division was overcome in Christ.[32] For our purposes, what is remarkable about this distribution of Calvin's uses of Ephesians 2 is the nearly complete absence of the passage from the sections of the *Institutes* where Calvin directly treats the atonement.[33] The one place where the Pauline text appears, Calvin interprets it not as a reference to reconciliation among human beings or the constitution of a new humanity, but as a text about the reconciliation of God and humanity. "God loves us and yet was angry toward us at the same time, until he became reconciled to us in Christ," Calvin writes, and then offers a catena of New Testament texts in support: 1 John 2:2 (Christ is "the expiation for our sins"); 2 Corinthians 5:19 ("God was in Christ reconciling the world

---

[30]Calvin, *Institutes* 1.7.2; 4.1.9; 4.2.1, 4. These appeals are ironic, since Paul does *not* mention "teaching" in the passage. According to Eph 2, the foundation of the church is not doctrine but people—Jesus Christ the cornerstone, and the apostles and prophets in their ministry of teaching and leading and evangelizing as the other foundation stones.

[31]Calvin, *Institutes* 4.16.31: "Abraham, he says, was in uncircumcision justified by faith. Afterward, he received the sign of circumcision, the seal of the righteousness of faith, that he might be the father of all believers, both of uncircumcision and of circumcision, not of those who boast of circumcision alone, but of those who follow the faith which, in uncircumcision, our father Abraham had [Rom. 4:10-12]. Do we not see that both kinds are made equal in honor? For, during the time set by God's decree, Abraham was father of the circumcision. After the wall was broken down (as the apostle elsewhere writes [Eph. 2:14]) which separated Gentiles from Jews, the Gentiles too were given access to God's Kingdom, and Abraham became their father—and that apart from the sign of circumcision, for they have baptism in place of it. But in order to crush the haughtiness of some who, neglecting all concern for piety, preened themselves on ceremonies alone, Paul expressly denies that Abraham is the father only of those who are of the circumcision [Rom. 4:12]."

[32]Calvin, *Institutes* 2.11.11: "Israel was then the Lord's darling son; the others were strangers. Israel was recognized and received into confidence and safekeeping; the others were left to their own darkness. Israel was hallowed by God; the others were profaned. Israel was honored with God's presence; the others were excluded from all approach to him. 'But when the fullness of time came' [Gal. 4:4] which was appointed for the restoration of all things, he was revealed as the reconciler of God and men; 'the wall' that for so long had confined God's mercy within the boundaries of Israel 'was broken down' [Eph. 2:14]. 'Peace was announced to those who were far off, and to those who were near' [Eph. 2:17] that together they might be reconciled to God and welded into one people [Eph. 2:16]. Therefore there is now no difference between Jew and Greek [Gal. 3:28], between circumcision and uncircumcision [Gal. 6:15], but 'Christ is all in all' [Col. 3:11]."

[33]There is one citation of Eph 2:11-21 in Calvin, *Institutes* 2.12-17.

to himself"); Ephesians 1:6 ("He bestowed his grace on us in his beloved Son"). In this context, he quotes Ephesians 2:15-16, "that he . . . might reconcile us both . . . in one man through the cross."[34] The fragmented quotation marginalizes the ecclesial dimension of the passage, and Calvin moves on quickly to God's reconciliation of sinners to himself through Christ, God as the fount of righteousness and ultimately, inevitably, justification.

Nowhere else in his treatment of the atonement does Calvin give any indication that the atonement has a direct social or ecclesial effect. Structured by the Apostles' Creed, Calvin's atonement theology is largely Anselmian, focusing on Christ's obedient life and death as "satisfaction" for sins, a payment of an adequate price and a fulfillment of the penalty due to sin.[35] At several places *Christus Victor* themes are embedded within his theory. Jesus was not overwhelmed by the curse that was imposed on him but "in taking the curse upon himself—he crushed, broke, and scattered its whole force."[36] He submitted to death, but not "to be engulfed in its abyss, but rather to engulf it."[37] When Calvin moves outside the "objective" work of Christ in history to the application of Christ's work, the focus is usually on the fruits of Christ's death and resurrection in the lives of individual believers. Christ's death not only satisfies God's justice and propitiates his wrath but also possesses an efficacy that enables Christians to mortify the flesh.[38] The resurrection has power to bring righteousness and life into the life of the believer.[39] Together the death and resurrection of Jesus enable the believer to kill the sinful flesh and to walk in newness of life, what Reformed theology has generally called "mortification" and "vivification."

Given Calvin's emphasis on the covenant, and his extensive treatment of the similarities and differences between old and new covenants,[40] it would seem natural for Calvin to connect the death of Christ to the transition from old to new. If he does this, it is certainly not central to his account of the atonement. He agrees with Augustine that there is a transition from the many, complicated and less powerful rites of the old covenant to the fewer,

---

[34]Calvin, *Institutes* 2.17.2.

[35]For discussion, see Richard Muller, *Calvin and the Reformed Tradition: On the Work of Christ and the Order of Salvation* (Grand Rapids: Baker Academic, 2012); van Buren, *Christ in Our Place.*

[36]Calvin, *Institutes* 2.16.6.

[37]Calvin, *Institutes* 2.16.7.

[38]Calvin, *Institutes* 2.16.7

[39]Calvin, *Institutes* 2.16.13.

[40]Calvin, *Institutes* 2.10-11.

simpler and more potent rites of the new, but that transformation of ritual life is not connected directly to the death and resurrection of Jesus. This seems partly due to his use of the distinction between the "substance" of the covenant and its "administration." Substantively, the covenant remains the same throughout history; only the administration changes. That may be another indication of an implied nature/grace paradigm: the substance of the covenants is on the "supernatural" side of the divide, while the sensible, ritual "administration" is on the natural side. Whether or not this is an accurate explanation of Calvin's atonement theology, the absence of any integration of atonement with ecclesiology and political theology is noteworthy.

Overcoming fear of death. For Athanasius, Jesus' death is fundamentally a triumph over death, and as such the death of Christ delivers human beings from their natural fear of death. Human nature is mortal, and in the condition of sin we are fearful of death. Deification is liberation from the fear of death, which is essentially a human form of immortality, to be consummated at the resurrection. Deliverance from death manifests itself in human overcoming of the passions of fear and timidity, a triumph that must, on Athanasius's premises, be manifest in bodily action, not simply in intellectual assent. *On the Incarnation* points to the lives and deaths of martyrs as evidence that the Spirit of the incarnate Son, the Spirit of the crucified and risen Deliverer, is beginning to pervade the human race: "Is it a slight indication of the Savior's victory over [death], when boys and young girls who are in Christ look beyond this present life and train themselves to die? Every one is by nature afraid of death and of bodily dissolution; the marvel of marvels is that he who is enfolded in the faith of the cross despises this natural fear and for the sake of the cross is no longer cowardly in the face of it."[41] Is it possible to doubt Christ's "conquest of death" after "so many martyrdoms in Christ and such daily scorn of death by His truest servants"?[42]

Whole societies had been devoted to death, violence and murderous competition. Now all the deathliness that has corrupted human existence from within is being overcome in the Spirit. Barbarians "are naturally savage in their habits," and while they sacrifice to idols, "they rage furiously against

---

[41] Athanasius, *On the Incarnation* 28. I have examined Athanasius' soteriology at greater length in *Athanasius*, Foundations of Theological Exegesis and Christian Spirituality (Grand Rapids: Baker Academic, 2011), chap. 6. Quotations are taken from St. Athanasius, *On the Incarnation*, trans. C. S. M. V., Popular Patristics (Crestwood, NY: St. Vladimir's Seminary Press, 1993).

[42] Athanasius, *On the Incarnation* 28.

each other." As soon as they hear the teaching of Christ, "they turn from fighting to farming, and instead of arming themselves with swords extend their hands in prayer."[43] Bodily actions change, and they change within the present world of mortality and evil. Christ, the one who fulfills the *typoi* of the prophets, impresses his image back onto the human race, and as a result "they shall beat their swords into ploughshares and their spears into sickles, and nation shall not take sword against nation, neither shall they learn any more to wage war."[44] Athanasius sees Jesus' triumph over death as having quite immediate cultural consequences.

    Christ's fulfillment of Torah and temple. Thomas Aquinas is sometimes grouped loosely with Anselm as an advocate of a "satisfaction" model of the atonement, and specifically as an advocate, if not directly of penal substitution, at least as a precursor to the penal substitution view. This is no more accurate for Thomas than it is for Anselm.[45] Thomas inherited two ways of understanding satisfaction. On the one hand, there is the relatively recent Anselmian idea that satisfaction restores honor to God that has been damaged by sin. The deeper, Augustinian notion of satisfaction, reflected in the penitential system of the medieval church, is concerned with dealing with the *root* of sin. Satisfaction in this sense does not merely restore a balance that has been upset but aims at healing and restoring the damaged image of God in human beings.[46] Satisfaction in both senses aims at restoring justice, but justice is conceived differently. When satisfaction is understood as returning damaged honor, justice is thought of in mercantile terms of balance. Jesus pays a price that no one else could pay. When satisfaction is understood as healing and restorative, justice has to do with restoring just relationship.[47]

    Thomas, like Anselm, employs *satisfactio* to describe an *alternative* to punishment rather than a form of punishment. In Thomas it is clear that the

---

[43]Athanasius, *On the Incarnation* 52.

[44]Athanasius, *On the Incarnation* 52, quoting Is 2:2-4.

[45]This needs to be qualified by recognizing the diachronic development of Thomas's atonement theology. Romanus Cessario argues that Thomas moves from a legal and juridical account of the atonement in his early work to a more "personalist" perspective in his mature work. See Cessario, *The Godly Image: Christ and Salvation in Catholic Thought from Anselm to Aquinas* (Petersham, MA: St. Bede's Publications, 1990). See also Rik van Nieuwenhove, "'Bearing the Marks of Christ's Passion': Aquinas' Soteriology," in *The Theology of Thomas Aquinas*, ed. Rik van Nieuwenhove and Joseph Wawrykow (Notre Dame, IN: University of Notre Dame, 2005), 283.

[46]On the two conceptions of *satisfactio*, see Cessario, *Godly Image*, esp. 42-44, 55.

[47]Ibid., 60, 63.

concept of satisfaction is taken from the penitential system, which is also a source for Anselm's theory. For Thomas satisfaction differs from punishment first because it is voluntary rather than involuntary. Renunciation of sin is inherent in penance, so that satisfaction is not merely a transaction restoring balance but part of a return of the offender to the one offended. Sinners might be purified by punishment as well as by penance, but punishment is not itself part of that purification of the will. Penance does restore right order—not in the external, juridical sense of restoring a balance, but because it turns the sinner from idols to his genuine good, God. Satisfaction also differs from punishment because, unlike punishment, satisfaction can be fulfilled by someone other than the offender. According to Aristotle, the "things we can accomplish through the efforts of our friends we seem to do ourselves." In fact, the act of a friend on another's behalf is *more* pleasing to God than punishment of the offender because it is done out of love rather than necessity. Like loves like, and the God of love loves love.[48]

This is, in fact, the basic principle that drives all of Thomas's reflections on the atonement. What makes Christ's sacrifice a genuine satisfaction is not the depth of his suffering, or some balancing of the crime with the punishment, or the dignity of the Person of the sufferer. Rather, for Thomas, it is Christ's *love* that makes the sacrifice an adequate satisfaction for sin. Christ's is a sacrifice in the Augustinian sense, an act that aims toward union with God in holy society.[49] Because he offers himself to be united in communion and friendship with God, he restores friendship between God and humanity. Thomas's understanding of the atonement is not primarily legal but personalist. Legal concerns, including punishment, arise, but they are

---

[48]This paragraph summarizes the discussion of Thomas's view of *satisfactio* in Nieuwenhove, "'Bearing the Marks,'" 289-90. See *Summa theologiae* [hereafter *ST*] I-II, 87, 6: "A sinful act makes a person punishable in that he violates the order of divine justice. He returns to that order only by some punitive restitution that restores the balance of justice, in this way, namely, that one who by acting against a divine commandment has indulged his own will beyond what was right, should, according to the order of divine justice, either voluntarily or by constraint be subjected to something not to his liking." As Thomas says later in the same question, *poena* is not the same as *poena satisfactoria*. The latter removes the stain of sin precisely because it restores the soul to God: "As to the taking away of the stain of sin, clearly this cannot be wiped out except by the soul being rejoined to God; it was by drawing away from him that it incurred the impairment of its own splendor which constitutes the stain of sin. Now the soul is joined to God through an act of the will which embraces the order of divine justice" (trans. Fathers of the English Dominican Province, 1920, available at www.newadvent.org/summa).

[49]Augustine, *City of God* 10.6.

set in the context of Christ's love for the Father and the "capital" charity of the Christ for his people.[50]

For Thomas, though, this is not a matter of an "objective" ground of a later "subjective" application. Christ's actions are the actions of the head of the body of humanity. Even in his atoning work, Christ cannot be isolated from the rest of humanity, particularly from his body, the church. The Augustinian idea of the *totus Christus*, the whole Christ, is critical to Thomas's understanding of the atonement. As Thomas said, "Christ was given grace not only as an individual but insofar as he is head of the church, so that grace might pour out from him upon his members."[51] For Thomas, "the head and members form as it were (*quasi*) a single mystical person," and for this reason "Christ's satisfaction extends to all the faithful as to his members." The reason Christ's satisfaction "works" for others is that "when two men are united in charity one can satisfy for the other."[52] It is even true that the satisfaction of Christ is echoed by a satisfaction in the life of the members of the body. Through the penitential disciplines of almsgiving, fasting and prayer the roots of sin are killed and the will is directed back to friendship with God. These penitential disciplines are not, in Thomas's view, semi-Pelagian efforts at justification by works; rather, they have the fruit they do only because the satisfaction of the members is incorporated by the grace of the Spirit into the satisfaction of the head.[53]

---

[50]For Nieuwenhove, this means that Thomas cannot offer a "substitutionary" view of the atonement. Union of the head and body precludes the substitution of the head for the body: participation, not substitution, is the keynote of Thomas's soteriology ("Bearing the Marks," 296). Cessario says that the capital merit of Christ, with its ecclesiological import, is Thomas's main contribution to soteriology (*Godly Image*, 158; cf. 142-45).

[51]*ST* III, 48, 1.

[52]*ST* III, 48, 2.

[53]On satisfaction in the members, see Cessario, *Godly Image*, 98-99. It is not surprising that Abelardian elements are nearly as prominent in Thomas as Anselmian ones. When Thomas asks, how does Christ's passion liberate from sin? his first answer (*ST* III, 49, 1) is entirely Abelardian: "Christ's Passion is the proper cause of the forgiveness of sins in three ways. First of all, by way of exciting our charity . . . it is by charity that we procure pardon of our sins." And this is set side by side with a second answer that is Augustinian, reliant on the concept of the *totus Christus*: Christ's passion causes forgiveness because "He is our Head," and thus out of love "He delivered us as His members from our sins, as by the price of His Passion." He gives the oddly charming illustration of a man who pays off a "sin committed with his feet" by doing good work with his hands, but the point is clear. He also claims that the passion causes forgiveness "by way of efficiency," since the flesh of Jesus is the instrument of the Godhead, full of divine power to "expel" sins. The atonement works because Jesus is the head of a body, so that whatever he does and achieves benefits the members. See Matthew Levering, *Christ's Fulfillment of Torah and Temple: Salvation According to Thomas Aquinas* (Notre Dame, IN: University of Notre Dame Press, 2002), 60.

Already we can see an ecclesiology embedded in Thomas's understanding of the atonement. The work of Christ has no effect apart from a participation of the members in the love of the body. That participation is not simply in the historical work of Jesus in his life, death and resurrection, but by the grace of the new law, which is the Holy Spirit himself, the members *continue* to participate in the head. Sacramentally joined to the head and nourished by the head, they produce the virtues of faith, hope and love. Justice is restored as harmony and friendship between God and human beings, and as human beings participate in the loving sacrifice of the Son, they become just.[54]

We get the flavor of Thomas's discussion in his answer to the question, Whether Christ's Passion is a sacrifice.[55] It does not seem so, Thomas says, because "human flesh was never offered up in the sacrifices of the Old Law," and such sacrifices were condemned (citing Ps 105:38). Thomas replies by emphasizing the figural character of the old covenant. Christ's death was prefigured or typified in the sacrifices of the old law, but the similarity is not total: "Truth must go beyond the figure." It is the most perfect sacrifice because, being flesh, it is offered for humans and to them at the Table; because it is passible and therefore "fit for immolation"; because, being sinless, it can cleanse sin; because, being Jesus' own flesh, it is acceptable to God. Nothing could be more appropriate than "this immolation of mortal flesh." Christ

---

[54]Thomas is able to fill out this ecclesial/corporate understanding of the atonement through a figural reading of the Old Testament, which he designates as the "Old Law." Following earlier medieval precedent, Thomas divides the Torah into ceremonial, moral and judicial, which regulated Israel in its different relations—the ceremonial in its relation to God, the moral in individual's relation to one another and the judicial in Israel's civic constitution. The three dimensions of the law are not wholly separate from each other. There are moral concerns embedded in the symbolisms of the ceremonial law. Human life has right worship in charity as its ultimate end, and so the ceremonial law that directs Israel to right worship under the conditions of the old covenant directs Israel to its ultimate end of love for God. But because Israel lives in three different dimensions, its law can be distinguished according to this tripartite scheme. Christ fulfills the law, and Thomas specifies that he fulfills the law in each of these dimensions. His perfect love for the Father fulfills the moral precepts of the law; his self-sacrifice is the reality to which all the animal sacrifices of the old law pointed; and Jesus suffers the penalty due to sin on behalf of sinners. Adam stole the fruit from the tree; Jesus attached himself to a tree in order to pay what he had not stolen. Fulfillment is not the same as repetition. In his death and resurrection, Christ exceeds the law, doing and accomplishing what the law always pointed to. Torah was given as pedagogy to prepare for the coming of Christ, and as such prefigures the communion and union that believers have, in Christ and the Spirit, with the Triune God. See Levering, *Christ's Fulfillment*, 119.

[55]*ST* III, 48, 3.

thus fulfills the old law precisely by exceeding the demands of the law in a supreme act of love that satisfies the Father.[56]

Given Thomas's *totus Christus* framework, the fulfillment of the law cannot be confined to the actions of Jesus in his life, death and resurrection. The grace of the new law, which is the Holy Spirit, flows from the head and incorporates the members of Christ's body into his fulfillment. His fulfillment of the law is not, as in later Protestant theology, merely "imputed" to sinners, who then are able to stand as righteous before God. Rather, the members share in the actions of the Son, so that they too begin to fulfill the law in their personal experience. United to the head, and by the grace of the head bestowed by the Spirit that animates the body, they offer themselves as living sacrifices to God and keep themselves unstained from the world, fulfilling the ceremonial law; filled with the Love that is the Spirit, they are conformed to the love of the Son, and so fulfill the weightier matters of the moral law; the saints fulfill the demands of the judicial law by following Christ in bearing burdens for their brothers. Thomas's treatment of the effects of the atonement might be seen as a gloss on the first verses of Romans 8: Christ died so that the Spirit of life might lead us to fulfill the righteous requirements of the law. Shifting the angle slightly, Thomas's soteriology can also be seen as a fulfillment of Israel's temple and temple system. Christ himself is the temple of God, fulfilling Israel's sanctuaries, and by his "capital" grace, the church also becomes a dwelling of God in the Spirit. Believers participate in Christ's fulfillment of the temple as they receive the graces of the sacraments and grow in the virtues that were symbolized in the temple.[57]

Though Thomas, famously, never wrote a separate treatise on ecclesiology, the church is integral to his understanding of the cross and resurrection of

---

[56] At a formal level, Thomas is exactly right. Yet I am not convinced that he is as clear about the substance of Christ's fulfillment of old covenant sacrifices as he could be. He spends a great deal of time detailing the forms of sacrifice in the old covenant, but he does not provide a persuasive rationale for saying that the antitype must be a *human* self-sacrifice. He answers the question of why Christ offered a human sacrifice, but steps out of the realm of a figurative reading of the old law in order to do so. To make such a case, he would have to attend to more of the details of the sacrificial system—the role of the Aqedah as the foundation and background for all sacrifice; the Levitical designation of sacrificial animals as "sons"; the analogies between sacrifices and priests in Lev 21–22. When these details are taken into account, there are clues and hints woven throughout the system that point to the sacrifice of a second Isaac, a son of Abraham. From one angle, the discussion of Torah in chap. 4 above is an effort to perfect Thomas's treatment of the atonement by incorporating recent work on sacrifice and Levitical law into atonement theology.

[57] Levering, *Christ's Fulfillment*, 108.

Jesus. Jesus' death remakes human sociality because it fulfills the law and enables the fulfillment of the law among those who are united to the head by the Spirit. The formation of the community of love united in devotion to the Triune God is the aim of Christ's suffering as it fulfills the aims of the law. For Thomas this is not a generic fulfillment in community as such, but specifically in the eucharistic community, which is the fitting culmination of what Torah and temple prepared Israel for.[58]

---

[58]Ibid., 97-98, 101.

NATURE, THE SUPERNATURAL AND JUSTIFICATION

†

Protestants and Catholics gave, and still often give, different meanings to nearly every significant term in the debate over justification. *Faith, justify* and sometimes *works* have different denotations and certainly different connotations. When Protestants say that the sinner is justified "by faith alone," Catholics sometimes fill in their own definition of faith as intellectual assent and are suitably appalled at the result: How could anyone be acceptable to God by mere assent, loveless belief, *un*formed faith? Protestants, for their part, insist that faith is more than intellectual assent and, in Luther's terms, has the power to unite the believer to Christ for justification.[1] Catholics believe that Protestantism is antinomian, for it seems to rule out the necessity and importance of good works. Protestants answer that though works do not make the Christian, no one can be a Christian without producing the fruit of good works, and charge Catholics with teaching a form of self-salvation. Protestants insist that good works characterize the Christian life, but locate good works under the heading of sanctification rather than justification. The central contention is over the term *justify* itself. Inspired by Augustine, Catholics defined justification etymologically as "making-just" (*iustum facere*), while Protestant confessions teach that justification is a judicial, legal or forensic term that means "to declare just."

The Reformation debates about justification sometimes appear to be nothing more than debates about terminology.[2] For some, the debates are

---

[1] Luther discusses the "three powers" of faith in "The Freedom of a Christian," in *Three Treatises,* trans. Charles M. Jacobs et al. (Philadelphia: Fortress, 1970), 284–87.

[2] Though he does not make this argument, this impression is left by the discussion of justification during the Reformation era in Alister McGrath, *Historical Theology: An Introduction to the History of Christian Thought* (Oxford: Blackwell, 1998), 184–95.

surpassingly tedious, and it is sometimes hard for nontheologians to see that what was at stake was a difference between life and death, true gospel and false, heaven and hell. This is short-sighted. Terminological disputes were part of the Reformation conflict. There was some degree of "talking past," but this very fact suggests that there were underlying systematic differences that manifested themselves in the terminological disputes. Augustine's debates with the Pelagians were not only about grace, free will, original sin and so on, but also about the nature of God, his relation to the world and creation;[3] the same was true in the Reformation debates. Intertwined with the soteriological debates of the Reformation were cosmological, anthropological and theological concerns, often involving issues of nature and the supernatural that we discussed in appendix one.

CAUSATION

Some medieval theologians applied the logic of natural/supernatural to posit a "twofold operation" in justification: first, grace operates on the will to produce moral good (natural), and then grace raises human acts from natural goodness to a supernatural plane where they are meritorious.[4] But the effect of the natural/supernatural scheme on medieval soteriology went deeper than this semi-Pelagian doctrine of justification. It extended to the question of whether humans can be an independent "cause" of their own salvation.

High Scholastic theology did not, as a rule, posit an actual realm of pure nature or operate by a rigid natural/supernatural system. As a result, the high Scholastics like Aquinas did not believe that human nature was ever actually independent of grace, nor did they see much value in theorizing about a human nature devoid of grace. Nor did they think that human beings could in any way escape the oversight and providence of God. Human beings are ontologically incapable of being *independent* causes of *anything*. For Thomas at least, cooperation between God and humans is not competition, and causation is *not* a sum total of divine and human causation.[5]

---

[3]Michael Hanby, *Augustine and Modernity*, Radical Orthodoxy Series (London: Routledge, 2003), chap. 3.

[4]Alister McGrath, *Iustitia Dei: A History of the Christian Doctrine of Justification*, 3rd ed. (Cambridge: Cambridge University Press, 2005), 131.

[5]According to Fergus Kerr, this theme "takes us right to the heart of Thomas's theology. He often quotes Isaiah 26:12: 'Lord, thou hast wrought all our works in us'—which he takes . . . precisely

After 1250, however, theologians began to develop quite different views of causation, reflected in the changing meanings of the word *influentia*.[6] Prior to the mid-thirteenth century, *influentia* was understood in its etymological sense as a "flowing-in" from God to creatures. From this viewpoint, God's general providence and his special providence, including the providences associated with redemption, were intricately intertwined. God is the universal cause of everything, but, in John Milbank's words, since

> he causes by sharing his own nature, by giving his gifts to-be, the lower levels exert within their own sphere their own secondary and equally total causality. There is a kind of "exchange without reciprocity." There is reciprocity in the Trinity, and reciprocity within the Creation, but not between the Creation and God, because even though there is "exchange" in the sense that creatures receive by returning, God properly receives nothing.[7]

On this early understanding, God does not merely influence by setting the general boundaries and shaping the contours of history and the actions of creatures. Rather, he is the ultimate cause of the specific actions and events that happen within the creation, and general providence is "the sum of specific instances, even though it is a *dynamis* in excess of those instances."[8] Divine and human causation are never in competition; causation is not a

---

as excluding all competitiveness between divine and human agency." Cooperation for Thomas does not picture "two rival agents on a level playing field," but rather he "sees it as a mark of God's freedom, and ours, that God 'causes' everything in such a way that the creature 'causes' it too." Quotations from Fergus Kerr, *After Aquinas: Versions of Thomism* (Oxford: Blackwell, 2008), chap. 8. According to Kerr, Thomas consistently contests the notion that "if God produces the entire natural effect, surely nothing is left for the human agent to do," emphasizing instead a doctrine of "double agency," in which God and humans act to produce the same effect, though in different ways. Thomas rightly sees this as an implication of the doctrine of creation: "It is always by divine power that the human agent produces his or her own proper effect: that is the doctrine of creation. It is not superfluous, even if in principle God can by himself produce all natural effects, for them to be produced by us as causes. Nor is this a result of the inadequacy of divine power, as one might be tempted to think, thus giving way to the charms of process theology. On the contrary: it is a result of the immensity of God's goodness (*bonitas*: "bounty"). It is another implication of the doctrine of creation that God wills to communicate his likeness to things not only so that they might simply exist but that they might cause other things. Indeed, this is how creatures generally attain the divine likeness—by causing" (ibid., 143).

[6]John Milbank, *The Suspended Middle: Henri de Lubac and the Debate Concerning the Supernatural* (Grand Rapids: Eerdmans, 2005), 89-90. Milbank is drawing on the work of Jacob Schmutz, "La Doctrine medievale des causes et la theologie de la nature pure (XIII2–XVII2 siecles)," *Revue Thomiste* (Jan./June 2001): 217-64.

[7]Milbank, *Suspended Middle*, 91.

[8]Ibid.

"zero-sum game" in which creaturely causation can only be affirmed at the expense of divine causation. Every event in creation is wholly the product of God's action, and yet at the same time it is totally caused by creatures. God causes by influencing from within the creation, not by exerting power externally from without. This is the view, as noted above, of Thomas Aquinas.

By the late thirteenth century, this view was disrupted as *influentia* came to connote an external pressure or causation rather than God's action working *within* the creation. On the older view, "the higher and especially the highest cause is always more deeply active at a lower level than any secondary cause," so that God is more deeply the cause of my sneezing than the particles in my nose. On the newer view, "a higher cause operating on a lower level is just 'one other' causal factor."[9] Divine causality came to be seen as a "general" influence that is supplemented by the special influence of miracles. Primary and secondary causes are separated, and then join forces in a shared *concursus*. For Aquinas, the mind of a maker gives a thing the form it has because the maker plans its construction. Though a saw has causal force in making a table, the form the table takes comes from the mind of the woodworker using the saw. The saw is not an "additional" causal force but the instrumental tool of the prime cause. Duns Scotus, by contrast, saw the tool as an *additional* causal power, arguing, for example, that the heart cannot write letters without the added power of the hand. Aquinas saw the table coming to reality as the primary cause employed tools to achieve the final cause; Scotus saw a letter coming to reality by the addition of the primary cause with a secondary cause.[10]

Bonaventure applied this later notion of causation in the realm of soteriology, arguing that humans are capable of doing good by their own power and need only the help of God's general providence, not the help of "supernatural" grace. In this Bonaventure followed Alexander of Hales, "who had spoken of the natural *concursus* as being at work even in the case of *gratia superinfusa*. In the case of both general and specific divine causality, a sphere of independent and partial causality had been reserved for the creature. And this is already the space of *natura pura*." By rejecting, or at least circumscribing, the place of pure nature, Aquinas was "*more* Augustinian than the Augustinians."[11]

---

[9]Ibid., 92.
[10]Ibid., 92-93.
[11]Ibid., 97.

PREPARATION AND COOPERATION

On the ground of these faulty notions of nature, causation and grace, medieval theology debated the possibility of preparation for grace and cooperation with grace. *Habitus* could be used to construct a doctrine of merit, since *habitus* ensured that good works were works of sinners themselves, not God's works within sinners. The connections between these different themes can be seen in the *Summa Fratris Alexandri*, which Alister McGrath calls "the first systematic discussion of the nature of created grace."[12] Notions of created grace and preparation for grace are worked out in this treatise through the biblical paradigm of the soul as a temple of the Spirit. Since the soul is finite and has no natural capacity for the infinite Spirit, there must be something added to the soul to make the soul into a temple of the Spirit. This addition is created grace, but it is only needed because of the prior assumption that the human soul has not been created with the capacity to receive the Spirit. This is not, it is once again crucial to notice, a claim that God must clean out a sinful soul before he is willing to inhabit it. The argument is not about sin; it is about the capacity of human beings as creatures to receive the Spirit. As creatures, we are sieves. Created grace stops the holes so we can become containers.

Dominican theologians generally disagreed, arguing that "the soul naturally has a capacity for grace" (*anima naturaliter est gratiae capax*).[13] Even among Dominicans, this was undercut by anthropological assumptions. Aquinas rejected Peter Lombard's straightforward claim that the "*caritas* infused into the soul in justification" is the Spirit, and this was partly because "the union of the uncreated Holy Spirit with the created human soul appeared to him to be inconsistent with the ontological distinction which it was necessary to maintain between them."[14] Medieval notions of preparation for justification thus rest on the assumption that human beings are not, by virtue of creation, capacious enough to receive the Spirit. And this assumption arises from an underlying notion of pure nature, an idea that there is some strata of human existence that is not created as a receptor of grace. Humans are created canaries; to receive the crowning gift of the Spirit, they must first be remolded as humans.

---

[12]McGrath, *Iustitia Dei*, 103.
[13]Quoted in ibid.
[14]Ibid., 176. This is a controverted point. Some passages in Thomas indicate a position closer to Lombard's.

Similar problems arise in connection with medieval theories concerning cooperation with grace. So long as divine and human causation were not seen to be competitive, and as long as a human action was not conceived of as the product of human causation *added to* divine causation, human contributions to salvation could not be conceived of as independent contributions. On this view, there might be a *proper* synergism: We work out our salvation not *in addition to* God working in us, but *because* God works in us. We work and love because his Spirit who is love is poured into us and his power works in us. As soon as the notion of causation assumes an area of pure nature in which human beings act and exist in semi-independence of God's action, then synergism becomes a Pelagian nightmare. This is the kind of cooperation posited by late medieval theology, and the kind of cooperation the Reformers were correct utterly to reject.

PROBLEMS OF PROTESTANT SOTERIOLOGY

The Augustinian, medieval Scholastic and Tridentine theology of justification suffers from one fatal fault: Paul does not mean by the word "justify" what they claim he means by the word "justify." As some modern Catholic exegetes now concede,[15] Protestant soteriology is correct to emphasize the "forensic" character of justification. That does *not* mean that Protestant soteriology is free from problems.

Alister McGrath argues that there was a consensus among the theologians of Trent that justification is "factitive," a view that excluded the possibility that "a sinner may be justified solely as a matter of reputation or imputation, while remaining a sinner in fact."[16] But that raises the question, what is a fact? If (as Cornelius Van Til everywhere says) facts and interpretations are inseparable, and if facts are what they are ultimately because of *God's* interpretation of them, then God's interpretation should trump everything else. A sinner who is reputed and named by God as righteous is *in fact* righteous, just as a child whose parents name him "Jacob" is *in fact* Jacob.[17] A doctrine of justification that rests on imputation is as much a factitive doctrine as the

---

[15]Joseph A. Fitzmyer, *Romans*, Anchor Bible 33 (New York: Doubleday, 1993); Brendan Byrne, *Romans*, Sacra Pagina (Collegeville, MN: Liturgical, 1996), 57.

[16]McGrath, *Iustitia Dei*, 326.

[17]This is what I take Reformed theologian John Murray to mean when he says that justification "constitutes" a righteous relationship with God. See *Redemption Accomplished and Applied* (Grand Rapids: Eerdmans, 1955) 74-75.

Catholic view. Protestants should claim to present a different—what may turn out to be a more *biblical*—notion of fact than the Tridentine view.

The implied Protestant notion of fact is linked to an anthropology. As Oswald Bayer has written,

> There is no such thing as an autocratic individual, totally independent of the surrounding world and its recognition. The individual is always socially formed. It is self-consciousness as it has formed itself and continues to be formed in the process of mutual recognition. Striving to find approval in the eyes of others, being noticed and not being dismissed as nothing by others, demonstrates that I cannot relate to myself without relating to the world. . . . What I am, I am in my judgment about myself, intertwined with the judgment made of me by others. Person is a "forensic term."[18]

Bayer expresses a fundamental Christian confession: individuals are what they are *not* because of what they are in themselves but by virtue of God's regard for them.[19] Following Paul, Bayer stresses that sinners find themselves not in themselves but in another, for we died, and our life is now hid with Christ in God (Col 3:3). Believers' true selves are the selves found *outside* themselves, in Christ.[20] *Person* is a "forensic term" in the strict

---

[18]Oswald Bayer, *Living By Faith: Justification and Sanctification*, Lutheran Quarterly Books (Grand Rapids: Eerdmans, 2003), 3-4.

[19]This is especially true of Reformed theology, with its strong stress on election. Bruce McCormack writes, "What we are essentially is a divine act which establishes a covenant relation—a relation which perdures and makes us to be what we are even when, in our perversity, we choose to live on the basis of a lie rather than the truth. I am I, I am identical with myself in all the random and unrelated moments of my existence, because God has chosen to make me his covenant-partner in Jesus Christ. That is my true identity. . . . Human being is the function of a decision God *made* in eternity past in his electing grace. And it is a function of a decision God *makes* in time in justifying the ungodly. The former is the ground of the latter; the latter actualizes the content of the former in time" (McCormack, "What's at Stake in Current Debates over Justification: The Crisis of Protestantism in the West," in *Justification: What's at Stake in the Current Debates*, ed. Mark Husbands and Daniel Treier [Downers Grove, IL: IVP Academic, 2004], 115).

[20]The alternative is to say that some exterior reality *other* than God forms the individual's deepest existence, or that the individual is self-formed. Neither of these is a Christian alternative. If there is an external determinant of my identity that is *not* God, then God is no longer sovereign, no longer Lord, no longer God. He is instead replaced by that other external determinant. And no matter how popular it is to suggest that the individual is what he is "in himself," considered in isolation from all relationships, it is equally wrong and equally idolatrous. For it finally makes *me* the determiner of my own identity. The notion that we are what we are by external relation is embedded in the most basic Christian affirmation about humanity, that is, that humans are the image of God. Gil Baillie, working in a Girardian framework, suggests that the claim that humans are made in the image of God means "this creature can only fulfill its destiny by becoming like someone else." This is the root of the mimetic character of human desire: "The likelihood

theological sense of "forensic." We are what we are because of how we stand with God our Judge.

If this is the case, then justification—which by strict Protestant definition is a change in my status before God—changes *me* in the profoundest way possible. If I *am* what God judges me to be, then justification marks a transition and change in my identity, a change in my being and person—not *in addition to* a change of status but *precisely because* it is a change of status. It can even be said that the verdict changes the answer to the question of *essence*: if a thing is what God names it to be, if it is what it is in relation to God, then when God names me as "righteous" and counts me as righteous, I am *essentially* different. When God says "this sinner is just," I am no longer the same man I was before that declaration. I continue to sin; but I now sin as one who has been redefined as a righteous man, and so remade. Once God declares me righteous, I simply *am* righteous. This is not because of any "infusion" of grace, and the declaration is not based on anything I have done by my "natural" powers. The declaration is pure declaration, but because it is the declaration of the God who determined all things before the foundation of the world, the God whose names for things *determine* their reality, it cannot but be a declaration that changes *me*.[21] This reflects a more strictly Pauline usage of *physis*, as argued in several places in this book.

All this should be *easy* for Protestant theology to say. Protestant soteriology supposes a radically decentered self, a self whose real, *factual* existence is determined by the free and gracious word of God. But at a certain point, Protestantism often backs off from its own premises. Protestants have not always recognized that their doctrine of justification is "factitive." Instead, we have often accepted the Tridentine claims and conceded that our doctrine

---

of this creature actually fulfilling such a destiny would be slim, indeed, unless the creature were somehow endowed with a desire to do so, a desire equally counterinstinctual and counterintuitive, a desire to be itself by becoming like someone else." From this perspective, he argues, "the postmodern assumption that the self is an artificial social construct," though "naïve" and though "it usually harbors hidden agendas," still "might help awaken Christians to the fact that something at least as shocking lies at the heart of Christian personhood. In a very real sense, at the burning center of Christianity is a person who emphatically insists that he exists only to bear witness to another person, a person whose life is therefore iconic in the extreme, an icon of the invisible God, the God, moreover, in whose image and likeness Genesis tells us we are made" (Gil Baillie, "The Imitative Self: The Contribution of Rene Girard," in *The Self: Beyond the Postmodern Crisis*, ed. Paul C. Vitz and Susan M. Felch (Wilmington, DE: ISI, 2006], 3-6).

[21] It is true, as N. T. Wright says (*Paul and the Faithfulness of God* [Minneapolis: Fortress, 2013], 945), that justification *creates* a new status. But we need to take a step further to say that the creation of a new status before God *is* the creation of a new *person*.

is *not* "factitive" but merely "legal." That Protestant concession, as much as the Tridentine formulation, assumes a realm of nature and human existence whose meaning and reality is not determined by God's judgments concerning it. To the extent that they implicitly set "repute" and "fact" in opposition, these formulations suggest that Protestantism has not inoculated itself from notions of brute facticity and pure nature. A nature/supernature scheme returns in Protestant guise, sometimes quite explicitly, and, as in medieval theology, is treated as the only way to guarantee the gratuity of grace. As a result the anthropological assumptions in some Protestant soteriology are incoherent: Protestantism often proposes a forensic person, but then allows a "natural" self to sneak back in by an unlocked back door, a natural self who presents himself as the *factual* self, albeit clothed in the garments of Christ, a natural self who wears the status of righteousness like a hobbit in a giant's robe.[22]

Practically, the anthropological inconsistency of Protestant soteriology is behind Protestant oscillation between antinomianism and legalism.[23] Once status and moral character, legal standing and fact, are distinguished in the way they sometimes are in the Protestant doctrine of justification, that oscillation is difficult to avoid. On the one hand, one can emphasize the justified status, but then it becomes difficult to explain why works are necessary or important if neither sin nor virtue has any effect on one's status. On the other hand, one can emphasize the necessity of a life of holiness and good works, but then it is no longer clear how one is *securely* saved by the status-declaration of justification that precedes the life of holiness, and Protestant piety can collapse into something resembling the tortured penitence of medieval Catholicism from which Protestantism was designed to rescue

---

[22]The difficulties are evident, for example, in confusions about the relation between regeneration, which results in repentance and faith, and justification. Justification is supposed to be "justification of the ungodly," yet in some treatments faith and repentance (understood, of course, as a gift from God) are said to be the presuppositions of justification (John Fesko, *Beyond Calvin: Union with Christ and Justification in Early Modern Reformed Theology (1517–1700)* [Göttingen: Vandenhoeck & Ruprecht, 2012], 90, quoting Edward Leigh). If that is the case, then justification is not a declaration concerning the ungodly, but a declaration concerning those-who-are-beginning-to-be-godly, the justification of the nascently penitent. Apart from some distracting shuffling around of terms, it is not clear how this differs from medieval soteriology. Wright falls into a similar tangle when he defines justification as God's "recognition and declaration" that the called and faithful are in his family (*Pauline Perspectives: Essays on Paul, 1978–2013* [Minneapolis: Fortress, 2013], 215). Wright can at least escape the incoherence by claiming that "ungodly" in Rom 4 refers not to unsaved sinners but specifically to Gentiles.

[23]This is particularly evident in Reformed theology and church practice.

the church. Classic Protestant soteriology has had ways of dealing with this problem. Dogmatic formulations emphasize the inseparability of justification and sanctification as the *duplex gratia* that comes from Christ. Though true, this point has not been resilient enough to prevent theological and pastoral ambivalence.[24]

JUSTIFICATION AND SANCTIFICATION

Similar problems arise in connection with one of the distinctive claims of Protestantism: its distinction between justification as a strictly forensic act, and the morally and spiritually transforming event of regeneration and sanctification.[25] Protestants sometimes assume an anthropological and cosmological dualism that is less than biblical, and arises, in my judgment, from the Reformers' imperfect extrication from the natural/supernatural schemes of medieval theology.[26]

Protestants define justification as "strictly forensic," and classify the Spirit's work as a further act of "sanctification," "regeneration" or "renewal." The declaration and the beginnings of renewal are sometimes said to occur simultaneously, and sometimes seen as dual aspects of the more basic reality of union with Christ in his resurrection.[27] Still, Protestant theologians insist that the declaration of justification does not change the sinner's character, but only their status before God.[28]

---

[24]The problem is often that the status and moral character of the person are treated individualistically. One's legal standing has little to do with membership in the body of Christ, and one's moral character is considered independently of one's embedding in the concrete historical reality of the *ecclesia*.

[25]It is hardly necessary to cite evidence. Still, for completeness: see the helpful compilation of Reformed creeds and confessions in Joel R. Beeke and Sinclair Ferguson, *Reformed Confessions Harmonized* (Grand Rapids: Baker, 1999), 98-106. As for the theologians, see Charles Hodge, *Systematic Theology* (repr.; Grand Rapids: Eerdmans, 1986), 3:118-33, 213; Heinrich Heppe, *Reformed Dogmatics*, ed. Ernst Bizer, trans. G. T. Thomson (London: Wakeman Trust, 1950), 543-44, 565-66; Louis Berkhof, *Systematic Theology* (Grand Rapids: Eerdmans, 1938), 513-17, 536-37; Millard Erickson, *Introducing Christian Doctrine*, 2nd ed. (Grand Rapids: Baker, 2001), 318-21, 326; Robert L. Reymond, *A New Systematic Theology of the Christian Faith* (Nashville: Thomas Nelson, 1998), 743-45, 757-59, 767-81 (Reymond helpfully emphasizes the reality of "definitive sanctification").

[26]Along similar lines, Bruce McCormack considers the influence of Greek ontologies on conceptions of union with Christ, and in regard to the ontology implicit in doctrines of justification, in "What's at Stake?," 111-17.

[27]See, for instance, Richard B. Gaffin, *Resurrection and Redemption: A Study in Paul's Soteriology*, 2nd ed. (Phillipsburg, NJ: P&R, 1987).

[28]A few quotations, if they are needed, will support the point: "Justification *per se* says nothing about the subjective transformation that necessarily begins to occur within the inner life of the Christian through the progressive infusion of grace that commences with the new birth (which

This can lead to incoherence. Martin Chemnitz claims that within all the deceits and trickeries of the Tridentine decree on justification are a few moments of honesty and clarity: "In ch. 4 they say that in this dispute about justification the question is how a man is transferred from that state in which he is a child of wrath into the state of grace and adoption of children of God."[29] In justification we are transferred from a place of wrath to a place of grace. But if this is the case, can it still be denied that justification is "life-changing"? To deny that a change of "realm" is a change of "inner character" assumes that human beings are what they are regardless of the "realm" in which they are found. And this in turn assumes the view that human *existence* is isolated from its surroundings, defined *in itself* rather than in relation to what is outside itself. Once again, we find the tensions of Protestant anthropology arising: on the one hand human salvation is defined exoterically, as union with Christ; but on the other hand this union with Christ is not determinative *after all*, at least for the "inner" human being.[30] If forensic

---

subjective transformation Scripture views as progressive sanctification). Rather, justification refers to God's *wholly* objective, *wholly* forensic judgment concerning the sinner's standing before the law. . . . The faith-righteousness of justification is not personal but vicarious, not infused but imputed, not experiential but judicial, not psychological but legal" (Reymond, *New Systematic Theology*, 741-43). Berkhof states the point less stridently and extremely, acknowledging a place for "subjective justification," which is the sinner's sense of release and peace of conscience that follows from trust in God's declaration of acceptance (*Systematic Theology*, 516-17). "Justification is the opposite of condemnation. To condemn is not to turn someone into an evildoer but to find him or her guilty. Similarly, justification is not to turn someone into a good person but to declare that person innocent. Regeneration transforms us. Justification says something about us. Regeneration is life-changing. Justification is forensic" (William Edgar, *Truth in All Its Glory: Commending the Reformed Faith* [Philipsburg, NJ: P&R, 2004], 196). Later Edgar claims that justification is not a matter of "as though." Rather, it is really so: "It is not only that we are considered innocent, but that we are actually constituted righteous" (ibid., 196). If this is true, however, it is difficult to see how his contrast of regeneration and justification stands; after all, being constituted righteous would seem to be a life-changing and transforming event. Hodge writes, "Justification is a forensic act, God acting as judge, declaring justice satisfied so far as the believing sinner is concerned, whereas sanctification is an effect due to the divine efficacy. . . . Justification changes, or declares to be changed, the relation of the sinner to the justice of God; sanctification involves a change of character. . . . The former, therefore, is objective, the latter subjective" (Hodge, *Systematic Theology*, 3:213). Heppe summarizes the tradition: "Justification is an act of God resulting outwith man, by which God assigns to him an alien righteousness; whereas sanctification is an activity of God in man's inward part" (Heppe, *Reformed Dogmatics*, 565).

[29]Martin Chemnitz, *Examination of the Council of Trent*, trans. Marin Kramer and Fred Kramer (St. Louis: Concordia, 1971), 1:517.

[30]The turn to a "substance" or "nature" anthropology represents an odd turn in Protestant theology, for part of the genius of the Protestant doctrine of justification is that it sees justification as a purely relational reality. As Berndt Hamm puts it, "To the godless . . . grace becomes real in the form of groundless acceptance into the family of God, the beginning of a new relationship.

justification is not a change in identity, then my outward "status" is independent of my inward "character." And, more obviously, it assumes that my being is not defined in relation to God, but in itself or in relation to something else, perhaps my sins.

Rather than considering justification "exterior," it should be seen as a status-change and a change of situation that affects the whole person. Justification even changes the character of my actions. This is the case even if there is no apparent change in my actions themselves. A man who sleeps with a hooker the night before his wedding has committed fornication; the night after his wedding he commits adultery. A private man who opens fire on a murderer in court will be tried for murder himself; a member of a firing squad may be commended for killing a traitor. Actions are not separable from the status or life situation of the person performing the action. Murder and execution are not two forms of the same act, "killing." They are *different* acts. So also the fornication of a nonjustified man differs from the fornication of the justified man. The justified man's fornication is compounded by the fact that he has joined the members of Christ to a harlot, while, on the other hand, his fornication is forgiven in Christ. For a justified person, using his body for fornication is sacrilege in a way that fornication can never be for one who is not indwelt by the Spirit.[31]

A conceptual approach in terms of relationship replaces the traditional qualitative and moral attitude. Sin remains real in ourselves, but outside ourselves (*extra nos*), in the relationship, that is to say, we are justified in the way in which we are seen by God (*coram Deo*). . . . The propitiatory righteousness of Jesus Christ acting vicariously for us is of fundamental importance. It alone is the cause of justification, it alone provides satisfaction and wins merit. The new relationship in which grace justifies us means that God sees man in the light of Christ's righteousness, and allows it to stand for the righteousness of sinners" (Hamm, "What Was the Reformation Doctrine of Justification?" in *German Reformation: The Essential Readings*, ed. C. Scott Dixon [Oxford: Blackwell, 1991], 70).

[31]Protestant teaching on justification has perennially been dogged by the objection that Protestants turn justification into nothing more than a "legal fiction," a purely extrinsic and arbitrary act where God pretends that someone is righteous who is manifestly *not*. The choices seem to be stark: Either God must acknowledge some degree of "inner" righteousness in the sinner (however slight) and judge the sinner righteous on that basis, or God's declaration must be purely an "external" judgment that neither acknowledges nor affects the inner state of the sinner. But this polarization is *entirely* the product of the underlying anthropological dualism. Protestantism has simply switched from one side of the dualism to the other. Catholics say, "Justification is based on inner renewal and is not merely outer status," while Protestants reply, "Justification is purely about outer status and neither arises from nor produces inner renewal." If, however, humans are unified beings, and if human beings (down to the deepest layer) are utterly dependent on the mercy of God and completely defined by the judgment of God, then God's declaration about our status before him *must* make us different men and women. Here we can

JUSTIFICATION AND REDEMPTIVE HISTORY

For Luther, Paul's claim that "Christ was raised for our justification" is not some strange departure from his normal doctrine but stands at its heart. As Luther put it in the *Babylonian Captivity of the Church*, "Baptism signifies two things—death and resurrection, that is, full and complete justification." Thus one may "say that baptism is a washing away of sins, but the expression is too mild and too weak to bring out the full significance of baptism, which is rather a symbol of death and resurrection."[32] In much of mainstream Protestant soteriology, the resurrection has been an afterthought, often linked with sanctification rather than justification.[33]

---

say without qualification that the sinner is "*constituted* righteous" by the declaration of justification, without at all suggesting that the declaration is *based* on some preexisting righteousness in the sinner. When asked, "Does the inner person change when they're justified?" we should simply reply, "I know no inner person who exists in a zone that is not governed by the Word and judgment of God. The person—the whole person—is changed because of their change of status in the court of God. As soon as God declares them just in Christ, they are a new person. *For there is nothing more fundamental about human beings than how God regards them.*"

[32] Quoted by Gerald Foote, *Justification by Faith: A Matter of Death and Life* (Mifflintown, PA: Sigler, 1991).

[33] A few representative quotations will illustrate the point. The Augsburg Confession focuses its attention completely on the death of Jesus: "Our churches also teach that men cannot be justified before God by their own strength, merits, or works but are freely justified for Christ's sake through faith when they believe that they are received into favor and that their sins are forgiven on account of Christ, who by his death made satisfaction for our sins. This faith God imputes for righteousness in his sight." Likewise, the Westminster Confession defines justification without reference to the resurrection of Jesus. Justification is accomplished "not by infusing righteousness into them, but by pardoning their sins, and by accounting and accepting their persons as righteous; not for any thing wrought in them, or done by them, but for Christ's sake alone; nor by imputing faith itself, the act of believing, or any other evangelical obedience to them, as their righteousness; but by imputing the obedience and satisfaction of Christ unto them, they receiving and resting on Him and His righteousness by faith." Chapter 11 talks about the debt discharged by Christ's satisfaction, but says nothing about the resurrection. Similarly, the Larger Catechism (q. 69) says that the "communion in grace" that members of the invisible church have with Christ is the means for their receiving "the virtue of his mediation, in their justification, adoption, sanctification, and whatever else in this life manifests their union with Him." Question 70 says that justification is God's act of pardon, acceptance and accounting as righteous; and this not for any work in them or by them, but only for the obedience of Christ imputed to them and received by faith. It is intriguing to contrast such statements with the earlier Protestant treatments of justification, which frequently refer to the resurrection of Jesus as well as to his death. The Heidelberg Catechism (q. 45) asks, "What is the benefit of Christ's resurrection?" It answers, "First, by His resurrection He has overcome death, that he might make us partakers of that righteousness which He had purchased for us by His death; secondly, we are also by His power raised up to a new life; and lastly, the resurrection of Christ is a sure pledge of our blessed resurrection." Righteousness is "purchased for us by His death," but we are made partakers of it only by the resurrection. The Second Helvetic Confession (article 15.3; 1566) is less emphatic, but there is still a connection between resurrection and justification: "Christ took upon Himself

The elision of the resurrection is one aspect of a more general detachment of justification from redemptive history. For Scripture, justification occurs not only in the private space where God meets secretly with the sinner, but also in the public square of history, where there is, as Bayer puts it, an ongoing struggle between God and rebellious humans for justification, for proving oneself right. God enters into history to vindicate his people by delivering them from sin, death and all enemies. Peace in Scripture has a broader connotation than peace of conscience or reconciliation with God. Peace encompasses the entire cosmos, and that cosmic shalom also belongs to the doctrine of justification.[34]

---

and bare the sins of the world, and did satisfy the justice of God. God, therefore, is merciful unto our sins for Christ alone, that suffered and rose again, and does not impute them unto us. But He imputes the justice of Christ unto us for our own; so that now we are not only cleansed from sin, and purged, and holy, but also endued with the righteousness of Christ; yea, and acquitted from sin, death, and condemnation."

[34]This is where some of the theologians associated with the new perspective on Paul, by emphasizing Paul's interest in the condition of Israel and the Jew-Gentile question, offer a crucial corrective. One sign of the eclipse of redemptive history in the doctrine of justification is the eclipse of the Old Testament. Most Protestant treatments of justification examine the Old Testament usage of ṣedeq ("righteous"), but the use of the Old Testament is usually confined to a philological discussion or examination of the background to Paul's use of Gen 15:6 or Hab 2:4. Few attempt to develop a theology of justification from the Old Testament, or to put it into the context of a biblical theology of judgment and justice. Mark Seifrid has recently attempted such a project in a number of articles. His results, while not always persuasive or even clear, are always stimulating. See, e.g., *Christ, Our Righteousness: Paul's Theology of Justification*, New Studies in Biblical Theology (Downers Grove, IL: InterVarsity Press, 2000); Seifrid, "Righteousness Language in the Hebrew Scriptures and Early Judaism," in *Justification and Variegated Nomism*, vol. 1, *The Complexities of Second Temple Judaism*, ed. D. A. Carson, Peter T. O'Brien and Mark A. Seifrid (Grand Rapids: Baker, 2001), 415-42.

ATONEMENT BY DELIVERDICT

Romans

✝

In chapter seven I argued that in Paul "justification" means a favorable judgment that delivers from the reign of sin, death and flesh, and that it refers in many passages not to a judgment rendered in the life experience of individual sinners but in the life history of Jesus. Justification happens in the cross and resurrection, and we participate in that historical deliverdict, die to sin and rise to life, as we are united to Christ in baptism and faith.

In chapter seven I focused on Galatians, supporting my case with brief references to other texts from Paul's letters. This appendix offers further supporting evidence from Romans. My goal is to show that Paul consistently uses "justify" to mean "deliverdict" and that "justification" frequently refers to the historical event of Jesus' resurrection.

REDEMPTION AND JUSTIFICATION, ROMANS 3:21-30

Romans 3:21 resumes the themes of the theme statement of Romans, using the phrase "righteousness of God" for the first time since Romans 1. All that we have said about *dikaiosynē* in chapter five applies here: Paul is announcing the good news of a Davidic king revealing, demonstrating and realizing the justice of God as a fulfillment of the hopes of Israel's prophets. God is at long last acting in his disordered creation to set things right. In Romans 3 Paul makes clearer *how* this Davidic king manifests this justice: through a faithful act that results in what Paul calls "justification."

In Romans 3:22 Paul describes this righteousness as coming *dia pisteōs Iēsou Christou*. That phrase is our first clue to the context of Paul's argument. As I argued in chapter six, that phrase often refers *not* to the trust of a sinner in Jesus or in God but to the faithful loyalty of Jesus to his Father. It is a way of summarizing Jesus' life of redemptive righteousness, his embodiment of the justice of Torah that surpassed the justice of the scribes. Above all, it refers to his relentless faithfulness to his Father and to his Father's word, even in the face of condemnation and death. Paul states that through his faithful life and death, Jesus manifests the justice of God. Jesus' faithfulness is evident in his self-offering in death, his completion of Torah in a fully realized sacrifice, the sacrifice of open-eared obedience that pleases the Father.

If Paul is talking about the justice of God in the sense he uses the term in Romans 1, and *if pistis Christou* refers to the faithful life and death of Jesus, then Paul's argument cannot be *merely* about how a guilty sinner gets saved from guilt. In Romans 3:25-26 *dikaiosynē autou* includes just condemnation of evil, and in this passage it is preeminently that.[1] Luther to the contrary, Paul follows the Psalms and Prophets in viewing God's punitive justice to be *good* news. That makes sense because Paul's concern is with theodicy, with the unveiling of God's justice in a disordered creation.[2] What kind of God can allow the evils cataloged in Romans 1:18-32? Paul's gospel announces that God is taking care of his judicial business, and he does so in Jesus. In Jesus' death, God demonstrates that he is Judge and will not sit idly by as sin and idolatry ruin his world and deface his image.[3] Romans 3:26 repeats the point, and again emphasizes that in the death of Jesus God deals with sin more decisively than he had dealt with sin in the past. The death of Jesus is the end of God's forbearance, the climax of his drive to destroy sin and arrest

---

[1]The chiastic structure of Rom 3:21-28 is illuminating in this regard, centering as it does on God's need to demonstrate his hatred of sin:

  A Apart from law, the righteousness of God manifest
    B No difference; all sinned (that is, Jews and Gentiles)
      C Justified as gift by grace through redemption in Christ
        D God displayed Jesus as *hilastērion* in blood
          E To demonstrate his justice in the now time
            F Because God had previously passed over sin
          E′ For the demonstration of his justice
        D′ That he might be just
      C′ And the justifier
    B′ Of the one who is of the faith of Jesus
  A′ Apart from law, humanity is justified

This structure will be useful for unraveling some other points later on.

[2]Following his father's lead, Markus Barth stresses the interconnections of justification and theodicy (*Acquittal by Resurrection* [New York: Holt, Rinehart, & Winston, 1964], 88).

[3]As noted in chap. 7, this strikes a Grotian, governmental note in Paul's atonement theology.

its damage once and for all. He can no longer be accused of being an absentee God who leaves the world to its dismal devices. He is not going to let fleshly fear, desire and impulses control humanity forever.

Christ's work is described as "redemption" (*apolytrōsis*), an act of deliverance, manumission or release of a slave, accomplished by the payment of a ransom (cf. Ex 21:8, 30 in LXX) or by offering a substitute (Ex 13:13, 15). In the Old Testament, "redemption" took on the meaning of "liberation by an act of power." The exodus was a redemption (Ex 15:13), though Yahweh paid nothing to Pharaoh when he released Israel from bondage.[4] In the immediate context of Romans 3, the bondage is a bondage to sin, and Jesus' faithful work "buys" sinners from that bondage and, implicitly, brings them to the glory that they could not reach while under sin. This happens because of God's just judgment accomplished in the death of Jesus, his demonstration of his justice in dealing with human rebellion. To anticipate what Paul says a few chapters later, God condemns, judges and destroys sinful flesh in the death of Jesus. Once sin is killed, it has no more hold over human beings. Those who are redeemed by Jesus no longer fall short of the glory of God, but share in it.

This redeeming death of Christ accomplishes what Paul calls justification.[5] Here, as in 1 Timothy 3:16, *dikaioō* names what happens in the life, death and resurrection of Jesus, and in the context, *dikaioō* has liberative overtones.[6] Interpreters often read Christ's liberating redemption, the deliverance from sin that he accomplishes by his death, as the *ground* or *basis* of an act of justification that takes place at a later time, not on the cross but in the life experience of sinners. There is nothing in Romans 3 that requires that shift of time frames or contexts. Even if Paul *does* subtly change focus from Christ's death to later happenings in the lives of individuals, both

---

[4]This point was made many years ago by Leon Morris, *The Atonement: Its Meaning and Significance* (Downers Grove, IL: InterVarsity Press, 1984), 106-31.

[5]It has been common to distinguish the redemption accomplished on the cross from the application of that redemption in justification. That may be what Paul has in view here, but see Douglas Campbell, *The Deliverance of God: An Apocalyptic Rereading of Romans* (Grand Rapids: Eerdmans, 2009), 663, for the argument that "justify" and "redeem" are essentially synonyms here.

[6]Campbell (*Deliverance*, 663) argues that the situation Paul has described demands a liberating response: If there is universal slavery in Adam, there is also a universal need for rescue. If God's action meets the need, then it must be a manumission from slavery to sin, which Paul describes here as both redemption and justification. Campbell also observes that *dikaioō* has a liberative sense later in Romans (e.g., Rom 6:7-8) and thus likely does here as well.

events are deliverances. If justification is an application of the redemptive liberation of Jesus' death, justification must also be a liberation from sin. A redeeming that is applied to slaves without freeing said slaves is not much of a redemption.

It is also possible that there is no time shift in the passage at all, but that the "justification as a gift by grace" comes *at the time* that Jesus accomplishes redemption in his death. Justification is the legal, judicial way to describe the event of the cross, which involves God's judgment of sin that liberates from sin. The structure noted above (see note 1) supports this reading. Paul begins his account of the "now" by saying that the justice of God is manifested *chōris nomou* (Rom 3:21), and the passage climaxes with the parallel claim that humanity[7] is justified by faith (implied, the "faith of Christ") *chōris ergōn nomou* (Rom 3:28). Justification of humanity comes by the faith of Jesus rather than by something the law does, or by something human beings do with law. In the structure, "justification" is parallel to the "manifestation of justice." If we press the parallel, then "justification" is *just* God's manifestation of his justice, which is what he does in the death and resurrection of the Messiah. Even if they are not identical in meaning, they appear to be related as cause and effect: God manifests his justice *in that* he accomplishes justification.

If justification refers to the justification of individuals, it is not clear how the belief of sinners manifests God's just judgment against sin, or how it answers the problem of theodicy that dominates this passage.[8] If God manifests his justice by an act of liberation, delivering humanity through the faithful death of Jesus, then we can see in the cross an act of God's justice. In the justifying death of Jesus, God's righteousness is manifest. In the death of Jesus, God demonstrates his hostility to sin: he is so hostile to sin, and so passionate in his love for humanity, that he shoulders the

---

[7]The anarthrous *anthrōpos* is typically translated as "a man," but that is certainly not a necessary translation, and given the surrounding concerns with the justification of Jew and Gentile, it is not the best translation. At the very least, by "a man" Paul means "a man, whether he is Jewish or Gentile." Otherwise, the question of Rom 3:29 does not follow. The question of whether God is God of Jews only arises because Paul has implied that every human, or all humanity, is justified apart from law.

[8]I argue just below that the justice of God *is* manifested in the lives of believers, but not simply in their believing. It is manifest when, by faith, they begin to embody the life of justice to which God calls them. Once we include that ecclesial dimension, Rom 3 can be taken as a statement about the "application" of redemption. Without that ecclesial dimension, it does not.

burden of sin and death on our behalf, as he had been doing since Sinai. More on this point below.

All this does not make individual belief irrelevant or turn Paul into a "political" rather than a "pastoral" theologian.[9] The distinction makes nonsense of the way Paul's mind moves. In Romans 3 Paul makes clear that, while God displays his justice and justifies in public history, in a Roman execution outside Jerusalem, that justice is not evident to everyone. Jesus' life and death of faithful obedience manifests the justice of God to those who believe (*eis pantas tous pisteuontas*).[10] Paul may be speaking of perception: the *pistis* of Christ that manifests God's justice is evident only to those whose response co-responds to Christ's *pistis*. After all, God's justice does not look like justice any more than his wisdom looks like wisdom and his strength like strength (see 1 Cor 1). It is more likely, however, that Paul means that the righteousness of God is manifest *among* or *with* those who, by their trust in Jesus, are "*of* faith," who take their origin, life and trajectory not from flesh or from Torah but from the faithful work of Jesus (*ton ek pisteōs Iēsou*, Rom 3:26). The justice of God is not merely displayed publicly in the faithful life and death of Jesus but realized in human life among those who are of the faith of Jesus (Rom 3:26) rather than among those who are "of the law." The liberation to justice must be by faith because God is the one God of all human beings, and thus must offer a way of justice that includes all. "Circumcision" and "uncircumcision" receive the liberating verdict in the same way: through the faith of the Christ that is received by faith.[11] Among both Jews and Gentiles, God's justice comes to expression among those who are of the faith of Christ.

---

[9]There is no polarization of social and individual here *in either direction*. In terms of later conceptualities, Paul is neither an individualist nor a communitarian, but displays a trinitarian imagination in which individual and body are mutually defining (see his discussions of body and members in Rom 12 and 1 Cor 12). What God does in Christ in redemptive history changes the course of history, and just so effects a radical renewal in the life experience of those who trust in Christ. The problem is not that traditional Protestant and Catholic readings have looked to these passages to answer questions about individual salvation. Paul addresses those questions. The problem is that traditional readings have often looked *only* for answers to those questions.

[10]The grammar of the sentence beginning in Rom 3:21 is obscured by the clauses that intervene. If we remove the clauses, Paul claims that "the righteousness of God has been manifested . . . for all those who believe."

[11]Translations are somewhat misleading in rendering *peritomē* and *akrobystia* as "circumcised" and "uncircumcised." That translation implies that Paul is talking about two collections of people, some circumcised and some not. Paul's terms are more abstract, referring not just to circumcised and uncircumcised persons but to circumcision and uncircumcision as "systems." Both need to be judged and renewed, and both are judged in the same fashion: by the faithful work of Christ.

The connections of justification, redemption and the formation of a body may be even more direct. The "*one* who is of the faith of Jesus" (*ton* is singular in Rom 3:26) may be the one new person formed by the blood of Christ.[12] Paul implicitly refers to the breakdown of the dividing wall, the overcoming of the Babelic curse, through the work of Christ. In the church the communal life of the Jews and Gentiles who are of the faith of Jesus displays the justice that Torah aimed at. Out of the fidelity of Jesus is born a united humanity, a people that has been justified as the delivering verdict that God pronounced in the death and resurrection of Jesus has been replicated in their experience. By his fidelity to death, Jesus forms a new humanity of Jews and Gentiles, no longer living by flesh but knit into one body by the Spirit (see Eph 2:11-22).[13]

God's method for justifying by redemption is to put Jesus forth as a *hilastērion*. The term is much disputed, interpreted as "atonement" or "propitiation," or a "place of atonement" or specifically the "mercy seat." Given Paul's emphasis on wrath against sin in the earlier part of Romans,[14] the word must carry something of its typical Greek sense of "propitiation." The Father sets Jesus up so that the wrathful God might become propitious to human beings.[15] In Jesus, God suffers the penalty that Israel, and humanity, deserves, on behalf of Israel, and therefore on behalf of humanity.

It is critical to work through this point carefully. Scripture nowhere polarizes wrath and love. Wrath is, on the contrary, the *expression* of offended love, love bewildered and grieved that it is not reciprocated. Yahweh's wrath at the violence of flesh before the flood is regret about creation itself, pain over the mess that human beings have made of his good and loving gifts. Wrath is jealousy, the protectiveness of love that claims the beloved and desires a response of love. Jesus' death overcomes God's wrath. But that does not mean that the Father is angry with *Jesus* or that the divine communion

---

[12]Campbell (*Deliverance*, 673) notes that "Jesus" is not found at the end of Rom 3:26 in some manuscripts, and suggests that even if it is original, it is epexegetical rather than part of a genitive phrase. Thus God is justifier of "those who are of faith, that is, of Jesus."

[13]Note the flow of the argument as displayed in the chiastic structure noted above (n. 1). Paul begins from a universal premise about the human condition: all sinned. He ends with another premise: that God justifies every human being, Jew or Gentile, in the same fashion, by the faithful work of Jesus.

[14]Campbell dissolves the question by claiming that the wrath-preaching of Rom 1 does not express Paul's own views, an ingenious and terribly convenient solution.

[15]See John Dunnill, *Sacrifice and the Body: Biblical Anthropology and Christian Self-Understanding* (Farnham, UK: Ashgate, 2013), 94.

is torn apart at the cross.[16] It *cannot* be the case that the gentle Son propitiates his angry Father, because the Son is on the cross only because "God so loved the world that he sent" him. If Jesus' Father is angry with sin, he is angry with the same passionate Spirit that breathes the Word. If the Father speaks a No of condemnation against flesh, the eternal Word pronounces that No. The cross is designed and worked out by the tripersonal God. Barth is at his paradoxical best in claiming that God plunges into his own wrath on the cross in order to dissipate it, and this is possible because of God's self-differentiation as Trinity.[17]

We can gain a firmer handle on this by recognizing that wrath involves "handing-over," explicitly so in Romans 1, where wrath is expressed in the handing-over of sinners to sin, the delivering of flesh to its own evils. Fleshly desires produce violence and mayhem, and God punishes flesh by giving it what it wants, by handing flesh over to fleshliness. Wrath commonly has this same shape in the Old Testament. In wrath, Yahweh gives Israel into the hand of Midian and Moab, Babylon and Philistia. Now, in the fullness of time, he has handed Israel over to demons. The situation of vengeance, strife, conflict, rivalry and violence—this is not only what angers God but also an expression of that anger. Stoicheic order is accommodated to the prior wrath of expulsion from Eden and scattering of nations. Sent by the Father, the Son willingly enters the foreign kingdom of sin and death to which Father and Son have delivered the human race. As soon as Jesus enters this world, he enters a world under wrath, estranged *by* the jealous love of God *from* the God who is love. God expels in wrath. Then he chases his beloved into exile to bring her back to himself.

To the extent that *hilastērion* refers to a "place" of atonement, Paul is claiming that Jesus, not the temple, becomes the new location for the work of purification, removal and riddance; by his blood alone is Israel and the

---

[16]As is suggested at times in the work of Jürgen Moltmann; see, e.g., *The Crucified God* (Minneapolis: Fortress, 1993), 244.

[17]Karl Barth, *Church Dogmatics*, IV/1, *The Doctrine of Reconciliation*, ed. Geoffrey W. Bromiley and T. F. Torrance, trans. Geoffrey W. Bromiley (Edinburgh: T&T Clark, 1956), 253-54. See also Barth's claim that God accepts responsibility for the being of humanity (ibid., 158), and his claim that in Christ God suffers Israel's suffering, allowing his own divine sentence to fall on himself (ibid., 175). Two recent expositions of Barth's atonement theology are illuminating: Nathan D. Hieb, *Christ Crucified in a Suffering World: The Unity of Atonement and Liberation* (Minneapolis: Fortress, 2013); Matthias Grebe, *Election, Atonement, and the Holy Spirit: Through and Beyond Barth's Theological Interpretation of Scripture* (Eugene, OR: Pickwick, 2014).

world cleansed. As Mount Moriah became the place of future atonement rituals because of the near death of Isaac, so the death of Jesus, the new Isaac, founds a new place of atonement and a new temple system outside the camp.[18] One of the key points is that God has now done this out in the open. He has been absorbing the sins of Israel for centuries, through his priests and sanctuary, through his bearing of sin on the Day of Atonement. That, however, has all been done in secret. God's way of being just and the justifier has been hidden, but in Jesus what has been whispered in the inner sanctuary of Yahweh's house is done out in public.[19] Because it is in public, it creates a seismic shift in the structures of Israel's religion. If the sanctuary is turned inside out, everything changes. The physics of Israelite religion is being transformed; Israel is receiving a new nature through the justifying act of redemption in the cross of Jesus.

James Jordan is also suggestive in tracing out the cosmic symbolism of the ark of the covenant, linking the throne with heaven, the cover with the firmament and the box with earth. On this understanding, Jesus is set out as a *hilastērion* in the sense that he is displayed as a new firmament stretching over the earth, the one mediator between heaven and earth. That captures the universal scope of Paul's argument. In whatever sense we take the term, the effect is clear: through the blood of Jesus, shed in his faithfulness to death, God judges sin, redeems, liberates—in short *justifies* Jews and Gentiles.

Once again the claim is that when Paul is talking about justification, he is talking about the history of salvation, about atonement theology. Paul does not say, "The atonement happens at the cross, and justification takes place on the basis of this historical event." Rather, justification is a name for what happened in the historical event of the cross and resurrection of Jesus. It was in those events that God pronounced his delivering verdict, condemned sin and formed a new spiritual man, Jesus, in whom we participate when we believe and entrust ourselves to the Faithful One.[20]

---

[18]Campbell, *Deliverance*, 640-56, argues for a multilayered reading of the term, referring first to the place of atonement in the Levitical system and, behind that, to the Aqedah.

[19]See Peter Stuhlmacher, *Paul's Letter to the Romans: A Commentary* (Louisville: Westminster John Knox. 1994), 60-61.

[20]N. T. Wright (*Paul and the Faithfulness of God* [Minneapolis: Fortress, 2013], 950) and Michael Gorman (*Inhabiting the Cruciform God: Kenosis, Justification, and Theosis in Paul's Narrative Soteriology* [Grand Rapids: Eerdmans, 2009]) have both rightly emphasized "incorporation" into the Messiah as a central theme in Paul's thought.

JUSTIFIED BY RESURRECTION, ROMANS 3:31–4:25

What Paul says to introduce his allegory of Isaac and Ishmael in Galatians 4 is implied as he makes the transition from Romans 3:31 to Romans 4:1. The tone is not as polemical as in Galatians, but the point is the same: You who want to establish justice by Torah, do you *listen* to Torah? Abraham is introduced to prove that Paul's gospel of justice by Christ's faith fulfills what Torah had always anticipated, just as it is a fulfillment of prophetic promise.

Paul introduces Abraham especially to demonstrate that the union of Jew and Gentile in justification is what the Torah promised from the beginning.[21]

---

[21]Paul quotes from Gen 15:6 (Rom 4:3), a passage that does *not* describe Abram's conversion or the beginning of Abram's role as God's partner in covenant. That creates some difficulties for interpretations that read Rom 4 exclusively as a text about individual salvation. Protestant theologians have acknowledged this but sometimes have forced the narrative of Genesis into an *ordo salutis*: Abram was called in Ur but was justified after, proof that vocation comes before justification in the *ordo salutis*. But the gap is decades-long, and the gap is temporal, not logical. It would be best to abandon the attempt to force Abram into the *ordo* paradigm. Given the context of Gen 15, it seems very odd to describe Abraham as "ungodly." He has left his home and his father's house in obedience to Yahweh's promise; he has been establishing altars throughout the land. How exactly is he ungodly? New perspective writers take this as Paul adopting typical Jewish language to refer to Gentile outsiders (similar to "sinners from among the Gentiles" in Gal 2). That does fit into the flow of Paul's later argument in the chapter, and in that sense the term describes Abraham, who was not yet circumcised.

Let me offer an alternative. Paul never explicitly says that Abraham was *justified*. Abraham was not justified by works, Paul says, which may imply that he was justified in some other fashion. But Paul never closes the circle and states positively that Abraham *was* justified. Abraham believed in the God who justifies the ungodly (Rom 4:5), but Paul does *not* explicitly indicate that Abraham himself was one of the ungodly who was justified. In fact, there is only one place in the New Testament where the name "Abraham" is the subject of the verb "justified," and that is not in Paul at all but in James 2:21, where James takes it as obvious that "Abraham our Father [was] justified by works when he offered up Isaac his son on the altar" (NASB). My point is not to question whether Paul believed that Yahweh counted Abraham as a righteous one, nor to question whether Abraham was counted or credited as righteous because he believed God's promise. Paul is quite explicit that Abraham did not earn his status as righteous as a worker earns wages. Nor am I denying that what Paul means by "justification" includes something along the lines of being credited as righteous, being reckoned as righteous or having a right standing in the presence of God. Abraham's faith *is* an example to Paul's readers, and the fact that Abraham was credited with righteousness is written for our sake, for we too will be credited as righteous by believing in the God who raised Jesus from the dead (Rom 4:24). I simply highlight a factual point: Paul *never* says that Abraham himself was *justified*. And that raises the possibility that, whatever blessings Abraham enjoyed as a believer in Yahweh's promises, he did not enjoy the blessing of justification, and that because justification was not yet *available* to be enjoyed. If justification comes by the work of Christ, after all, Abraham could not have enjoyed that blessing until Christ died and rose again. In the Christian tradition, the death and resurrection of Christ is understood to be efficacious in reverse, to save those who looked for the Messiah in hope. That is correct, but Paul's subtle variations in terminology may point both to the reality of blessings to the saints of old and also to the limitations of those blessings. Abraham was reckoned righteous because he trusted the God who would ultimately raise Jesus; but he did not enjoy the full reality of Jesus' resurrection because the resurrection had not yet happened.

If Abraham had been justified by works, he would have had something to boast about (Rom 4:2). The "works" here are implicitly the "works of Torah" mentioned in Romans 3:21, 28. Abraham could not have been justified by the works of Torah, not least because he believed God and was reckoned righteous *before* Torah was given, even before he received the commandment concerning circumcision, a point Paul emphasizes in Romans 4:11. Abram was *not* justified by works (Rom 4:2), *however* "works" is defined. He did not merit God's favor; he was not reckoned righteous because he performed what Torah required or because he wore the badge of circumcision; he was not reckoned righteous by what Torah accomplished. Abraham does no work to be reckoned righteous. Rather, he relies on *God's* work.

To be reckoned righteous (Rom 4:3) is to enjoy the blessing of having sins forgiven, covered and not imputed (Rom 4:6-8), but Paul does not abandon the liberative, "deliverdict" understanding of justification that he introduces in Romans 3. "Justify" in Romans 4:2 and Romans 4:5 still carries the same connotation it had in the previous chapter. In fact Paul reserves the actual term *dikaioō* for something else than "being reckoned righteous." That is evident at the close of the chapter. In more than one place, Paul explicitly links justification with the resurrection of Jesus (Rom 4:25; 1 Cor 15:16-17). A dead Christ is not a savior; a dead Christ cannot justify. If Christ is still dead, we are still in our sins.[22] In Romans 4 resurrection is not only the

---

It seems plausible, if not unquestionable, that Paul sees Abraham as one who *hopes* for justification rather than as one who actually *receives* it. Abraham's faith is credited (*elogisthē*) as righteousness, and that may connote not that God granted righteousness to Abraham but that he gave a promissory note to pay in the future. (This is how the verb is taken by Campbell, *Deliverance of God*, 730-32.) It is plausible, if not unquestionable, that Abraham's faith in the "justification of the ungodly" is not confidence in his *own* standing before God but confidence in the promise that Yahweh would issue a verdict at some point in the future to deliver ungodly Gentiles from the curses of Eden and Babel. Both in Rom 4 and in Gal 3, Paul emphasizes that the content of the promise to Abraham has to do with blessing to Gentiles (Gal 3:17). The specific promise in Gen 15 is that Abraham's seed will be like the stars, and that is extended in Gen 17:5 with the promise that Paul quotes in Rom 4:17: that Abraham would be the "father of many nations." *This* is what Abraham believed when he trusted "him who justifies the ungodly," and that means that "justification of the ungodly" is equivalent to "God extending the Abrahamic blessing to the nations." More immediately, the content of Abraham's faith was *not* that God reckoned him just; he was reckoned righteous, but he was reckoned so by believing Yahweh's promise to bring life from his dead body (Rom 4:19-21). Yahweh credited righteousness to Abraham *not* because Abraham believed God credited righteousness to him but because Abraham believed a promise about a future resurrection, a future son who would rise from the grave of Sarah's womb. Or, to say the same thing, Abraham was reckoned righteous because he believed a promise about a future justification-by-resurrection.

[22]Evangelical Protestants often have difficulty integrating the resurrection into their theology of

"ground" of justification but the object of faith and the *form* of justification. Romans 4:25 describes the purpose of Christ's death and of his resurrection. By his death Jesus dealt with our transgressions, our violations of God's law. By his resurrection Jesus establishes us in righteousness, justifying us. As we have seen, Paul's logic is illumined by 1 Timothy 3:16, examined in chapter seven. When all human courts had found Jesus guilty and sentenced him to death, the Father intervened to reverse the verdict and the sentence. The resurrection is the Father's enacted declaration that his Son is the Righteous One, and the "deliverdict" that raises Jesus from the dead.[23]

In the light of Romans 4:25, we can see that the whole of Romans 4 is leading up to a statement about resurrection. Abraham's crisis in Genesis 15 has nothing directly to do with forgiveness of sins. Abraham surely sinned; there is no one who does not sin. Paul brings sin explicitly into Romans 4 by quoting from Psalm 32, David's pronouncement of blessing on the one whose sins the Lord covers.

Yet sin is only *indirectly* in view in that portion of the Abraham narrative. Abraham's problem is more directly to do with the dominion of death (which is, of course, the result of sin, Rom 5). Yahweh has promised that Abraham's seed will be like the stars (Gen 15:5) and that they will receive the land of Canaan (Gen 15:7), and those are the promises confirmed in the covenant ceremony in Genesis 15:9-21. Abraham believes promises about seed and land, and Yahweh reckons him as righteous. But there is an obstacle in the way of these promises: Abraham and Sarah are old. Abraham's own body is "as good as dead," and Sarah's womb is also "dead" (Rom 4:19). In the face of these impossibilities, Abraham trusts God to keep his word and make his

---

justification, a difficulty directly linked with the failure to integrate the Spirit's work into justification. In his popularly written "comprehensive study" of justification, for instance, James White discusses Rom 4:25 in less than a page, and much of his discussion consists of a block quotation from Charles Hodge saying that as "evidence of the acceptance of his satisfaction on our behalf, and as a necessary step to secure the application of the merits of his sacrifice, the resurrection of Christ was absolutely essential, even for our justification" (*The God Who Justifies* [Minneapolis: Bethany House, 2007], 235-36). Wright forcefully stresses the role of the Spirit in justification (e.g., *Paul*, 956), which makes justification a fully trinitarian event. Kevin Vanhoozer makes a similar point concerning the central importance of the Spirit in atonement theology ("The Atonement in Postmodernity: Guilt, Goats and Gifts," in *The Glory of the Atonement: Biblical, Theological and Practical Perspectives*, ed. Charles Hill and Frank A. James III [Downers Grove, IL: InterVarsity Press, 2004], 400).

[23]Richard B. Gaffin, *Resurrection and Redemption: A Study in Paul's Soteriology*, 2nd ed. (Phillipsburg, NJ: P&R, 1987), 119-24. See the similar exegesis in John Reumann, *Righteousness in the New Testament: Justification in the Lutheran-Catholic Dialogue* (Minneapolis: Fortress, 1982), 30.

descendants like the stars of heaven: "With respect to the promise of God, he did not waver in unbelief but grew strong in faith, giving glory to God" (Rom 4:20 NASB). He believes because he is confident that Yahweh is "able also to perform" what he has promised (Rom 4:21). Abraham, in short, exhibits faith in the God of resurrection, which, in context, seems to be identical to faith in the God who justifies the ungodly (Rom 4:5). Abraham trusts that Yahweh is the Lord of life who triumphs over death. Abraham is reckoned righteous for believing in resurrection (Rom 4:22). Resurrection is a central theme of the chapter. It is the content of the faith of the justified. God's delivering verdict comes to those who trust God to issue the delivering verdict.

Jesus' justification takes the form of a resurrection, a transforming judgment that is also his deliverance from the realm of death. For Abraham too, the hope of justification was the hope for resurrection, the hope that God would throw down death itself in order to keep his promises. Abraham was reckoned righteous because of his trust in Yahweh's promise, but that promise, Yahweh and Abraham's confidence were all vindicated by the resurrection of Isaac's birth. Abram's justification was as public as Isaac's birth. Isaac's birth is a type of the resurrection of Jesus from the dead womb of the earth, from the dead womb of humanity and the dead womb of Sarah-Israel. Abraham's faith is a model for believers, but it is a model because it is faith in resurrection. It is an example of faith that is justified, proved valid, by the birth of a son from the dead.

Justified from Sin, Romans 5–6

Having written that we are justified in the resurrection of Jesus, implying that the resurrection is God's favorable judgment to new life, Paul is unlikely to use the same word in a different sense in the following sentence. We are justified by the resurrection of Jesus, and *having been justified* we have peace with God. God's favorable judgment, rendered in the resurrection of Jesus in which believers participate, brings renewed peace with God, and that assures believers that in the midst of tribulations the Lord is working character and hope into us. By his favorable judgment, God liberates us from death so that we can be at peace with him.

In a proto-Abelardian vein, Paul claims that the love of God is manifest in the fact that he sent his Son to die for ungodly sinners, not for the righteous (Rom 5:6-8). Paul speaks in Romans 5:8-9 of a *delivering* justification. When we were still sinners, Christ died for our transgressions, so that we might be raised up with him to justification. He died and rose to make us righteous in the same way *he* is righteous in his resurrection—by deliverance from the sentence of death, by deliverance from death itself, from the mortality of flesh and from the sin that brought death into the world in the first place.[24]

The Adam-Christ parallel in Romans 5 clarifies some of the "mechanics" of what Paul has talked about in more compressed and vague terms earlier in the letter, and also broadens out the scope of justification. That God's justice is evident in his condemnation of sin, and that this condemnation of sin takes place in the cross, is already implied in Romans 3:23-26. In Romans 5 Paul's personification, or cosmicization, of *hamartia* and *thanatos* makes this point more sharply. Sin and death are powers, ruling in dominance over the sons of Adam in some of the ways we described in our treatment of "flesh" above. Sin enters the world through the disobedient act of the one man Adam. Judgment against the one disobedient man is "unto condemnation" (Rom 5:16; *eis katakrima*), but condemnation is more than a "guilty" verdict. It is condemnation to slavery under the domination of sin. More particularly, "death reigned" (Rom 5:17) because of the sin of Adam, with the result that all sinned.[25] The action of Adam results in a regime of death, and as Romans 7 will explore at length, Torah was powerless to curb that regime's power. Torah was powerless to justify, to deliver the destroying condemnation of destruction and to deliver the life-giving verdict of justification. Instead the law became an instrument of death, killing the fleshly Israel to whom it was delivered.[26]

---

[24]This text also indicates a connection between justification and a future deliverance from wrath. Justification has occurred in the present, and those who share in the justifying verdict of Jesus are saved from the wrath that is coming. I take this as a reference to the wrath that is coming on Jew and Gentile at the end of the age in the final destruction of the old stoicheic order. Those who have been delivered from death in the present by the death of Jesus will be safe from that destruction when it comes. Having already left the Egypt of stoicheic order, they will suffer no loss when it collapses utterly.

[25]I've defended this understanding of the controversial clauses of Rom 5:12 in "Adam, Moses, Jesus," *Calvin Theological Journal* 43, no. 2 (2008): 257-72. See also the important psychological study by Richard Beck, *The Slavery of Death* (Eugene, OR: Wipf & Stock, 2013).

[26]See the superb summary of N. T. Wright in *Pauline Perspectives: Essays on Paul, 1978–2013* (Minneapolis: Fortress, 2013), 373: Torah draws sin out to do its worst.

All this is evident from the way Paul uses "condemnation" interchangeably with "death" or the "reign of death":

by the transgression of the one the many died (Rom 5:15 NASB)

the judgment arose from one [transgression] to condemnation (Rom 5:16)

if by the transgression of the one, death reigned through the one (Rom 5:17 NASB)

as through one transgression to condemnation to all men (Rom 5:18)

through the one man's disobedience the many were made sinners (Rom 5:19 NASB)

"Condemnation" means "condemned to be under the mastery of sin and death."

Adam was created to rule, but by sin he became a slave. The opposite effect comes from the obedience of the Last Adam. By his faithful death (perhaps also including his resurrection), Jesus has overcome sin and death, and the result is "justification" (*dikaiōma*), here quite directly the opposite of "condemnation." Since condemnation involved the establishment of a regime of death, the justification that replaces it must involve more than forgiveness. It must involve liberation from Egypt and the establishment of a regime of life. That is precisely what Paul goes on to say: "Through one act of righteousness unto all men unto justification of life" (Rom 5:18; *di' henos dikaiōmatos eis pantas anthrōpous eis dikaiōsin zōēs*). What Paul describes as "justification to all men" is equivalent to the situation he describes in Romans 5:17 as the reign in life of "those who receive the abundance of grace and the gift of righteousness." The regime change is not simply the elevation of abstract properties—life and righteousness—but specifically the exaltation of those who receive the righteousness of God, who share his justice in Christ. Justification describes, in short, the once-for-all event of the obedience of the Last Adam and the regime he established by his death (and resurrection). Justification here does not refer to the right standing of the believer but to the condition of *humanity* ("all men") after Christ.

At base, justification has a very particular referent: one man is justified, and that is Jesus (Rom 4:25; 1 Tim 3:16). For Paul, though, there is also a *universal* dimension to justification: the "world" is justified, delivered by judgment from the reign of death, by Jesus' obedience to death and by the Father's raising him from the dead. That is true because one man has been liberated from death and sin, and because that one man is the chief Man, the head of the eschatological humanity. The death and resurrection of Jesus brings in a cosmic regime change, and Paul describes the new regime as the "justification" of the human race (Rom 5:16, 18).

In response to a false charge of antinomianism, Paul goes on to emphasize that those who have been united by baptism with Christ are liberated from sin to serve God in justice (Rom 6). Baptism incorporates the baptized into the justifying death of Jesus; the baptized participate in God's No to sin and death that he enacted in Jesus' death. Union with Jesus' death in baptism leads to freedom from sin, a share in the deliverdict that the Father pronounced over Jesus in his resurrection. Thus in Romans 6:7, Paul writes, *ho gar apothanōn dedikaiōtai apo tēs hamartias,* "for the one who has died is *justified* from sin."[27] The context makes clear that Paul is not talking about forgiveness of sin or removal of guilt, but rather about the death of Jesus that, operating through baptism, delivers sinners from sin's power.[28] He is talking about life, not merely about legal status; he describes the transition from life under sin to life under grace as a "justification."[29]

---

[27]This verse has apparently played little role in historic theologies of justification. There are no references to Rom 6 at all in Alister McGrath's magisterial *Iustitia Dei: A History of the Christian Doctrine of Justification,* 3rd ed. (Cambridge: Cambridge University Press, 2005), and John Fesko's compendious study of Reformed notions of the *ordo salutis* and union with Christ (*Beyond Calvin: Union with Christ and Justification in Early Modern Reformed Theology (1517-1700)* [Gottingen: Vandenhoeck & Ruprecht, 2012]) includes no reference to Rom 6:7.

[28]The scriptural depth of the passage is greatly enhanced if we recognize the exodus typology running through this portion of Romans. Romans 5 describes the "Egypt" of sin and death; through the waters of baptism, believers are brought out of Egypt, liberated/justified from Pharaoh and hoping for the promised land of a new creation. For further development, see N. T. Wright, "Romans," in *The New Interpreter's Bible,* vol. 10, *Acts–1 Corinthians,* ed. Leander E. Keck (Nashville: Abingdon, 2002), 513-14. Theodore Jennings Jr. (*Outlaw Justice: The Messianic Politics of the Apostle Paul* [Stanford: Stanford University Press, 2013], 101) rightly stresses that baptism has ethical consequences, though he unfortunately sets "ethical" in opposition to "cultic," yet another expression of the distorting nature/supernature paradigm.

[29]Even unreconstructed Protestants frequently recognize that Paul's use of *dikaioō* does not correspond to Protestant confessional usage. John Murray nicely describes deliverance from sin as a judicial act (*The Epistle to the Romans,* New International Commentary on the New Testament, 2 vols. [Grand Rapids: Eerdmans, 1965], 1:222). Murray still hedges here; he maintains the traditional Protestant distinction of justification and sanctification by saying that the "justification" in view here is the "basis" of sanctification, rather than what Murray elsewhere calls "definitive sanctification." Douglas Moo, whose massive and careful commentary is one of the most traditionally Protestant of the recent spate of Romans commentaries, hedges in a similar fashion, noting that "Paul is pointing to justification through participation in Christ's death as the basis for the freedom from sin enjoyed by the believer." Despite the oddity of the usage, Moo concludes

That this follows on the regime-change discussion of Romans 5:12-21 is worth noting. Romans 6 is not *simply* a qualifying passage designed to rebut the antinomian misinterpretation of Paul's gospel. It continues Paul's argument. In Romans 5 Paul insists that those who receive the gift of righteousness and grace reign in life, and that this situation of the reign of those who have received righteousness can be described as the enactment of "justification." How is that new situation realized in human existence? How do we receive the gift of righteousness so as to reign in life? Romans 6 tells us: By death to sin's reign, the baptized are "justified"—delivered by judgment—to a life under Christ, no longer under the reign of sin and death. Having been crucified with Christ, and sharing in the righteousness of his resurrection, the baptized are to consider themselves dead to the reign of sin, dead to death and flesh, and alive instead to God in Christ (Rom 6:11). In the power of the resurrection that comes to them in their baptismal death, they put sin to death. Sin's reign has been broken in the world by the death and resurrection of Jesus. Resurrection has happened, which means that the world of sin and death has been condemned and Jesus has been justified. Justification has happened to "all men" (Rom 5:18) because *everyone* lives in a world where God has condemned sin in the cross and justified Jesus and his kingdom. Justification happens to the world because God joins people to Christ's delivering death and resurrection by his Spirit, in baptism and faith.

Those who die with Christ already participate in the resurrection *of the body*, offering the members of their bodies as instruments and weapons of God's justice. Once they lived according to the flesh, pursuing pleasure and avoiding pain, establishing societies on the basis of the fear of death and loss, erecting the reign of the phallus. For those who have been baptized into Christ, that world is dead. They have died to flesh and now live to God, which means living toward justice, since God is Justice in himself. The baptized live the life of the justified—that is, of those who share in Jesus' death

---

that here "'justified from sin' means 'set free from the [power of] sin'" (Moo, *The Epistle to the Romans*, New International Commentary on the New Testament [Grand Rapids: Eerdmans, 1996], 376). He points out that "the forensic term 'justify' is used with reference to the judgment executed upon the power of sin in the death of Christ. The result is that all who have died with Christ are the beneficiaries of this judgment executed and are therefore quit of sin's dominion. This is the force of the expression 'justified from sin.' In like manner the forensic term 'condemn' can be used in this instance to express the judicial judgment executed upon the power of sin in the flesh of Christ" (ibid., 279).

to death and his justifying resurrection. Though it is clear from the rest of the New Testament that believers continue to commit sins (e.g., 1 John 1), the life of the justified is *not* properly summed up as *simul iustus et peccator*. The justified are *dead* to sin, justified from sin in their baptismal death, and are to conform their self-conception to what baptism declares about them: "All of us who have been baptized into Christ Jesus have been baptized into His death. . . . Even so consider yourselves to be dead to sin, but alive to God in Christ Jesus" (6:3, 11 NASB).[30] In this way the justification that occurs in Jesus' death and resurrection initiates the reign of the justice of God, the reign in life of those whose bodies share in the new life that is Christ, and so share in his righteousness. The *dikaiosynē theou* comes to realization through the justification of Jesus in his resurrection as he shares his new life and new status with those who are joined to him in faith and baptism. Thus God's justice comes *not* through the working of law but through the faith of Jesus and the faithfulness of his Father.[31] In fact they have to be justified *from* the law itself, since according to Paul Torah provoked sin and stirred it up into hyperreality.[32]

WHAT TORAH COULD NOT DO, ROMANS 7:1–8:4

Romans 8 opens with Paul's declaration that there is "no condemnation" (*katakrima*), a phrase that in Paul's usage is equivalent to a declaration of "justification." That "condemn" is the opposite of "justify" is evident already in Romans 5:16-18. Through the transgression of Adam came "condemnation," but through the gift of God comes "justification" (Rom 5:16), and just as "condemnation" comes to all men through one transgression, so one act of righteousness results in "justification of life for all men." As in Romans 5, condemnation in Romans 8 is an *enacted* verdict, not merely a verbal declaration. Paul's declaration that there is "no condemnation" means the same as the declaration "those who are in Christ Jesus are justified"; and as "no condemnation" implies "no longer condemned to slavery to sin and

---

[30]We may well ask at this point if the conventional Protestant soteriology does not flirt with a form of Galatianism, betraying a lack of faith in the baptismal declaration of the gospel. If God says in baptism, "You are dead to sin," and exhorts us to "consider ourselves dead to sin," is it not an act of pastoral malpractice to tell the baptized that they are "sinners"?

[31]Markus Barth stresses how the resurrection publicly demonstrates the Father's faithfulness to his faithful Servant (Barth, *Acquittal by Resurrection*, 50-52).

[32]The term is from Jennings, *Outlaw Justice*.

death," so the implied positive verdict of justification is both deliverance from sin's power and a verdict of innocence.

Romans 7 ends with Paul looking forward to a deliverance from the power of sin and death that holds him.[33] His wretchedness is not relieved by the law, but only made worse, and he hopes in anguish for deliverance that he characterizes as future: "Who *will* set me free from the body of this death?" (Rom 7:24). The statement in Romans 8:1, however, is about a "now," and Romans 8:2 makes it clear that what happens "now" is the "setting free" that Paul said he was hoping for in the future. The word for "set free" in Romans 7:24 is not the same as in Romans 8:2, but the notion is the same: both speak of liberation from death, of rescue and deliverance. For those who are in Christ Jesus, deliverance is realized; there is now a rescue, now a new exodus.[34] In Paul's terminology this new exodus is an act of "justification," a liberation by judgment from sin, death and flesh.

Paul describes how this works with two connected phrases in Romans 8. First, Paul describes Jesus' death as *peri hamartias*, a technical term for the "purification offering" (Hebrew: ḥaṭṭāʾt; Lev 4).[35] As I noted in chapter four, the purification offering was distinctive in its use of blood and in its disposal of flesh. When a priest or the whole congregation offered a sin offering, the blood was smeared on the horns of the golden altar in the Holy Place, and the animal's flesh was destroyed outside the gate. According to the letter to the Hebrews, Jesus is just such a sin offering to purify the entire people, suffering in the flesh outside the gate (Heb 13:11-12). Jesus' death purifies in a way that the purifications of the law could not. Torah purifications were performed through animals, who rose along the path of blood into Yahweh's presence. Jesus lays down his own life in complete obedience, in true sacrifice, and so enters *as a man* into the garden. He is the first to pass through the cherubic fire and find life on the other side. Thus Jesus did what all legal sacrifices could not do: he has actually destroyed flesh in his death and taken up the new life of the Spirit.

---

[33] I recognize that the identification of the "I" of Rom 7 with Paul is controversial, and I do not mean a simple equation of the two. Paul's main point in Rom 7 is to highlight the destructive effects of Torah in a world under the dominion of sin and death, and thus the "I" surely plays the role of a representative Israelite. But it is difficult to avoid the sense that Paul is also speaking somewhat autobiographically.

[34] I am dependent here on Thomas Schreiner, *Romans*, Baker Exegetical Commentary on the New Testament (Grand Rapids: Baker, 1998), 398-408.

[35] Moo, *Epistle to the Romans*, 480. Moo claims that the phrase refers to a sin offering in forty-four of fifty-four uses of the phrase in the LXX. Cited in Dunnill, *Sacrifice and the Body*, 93.

The point that Paul highlights about the sin offering is that it involved the condemnation of flesh. With Jesus as an offering for sin, God condemned sin in flesh (Rom 8:3: *katekrinen tēn hamartian en tē sarki*).[36] The specific target of condemnation should be noted. Jesus is not the subject of God's condemning judgment. Gripped by the fear of death that is flesh's motivating power, as robotic servants of death and so of sin, Jews and Gentiles combine to condemn Jesus to death. Jesus' persecutors claim that he is "stricken, / smitten of God, and afflicted" (Is 53 NASB). Anyone who suffers so much must, like Job, be guilty of some horrific wrong. They are wrong about Jesus, and, as we saw in chapter six, put Jesus to death for the sins that they themselves have committed. Their very act of putting Jesus to death is a blasphemy for which they deserve to be wiped off the face of the earth as thoroughly as the Nephilim at the time of the flood. They put Jesus in the dock where they should be standing. Not only are they wrong about Jesus, but they are also wrong about God's regard for Jesus. For the Father never, *ever* joins Jesus' enemies in judging Jesus to be guilty. The Father sends the Son in the flesh as a son of David (see Rom 1:4), and willingly delivers his willing Son over to thugs and murderers.

Paul (like John) highlights the ironic turnaround at the cross. The Jews urge the Romans to put Jesus in their place to suffer the penalty of blasphemy they deserve, but the ones really on trial are the Jews and Romans themselves. "Now is the judgment of this world," Jesus says in John 12:31. And Paul says the same in essence: now is the judgment *of flesh*. It looks as though Spirit is under the judgment of flesh in the trial of Jesus and at the cross; what is in fact happening is that flesh is being condemned, judged, put to death.

That is partly a matter of flesh's own self-condemnation. "Whoever does not believe is judged already" (Jn 3:18). Torah had become so much a tool of flesh in the hands of the Jews that they were able to use Torah to condemn the Torah-giver. Roman justice was so thoroughly fleshly that Romans put

---

[36]Paul is talking about the cross, and it is obvious enough that the "condemnation" of sin that took place on the cross was not merely a matter of pronouncing a verdict. At the cross, God *destroyed* sin, judged it, condemned it by placing/taking all its burden on his Son/himself. If the verb "condemn" in Rom 8:3 means an act of God to triumph over sin, that same range of meaning is likely present in Rom 8:1, since Paul clearly intends a verbal play on the two uses of the word, as pointed out by Chuck Lowe, "'There Is No Condemnation' (Romans 8:1): But Why Not?" *Journal of the Evangelical Theological Society* 42, no. 2 (1999): 241.

a man they knew was innocent to death in order to protect a little piece of imperial order (and that for only a brief time!). In the death of Jesus, flesh stands condemned because flesh—fear of death, fear of loss, desire for glory—inspires the human race to kill the Creator of flesh, the one irrefutably righteous man, the One man who lived in flesh but not according to flesh, the Man who lived in the flesh by the Spirit. *Now* is the judgment of this world—the world of old, the world of flesh, the world of the First Adam under the reign of sin and death. In the cross, sin does its worst and is exposed for what it is: anti-good, anti-life, anti-God.

Not only is the death of Jesus the exposure of the evil of sin and flesh but also, because the death of Jesus is fulfilled in his resurrection, it cancels the power of sin. The cross does not merely *expose* or *disclose*. It *delivers* because it is followed by new life, the justifying verdict enacted in Jesus' resurrection. It deletes the power of sin past, the power of past wrongs to determine the present and the future. By the resurrection of Jesus, the world is given a new past and a new future because humanity is given a new Adam as head. Passing through death, Jesus is raised and ascends to the Father, overcoming the exclusion of Eden. Thus God delivers his Son to sin and death, lets them do their worst and uses their highest triumph to defeat them.

Though Torah could not achieve this judgment against sin, much less the life-giving verdict of justification, Torah has an essential role in Paul's presentation. What Paul says about Jesus as sin offering in Romans 8 depends on his prior discussion of the "working of Torah" in Romans 7. Torah kills fleshly Israel by tearing Israel, and each Israelite, in two. Torah performs a circumcision, exposing the flesh that resists Torah and tries to turn Torah to its own purposes, but by the same token bringing to light the "inner person" who delights in the Torah. Torah's role has been to flush out flesh, to demonstrate that there is no good in human flesh, so that flesh can be targeted for condemnation and destruction in the cross. Because it creates a divided Israel, and divided Israelites, Torah makes it possible for Jesus' sin offering to condemn flesh without killing Israel. When Jews clamor to put Jesus, living Torah, on the cross, it is their flesh that acts and controls; their flesh blinds them to Jesus so that they do what they do in ignorance, not recognizing the Lord they claim to serve. When the Father then reverses their verdict, when he completes the condemnation of flesh by raising Jesus in the Spirit, they can be brought to recognition and repentance. What looked to them like a pariah, an outcast and leper, barely human, is revealed in the resurrection to have been, all along, the Lord of glory, showing the glory of his covenant love in giving himself for his people.[37]

By condemning flesh to death in the death of Jesus, by raising Jesus up in the Spirit, God has introduced a new *nomos* into the world, a new cultural order. It is neither the Torah of Israel nor the *civitas* of Rome but a law of the Spirit who brings life. It is only this law that establishes true justice, because "the just requirement of the law"—the justice that the law always aimed at—is brought into reality not among those who walk in flesh but among those who walk by the Spirit (Rom 8:4). Romans is far from finished, but Paul's argument has circled back to his opening theme: The justice of God is manifested in the faithfulness of Jesus because by his faithful, obedient life and death, flesh is condemned and the Spirit is unleashed, and a new human possibility is planted within the human race: to walk not in the flesh, enslaved to death and therefore to sin, but to walk in the fearlessness of the Spirit.

Jesus' death is a sin offering by which flesh is condemned, the climactic campaign and final triumph in Yahweh's war with flesh. By the death and resurrection of Jesus, flesh is dealt a death blow and Spirit is unleashed on the world. As in the Levitical system, that sin offering is followed by a *thysia*, a sacrifice of peace offerings (Rom 12:1).[38] Readmitted to Eden by the sin offering of Jesus, and incorporated into his self-offering by the Spirit, believers perform a new liturgy (*latreia*) that consists of a continuous peace offering, which is to say, a continuous feast. That feast is not confined to ritual celebrations but rather spills over to infuse all of life with eucharistic

---

[37]Though Paul is describing a deliverance from Israel's (and his) schizophrenic existence under Torah, he describes this deliverance in judicial terms, as a "verdict" of "no condemnation." This point is reinforced by the following verses, where Paul roots the declaration of "no condemnation" in the fact that the Spirit has "set free" from the law of sin and death. This is not, be it noted, a deliverance from law, command and order as such, but from the Torah as a system and especially from Torah as it was co-opted and hijacked by sin and death. The goal of this deliverance from the "law of sin and death" is to make it possible for the Torah to be fulfilled by those who walk by the Spirit (Rom 8:4). For superb critical reflections on the modern misconstruals of law and grace in Lutheran theology, see David Yeago, "Martin Luther on Grace, Law, and Moral Life: Prolegomena to an Ecumenical Discussion of *Veritatis Splendor*," *The Thomist* 62, no. 2 (1998): 163-91; Yeago, "Gnosticism, Antinomianism, and Reformation Theology: Reflections on the Costs of a Construal," *Pro Ecclesia* 2, no. 1 (1993): 37-49.

[38]Sarah Whittle, *Covenant Renewal and the Consecration of the Gentiles in Romans*, Society of the New Testament Monograph Series 161 (Cambridge: Cambridge University Press, 2015), 79-90, convincingly argues that Paul refers specifically to the peace offering in Rom 12.

joy. The confinement of sacrifice to the sanctuary, and one sanctuary, under stoicheic order confined festivity to one place. Now that the veil is torn, the cherubic curse lifted and Eden reopened, the church celebrates a continuous sacrificial liturgy, a liturgy of sacrificial life. That takes form in the harmonious mutual service of the members of the body (Rom 12:4-8). It takes form as brotherly love, mutual honor and glorification, humility, charity, hospitality, generosity to enemies, renunciation of vengeance (Rom 12:9-20). The peace offering is communion with God in all of human life, the just society that God promised to Abraham, an *ekklēsia* that gives form to the *nomos* of the Spirit and fulfills the justice of Torah, as it lives in the confidence that flesh and death itself are dead, as it walks by the Spirit.

AUTHOR INDEX

SUBJECT INDEX

SCRIPTURE INDEX